THE LIBERAL TRADITION
IN EUROPEAN THOUGHT

The Liberal Tradition in European Thought

EDITED WITH INTRODUCTORY ESSAYS

by David Sidorsky

G. P. Putnam's Sons

New York

CONTENTS

INTRODUCTION

European liberalism is a continuing effort to interpret the idea of freedom and to examine the conditions for the realization of freedom within the framework of changing political and social institutions. This abstract and general formulation of liberalism suggests the complexity of the liberal tradition. The idea of freedom is inevitably ambiguous, and liberals have advanced differing interpretations; the conditions for its realization are necessarily diverse, and liberals have advocated competing strategies; the changes within major European social institutions have been so extensive that it is not only plausible but mandatory that a liberal program in one period be amended or repudiated in another.

The most familiar example is the identification of liberalism with an economic policy of laissez-faire, as well as with support of state intervention in the economy as a condition for social freedom. Liberalism embraces the defense of the principle of popular sovereignty, although one of its most recurrent themes has been the setting of limits to the popular will. Liberalism is the classic source of doctrines of natural rights, and yet one of its major theoretical architects condemned this doctrine as nonsensical. The liberal tradition includes significant justification for revolution, although its characteristic stress is upon the primacy of peaceful methods of social change.

The incoherence of the liberal tradition suggests two methods of approach to the interpretation of liberalism. On the one hand, the road to clarity lies in qualification. French liberalism is distinguishable from British or Spanish liberalism. Even within a particular national tradition, the liberalism of Locke differs from that of Mill or Gladstone. More

1

prosaically, the programs of a liberal party in power usually vary widely from those of a liberal party which is powerless. Any presentation of the liberal tradition involves a concatenation of particular liberal policies, ideas, or programs, each of which is embedded in its unique historical context.

The historical approach to the liberal tradition itself, however, shows that when liberals have advanced programs or policies, they have argued for them on the basis of a coherent set of values. It is by reference to such values, for example, that John Locke is considered a liberal, even though his writings antedate the introduction of the term to England by more than a century. Similarly, in our time, when the "traditional" liberal parties of Europe are in eclipse, we understand discussions of the continuity of liberal principles in changed circumstances or the need for a new formulation of liberalism. There is presupposed some sense in which liberalism reflects, in the phrase of its most gifted historian, Guido Ruggiero, "a deep lying mental attitude." In this broad sense liberalism may be considered a major secular faith of Western Europe. For the understanding of liberalism, just as for the understanding of any major social movement or religious faith, both methods of approach are necessary: the recognition of historic variation in matters of doctrine and program, and the search for a residual core especially of attitude or value.

When liberalism is considered as a secular faith, its central vision is a conception of the nature of man, of society, and of history. In simplest terms, it is, first, a conception of man as desiring freedom and capable of exercising rational free choice. Second, it is a perspective on social institutions as open to rational reconstruction in the light of individual needs. It is, third, a view of history as progressively perfectible through the continuous application of human reason to social institutions.

Although it is not possible to logically deduce any of the specific programs of liberalism from its conception of human nature, these programs would seem to presuppose that man is capable of freedom. For unless he were, there would seem to be no point to the whole range of liberal effort, from acts of toleration in the seventeenth century to the extension of suffrage to women in the twentieth, which defend a person's right to exercise his freedom or extend the areas in which it can be exercised. Unless men wanted freedom and could make reasonable use of it, there would seem to be no passionate preference for the elimination of censorship or of prescribed belief or even of many forms of coercion.

This liberal vision of the nature of man is cast in bold relief in those characteristic and revealing "myths" of isolated independent individual man which appear in certain classic formulations of liberal doctrine. We have the example "natural man," in social contract theory, prudentially deciding whether to close contract with sovereign political society; or the myth of "economic man" in a free market determining what to produce, to buy, to sell, or even to work at, through the calculation of marginal utilities; and, again, the ideal of "rational man" freely deciding to assent or to withhold assent on fundamental beliefs about the nature of the world, the soul, or God.

Most fundamentally, the significance of this conception emerges when it is challenged. Some utilitarians, for example, seem to have believed that freedom is only a means for the achievement of happiness. When faced with the possibility of a contented society of slaves, however, they have suggested that human happiness is possible only through the exercise of the potentiality of freedom. Critics of liberalism, such as Dostoyevsky or de Maistre, have suggested that men fear freedom and are anxious to escape it through the acceptance of tradition or authority, but have found their empirical evidence discounted. Men reject freedom, the liberals reply, because they are sick or coerced or ignorant or desperate or believe that they are attaining a greater measure of freedom. Men could never knowingly choose not to be free, in the liberal view, without ceasing to be human.

Secondly, for men to exercise the degree of rational free choice which liberalism envisages, the major institutions of society must admit of reform and revision. The rationalist attitude of liberalism is in conflict with any historicist conservatism which sets sharp limits to the possibilities of social reconstruction or social engineering or with any historical determinism which denies to rational intelligence the possibility of transformation of the social process. Liberal theory traces this priority of the individual over the social institution in such fundamental social institutions as the church, the state, and economic order.

In most religious theory, men are born into a church which then determines their appropriate place in the cosmic order of things. For liberalism, the church becomes a voluntary society which the individual joins or leaves depending upon the light of his reason or conscience. The status of the church then becomes transformed as one of several voluntary associations in society with significant implications for the doctrine of separation of church and state and for the theory of religious toleration.

In most classical political theory, the state was a natural condition of man's social development. His relationship to it was necessary and organic. Although the liberal sovereign state is not a voluntary association, the individual's relationship with it is a contractual one. A person in theory may terminate the relationship either through emigration or through actions aimed at dissolution of the state if his self-interest requires it.

Further, man's position in the social order, that is, his status, power, vocation, and wealth, in the traditional view before the period of modern liberalism, were considered to be, in great measure, the product of birth and custom. In liberal theory, the doctrine of rationality of men is developed to suggest that all men are equal; hence, the stress upon equal opportunity with careers open to talents without antecedent determination of political or social position. Any fixed social or economic order could be restructured in the light of individual effort or by the aggregating of individual preferences.

This liberal attitude to church, state, and social hierarchy of course reflected the transformation of these institutions in Western Europe in a period of the rise of science, secularism, and capitalism. Liberalism was both the product and, in part, the shaper of that transformation. The record of that transformation and the optimism it engendered is revealed in liberal historiography.

The third aspect of liberalism as secular faith is its approach to understanding human history. The interpretation of the past provides the frame of reference for its political and social programs. For liberalism, history is the arena of human progress and perfectibility. In the background of many of the specific programs or theses of liberalism there is implicit the doctrine that the correct and repeated application of human reason to any social evil—war, poverty, illness, prejudice, or any of the terrors of the apocalypse or primal curses of the human estate—can mitigate their ravages and gradually but effectively eliminate each and all of them without any foreseeable limit to the process. If human history is full of atrocity and evil, it is because man has not yet educated himself to overcome the ignorance imposed by corrupt institutions. No "motiveless malice" or lurking "death instincts" intrude on the goodness of human nature. Condorcet, the author of the classic formulation of liberal doctrine of perfectibility, expresses the liberal attitude when he argued "all errors in politics and morals are based on philosophical errors and there in turn are connected with scientific errors." These errors are then progressively eliminable, for "All the causes that contribute to the perfection of the human race . . . exercise a perpetual influence and always increase their sphere of action." The scope of this progress is not limited to politics but involves social and human transformation through the progress of science. "Certainly man will not become immortal," Condorcet concedes, but he goes on to ask "will not the interval between the first breath that he draws and the time when in the natural course of events, without disease or accident, he expires, increase indefinitely?"

The daring and vision of that rhetorical question can help explain why liberalism provided a secular faith for its adherents. In recent decades, there has been an understandable hesitation by liberals in affirming this vision of perfectibility. Critics of liberalism, both the secular like Camus or the religious like Tillich, have not been hesitant in pointing to such realities as the rational use of terror and the techno-logical expansion of destructive capabilities as definitive refutation of the shallowness and superficiality of the liberal view of man and history. It may be that the viability of the liberal faith depends upon the re-formulation of some thesis of human perfectibility in responsible and believable terms.

The preceding sketch of three fundamental liberal attitudes, even if drawn in much greater detail, represents a partial approach to the inter-pretation of liberalism as a major European political and social move-ment. At the other extreme, it could be matched by a survey of the acts of legislation or governmental policies proposed or supported by European liberal parties. A balancing of these two approaches is found in those major classics of liberal philosophy or ideology which both formulate or reflect liberal values or attitudes and indicate or derive the relationship of those values to liberal programs. The history of liberal thought, perhaps because of the commitment to rationalism that has been characteristic of liberalism, includes a significant number of such classic statements.

The liberal tradition manifests itself in four areas. First is the concern with freedom of thought, conscience, and expression. The second area is the development of political freedom in the context of the modern sovereign state. Third is the social, and particularly the economic, framework for freedom. And fourth are those concerns with the ideal of national freedom which raised for liberalism dilemmas about self-determinism, revolution, and international order.

TOLERATION AND FREEDOM OF THOUGHT

Modern European liberalism has been unique in the importance it has placed upon liberty of conscience, thought, and expression as fundamental to the idea of freedom.

Many aspects of European history and thought are related to the development of the liberal interpretation of freedom of thought, conscience, and expression. The notion of ascribing rights to an individual is itself the product of an historical movement. The assertion and defense of the rights of an individual are a part of a broad social change which replaces the previous characteristically feudal practice of asserting corporate rights vested in group status. Locke, Spinoza, and Rousseau, may have disagreed about the rights of man or about the justification of those rights, but they shared this ascription of rights to the individual.

Further, the idea of liberty of conscience was linked to a major political movement which had begun to come to full expression by the seventeenth century: the European secular nation-state. The framework of liberal argument reflects the legitimacy of the secular state as sovereign without ultimate sanction of any ecclesiastical authority.

In the seventeenth century, liberty of conscience was a religious ideal advanced in an age of intense religious concern and horrendous religious warfare. The contemporary political theorist, John Plamenatz, has suggested that it is only in a period when religious belief is taken seriously that religious intolerance is likely and tolerance then becomes formulated as a positive ideal. Further, in a society where uniformity of belief and attitude has been abandoned, toleration of dissent becomes a strategic necessity. This pragmatic argument was augmented by the religious view that coercion is impossible on questions of religious conscience since authentic and sincere belief can never be the product of coercion. To a lesser extent, in the defense of religious toleration, there also was advanced the claim of intrinsic value of plurality of beliefs. Locke, for example, did not assert the view of Mill and later liberals that plurality of opinion generates truth, but he did recognize plural beliefs as the desirable outcome of permitting differing individuals to follow their own consciences and reason.

The seventeenth century was, however, crucial for the ideal of liberty of thought—and not just because the emergence of warring religious groups was a catalyst for religious toleration. It was also the first great period of modern science with its accompanying philosophical method of rationalism. Although faith in reason is logically consistent with coercion of belief, the philosophical rationalists, perhaps because they were a barely tolerated minority, argued that since individual reason is alone competent to decide all questions, toleration must be universal.

The claim that truths sanctioned by revelation, tradition, or authority can be rejected by the natural light of individual reason is a declaration of intellectual independence. Pierre Bayle applied in a limited manner to the specific issue of religious tolerance the method of rationalism which Enlightenment liberalism was to universalize as a model of free inquiry. The argument that the moral positions of Scriptural texts must be interpreted in the light of natural reason, an argument with respectable antecedents in the religious tradition itself, was extended throughout the rationalism of the seventeenth century and the Enlightenment of the eighteenth century. That extension, in the argument of Bayle's *Philosophic Commentary*, means that the specific texts which justify religious intolerance are to be rejected or reinterpreted since any effort to instill sincere faith by force is contrary to the natural light of reason.

At the same time, a fundamental argument for religious tolerance is not confidence in reason, but skepticism of knowledge. If one person is to convert another, he must have a high degree of confidence in the truth of his beliefs. Many liberals have argued, as Bayle did, the impossibility of certitude of the "particular truths of religion." This argument of fallibilism has often been used as a justification of tolerance and is particularly persuasive in periods, as in the seventeenth century, when large numbers of people sincerely hold conflicting beliefs. Historically, it seems that the growth of fallibilism almost always follows the coexistence of differing beliefs and becomes the common rationale for tolerance.

It might seem paradoxical that fallibilism was advanced by many who believed that each man is capable of knowing the truth independent of any authoritative tradition. One reconciliation of this apparent contradiction was that the individual light of reason may be sufficient for interpretation of Scriptures or moral truths, or factual questions or mathematical principles, though it fails in questions of abstruse doctrine. The early tradition of liberalism argued that wherever reason fails, we have no better alternative than to allow each to follow his own inner light. Later on, the areas where the light of reason fails are usually recognized as the domain of individual taste or sentiment where coercion is inappropriate. Liberals have used both rationalism and fallibilism as arguments for religious tolerance.

The earliest complete statement of the liberal position developed from rationalist premises was that of Benedict Spinoza. Spinoza presents a rational justification of the sovereign authority of the secular state, whose sovereignty logically requires the complete separation of church and state. Further, Spinoza is unique among early champions of a powerful secular state in arguing that a necessary condition for its survival is freedom of thought, speech, and conscience. According to him, total thought-control of rational men is unachievable. Therefore censorship needlessly brings about the alienation, hostility, or corruption of the talented citizens with probable stagnation of the sciences and the possibility of revolution.

Men have the capacity for rationality; but only in a state which has liberty of speech and expression can human nature become truly rational. In such a society, men are not made into "brutes or puppets," Spinoza wrote, but "use their reason freely." Spinoza thus formulates the characteristically liberal faith in the possibilities of progressive development of rational human nature if only political institutions will allow this development through complete liberty of thought and expression.

The work that has long been considered the canonic formulation of seventeenth century liberalism on religious toleration is John Locke's *Letter Concerning Toleration*. Locke's statement of the argument is part of the received doctrine of the Enlightenment. It represented the orthodoxy of liberalism until the time of John Stuart Mill in the nineteenth century.

In Locke's work we find the classic source of the liberal doctrine that the church is a "voluntary society." Civil authorities cannot justifiably intrude into the internal affairs of any private voluntary association, except as these impinge clearly upon the public interest. The church cannot appeal to the state for coercion of citizens on any religious question, but must restrict itself to expulsion from is body of those who refuse to accept its authority. Later this conception of the nature of private society and the sovereign, and this drawing of the boundaries between public and private affairs applied not only to the church but to the university, the trade union, the corporation, and other private associations of the liberal state. In the current turmoil of the universities, it explains, in part, the reluctance of university authorities to appeal for police protection; it also supports the traditional legitimacy of the penalty of expulsion from a "voluntary society." The boundary lines which Locke drew may represent an artificial or inappropriate distinction between the domain of private and public. Some assertion, however, along Locke's lines of the autonomy of the private association, and accordingly some boundary to state intervention, remains a criterion for a liberal philosophy of the state.

Locke discussed in an extraordinarily direct and forceful manner the limits of toleration within the secular, liberal framework. The perennial dilemma of liberalism has been whether toleration is to be extended to the intolerant or limited to those who are committed to agreed rules of the society. The difficulty with the first option of the dilemma is that the free society may be undermined by toleration of those who would destroy it; the difficulty with the second option is that the freedom of the society may be eroded by exclusion of its critics from the community. Locke's formulation runs heavily to the risks of the second option. He excludes freedom of opinion for four groups of dissenters: (1) those who reject ordinary moral canons of morality, (2) those who organize to subvert the civil rights of others, (3) those who are in the service of a foreign power, and (4) atheists. Liberals have usually considered Locke's criteria too restrictive even though they recognize the necessity of setting the limits of tolerance for a free society, especially in the context of the rise of totalitarian movements.

Political thinkers, as we have seen, often trace their specific proposals to the fundamental nature of man. Spinoza argued that total coercion of thought is impossible; Locke, that complete coercion of religious conscience is impossible. Immanuel Kant believed that it is the coercion of the rational self which is impossible; for Fichte or the Romantics, the coercion of the expressive ego is impossible. In each case, it is maintained, some fundamental and residual portion of the individual defies the reach of external force. The disagreement as to what constitutes this essential residue of the self seems to have direct analogues in the political theory of freedom. It was Spinoza's view that freedom of thought is a political necessity just as Locke argued that the denial of freedom of conscience is politically irrational. For the Romantic, any censorship of authentic expression is beyond the proper power of the sovereign. For Kant, who is a major architect of Continental liberalism, there can be no coercion of the domain of the autonomous rational self.

"The touchstone," Kant wrote, "of everything that can be concluded as law for people lies in the question whether people could have imposed such law on itself." The application of this touchstone, Kant believed, would permit censorship for reasons of public welfare. It could permit restrictions on the free expression of persons hired in particular institutions, so that a civic employee may not participate freely, while holding office, in certain forms of public expression. It could never allow, and here is the particular force of Kant's position, any censorship which would distort the process of rational inquiry. Kant argued that if a rational being consented to censorship of the process of reason, he would be denying the condition of his own self-determination. It would therefore be self-contradictory for a human being to propose, or consent to, censorship of rational inquiry.

There are, of course, many liberals who do not concede the merit of Kant's argument and who argue that freedom of inquiry is always a question of competing values, not a logical necessity of the human condition. Yet liberalism has, since Kant, been particularly sensitive to censorship in areas of intellectual inquiry. In part this represents the impact of the belief in progress, especially as formulated during the Enlightenment. In that view, to block inquiry is to deny the process of human rationality, and so to block the possibility of continuous progress through the application of reason. The logic of the Kantian argument is applied historically. Defense of the freedom of inquiry then became both the condition of human rationality and the condition of human progress. It is against this background that the special priority within liberalism, and within German liberalism particularly, of the tradition of academic freedom and untrammeled scientific exploration can be understood.

There is an illuminating contrast between this view, which is expressed in Kant's essay *What is Enlightenment?* and John Stuart Mill's *On Liberty*. Kant and Mill are at one in their condemnation of any state intervention to censor or to abridge the process of freedom of opinion and inquiry. Yet while Kant viewed such censorship as logically contradicting the rationality of human nature, Mill held that freedom is justified by calculations of utility. Mill did not, however, actually calculate the consequences in units of pleasure and pain of particular acts of censorship. Instead he develops the general arguments which lead to the belief that censorship would generate disutility.

Some of these arguments have attained classic status within liberalism. For example, Mill argued that since the individual usually knows his own best interests, the risks of misplaced intervention on behalf of the individual's interests are greater than the risks of his own error. Again, the empirical risk of abuse by persons who have broad grants of power outweighs the potential benefits of exercise of such power in areas of morals or thought. One especially interesting argument which Mill used to exclude public intervention in any area of opinion, is the claim that a necessary condition for accepting any opinion as true is that all the relevant counterevidence and counterargument has been examined. Since censorship limits the availability of such counterevidence, it cannot direct the advance, but can only impede the search for truth.

Mill was, however, committed to the view that where censorship or public intervention would in fact maximize utility or the greatest good for the greatest number, it would be justified. In the practice of liberalism this utilitarian justification for state intervention in the sphere of the individual's moral or economic activities has often been adopted.

John Stuart Mill's *On Liberty* is, however, the source of another liberal criterion for limiting legislation that affects the individual which is not utilitarian. Mill seeks to draw a sharp distinction between self-regarding acts, which affect only the agent, and other-regarding acts. Mill's position is that there ought not to be any legislative intervention with respect to self-regarding acts. The validity of this criterion and its application to an entire range of legislative questions—the use of narcotics, compulsory education, sexual acts between freely consenting adults—have been the subject of controversy throughout the history of modern liberalism. A strikingly similar position to that of Mill was developed by the liberal Prussian Minister of Public Worship and Instruction, Wilhelm von Humboldt.

On the other hand, almost continuously from its publication, Mill's *On Liberty* has been the subject of criticism. In particular, the critics have charged that Mill's liberalism involves a conception of society as a set of atomic individuals not related to any particular moral fabric—for it is only with such a view that the notion of self-regarding acts becomes significant. Liberal theory for more than a century has ranged between a defense of Mill's position, including its practical implications, and an attempt to formulate an approach to social freedom which would accept a more "organic" conception of the relationship between the public and the private.

With the rejection of laissez-faire economics in late nineteenth-century liberalism, there developed a parallel skepticism of Mill's conception of the relationship between the state and the individual. In part this reflected the influence of Hegelian thought which sought to show how individuals, without being aware of it, were participating in the spirit of their culture and their time. It also expressed a greater sensitivity to the role of public policy in creating the social climate for intellectual and moral achievement. Socialist thought influenced many liberals in its stress upon the economic or social forms of coercion. State intervention might then be justified on liberal grounds as minimizing other kinds of extra-legal coercion. In every European country, as well as in the United States, we see a self-conscious effort to reexamine and to reinterpret the principles of liberalism in the light of these criticisms.

The view of the new liberalism is that many governmental actions of social control, ranging from redistribution of wealth through subsidization of the arts, are compatible with individual freedom in society. They may even be necessary for the furthering of individual freedom. The liberal ideal of freedom of conscience, thought, and expression, so controversial in its origin, had become a commonplace by the second half of the nineteenth century. "The nineteenth century might be called the age of Liberalism," Leonard Hobhouse, one of the proponents of the new organic liberalism wrote at the turn of the century, "yet its close saw the fortunes of that great movement brought to its greatest ebb." Since then, the defeat of Nazism and Fascism in the heart of Europe in World War II and the recent appearance of liberalism as a spectre haunting Communist Europe suggest a continuing significance of the ideals of liberty of thought, conscience, and expression on the continent of their birth.

CONSTITUTIONALISM AND DEMOCRACY

In the literature of liberalism, there is a familiar and useful distinction between negative and positive freedom. In an important sense, a person is free, whatever be his desires or capacities, if he is not subject to coercion by another. Champions of negative freedom, like Humboldt, Mill, or Constant, recognizing this aspect of freedom have sought to set limits to state intervention in the sphere of individual activity. In the context of political institutions, this has involved the protection of the rights of the individual from the potential abuses of arbitrary power. Hence the support by liberals of the traditional safeguards embodied in the system of checks and balances or in the rule of law. Here also is the source of the tradition of liberal mistrust of concentration of power even when the power is necessary, rational, benevolent, or progressive.

In another important sense of freedom, a person is free when he can achieve what he wants to do. Champions of the concept of freedom, such as Rousseau, Kant, or Hobhouse, have advanced a conception of freedom in which the individual's or society's true needs or ends must be identified and the means necessary for their realization must be developed. In that view, the ignorance of true needs or the lack of appropriate means for their satisfaction, even when there is no explicit element of coercion, constitutes a denial of freedom. In the context of governmental structure, this conception has required liberals to move far beyond a concern with limits to state intervention toward a concern that the state satisfy the demands, and express the will, of the people. The historical process has been the identification of the idea of liberty with the idea of democracy.

It seems that a straightforward political realization of the value of liberty requires as a minimum that laws have the consent of the governed on the general ground that a person is not free if he is subject to coercion by laws which he opposes. The notion of consent, however, ranges over a broad continuum. For Locke, a founding father of liberal political theory, a person who has the right to leave a country but chooses to remain and participate in its activities has tacitly consented to its laws. No democratic election or representation is required to guarantee the citizen's freedom, although Locke therefore was led to grant the citizen's right to emigration and his ultimate right to revolution as the method for withholding or denying consent. At the other end of the spectrum, consent of the governed would require direct express participation and unanimous approval for all coercive action. Liberals with anarchic sympathies have advanced this only as a limiting ideal. Most liberal theorists require explicit, periodic consent of the majority through the devices of election or representation as necessary to satisfy the condition of freedom. A non-democratic society would, therefore, not be a liberal society.

A commitment to democracy does not appear in the early medieval sources of European liberal theory. The defense of freedom there was then related to the right of resistance to tyranny. Some of the justifications of this right rely upon the ancient arguments of the right to oppose the law of the state in the name of divine law. In the development of liberalism this right was transposed. With the growth of the secular state which tolerated different religions within its boundaries, there could be no right to revolt in the name of divine truth. Yet if the secular state was reciprocally denied power to intervene in affairs of religion, conscience, or thought, there could be continual grounds for revolution in the resistance to encroachment of public authority into any private domain.

Most doctrines of natural rights implied a right to revolution. Even an authoritarian like Hobbes conceded that if the social state is deemed not superior relative to the right to life over the terrible state of nature, the individual has the residual right to revolution. For Locke or Rousseau and the more liberal theorists of natural rights, the violation of fundamental natural rights justifies revolution.

With the development, however, within later liberal theory, of representative democracy as an adequate fulfillment of liberal society, the right to revolution is restricted. In one standard argument, since a minority can become a majority through democratic process, it is only a denial of democratic process that justifies revolution. Within a democratic society, therefore, one can have no right to revolution.

A right to revolution is an extreme check to tyranny. Like all threats of the use of ultimate weapons, it is not viable in limited situations for it is much too dangerous and much too implausible a response to continuous but minor abuses of power. A concern with translating the idea of human freedom into the fabric of political institutions must then rely on more limited approaches.

Political experience seems generically to invent checks and balances in all political situations. What is unique to liberalism in its doctrine of separation of powers is the abstract and explicit formulation of the separation as a condition of freedom. Montesquieu, for example, to whom this interpretation of British political practice of separate legislative, executive, and judicial checks is usually traced, may be regarded as either a conservative or a liberal. The formula of checks and balances among the agencies of government as a universal set of conditions for politically free society, however, became part of a liberal constitutionalism of the nineteenth century. Liberals have further conceived in general the possibility of an ideal constitutional model for free institutions to spread throughout the world. This general vision has become the target of much criticism of liberalism. Critics such as Oakeshott, with an eye to uniqueness of temperament, tradition, and political education, have ridiculed the concept of exportation of a constitution or of a political framework. Yet if arbitrary exercise of power is an inevitable threat in all sovereign societies, some version of the wisdom codified in doctrines of separation of powers has seemed to liberals an ineliminable aspect of free society.

There is, as suggested, an interpretation of the positive sense of freedom according to which man is free only if he legislates the laws which he obeys. Immanuel Kant, more than any other thinker in history, has examined the concept of freedom as autonomous legislation in metaphysical and moral contexts. According to Kant, human rationality legislates the conceptual framework of our experience, and human morality consists in asserting imperatives which must be obeyed on pain of denying our own rationality. The political transposition of this theme marks Kant as a major influence in the development of European liberalism. These include a stress on majority rule, or an emphasis on limits of sovereign power or a doctrine of "general will."

Every person must legislate for himself the laws to which he submits. Literally interpreted, it would then seem that all laws require unanimous consent. Since one function of a legal system is to impose coercive sanction upon the recalcitrant, the notion of unanimous consent seems paradoxical. Continental liberalism worked out several resolutions of this paradox.

The votes of the majority would seem to provide the only practical method by which one approximates the will of the community, yet since every person has rights, the rights of a minority cannot be overruled by majority vote.

One liberal response is to restrict the sphere of possible legislation to those areas where universal consent is rational. All rational car drivers, though they dislike to be punished, want some rules of the road. Any rational egalitarian entering a competitive race he would wish to win for himself would want to prescribe an unbribable judge. Legislation then can be universal when it is of this character, binding on minority or majority.

The implications for liberalism of this argument have been enormous. It is this kind of argument that reinforced the view, also held on grounds of economic theory of the market, that state legislation must be limited to general rules, and must avoid intervention for particular interests. It contributes to the general liberal conception of the relations between the state and the individual where the state must provide the framework of a rule of law, legal equality, and hence equality of opportunity for the individual who in turn must then function within the framework of the law.

Critics of liberalism have often asserted this conception shows the excessively formal character of political freedom in the liberal state. Champions of liberalism have argued that in making rule of law the necessary condition of the free state, liberalism provides the political framework which guarantees civil rights and provides safeguards to the arbitrariness of despotism.

The concept of freedom as prescribing the laws which one obeys has also been significant for the theory of popular sovereignty. For

Rousseau even unanimity ought not to prescribe laws since a person could have his judgment of what should be the public law distorted by special interest. Rousseau's solution lies in the doctrine of the general will as the ultimate infallible legislator of a free society, that is, as legislating exclusively those laws which each rational citizen would prescribe to himself. Rousseau argues that the general will of a society does not emerge from a balance among its express and vested interests but from eliciting the authentic and disinterested voice of the people. It is this conception of the general will more than any other doctrine which influenced the emergence of a conception of a free society as the democratic society, that is, the society in which the laws approximate most closely the "will of the people." But since Rousseau's conception of the general will of the society is independent of harmonization of interests of the different groups of society, he is often considered a precursor of that aspect of democratic theory which leads through support of revolutionary mass movements to the "totalitarian democracy."

There are many points of contrast between British liberalism and the liberalism of the Continent. These differences are usually traceable to differences between the development of British institutions and those of the Continent. In contrast to Continental development, the classic statements of British democratic liberalism were not written in the context of the Enlightenment and are related to utilitarian theory.

Utilitarianism provides, in principle, a method for evaluating systems of government. Every system of government ought to maximize the greatest good for the greatest number, counting each person as one. Of course, it does not follow that each person should have one vote: if persons are not capable of knowing their own best interests, there would be a strong case on utilitarian grounds for benevolent despotism. As an interesting historical example, James Mill, a founder of the British Liberal Party, wrote in 1832 that representative government for India, which had been urged by some liberal enthusiasts including Sir Andrew Johnston, a former Chief Justice of Ceylon, was wholly out of the question. The fundamental argument of James Mill's *Essay on Government* does not assume that each individual knows his own best interests. Rather, it assumes that each person will pursue what he *believes* to be his interests at the expense of another person's interests. Accordingly no one should turn over to another the guardianship of his own interests. The principle of democracy provides the method whereby each person preserves control of his own interests.

James Mill and the utilitarians realized that direct democracy was impossible. It followed that governmental institutions must admit of delegated authority and yet must not permit the abuse of the interests of the individual by his delegates. In this way much of the agenda of liberalism for the first half of the nineteenth century was set.

Since no person can abdicate his right to select his representatives, universal suffrage is a priority item of this agenda. Since representatives must be controlled by the electorate, the practice of periodic elections is a minimal requirement for liberal democracy. John Stuart Mill, the great spokesman of nineteenth-century British liberalism, accepts as the fundamental justification of democracy the risks of abuse of the person's interests in any non-democratic system of government. Mill supports universal suffrage since participation in government constitutes the best form of political education. The participation of the masses in democratic government will, he argued, develop the social character of the citizens.

French liberalism, in the writings of Benjamin Constant and Alexis de Tocqueville, was more concerned with the threat to freedom from a democratic society. The greater concentration of political power in democracies; the willingness, and perhaps even the necessity, to jettison traditional safeguards for the sake of social achievement; the power of public opinion to silence dissent, are among the factors de Tocqueville enumerated in showing the risk to freedom from democracy.

Benjamin Constant, with the rule of Napoleon as paradigm, argued that the despotism of the modern age supported by mass enthusiasm could surpass ancient tyranny. The rise of mass movements in major western European democracies which advocated dictatorial rule has confirmed in surprising ways the vision of Tocqueville and Constant. At the same time contemporary political sociologists have stressed the power exercised by bureaucratic minorities within both democratic and totalitarian societies. Consequently, the desire to preserve individual freedom within "mass society" has led to efforts to reformulate the principle of liberal democracy.

The development of this theory of democracy, which is primarily the fruit of bitter experience with totalitarianism, has not been the monopoly of liberals. Theorists of democracy have sought to formulate the criteria which distinguish democracy from the tyranny of the majority. These criteria include the existence of plural elite groups in the society so that countervailing powers operate, a degree of social mobility so that there is open access to elite groups within a society, and no monopolistic control of mass media. The single most fundamental criterion remains what the traditional proponents of liberal democracy claimed: periodic free elections among competing candidates for political leadership.

PROGRESS, ECONOMIC LIBERALISM, AND SOCIAL DEMOCRACY

The programs of liberalism have constantly sought to apply fundamental knowledge of man and society to the improvement of the human condition. There have been, however, great changes in what counts as fundamental knowledge of man and society. The development of economic theory, for example, has had decisive impact on liberalism in the two centuries since philosophers of the Enlightenment first sought to derive programs of social reform from their interpretations of history, psychology, and economics.

The classic statement of perfectibility against the background of a theory of social change is Antoine Nicholas de Condorcet's *Sketch for a Historical Picture of the Progress of the Human Mind*. Condorcet was able, because of the wide learning in several fields of knowledge, to present a plausible and extremely dramatic account, replete with heroes and villains, of the major episodes of the human spirit. He evaluated, for example, with measured reasons, the negative influence of Christianity on natural science or the limited scope of the Islamic renaissance. He assessed, as history's chief magistrate, the status of the medieval university or the limits of Cartesian science. In so doing, Condorcet provided liberalism with a point of view, a reasoned attitude on the major events and institutions of Europe.

In projecting that history into the future, Condorcet also provided, in the words of Stuart Hampshire, "the first and most complete statement of that radical programme which was gradually to be translated into fact in the democracies of Western Europe." That program included such characteristic liberal planks as universal education, universal suffrage, increase in economic productivity through the application of the sciences, self-determination for colonial peoples, and equal rights for women.

Condorcet's optimism, however, seemed to run counter to the dismal truths of economics which were formulated by liberals of the nineteenth century. The liberal tradition includes not only Condorcet but Malthus, and Malthus wrote in his *Essay on Population*, which derives directly from his reading of Condorcet, that his "object was . . . to try the truth of those speculations on the perfectibility of man and society." The historian of liberalism, Élie Halévy, has pointed out how Malthus reinterprets rather than refutes the concept of perfectibility, so that both, the optimism of Condorcet and the pessimism of Malthus, set the boundaries for nineteenth-century liberal thought.

Malthus explicitly argued for the idea of progress, but insisted that progress is limited by knowledge of the laws of nature, including the inevitable pressure of population in resources. That this argument was in a liberal context is confirmed by John Stuart Mill's *Autobiography:*

> Malthus's population principle was quite as much a banner, and point of union among us, as any opinion specially belonging to Bentham. This great doctrine, originally brought forward as an argument against the indefinite improvability of human affairs, we took up with ardent zeal in the contrary sense, as indicating the sole means of realizing that improvability by securing full employment at high wages to the whole laboring population through a voluntary restriction of the increase of their numbers.

For Mill and for Malthus, the lessons to be learned and applied were those of the new economic theory. The interpretation of the economic theories of Malthus, Ricardo, and Adam Smith determined the shape of liberalism throughout most of western Europe, and particularly in England. It was the "realism" of classical economics in England, just as much as it was the shock of terror and dictatorship in France, which brought about the sharp differentiation between the liberal faith in progress in the nineteenth century from that of the more utopian and visionary followers of Condorcet such as St. Simon or Comte.

Classical economics provided liberalism with much more than the liberal faith in gradual, even incremental, social progress. It was the source, either by correct interpretation or by distortion, of the belief that government intervention in economic affairs would, on the whole, harm rather than help its intended beneficiaries. This classical doctrine reinforced the traditional liberal preference for a limited state to the point where the views that the best government is that which governs least entered the liberal canon.

Liberal views then served as a rationale for the removal of restrictions on enterpreneurial economic activities. Adam Smith cast much of the argument of *The Wealth of Nations* as a criticism of the errors of mercantilists or agrarian economic systems in which tariffs, subsidies, or colonial monopolies were justified as assisting economic growth and welfare. Smith contrasted the mistaken benefits of those systems with the true benefits desirable with slight exceptions from a policy of free trade. Jeremy Bentham, who was a prominent popularizer of extreme laissez-faire economics argued, for example, that government intervention to set maximum interest rates by usury laws represents a necessarily misguided intervention in allocation of investment as well as a paternalistic interference with the liberty of the individual.

Disillusionment with the social consequences of laissez-faire economic policies has been a stimulus to liberals to reformulate liberalism so that it would be compatible with government intervention for economic welfare. In some accounts this intervention is justified as an extension of liberal democracy. The argument is that freedom means that every individual should control to the maximum degree possible the social institutions that affect his life. Democratic government must then intervene in the economy in order for the individual to assert some control over the major coercive institutions of modern society. This argument obviously leads liberals to a position which is very close to that of European social-democratic parties. It is not surprising therefore that many liberal groups in western Europe have been absorbed into labor or socialist parties.

On the other hand, it is not so often noted how important the influence of liberalism was in reshaping the direction of Marxist social-democratic parties. Eduard Bernstein, the leader of German social democracy, was one of many Fabians, or Social Democrats, who believe that socialism must be continuous with the ideals and programs of liberal democracy. The rapprochement between social democrat and liberal in economic policy, of course, has never been complete.

Economic liberals like Keynes or Beveridge who have argued for governmental intervention in the economy or for welfare state policies have never believed that social ownership of industry is the desirable method for such intervention. There has been no consensus even among the interventionists on the measures which a liberal economic policy should adopt. Hobhouse, whose reformulation of "positive" liberalism was probably the most widely shared view, wrote that "the manner in which the state is to exercise its controlling power [over property and industry] is to be learnt by experience and even in large measure by cautious experiment." Keynesian economics was obviously useful to liberals since it suggested the possibility of sufficient economic control over a capitalist economy to avoid stagnation and depression without direct economic control or widespread nationalization. Keynes' own agenda includes the growth of autonomous quasi-public corporations, currency and credit controls, and population policy.

At the same time, other economic liberals have insisted that the policies of classic laissez-faire liberalism ought not to be drastically modified. These liberals do not necessarily maintain that a free market economy will sustain optimal employment rates or maximize social welfare, although some are willing to defend the historical record and the continued value of a free market economy. Their argument is that only a market economy sustains individual freedom under a rule of law. The abolition of the capitalist economy or its erosion through the accretion of interventionist controls involves such a large concentration of political and economic power that it must bring about the decline of individual freedom and the evolution of a totalitarian state.

In the past two decades, however, the debate on state intervention has lessened. In part this suggests a narrowing of the spectrum of disagreement between liberal and conservative economic theorists on questions of social policy. It may also reflect the fact that the traditional dilemma between confidence in the application of science to social problems and fear of excessive concentration or abuse of power has shifted to more explosive issues raised by the new technological possibilities.

NATIONALISM, REVOLUTION, AND INTERNATIONAL ORDER

In our time, the most fundamental social question is the question of war and peace. This has also been true throughout the era of modern liberalism. Yet the problem of peace has not been central for modern social theory, not for liberalism or conservatism or socialism. The reason for this, however, is not that social philosophers ignore their most fundamental problems but that they consider war to be a consequence of other problems of social, economic, and political life.

For liberalism, the main cause of the wars of the seventeenth century was religious intolerance. Religious toleration was then a program for international peace. Similarly, liberals argued that the dynastic wars of Europe derived from mistaken or selfish desires of tyrants. The establishment of republican regimes was then a measure toward peace. The liberal program for sovereign authority in which no person's and no faction's interests or freedoms would be suppressed was a formula for ending civil warfare.

There are a number of important contexts for liberal policy and programs in which there is a more explicit and primary concern over the problems of war and international order.

Seventeenth-century philosophers, like Locke, Spinoza, and Grotius, asserted the existence of a law of nature discernible by right reason. Grotius first advanced specific rules of international law derived from the law of nature. This appeal to natural law by Grotius, Spinoza, and Locke replaced the appeal to custom or revealed authority as a sanction for moral rules. The medieval foundations for international order lay, broadly speaking, in the legitimacy of hereditary monarchies authorized by a religious covenant. In theory, the causes for war lay in usurpations of legitimacy or violation of religious sanction. Accordingly, rationally perceivable laws of nature, based upon the character of human interests, afforded new foundations for international order. This replacement of theological and traditionalist arguments by a rationalist interpretation of the order of nature characterizes the emergence of modern liberalism.

Liberals formulated the problem of world order as the harmonization of the rational interests among secular nation states into a system of rule and law. Some version of this "dream of reason" has continuously been advocated in the liberal tradition.

In Condorcet's sketch of human progress, the elimination of war was naturally seen as an aspect of human perfectibility. What is relevant, however, is not the abstract and utopian vision (Condorcet expressed his reservations about "those projects of eternal peace which have filled the leisure and consoled the hearts of certain philosophers") but the specific steps Condorcet advocated, which became an integral part of the liberal program for the elimination of war. Universal education, free trade, and international organizations are among the factors Condorcet listed that would "hasten the progress of the brotherhood of nations."

Rationalist projects for perpetual peace, like those of Kant and Bentham, reveal fundamental features of liberalism. Three components of Kant's natural "guarantee" for perpetual peace, for example, have usually been part of a liberal program. One is Kant's view that international peace depends upon the republican character (*i.e.*, a government based on *de facto* popular sovereignty) of individual nations. A second is the claim that standing armies are a bar to peace among nations. The third is his belief that the effect of international travel or commerce is to increase the possibility of peace among nations.

Liberals placed particular stress upon the "spirit of commerce" as ultimately in conflict with the wastefulness of war. One particular corollary which became a constant in liberal ideology was the economic disutility of colonialism. Adam Smith, Jeremy Bentham, and John Stuart Mill distinguished between the expansion of the trading market which has been a by-product of colonialism and the monopolistic development of the colonies which has been injurious to free trade, and, therefore, in their view, to the economic welfare of both the colony and the colonial country.

Economic considerations were only one of three major reasons liberals advanced in general support of emancipation of colonies. The second reason is political. Since legitimate government requires the consent of the governed, colonies should become self-governing or independent. The development of representative institutions then became the responsibility of the colonial power. One ironic result may be that in native countries which lack traditions of democratic rule, the liberal doctrine imposes such institutions in the name of self-determination.

The third liberal argument is that emancipation of colonies would help to eliminate war. It could do this both by reducing the irrational bellicose competition for control of colonies, and by eliminating any cause for war between native movements for national self-determination and colonial powers. In some interpretations of liberalism, since colonial rule was repressive of national freedom, a system of lasting peace could be achieved only after the emancipation of all colonies. Liberal theory does not stress the complexities of stabilizing a system of international order in post-colonial society. And as the liberal support for South African independence after the Boer War showed, problems of race were not examined.

Independence for colonial countries was universally advocated by liberals as a condition for peace or freedom. The argument that some countries were not prepared for self-government was accepted, for example, by John Stuart Mill even though he had advanced, in other contexts, the view that actual participation in the process of government was a legitimate form of education for self-government. Mill argued that the preservation of some residual bonds of empire is "a step . . . towards universal peace, and general friendly cooperation among nations." Among his reasons is the view that the emancipated colony could be absorbed by another foreign state and become "a source of additional aggressive strength" for a rival power which might be more despotic than the original colonial power had been.

The main stress of liberal thought and politics, however, was in favor of eventual independence for all colonial dependencies. The rapid and nearly total emancipation of the colonies of the major European countries shows in significant measure the influence of liberalism.

The tensions that may develop between forces seeking to conserve an international order and revolutionary nationalist movements have occurred in the past few decades primarily in Asia and Africa. In the nineteenth century those tensions were most intense in Europe.

The movements for national self-determination and political freedom in Poland, Germany, France, Italy, Ireland, Hungary, and Greece were in conflict with ruling European powers. Liberal rhetoric which had praised the universal human triumph of reason over particularistic backward cultural traditions in the eighteenth century, was exuberant in its support of the aspirations of authentic national groups in the nineteenth century. The ideal of freedom becomes identified with the liberation of the suppressed nationhood and the expression of the national spirit. The writings of Mazzini or the German Declaration of the Rights of Man in 1848 show that the assertion of national unity has been merged with the demand for freedom.

Some element of ambivalence always appeared in the liberal embrace of nationalism. Some of the Romantic and traditionalist justifications of particular nationalist movements clashed with the liberal vision of enlightened, progressive self-determination. Most significantly, liberals were supporters of international peace while they were also in the vanguard of revolutionary movements that wished to use force to change the map of Europe. The ultimate justification for that support was found in the principles of national self-determination and the defense of civil liberties against the repressive authoritarian government. It also required the faith, perhaps not always warranted, in a connection between internal liberty and internal peace, so that the overthrow of tyrannical regimes became by extension a plausible basis for a peaceful international order.

There is a useful analogy between the liberal ambivalence over revolutionary nationalism and the liberal attitude to social revolution. As champions of rights of the individual, liberals supported such revolutionary demands for social change as universal suffrage, constitutional governments, and later even greater economic equality. On the other hand, as believers in reform as the method of change, liberals opposed revolution. In revolutionary crises, liberals split between those who side with legality or order despite their sympathy with the causes that the revolutionaries champion and those who side with the revolution despite their misgivings over violence and extralegality. This perennial dilemma of liberalism in the face of social revolution is particularly acute, as the writings of the Russian exile and lover of liberty, Aleksandr Herzen, show in countries that lack a successful tradition of reform.

There is an inevitable discrepancy between the abstract formulation of the rights and duties of states and individuals toward the achievement of world peace and the necessities and expediencies of national policy in periods of international strife and disorder.

This has been dramatically shown in both great wars of this century. In the period before World War I, liberals asserted the illusory character of the benefits achievable by force of arms. The willingness of a state to undertake military commitments, for some liberals, was a distortion of the purposes of the state and represented a violation of the rights of the individual. T. H. Green, with Hobhouse, a major spokesman of the new liberalism, argued, for example, that most activities of the state in the field of national defense represented militaristic, imperial, or mis-guided patriotic activities which a liberal state ought not to undertake.

Yet when faced with the realities of military pressures, liberal regimes responded by efforts to achieve a balance of power necessarily includ-ing effective alliances and guarantees to neutrals or potential allies. The result was the willingness of the liberal governments of western Europe to commit themselves to the First World War. The postwar period also reveals this kind of oscillation between support of policies based on certain abstract liberal principles, intervention in support of democratic self-determination, for example, and support of policies based on a more realistic concern with collective security or national interest.

The two great catastrophes of the twentieth century—world war generated by Europen national hostility and the rise of totalitarian regimes—have disappointed the hopes of nineteenth-century liberal movements. Those who would pursue the liberal vision in political society have had to learn new lessons or relearn old lessons about the nature of man and power. Yet the eclipse of liberal ideals through totalitarianism and war can also increase the awareness of the values of liberal tradition.

I

Toleration and Freedom of Thought

The beginning of the liberal tradition is in the struggle for religious toleration and intellectual freedom. The selections that comprise this section show the range of discussion of the value of freedom of thought. They also exhibit the diversity of justification for that freedom that is the heritage of liberalism.

The first three selections, taken from Spinoza, Bayle, and Locke, which date from the seventeenth century, were published in Holland, a country which has been described as then the "working model of free institutions and the center of light for the rest of Europe." Each of these three authors suffered in varying degree from political or religious intolerance. There is a significant similarity in their approach to freedom of thought. Yet each derived from a different intellectual tradition of the age.

Spinoza, as the most consistent of the systematic philosophical rationalists of the seventeenth century, pursued the implications of a rationalist conception of human nature to derive the conditions for freedom in a secular sovereign state. In contrast, Bayle derived his concern for tolerance, to a marked degree, from that skepticism toward religious knowledge which was a product of European human-ism and the revival of the tradition of classical "Pyrrhonic" skepticism. Locke's justification of toleration recognizes the political necessity of toleration for the nation state. Its philosophical connections are neither with rationalism nor with skepticism but with the method of empiricism which was to become the dominant philosophical tradition of the Enlightenment.

The philosophers of the eighteenth-century Enlightenment adum-brated in sharp relief (most characteristically in the "sketch" of Condorcet which is anthologized in the third section of this book) the progress which flows from freedom of opinion with the backwardness which is a consequence of repressive regimes of monarchy and church. Immanuel Kant, in *What Is Enlightenment?* formulated this point of view in arguing for a logical connection between progress and freedom of thought.

The selections from another eighteenth-century German thinker, Wilhelm von Humboldt, do not derive from Enlightenment rationalism but from the "romanticist" concern with expression of individuality. Like the works of Constant or de Tocqueville, they are a significant portion of the liberal tradition which stressed the necessity of freedom of the individual and of the independence of the secondary association, particularly the universities, against the intervention of state or of public opinion.

Liberalism of the nineteenth century, especially in Britain, found in utilitarianism its fundamental creed. Jeremy Bentham gave this creed its most straightforward formulation and used it to determine the limits of the legislation of morality. The selection from Bentham presents both his statement of the principle of utility and his grounds for legislative nonintervention in matters of opinion and morals. Bentham's doctrines were critically recast by his disciple, J. S. Mill, in *On Liberty*, which immediately became part of the liberal canon.

The final selection in this section, excerpted from Hobhouse's *Liberalism*, is representative of later liberal criticism of the views of Bentham and Mill. It marks the concern of liberalism in the twentieth century with the social conditions for freedom of thought or individual freedom.

In the development of liberal thought there has been near unanimity on the value of tolerance or freedom of thought with widespread disagreement on issues of interpretation and application. This controversy is continuous. Two contemporary illustrations show this continuity.

First, the contemporary concern with changing sexual mores has brought to the fore the problem of legal intervention regarding homosexuality, obscenity, pornography, and prostitution. Critics of the "permissive" society have stressed the interconnected fabric of social order and, accordingly, the responsibility of the public for the varieties of individual behavior. On the whole, liberal spokesmen have reasserted the views of Mill on the impropriety of legislation to acts which affect consenting individuals and the harm of governmental legislation in areas of morality. No consensus within the courts or in the marketplace of ideas has emerged.

Second, the activities of totalitarian movements in subverting democratic government have recast with new urgency the problems raised by Spinoza, Bayle, and Locke on the limits of toleration. The tragedy of the German Weimar Republic and the failure of its sovereign authority to outlaw anti-democratic movements has been an over-whelming case example arguing for the rights of the state to protect democratic freedoms against attack. Yet the enormous growth in power of the state, its resources for invasion of privacy or influencing public opinion has made most liberals fear the stifling of dissent through devices which identify dissent with conspiracy.

Disagreement is expected, even inevitable, as to how or where we should draw the line of toleration and freedom of thought. What is more disturbing to liberalism is the emergence of fundamental challenge to the traditional justification of such freedom. The Marxist challenge has been the rejection of freedom of thought as a formal or vacuous freedom which rationalizes or masks the exploitative character of the bourgeoisie. This argument has been generalized along the following lines: Every value system including one which espouses tolerance or freedom reflects the ideals of an established group and depends upon the framework in which it exercises power; the rejection of freedom of thought, objectivity, or tolerance is then asserted as the prerequisite to the overthrow of a repressive framework of power. In this view, such permanent and irrational revolution is the price for the emergence of new self-determining, concrete, and participatory freedom of expression which can replace the old rationalist liberalism of Spinoza, Kant, or Mill.

The resolution of these practical and theoretical issues will determine the viability of the liberal tradition of the twentieth century.

1. SPINOZA

Freedom of Thought and Speech

Benedict Spinoza (1632–77) published his major work in political theory, *Tractatus Theologico-Politicus*, pseudonymously in Amsterdam in 1670. It was banned by the civil authorities in 1674. The full title of the work is "A Treatise on Religion and Politics Containing Several Discussions Which Show That to Philosophize Not Only Can Be Granted Without Detriment To Piety And Public Peace; But Cannot Be Destroyed Without Destroying

Them as Well." The present selection constitutes most of the concluding twentieth chapter.*

THAT IN A FREE STATE EVERY MAN MAY THINK WHAT HE LIKES, AND SAY WHAT HE THINKS.

If men's minds were as easily controlled as their speech, every king would sit safely on his throne, and no government would be oppressive. Then every subject would shape his life according to the intentions of his rulers, and would judge a thing true or false, good or evil, just or unjust, in obedience to their dictates. However, we have shown already that no man's mind can possibly lie wholly at the disposition of another, for no one can willingly transfer his natural right of free reason and judgment, or be compelled so to do. For this reason government which attempts to control minds is accounted tyrannical, and it is considered an abuse of sovereignty and a usurpation of the rights of subjects, to seek to prescribe what shall be accepted as true, or rejected as false, or what opinions should actuate men in their worship of God. All these questions fall within a man's natural right, which he cannot abdicate even with his own consent.

I admit that the judgment can be biased in many ways, and to an almost incredible degree, so that while exempt from direct external control it may be so dependent on another man's words, that it may fitly be said to be ruled by him; but although this influence is carried to great lengths, it has never gone so far as to invalidate the statement, that every man's understanding is his own, and that opinions vary as much as taste. . . .

However unlimited, therefore, the power of a sovereign may be, however implicitly it is trusted as the exponent of law and religion, it can never prevent men from forming judgments according to their intellect, or being influenced by any given emotion. It is true that it has the right to treat as enemies all men whose opinions do not, on all subjects, entirely coincide with its own; but we are not discussing its strict rights, but its proper course of action. I grant that it has the right to rule in the most violent manner, and to put citizens to death for very trivial causes, but no one supposes it can do this with the approval of sound judgment. Nay, inasmuch as such things cannot be done without extreme peril to itself, we may even deny that it has the absolute

* Translated by R. M. N Elwes, with minor revisions by the editor.

power to do them, or, consequently, the absolute right; for the rights of the sovereign are limited by his power.

Since, therefore, no one can abdicate his freedom of judgment and feeling; since every man is by indefeasible natural right the master of his own thoughts, it follows that men thinking in diverse and contradictory fashions, cannot, without disastrous results, be compelled to speak only according to the dictates of the supreme power. . . . Still we cannot deny that authority may be as much injured by words as by actions; hence, although the freedom we are discussing cannot be entirely denied to subjects, its unlimited concession would be most baneful; we must, therefore, now inquire, how far such freedom can and ought to be conceded without danger to the peace of the state, or the power of the rulers . . . .

It follows, plainly, from the explanation given above, of the foundations of a state, that the ultimate aim of government is not to rule, or restrain, by fear, nor to exact obedience, but, on the contrary, to free every man from fear, that he may live in all possible security; in other words, to strengthen his natural right to exist and work without injury to himself or others.

No, the object of government is not to change men from rational beings into beasts or puppets, but to enable them to develop their minds and bodies in security, and to employ their reason unshackled; neither showing hatred, anger, or deceit, nor watched with the eyes of jealousy and injustice. In fact, the true aim of government is liberty.

Now we have seen that in forming a state the power of making laws must either be vested in the body of the citizens, or in a portion of them, or in one man. For, although men's free judgments are very diverse, each one thinking that he alone knows everything, and although complete unanimity of feeling and speech is out of the question, it is impossible to preserve peace, unless individuals abdicate their right of acting entirely on their own judgment. Therefore, the individual justly cedes the right of free action, though not of free reason and judgment. No one can act against the authorities without danger to the state, though his feelings and judgment may be at variance with them. He may even speak against them, provided that he does so from rational conviction, not from fraud, anger, or hatred, and provided that he does not attempt to introduce any change on his private authority.

For instance, supposing a man shows that a law is repugnant to sound reason, and should therefore be repealed; if he submits his opinion to the judgment of the authorities (who, alone, have the right of making and repealing laws), and meanwhile acts in nowise contrary to that law, he has deserved well of the state, and has behaved as a good citizen should; but if he accuses the authorities of injustice, and stirs up the people against them, or if he seditiously strives to abrogate the law without their consent, he is a mere agitator and rebel.

Thus we see how an individual may declare and teach what he believes, without injury to the authority of his rulers, or to the public peace; namely, by leaving in their hands the entire power of legislation as it affects action, and by doing nothing against their laws, though he be compelled often to act in contradiction to what he believes, and openly feels, to be best.

Such a course can be taken without detriment to justice and dutifulness, nay, it is the one which a just and dutiful man would adopt. We have shown that justice is dependent on the laws of the authorities, so that no one who contravenes their accepted decrees can be just, while the highest regard for duty, as we have pointed out in the preceding chapter, is exercised in maintaining public peace and tranquillity; these could not be preserved if every man were to live as he pleased; therefore it is no less than undutiful for a man to act contrary to his country's laws, for if the practice became universal the ruin of states would necessarily follow.

Hence, so long as a man acts in obedience to the laws of his rulers, he in nowise contravenes his reason, for in obedience to reason he transferred the right of controlling his actions from his own hands to theirs. This doctrine we can confirm from actual custom, for in a conference of great and small powers, schemes are seldom carried unanimously, yet all unite in carrying out what is decided on, whether they voted for or against. But I return to my proposition.

From the fundamental notions of a state, we have discovered how a man may exercise free judgment without detriment to the supreme power: from the same premises we can no less easily determine what opinions would be seditious. Evidently those which by their very nature nullify the compact by which the right of free action was ceded. For instance, a man who holds that the supreme power has no rights over him, or that promises ought not to be kept, or that everyone should live as he pleases, or other doctrines of this nature in direct opposition to the above-mentioned contract, is seditious, not so much from his actual opinions and judgment, as from the deeds which they involve; for he who maintains such theories abrogates the contract which tacitly, or openly, he made with his rulers. . . .

I do not deny, however, that there are some doctrines which, while they are apparently only concerned with abstract truths and falsehoods, are yet propounded and published with unworthy motives. . . . If we hold to the principle that a man's loyalty to the state should be judged, like his loyalty to God, from his actions only—namely, from his charity toward his neighbors; we cannot doubt that the best government will allow freedom of philosophical speculation no less than of religious belief. I confess that from such freedom inconveniences may sometimes arise, but what question was ever settled so wisely that no abuses could possibly spring therefrom? He who seeks to regulate everything by law, is more likely to arouse vices than to reform them. It is best to grant what cannot be abolished, even though it be in itself harmful. How many evils spring from luxury, envy, avarice, drunkenness, and the like, yet these are tolerated—vices as they are—because they cannot be prevented by legal enactments. How much more then should free thought be granted, seeing that it is in itself a virtue and that it cannot be crushed! Besides, the evil results can easily be checked, as I will show, by the secular authorities, not to mention that such freedom is absolutely necessary for progress in science and the liberal arts: for no man follows such pursuits to advantage unless his judgment be entirely free and unhampered.

But let it be granted that freedom may be crushed, and men be so bound down, that they do not dare to utter a whisper, save at the bidding of their rulers; nevertheless this can never be carried to the pitch of making them think according to authority, so that the necessary consequences would be that men would daily be thinking one thing and saying another, to the corruption of good faith, that mainstay of government, and to the fostering of hateful flattery and perfidy, whence spring stratagems, and the corruption of every good art.

It is far from possible to impose uniformity of speech, for the more rulers strive to curtail freedom of speech, the more obstinately are they resisted; not indeed by the avaricious, the flatterers, and other numskulls, who think supreme salvation consists in filling their stomachs and gloating over their money-bags, but by those whom good education, sound morality, and virtue have rendered more free. Men, as generally constituted, are most prone to resent the branding as criminal of opinions which they believe to be true, and the proscription as wicked of that which inspires them with piety toward God and man; hence they are ready to forswear the laws and conspire against the authorities, thinking it not shameful but honorable to stir up seditions and perpetuate any sort of crime with this end in view. Such being the constitution of human nature, we see that laws directed against opinions affect the generous-minded rather than the wicked, and are adapted less for coercing criminals than for irritating the upright; so that they cannot be maintained without great peril to the state.

Moreover, such laws are almost always useless, for those who hold that the opinions proscribed are sound, cannot possibly obey the law; whereas those who already reject them as false, accept the law as a kind of privilege, and make such boast of it, that authority is powerless to repeal it, even if such a course be subsequently desired.

. . . And, lastly, how many schisms have arisen in the Church from the attempt of the authorities to decide by law the intricacies of theological controversy! If men were not allured by the hope of getting the law and the authorities on their side, of triumphing over their adversaries in the sight of an applauding multitude, and of acquiring honorable distinctions, they would not strive so maliciously, nor would such fury sway their minds. This is taught not only by reason but by daily examples, for laws of this kind prescribing what every man shall believe and forbidding anyone to speak or write to the contrary, have often been passed, as sops or concessions to the anger of those who cannot tolerate men of enlightenment, and who, by such harsh and crooked enactments, can easily turn the devotion of the masses into fury and direct it against whom they will.

How much better would it be to restrain popular anger and fury, instead of passing useless laws, which can only be broken by those who love virtue and the liberal arts, thus paring down the state till it is too small to harbor men of talent. What greater misfortune for a state can be conceived than that honorable men should be sent like criminals into exile, because they hold diverse opinions which they cannot disguise? What, I say, can be more hurtful than that men who have committed no crime or wickedness should, simply because they are enlightened, be treated as enemies and put to death, and that the scaffold, the terror of evil-doers, should become the arena where the highest examples of tolerance and virtue are displayed to the people with all the marks of ignominy that authority can devise?

He that knows himself to be upright does not fear the death of a criminal, and shrinks from no punishment; his mind is not wrung with remorse for any disgraceful deed: he holds that death in a good cause is no punishment, but an honor, and that death for freedom is glory.

What purpose then is served by the death of such men, what example is proclaimed? the cause for which they die is unknown to the idle and the foolish, hateful to the turbulent, loved by the upright. The only lesson we can draw from such scenes is to flatter the persecutor, or else to imitate the victim.

If formal assent is not to be esteemed above conviction, and if governments are to retain a firm hold of authority and not be compelled to yield to agitators, it is imperative that freedom of judgment should be granted, so that men may live together in harmony, however diverse, or even openly contradictory their opinions may be. We cannot doubt that such is the best system of government and open to the fewest objections, since it is the one most in harmony with human nature. In a democracy, the most natural form of government . . . everyone submits to the control of authority over his actions, but not over his judgment and reason; that is, seeing that all cannot think alike, the voice of the majority has the force of law, subject to repeal if circumstances bring about a change of opinion. In proportion as the power of free judgment is withheld we depart from the natural condition of mankind, and consequently the government becomes more tyrannical.

In order to prove that from such freedom no inconvenience arises, which cannot easily be checked by the exercise of the sovereign power, and that men's actions can easily be kept in bounds, though their opinions be at open variance, it will be well to cite an example. Such a one is not very far to seek. The city of Amsterdam reaps the fruit of this freedom in its own great prosperity and in the admiration of all other people. For in this most flourishing state, and most splendid city, men of every nation and religion live together in the greatest harmony, and ask no questions before trusting their goods to a fellow-citizen, save whether he be rich or poor, and whether he generally acts honestly, or the reverse. His religion and sect is considered of no importance: for it has no effect before the judges in gaining or losing a cause, and there is no sect so despised that its followers, provided that they harm no one, pay every man his due, and live uprightly, are deprived of the protection of the magisterial authority.

On the other hand, when the religious controversy between Remonstrants and Counter Remonstrants began to be taken up by politicians and the States, it grew into a schism, and abundantly showed that laws dealing with religion and seeking to settle its controversies are much more calculated to irritate than to reform, and that they give rise to extreme license: further, it was seen that schisms do not originate in a love of truth, which is a source of courtesy and gentleness, but rather in an inordinate desire for supremacy. From all these considerations it is clearer than the sun at noonday, that the true schismatics are those who condemn other men's writings, and seditiously stir up the quarrelsome masses against their authors, rather than those authors themselves, who generally write only for the learned, and appeal solely to reason. In fact, the real disturbers of the peace are those who, in a free state, seek to curtail the liberty of judgment which they are unable to tyrannize over.

I have thus shown:—I. That it is impossible to deprive men of the liberty of saying what they think. II. That such liberty can be conceded to every man without injury to the rights and authority of the sovereign power, and that every man may retain it without injury to such rights, provided that he does not presume upon it to the extent of introducing any new rights into the state, or acting in any way contrary to the existing laws. III. That every man may enjoy this liberty without detriment to the public peace, and that no inconveniences arise therefrom which cannot easily be checked. IV. That every man may enjoy it without injury to his allegiance. V. That laws dealing with speculative problems are entirely useless. VI. Lastly, that not only may such liberty be granted without prejudice to the public peace, to loyalty, and to the rights of rulers, but that it is even necessary for their preservation. For when people try to take it away, and bring to trial, not only the acts which alone are capable of offending, but also the opinions of mankind, they only succeed in surrounding their victims with an appearance of martyrdom, and raise feelings of pity and revenge rather than of terror. Uprightness and good faith are thus corrupted, flatterers and traitors are encouraged, and sectarians triumph, inasmuch as concessions have been made to their animosity, and they have gained the state sanction for the doctrines of which they are the interpreters. Hence they arrogate to themselves the state authority and rights, and do not scruple to assert that they have been directly chosen by God, and that their laws are Divine, whereas the laws of the state are human, and should therefore yield obedience to the laws of God—in other words, to their own laws. Everyone must see that this is not a state of affairs conducive to public welfare. Wherefore . . . the safest way for a state is to lay down the rule that religion is comprised solely in the exercise of charity and justice, and that the rights of rulers in sacred, no less than in secular matters, should merely have to do with actions, but that every man should think what he likes and say what he thinks. . . .

2. BAYLE

Reason and Tolerance

Pierre Bayle (1647–1706) wrote a series of works in the 1680's in defense of religious toleration. The *Philosophical Commentary*, published in Rotterdam in 1686, was the last of these.

Bayle's concern for religious tolerance was evidenced throughout his life. He was the son of a Protestant minister in Carla, a town in Southern France, which was a refuge for dispossessed Huguenots. In 1669, when Bayle was twenty-two, he studied at the Jesuit college in Toulouse and converted to Catholicism; a year later he renounced Catholicism and, as a lapsed Catholic in France, felt it was prudent to flee to Calvinist Geneva. Subsequently, he returned to France and taught at the Protestant Academy in Sedan. When the Protestant academies in France were closed in 1681, he went into exile in Rotterdam, where he taught philosophy and theology.

Bayle's *Philosophical Commentary* was published pseudonymously as a translation of an English work by a Mr. John Fox. The argument was attacked as excessively tolerant by Bayle's colleague and fellow exile from France, Jurieu. As a consequence of Jurieu's criticism of Bayle, Bayle was deprived of his professorship in 1693.

The selections are taken from the chapter entitled "Reason and Tolerance" in the *Commentary*.*

A PHILOSOPHIC COMMENTARY UPON THESE WORDS OF JESUS CHRIST: "COMPEL THEM TO COME IN," WHEREBY IT IS PROVED BY MANY DEMONSTRATIVE REASONS THAT NOTHING IS MORE ABOMINABLE THAN TO MAKE CONVERSIONS BY FORCE . . .

I leave it to the theologians and the textual critics to explicate this passage by examining what precedes and what follows, by showing

* As presented in *Great Contest of Faith and Reason*, translated and edited by Karl P. Sandberg. (New York: Frederick Ungar Publishing Co., 1963.) Used by permission.

the force of the terms of the original, and of their various possible meanings, and of the meanings which they indeed do have in several places in the Scripture. As for myself, I aspire to write a new kind of commentary and to found it upon principles which are more general and more infallible than anything which the study of languages and criticisms and commonplaces could furnish me. I will not even try to discover why Jesus Christ used this expression *compel*, nor will I try to ascertain its legitimate meaning, nor will I try to discover whether there be some mystery lurking beneath its surface. I will limit myself to refuting the literal meaning which the persecutors give to it.

In order to refute it incontrovertibly I will base my argument upon this principle of natural light, that any literal meaning which entails the obligation to commit crimes is false. St. Augustine himself sets down this rule for discerning between the figurative meaning and the literal meaning of the Scripture. Jesus Christ, he tells us, declares that if we do not eat the flesh of the Son of Man, we will not be saved. It seems that this interpretation enjoins us to commit a crime. These words must therefore be taken as a figure which enjoins us to participate in Communion and to bring to our remembrance for our edification that the Lord's flesh was crucified and wounded for us. This is not the place to examine whether or not these words prove that St. Augustine was not of the opinion of the Roman Church, or whether or not he applies his own rule appropriately. Suffice it to say that he bases his reasoning upon this fundamental principle of Scriptural exegesis that *if a literal interpretation of the Scripture obliges men to commit crimes* or (to be perfectly clear) to perform acts which natural light, the precepts of the Decalogue, and the morality of the Gospel prohibit, we must assuredly conclude that its proponents have given the Scripture a false meaning, and instead of a divine revelation, they offer us nothing more than their own imaginations, passions, or prejudices.

Far be it from me to wish to extend the jurisdiction of natural light and the principles of metaphysics as far as do the Socinians, who reject any meaning given to the Scripture which does not conform to this light and these principles and who because of this maxim refuse to believe the doctrines of the Trinity and the Incarnation. No, I do not believe that this maxim is without limits, [but] I know full well that there are axioms against which the most express and evident words of the Scripture would be powerless, as for example, the whole is greater than its parts; if from equal parts one takes away equal parts, the remainders are equal; it is impossible for two contradictory statements both to be true; or that the essence of a subject continues really to subsist after the destruction of the subject. Even if one were to show a hundred Scriptural passages contradicting these propositions, even if one were to perform thousands upon thousands of miracles, more than Moses and the Apostles, in order to establish a doctrine opposed to these universal maxims of common sense, people would still not be convinced. Rather, they would be persuaded either that the Scripture spoke only by metaphor or that these miracles came from the devil, for they cannot believe that the natural light of men which dictates these maxims is deceptive. . . .

Let us therefore be done with the idea that theology is a queen and that philosophy is her servant. The theologians themselves give evidence by their conduct that they regard philosophy as the queen and theology as the servant, for the source of all of their intellectual gymnastics is the desire not to be in contradiction with sound philosophy. Rather than so expose themselves they change their principles of philosophy, de-emphasizing this one or that one according to their particular need. But by all of these procedures they recognize clearly the superiority of philosophy and the essential need which they feel of its approval. They would not go to so much trouble to conform to its laws if they did not recognize that any dogma which is not, so to speak, confirmed, verified, and recorded by the Supreme Parliament of reason and natural light can be of only a very uncertain authority and fragile as glass. . . .

I say once again, far be it from me to wish to extend this principle as far as do the Socinians. But if it has certain limitations with respect to speculative truths, I do not think that it should have any with respect to practical and general principles which concern morals. I mean that without exception we must submit all moral laws to this natural idea of justice, which just as metaphysic light, "enlightens every man who comes into the world."

But if a man really desires to understand these ideas of natural justice or equity, I would ask him to consider them in general, divorcing them from his own personal interest and the customs of his country, for passions and prejudices obscure only too often our ideas of natural justice. When a man looks upon an action as very useful and agreeable for himself, he may easily be persuaded by a subtle and deeply-rooted prejudice that this action is reasonable. It is also possible that the strength of custom and the peculiar stamp given to the soul by early education will lead one to believe that a certain act is blameless when, in reality, it is not. Therefore, if one wishes to overcome these two obstacles and to ascertain the dictates of natural light concerning morality, I would ask him first to hold himself aloof from his own personal interest and the manners of his country and then to ask himself this question: If a certain custom were to be introduced into a country where it had not been in usage, would it be worthy of acceptance after a free and critical examination? I believe that this abstraction would dispel many of the clouds which sometimes come between our minds and this pure and universal light which emanates from God to make known to all men the general principles of equity, this light which is the touchstone of all precepts and individual laws, for I do not except even those which God has subsequently revealed to us extraordinarily, either by speaking to us Himself or by sending us His inspired prophets. . . .

This is the terminal point of all Roman Catholic writings against the way of reason and in favor of the authority of the Church. Without being aware of it, they only make a large circle and come back after much labor and fatigue to the point where the others go immediately. The others say frankly and without wasting words that we must hold to the meaning which appears to us to be the best. The Catholics, on the other hand, say that we must take care not to do so because our individual lights can deceive us. Our reason is only darkness and illusion, they say, and we must therefore defer to the judgment of the Church. But is this not coming back to reason? If one prefers the judgment of the Church to his own, does he not make the decision by virtue of this reasoning: the Church is more enlightened than I am; therefore, it is more believable than I am? It is consequently the individual's own enlightenment which determines the course to follow. If he believes that something is revealed, it is because his common sense, his natural light, and his reason tell him that the proofs offered of the revelation are sound.

But where will one be if he must distrust his reason as a dark and deceptive principle? Must he not then distrust his reason even when it tells him that "the Church is more enlightened than I am and therefore more believable than I am?" Must he not then fear that his reason is deceived both as to the principle and the conclusion derived from it?

And what will one do also with this argument? "All that God says is true. Now God says by Moses that He created a first man. Therefore, that is true." If we do not have a natural light to serve as an infallible rule by which to judge of everything that is called into question (including the question of whether a given idea is contained in the Scripture), will we not have reason to doubt the major premise of this argument and by consequence the conclusion? And because we would then find ourselves on the path to the most dreadful chaos and the most detestable skepticism imaginable, we must necessarily come to this conclusion: any individual dogma, whether it is said to be contained in the Scripture or whether it is otherwise advanced, is false when refuted by the clear and distinct ideas of natural light, and principally with respect to morality.

I have felt obliged to my readers to establish the universality of the foregoing principles, but now I come to the particular subject and the specific matter of my commentary on these words of the passage "Compel them to come in," and this is how I reason: the literal meaning of these words is contrary to the most distinct ideas which reason teaches us; therefore, it is false. . . .

It is then clear that the only legitimate way to inspire religion is to produce within the soul certain views and acts of will concerning God. Now since threats, persecutions, fines, exiles, beatings, tortures, and generally everything that is contained in the literal meaning of constraint cannot create these acts of will which constitute the essence of religion, it is clear that this use of constraint to establish a religion is false. Consequently, Jesus Christ did not command it.

I do not deny that the use of force produces within the soul certain views and acts of will, in addition to the external postures which are the usual signs of inward religion. These attitudes, however, are not toward God, but only toward the originators of the constraint. The persecuted judge that their persecutors are to be feared, and they indeed fear them. But those people who did not have the proper views concerning God beforehand and did not feel due respect, love, and fear for Him, do not acquire these ideas and feelings when someone forces them to go through the outward forms of religion. Likewise, those who held certain ideas of God beforehand and who believed that He was to be honored only in a certain way which was different than that of the persecutors, do not change their inward feeling toward God either.

Their only new thoughts are to fear their persecutors and to retain their goods which are in danger. Thus, these manifestations of force accomplish nothing with respect to God, for the inward acts they produce have no relationship to Him. And as for the outward acts, it is evident that they are accepted by God only as they are accompanied by the inward dispositions of the soul which are the essence of religion. This should be sufficient to assure the solidity of this proof.

The nature of religion is a certain persuasion of the soul with regard to God which produces in the will the feelings of love, respect, and fear which this Supreme Being deserves, and in the members of the body the signs appropriate to this persuasion and disposition of the will. Therefore, if the outward signs are accompanied by an inappropriate or contradictory disposition of the soul, they are acts of hypocrisy, bad faith, or infidelity and revolt against conscience. . . .

To try to convert people by force to a religion they do not profess is consequently in evident contradiction with common sense and natural light, the general principles of reason, and, in a word, with the original and basic rule of discerning the true from the false, the good from the bad. The clear and distinct ideas which we have of the essence of certain things persuade us invincibly that God cannot reveal to us anything which contradicts them. (For example, we are entirely certain that God cannot reveal that the whole is smaller than its parts; that it is proper to prefer vice to virtue; that we should esteem our dog above our friend and our country; that to go from one place to another by sea we should start out at a gallop on a horse; that in order to prepare a field for an abundant harvest we must not cultivate it.) It is then evident that God has not commanded us in His word to force acceptance of the Gospel upon people by means of beatings or other such violences. Thus, if we find in the Gospel a passage which commands us to do the contrary, we may be assured that the meaning is figurative and not literal, just as if we found in the Scripture a passage which commanded us to become very learned in languages and all kinds of capabilities without studying, we would believe that this passage should be understood figuratively, or that the passage had been falsified, or that we did not understand all of the meanings of the terms in the original, or that it is a mystery which speaks of a people unlike ourselves who are to come after us. Finally, we might believe it to be a precept given according to the oriental way of speaking, that is, by emblems, symbols, and obscure images. We would believe anything rather than be persuaded that God, wise as He is, commanded men literally and properly to acquire a profound knowledge without study. . . .

It is commonly said that there is no more dangerous plague in a state than the multiplicity of religions, because it causes dissension between friends and neighbors, fathers and children, husbands and wives, and sovereigns and subjects. I answer that far from working against me, this argument is a very strong proof in favor of tolerance. If a multiplicity of religions is harmful to a state, it is only because one religion does not wish to tolerate another and sets out to crush it by persecution. *Hinc prima mali labes*, this is the source of the evil. If each religion practiced the tolerance which I advocate, a state divided by ten religions would enjoy the same peace and harmony as a city where all the different kinds of artisans live together in peace in spite of their differences. The only result of religious toleration would be an honest effort on the part of each sect to distinguish itself by its piety, its virtuous acts, and its learning. Each one would make it a matter of pride to show by its good works that it was the most favored of God. Each would even show forth more devotion to the state if the sovereign protected all of them and judged them all with equity. Now such an honest emulation among them would obviously be the source of an infinite amount of good, and consequently nothing would be more apt to restore the Golden Age than toleration. Certainly the harmony which it would establish among several voices and instruments of varying tones and keys would not be any less pleasing than the uniformity of a single voice. But what stands in the way of this fine concert of diverse voices and sounds? It is the desire of one of the religions to exercise a cruel tyranny over the minds of others and to force others to sacrifice their consciences. It is the unjust partiality of kings who deliver the executive power of the state over to the raging and tumultuous desires of a populace of monks and religionists. In a word, all the strife comes not from tolerance, but from intolerance. . . .

If you ask a man to do any more [than to follow his conscience], it is clear that you are asking him to fix his love and zeal only upon the absolute truth, infallibly recognized as such. Now in our present human condition it is impossible for us to know with certainty that that which appears to us to be truth is in fact the absolute truth. (I am speaking here of the particular truths of religion, and not of the properties of numbers, nor of the first principles of metaphysics, nor of the maxims of geometry.) Indeed, all we can do is to be fully persuaded that we possess the absolute truth, that we are not mistaken, and that our opponents are mistaken. But this persuasion is an equivocal mark of the truth since it is found in the most hopelessly lost heretics. It is therefore certain that it is impossible for us to find any sure sign by which we might discern our true ideas, which we believe to be true, from our false ideas, which we also believe to be true. It is not by Cartesian evidence that we can make this discernment, because, to the contrary, everyone says that the truths which God reveals to us in His Word are profound mysteries which require us to make our understanding bow to faith. It is not by incomprehensibility that we can know the truth—what is there more false and at the same time more incomprehensible than a square circle, than a Supreme Being who is essentially evil, or a god which begets offspring by carnal generation, such as the Jupiter of paganism? It is not by the satisfaction of one's conscience, for a papist is as satisfied with his religion, a Turk with his, and a Jew with his, as we are with ours. It is not by the courage and zeal which an opinion produces, for false religions have their martyrs, their unbelievable austerities, a spirit of proselyting greater than the charity of the orthodox, and an extreme attachment to their superstitious ceremonies. In a word, there is nothing by which one can recognize the truth or falsity of his conviction. Thus, if you require that he discern infallibly between truth and error, you ask him to do more than he is able. All that he can do is to say that certain things appear false to him after examination and others true. We must therefore ask him to try to make true objects appear to be true to him. But whether he succeeds or whether he still mistakes error for truth, he must then abide by what he believes to be true. . . .

Ever since the Protestants left the Roman Church, they have constantly heard the objection that in rejecting the authority of the Church, they attempt to find the truth by examination of the Scripture and that this examination is beyond the means of an individual. . . . We complain about this argument being brought up again and again after we have answered it a thousand times, and yet we must admit that the Catholic writers are right in a certain way in continuing to bring it up, because it is not answered and cannot be answered without making the usual supposition that God requires each individual to know the absolute truth and to know that he knows it. Let us admit the debt: neither the learned nor the ignorant can attain such certainty by the way of examination. This way will never lead us to the criterion of truth, which is an idea so clear and distinct that after having considered all of the reasons to doubt we still feel keenly that it cannot be otherwise. It is not possible to arrive at such an idea with regard to this one point of fact, that a given passage of Scripture has been translated correctly, that the Word which is in Greek or Hebrew today has always been there; and that the meaning given it by the interpreters, the commentators, and the translators is the one intended by the author of the book. We can have a moral certainty of it, based upon very great probabilities. But in the final analysis, this certainty can be found in a multitude of people who are mistaken. Thus, it is not a sure mark of truth. It is not what is called a *criterium veritatis*, which is the irresistible evidence by which we know, for example, that the whole is greater than its parts; that if from equal things one subtracts equal portions, the remainders are equal; that six is half of twelve, etc. . . .

If you weigh these ideas carefully and meditate upon them profoundly you will no doubt see that the truth which I am attempting to establish here is that man in his present condition is required by God only to seek the truth as carefully as he can and, believing to have found it, to love it and take it for his guide. As everyone can see, this is a proof that we are obliged to have the same attitude toward the apparent truth as for the real truth. When this point is accepted, all the objections which are raised concerning the difficulty of individual examination disappear as mirages—it is certain that each individual, no matter how simple, is able to give a meaning to what he reads, or to what is read to him, and to feel that this meaning is true, and he then possesses his own truth. It is sufficient for each individual to consult sincerely and in good faith the light which God gives him, and after that to commit himself to the idea which seems the most reasonable and consistent with the will of God. If he does that, he is orthodox with respect to God, although by an unavoidable defect his thoughts may not be a faithful image of the reality of things, just as a child is orthodox in taking the husband of his mother to be his father, although he may not really be his son. The most important consideration is thereafter to act virtuously, and thus, each one must employ all of his means in honoring God by a prompt obedience to the precepts of morality. And as for the knowledge of our duties in questions of conduct, the revealed light is so clear that few people go astray when they seek it in good faith.

3.   LOCKE

Church and State

John Locke (1632–1704) wrote *A Letter Concerning Toleration*, his first published work, in Latin in 1685. He was then living in Holland because of his justified fear of imprisonment in England for participating in revolutionary political activity. The *Letter* was published anonymously at Gouda, Holland, in 1689. Translated into English by William Popple, it was published, again anonymously, in London that same year, the year of the passage of the British Toleration Act of 1689, and one year after the Glorious Revolution.

Locke's support of religious toleration was constant throughout his career. His first manuscript in 1666 was an unpublished essay on the need for religious tolerance, and the *Letter* is itself based on an essay drafted in 1667. Locke's death interrupted his writing of *A Fourth Letter for Toleration*, the last of his three replies to criticisms of *A Letter Concerning Toleration*.

A LETTER CONCERNING TOLERATION

. . . I esteem it above all things necessary to distinguish exactly the business of civil government from that of religion, and to settle the just bounds that lie between the one and the other. . . .

The commonwealth seems to me to be a society of men constituted only for the procuring, preserving, and advancing their own civil interests.

Civil interests I call life, liberty, health, and indolency of body; and the possession of outward things, such as money, lands, houses, furniture, and the like. . . .

Now that the whole jurisdiction of the magistrate reaches only to these civil concernments; and that all civil power, right and dominion is bounded and confined to the only care of promoting these things; and that it neither can nor ought in any manner to be extended to the salvation of souls, these following considerations seem unto me abundantly to demonstrate.

First, because the care of souls is not committed to the civil magistrate any more than to other men. It is not committed unto him, I say, by God; because it appears not that God has ever given any such authority to one man over another, as to compel anyone to his religion. Nor can any such power be vested in the magistrate by the consent of the people, because no man can so far abandon the care of his own salvation as blindly to leave to the choice of any other, whether prince or subject, to prescribe to him what faith or worship he shall embrace. For no man can, if he would, conform his faith to the dictates of another. . . .

In the second place, the care of souls cannot belong to the civil magistrate because his power consists only in outward force; but true and saving religion consists in the inward persuasion of the mind, without which nothing can be acceptable to God. And such is the nature of the understanding that it cannot be compelled to the belief of anything by outward force. Confiscation of estate, imprisonment, torments, nothing of that nature can have any such efficacy as to make men change the inward judgment that they have framed of things. . . .

It is only light and evidence that can work a change in men's opinions; which light can in no manner proceed from corporal sufferings or any other outward penalties.

In the third place, the care of the salvation of men's souls cannot belong to the magistrate; because, though the rigor of laws and the force of penalties were capable to convince and change men's minds, yet would not that help at all to the salvation of their souls. For there being but one truth, one way to heaven, what hope is there that more men would be led into it if they had no rule but the religion of the court, and were put under the necessity to quit the light of their own reason, and oppose the dictates of their own consciences, and blindly to resign themselves up to the will of their governors and to the religion which either ignorance, ambition, or superstition had chanced to establish in the countries where they were born? In the variety and contradiction of opinions in religion, wherein the princes of the world are as much divided as in their secular interests, the narrow way would be much straitened; one country alone would be in the right, and all the rest of the world put under an obligation of following their princes in the ways that lead to destruction; and that which heightens the absurdity, and very ill suits the notion of a Deity, men would owe their eternal happiness or misery to the places of their nativity.

These considerations, to omit many others that might have been urged to the same purpose, seem unto me sufficient to conclude that all the power of civil government relates only to men's civil interests. . . .

Let us now consider what a church is. A church, then, I take to be a voluntary society of men, joining themselves together of their own accord in order to the public worshiping of God in such manner as they judge acceptable to Him, and effectual to the salvation of their souls.

I say it is a free and voluntary society. Nobody is born a member of any church; otherwise the religion of parents would descend unto children by the same right of inheritance as their temporal estates, and everyone would hold his faith by the same tenure he does his lands, than which nothing can be imagined more absurd. Thus, therefore, that matter stands. No man by nature is bound unto any particular church or sect, but everyone joins himself voluntarily. . . .

It follows now that we consider what is the power of this church, and unto what laws it is subject.

Forasmuch as no society, how free soever, or upon whatsoever slight occasion instituted, whether of philosophers for learning, of merchants for commerce, or of men of leisure for mutual conversation and discourse, no church or company, I say, can in the least subsist and hold together, but will presently dissolve and break in pieces, unless it be regulated by some laws, and the members all consent to observe some order. . . . But since the joining together of several members into this church society, as has already been demonstrated, is absolutely free and spontaneous, it necessarily follows that the right of making its laws can belong to none but the society itself; or, at least (which is the same thing), to those whom the society by common consent has authorized thereunto. . . .

But, it may be asked, by what means then shall ecclesiastical laws be established if they must be thus destitute of all compulsive power? I answer: They must be established by means suitable to the nature of such things, whereof the external profession and observation—if not proceeding from a thorough conviction and approbation of the mind—is altogether useless and unprofitable. The arms by which the members of this society are to be kept within their duty are exhortations, admonitions, and advices. If by these means the offenders will not be reclaimed and the erroneous convinced, there remains nothing further to be done but that such stubborn and obstinate persons who give no

ground to hope for their reformation, should be cast out and separated
from the society. This is the last and utmost force of ecclesiastical
authority. No other punishment can thereby be inflicted than that, the
relation ceasing between the body and the member which is cut off.
The person so condemned ceases to be a part of that church. . . .

These things being thus determined, let us inquire, in the next place,
how far the duty of toleration extends, and what is required from
everyone by it?

And, first, I hold that no church is bound, by the duty of toleration,
to retain any such person in her bosom as, after admonition, continues
obstinately to offend against the laws of the society. For these being
the condition of communion and the bond of the society, if the breach
of them were permitted without any animadversion the society would
immediately be thereby dissolved. . . .

Secondly, no private person has any right in any manner to prejudice
another person in his civil enjoyments because he is of another church
or religion. All the rights and franchises that belong to him as a man
or as a denizen are inviolably to be preserved to him. These are not
the business of religion. . . .

This is the fundamental and immutable right of a spontaneous
society—that it has power to remove any of its members who transgress
the rules of its institution; but it cannot, by the accession of any new
members, acquire any right of jurisdiction over those that are not
joined with it. And therefore peace, equity, and friendship are always
mutually to be observed by particular churches, in the same manner
as by private persons, without any pretense of superiority or jurisdiction
over one another. . . .

Nobody, therefore, in fine, neither single persons nor churches, nay,
nor even commonwealths, have any just title to invade the civil rights
and worldly goods of each other upon pretense of religion. Those that
are of another opinion would do well to consider with themselves how
pernicious a seed of discord and war, how powerful a provocation to
endless hatreds, rapines, and slaughters they thereby furnish unto
mankind. No peace and security, no, not so much as common friendship, can ever be established or preserved amongst men so long as
this opinion prevails that dominion is founded in grace and that
religion is to be propagated by force of arms. . . .

In the third place, let us see what the duty of toleration requires
from those who are distinguished from the rest of mankind (from the
laity, as they please to call us) by some ecclesiastical character and

office; whether they be bishops, priests, presbyters, ministers, or however else dignified or distinguished. It is not my business to inquire here into the original of the power of dignity of the clergy. This only I say, that whencesoever their authority be sprung, since it is ecclesiastical, it ought to be confined within the bounds of the church, nor can it in any manner be extended to civil affairs, because the church itself is a thing absolutely separate and distinct from the commonwealth. The boundaries on both sides are fixed and immovable. He jumbles heaven and earth together, the things most remote and opposite, who mixes these two societies, which are in their original, end, business, and in everything perfectly distinct and infinitely different from each other. No man, therefore, with whatsoever ecclesiastical office he be dignified, can deprive another man that is not of his church and faith either of liberty or of any part of his worldly goods upon the account of that difference between them in religion. . . .

In private domestic affairs, in the management of estates, in the conservation of bodily health, every man may consider what suits his own convenience, and follow what course he likes best. No man complains of the ill-management of his neighbor's affairs. No man is angry with another for an error committed in sowing his land or in marrying his daughter. Nobody corrects a spendthrift for consuming his substance in taverns. Let any man pull down or build or make whatsoever expenses he pleases, nobody murmurs, nobody controls him; he has his liberty. But if any man do not frequent the church, if he do not there conform his behavior exactly to the accustomed ceremonies, or if he brings not his children to be initiated in the sacred mysteries of this or the other congregation, this immediately causes an uproar. The neighborhood is filled with noise and clamor. Everyone is ready to be the avenger of so great a crime, and the zealots hardly have the patience to refrain from violence and rapine so long till the cause be heard, and the poor man be, according to form, condemned to the loss of liberty, goods, or life. Oh, that our ecclesiastical orators of every sect would apply themselves with all the strength of arguments that they are able to the confounding of men's errors! But let them spare their persons. Let them not supply their want of reasons with the instruments of force, which belong to another jurisdiction, and do ill become a churchman's hands. Let them not call in the magistrate's authority to the aid of their eloquence or learning, lest perhaps, whilst they pretend only love for the truth, this their intemperate zeal, breathing nothing but fire and sword, betray their ambition and show that what they desire is temporal dominion. For it will be very difficult to persuade men of sense that he who with dry eyes and satisfaction of mind can deliver his brother to the executioner to be burned alive does sincerely and heartily concern himself to save that brother from the flames of hell in the world to come.

In the last place, let us now consider what is the magistrate's duty in the business of toleration, which certainly is very considerable.

We have already proved that the care of souls does not belong to the magistrate. . . . The care, therefore, of every man's soul belongs unto himself, and is to be left unto himself. But what if he neglect the care of his soul? I answer: What if he neglect the care of his health or of his estate, which things are nearlier related to the government of the magistrate than the other? Will the magistrate provide by an express law that such a one shall not become poor or sick? Laws provide, as much as is possible, that the goods and health of subjects be not injured by the fraud and violence of others; they do not guard them from the negligence or ill-husbandry of the possessors themselves. No man can be forced to be rich or healthful whether he will or no. Nay, God Himself will not save men against their wills. Let us suppose, however, that some prince were desirous to force his subjects to accumulate riches or to preserve the health and strength of their bodies. Shall it be provided by law that they must consult none but Roman physicians, and shall everyone be bound to live according to their prescriptions? What, shall no potion, no broth, be taken but what is prepared either in the Vatican, suppose, or in a Geneva shop? Or, to make these subjects rich, shall they all be obliged by law to become merchants or musicians? Or shall everyone turn victualler or smith because there are some that maintain their families plentifully and grow rich in those professions? But, it may be said, there are a thousand ways to wealth, but one only way to heaven. It is well said, indeed, especially by those that plead for compelling men into this or the other way. For if there were several ways that led thither, there would not be so much as a pretense left for compulsion. But now if I be marching on with my utmost vigor in that way which, according to the sacred geography, leads straight to Jerusalem, why am I beaten and ill-used by others because, perhaps, I wear not buskins; because my hair is not of the right cut; because, perhaps, I have not been dipped in the right fashion; because I eat flesh upon the road, or some other food which agrees with my stomach; because I avoid certain by-ways, which seem unto me to lead into briars or precipices; because, amongst the several paths that are in the same road, I choose that to walk in which seems to be the straightest and cleanest; because I avoid to keep company with some travelers that are less grave, and others that are more sour than they ought to be; or, in fine, because I follow a guide that either is, or is not, clothed in white or crowned with a miter? Certainly, if we consider right, we shall find that, for the most part, they are such frivolous things as these that (without any prejudice to religion or the salvation of souls, if not accompanied with superstition or hypocrisy) might either be observed or omitted. I say they are suchlike things as these which breed implacable enmities amongst Christian brethren, who are all agreed in the substantial and truly fundamental part of religion.

But let us grant unto these zealots, who condemn all things that are not of their mode, that from these circumstances are different ends. What shall we conclude from thence? There is only one of these which is the true way to eternal happiness: but in this great variety of ways that men follow, it is still doubted which is the right one. Now, neither the care of the commonwealth nor the right enacting of laws does discover this way that leads to heaven more certainly to the magistrate than every private man's search and study discovers it unto himself. . . .

But let us grant that it is probable the way to eternal life may be better known by a prince than by his subjects, or at least that in this incertitude of things the safest and most commodious way for private persons is to follow his dictates. You will say, what then? If he should bid you follow merchandise for your livelihood, would you decline that course for fear it should not succeed? I answer: I would turn merchant upon the prince's command, because in case I should have ill-success in trade, he is abundantly able to make up my loss some other way. If it be true, as he pretends, that he desires I should thrive and grow rich, he can set me up again when unsuccessful voyages have broken me. But this is not the case in the things that regard the life to come; if there I take a wrong course, if in that respect I am once undone, it is not in the magistrate's power to repair my loss, to ease my suffering, nor to restore me in any measure, much less entirely, to a good estate. What security can be given for the Kingdom of Heaven?

Perhaps some will say that they do not suppose this infallible judgment, that all men are bound to follow in the affairs of religion, to be in the civil magistrate, but in the church. What the church has determined, that the civil magistrate orders to be observed; and he provides by his authority that nobody shall either act or believe in the business of religion otherwise than the church teaches. So that the judgment of those things is in the church; the magistrate himself yields obedience thereunto, and requires the like obedience from others. I answer: Who sees not how frequently the name of the church, which was venerable in time of the apostles, has been made use of to throw dust in the people's eyes, in the following ages? But, however, in the present case it helps us not. The one only narrow way which leads to heaven is not better known to the magistrate than to private persons, and therefore I cannot safely take him for my guide who may probably be as ignorant of the way as myself, and who certainly is less concerned for my salvation than I myself am. . . .

But, after all, the principal consideration and which absolutely determines this controversy is this: Although the magistrate's opinion in religion be sound, and the way that he appoints be truly evangelical, yet, if I be not thoroughly persuaded thereof in my own mind, there will be no safety for me in following it. No way whatsoever that I shall walk in against the dictates of my conscience will ever bring me to the mansions of the blessed. I may grow rich by an art that I take not delight in, I may be cured of some disease by remedies that I have not faith in; but I cannot be saved by a religion that I distrust and by a worship that I abhor. It is in vain for an unbeliever to take up the outward show of another man's profession. Faith only and inward sincerity are the things that procure acceptance with God. The most likely and most approved remedy can have no effect upon the patient if his stomach reject it as soon as taken; and you will in vain cram a medicine down a sick man's throat which his particular constitution will be sure to turn into poison. In a word, whatsoever may be doubtful in religion, yet this at least is certain, that no religion which I believe not to be true can be either true or profitable unto me. In vain, therefore, do princes compel their subjects to come into their church communion, under pretense of saving their souls. If they believe, they will come of their own accord; if they believe not, their coming will nothing avail them. How great soever, in fine, may be the pretense of goodwill and charity, and concern for the salvation of men's souls, men cannot be forced to be saved whether they will or no. And therefore, when all is done, they must be left to their own consciences.

Having thus at length freed men from all dominion over one another in matters of religion, let us now consider what they are to do. . . .

Concerning outward worship, I say, in the first place, that the magistrate has no power to enforce by law, either in his own church or much less in another, the use of any rites or ceremonies whatsoever in the worship of God. And this, not only because these churches are free societies, but because whatsoever is practiced in the worship of God is only so far justifiable as it is believed by those that practice it to be acceptable unto Him. . . .

In the next place: As the magistrate has no power to impose by his laws the use of any rites and ceremonies in any church, so neither has he any power to forbid the use of such rites and ceremonies as are already received, approved, and practiced by any church; because, if he did so, he would destroy the church itself, the end of whose institution is only to worship God with freedom after its own manner.

You will say, by this rule, if some congregations should have a mind to sacrifice infants, or (as the primitive Christians were falsely accused) lustfully pollute themselves in promiscuous uncleanliness, or practice any other such heinous enormities, is the magistrate obliged to tolerate them because they are committed in a religious assembly? I answer, No. These things are not lawful in the ordinary course of life, nor in any private house; and therefore neither are they so in the worship of God, or in any religious meeting. . . .

By this we see what difference there is between the church and the commonwealth. Whatsoever is lawful in the commonwealth cannot be prohibited by the magistrate in the church. Whatsoever is permitted unto any of his subjects for their ordinary use neither can nor ought to be forbidden by him to any sect of people for their religious uses. If any man may lawfully take bread or wine, either sitting or kneeling in his own house, the law ought not to abridge him of the same liberty in his religious worship; though in the church the use of bread and wine be very different, and be there applied to the mysteries of faith and rites of divine worship. But those things that are prejudicial to the commonweal of a people in their ordinary use, and are therefore forbidden by laws, those things ought not to be permitted to churches in their sacred rites. Only the magistrate ought always to be very careful that he do not misuse his authority to the oppression of any church, under pretense of public good.

It may be said, what if a church be idolatrous, is that also to be tolerated by the magistrate? I answer, what power can be given to the magistrate for the suppression of an idolatrous church which may not in time and place be made use of to the ruin of an orthodox one? For it must be remembered that the civil power is the same everywhere, and the religion of every prince is orthodox to himself. If, therefore, such a power be granted unto the civil magistrate in spirituals, as that at Geneva, for example, he may extirpate, by violence and blood, the religion which is there reputed idolatrous; by the same rule another magistrate, in some neighboring country, may oppress the reformed religion, and, in India, the Christian. The civil power can either change everything in religion, according to the prince's pleasure, or it can change nothing. If it be once permitted to introduce anything into religion, by the means of laws and penalties, there can be no bounds put to it; but it will in the same manner be lawful to alter everything, according to that rule of truth which the magistrate has framed unto himself. No man whatsoever ought therefore to be deprived of his terrestrial enjoyments upon account of his religion. Not even Americans [Indians], subjected unto a Christian prince, are to be punished either in body or goods for not embracing our faith and worship. If they are persuaded that they please God in observing the rites of their own country, and that they shall obtain happiness by that means, they are to be left unto God and themselves. Let us trace this matter to the bottom. Thus it is: inconsiderable and weak number of Christians, destitute of everything, arrive in a pagan country; these foreigners beseech the inhabitants, by the bowels of humanity, that they would succor them with the necessaries of life; those necessaries are given them, habitations are granted, and they all join together and grow up into one body of people. The Christian religion by this means takes root in that country and spreads itself, but does not suddenly grow the strongest. While things are in this condition, peace, friendship, faith, and equal justice are preserved amongst them. At length the magistrate becomes a Christian, and by that means their party becomes the most powerful. Then immediately all compacts are to be broken, all civil rights to be violated, that idolatry may be extirpated; and unless these innocent pagans, strict observers of the rules of equity and the law of nature, and no ways offending against the laws of the society, I say, unless they will forsake their ancient religion and embrace a new and strange one, they are to be turned out of the lands and possessions of their forefathers, and perhaps deprived of life itself. Then, at last, it appears what zeal for the church, joined with the desire of dominion, is capable to produce, and how easily the pretense of religion and of the care of souls serves for a cloak to covetousness, rapine, and ambition. . . .

But idolatry, say some, is a sin and therefore not to be tolerated. If they said it were therefore to be avoided, the inference were good.

But it does not follow that because it is a sin it ought therefore to be punished by the magistrate. For it does not belong unto the magistrate to make use of his sword in punishing everything, indifferently, that he takes to be a sin against God. Covetousness, uncharitableness, idleness, and many other things are sins, by the consent of men, which yet no man ever said were to be punished by the magistrate. The reason is because they are not prejudicial to other men's rights, nor do they break the public peace of societies. Nay, even the sins of lying and perjury are nowhere punishable by laws, unless in certain cases in which the real turpitude of the thing and the offense against God are not considered, but only the injury done unto men's neighbors and to the commonwealth. And what if in another country, to a Mahometan or a pagan prince, the Christian religion seem false and offensive to God; may not the Christians for the same reason, and after the same manner, be extirpated there? . . .

Thus far concerning outward worship. Let us now consider articles of faith.

The articles of religion are some of them practical and some speculative. Now, though both sorts consist in the knowledge of truth, yet these terminate simply in the understanding, those influence the will and manners. Speculative opinions, therefore, and articles of faith (as they are called) which are required only to be believed, cannot be imposed on any church by the law of the land. For it is absurd that things should be enjoined by laws which are not in men's power to perform. And to believe this or that to be true does not depend upon our will. . . .

Further, the magistrate ought not to forbid the preaching or professing of any speculative opinions in any church, because they have no manner of relation to the civil rights of the subjects. If a Roman Catholic believe that to be really the body of Christ which another man calls bread, he does no injury thereby to his neighbor. If a Jew do not believe the New Testament to be the Word of God, he does not thereby alter anything in men's civil rights. If a heathen doubt of both Testaments, he is not therefore to be punished as a pernicious citizen. The power of the magistrate and the estates of the people may be equally secure whether any man believe these things or no. I readily grant that these opinions are false and absurd. But the business of laws is not to provide for the truth of opinions, but for the safety and security of the commonwealth, and of every particular man's goods and person. And so it ought to be. For the truth certainly would do well enough if she were once left to shift for herself. She seldom has received, and I fear never will receive, much assistance from the power of great men, to whom she is but rarely known and more rarely welcome. She is not taught by laws, nor has she any need of force to procure her entrance into the minds of men. Errors indeed prevail by the assistance of foreign and borrowed succors. But if truth makes not her way into the understanding by her own light, she will be but the weaker for any borrowed force violence can add to her. . . .

But some may ask, What if the magistrate should enjoin anything by his authority that appears unlawful to the conscience of a private person? I answer that if government be faithfully administered and the counsels of the magistrates be indeed directed to the public good, this will seldom happen. But if, perhaps, it do so fall out, I say that such a private person is to abstain from the action that he judges unlawful, and he is to undergo the punishment which it is not unlawful for him to bear. For the private judgment of any person concerning a law enacted in political matters, for the public good, does not take away the obligation of that law, nor deserve a dispensation. But if the law indeed be concerning things that lie not within the verge of the magistrate's authority (as, for example, that the people, or any party amongst them, should be compelled to embrace a strange religion and join in the worship and ceremonies of another church), men are not in these cases obliged by that law, against their consciences. For the political society is instituted for no other end, but only to secure every man's possession of the things of this life. The care of each man's soul, and of the things of heaven, which neither does belong to the commonwealth nor can be subjected to it, is left entirely to every man's self. . . .

But what if the magistrate believe such a law as this to be for the public good? I answer: as the private judgment of any particular person, if erroneous, does not exempt him from the obligation of law, so the private judgment (as I may call it) of the magistrate does not give him any new right of imposing laws upon his subjects which neither was in the constitution of the government granted him nor ever was in the power of the people to grant, much less if he make it his business to enrich and advance his followers and fellow sectaries with the spoils of others. But what if the magistrate believe that he has a right to make such laws, and that they are for the public good, and his subjects believe the contrary? Who shall be judge between them? I answer, God alone. For there is no judge upon earth between the supreme magistrate and the people. God, I say, is the only Judge in this case, who will retribute unto everyone at the last day according to his deserts, that is, according to his sincerity and uprightness in endeavoring to promote piety and the public weal and peace of mankind. But what shall be done in the meanwhile? I answer: The principal and chief care of everyone ought to be of his own soul first, and, in the next place, of the public peace; though yet there are very few will think it is peace there where they see all laid waste.

There are two sorts of contests amongst men, the one managed by law, the other by force; and these are of that nature that where the one ends, the other always begins. But it is not my business to inquire into the power of the magistrate in the different constitutions of nations. I only know what usually happens where controversies arise without a judge to determine them. You will say, then, the magistrate being the stronger will have his will, and carry his point. Without doubt; but the question is not here concerning the doubtfulness of the event, but the rule of right.

But to come to particulars. I say, first, no opinions contrary to human society, or to those moral rules which are necessary to the preservation of civil society, are to be tolerated by the magistrate. But of these, indeed, examples in any church are rare. For no sect can easily arrive to such a degree of madness as that it should think fit to teach, for doctrines or religion, such things as manifestly undermine the foundations of society, and are, therefore, condemned by the judgment of all mankind; because their own interest, peace, reputation, everything would be thereby endangered.

Another more secret evil, but more dangerous to the commonwealth, is when men arrogate to themselves and to those of their own sect some peculiar prerogative covered over with a specious show of deceitful words, but in effect opposite to the civil right of the community. For example: we cannot find any sect that teaches, expressly and openly, that men are not obliged to keep their promise; that princes may be dethroned by those that differ from them in religion; or that the dominion of all things belongs only to themselves. For these things, proposed thus nakedly and plainly, would soon draw on them the eye and hand of the magistrate, and awaken all the care of the commonwealth to a watchfulness against the spreading of so dangerous an evil. But, nevertheless, we find those that say the same things in other words. What else do they mean who teach that faith is not to be kept with heretics? Their meaning, forsooth, is that the privilege of breaking faith belongs unto themselves; for they declare all that are not of their communion to be heretics, or at least may declare them so whensoever they think fit. . . .

These, therefore, and the like, who attribute unto the faithful, religious, and orthodox, that is, in plain terms, unto themselves, any peculiar privilege or power above other mortals, in civil concernments; or who upon pretense of religion do challenge any manner of authority over such as are not associated with them in their ecclesiastical communion, I say these have no right to be tolerated by the magistrate, as neither those that will not own and teach the duty of tolerating all men in matters of mere religion. For what do all these and the like doctrines signify but that they may and are ready upon any occasion to seize the government and possess themselves of the estates and fortunes of their fellow subjects; and that they only ask leave to be tolerated by the magistrate so long until they find themselves strong enough to effect it?

Again: That church can have no right to be tolerated by the magistrate which is constituted upon such a bottom that all those who enter into it do thereby *ipso facto* deliver themselves up to the protection and service of another prince. For by this means the magistrate would give way to the settling of a foreign jurisdiction in his own country, and suffer his own people to be listed, as it were, for soldiers against his own government. Nor does the frivolous and fallacious distinction between the court and the church afford any remedy to this inconvenience; especially when both the one and the other are equally subject to the absolute authority of the same person who has not only power to persuade the members of his church to whatsoever he lists, either as purely religious or in order thereunto, but can also enjoin it them on pain of eternal fire. It is ridiculous for anyone to profess himself to be a Mahometan only in his religion, but in everything else a faithful subject to a Christian magistrate, whilst at the same time he acknowledges himself bound to yield blind obedience to the Mufti of Constantinople, who himself is entirely obedient to the Ottoman Emperor and frames the feigned oracles of that religion according to his pleasure. But this Mahometan living amongst Christians would yet more apparently renounce their government if he acknowledged the same person to be head of his church who is the supreme magistrate in the state.

Lastly, those are not at all to be tolerated who deny the being of a God. Promises, covenants, and oaths, which are the bonds of human society, can have no hold upon an atheist. The taking away of God, though but even in thought, dissolves all; besides also, those that by their atheism undermine and destroy all religion can have no pretense of religion whereupon to challenge the privilege of a toleration. As for other practical opinions, though not absolutely free from all error, if they do not tend to establish domination over others, or civil impunity to the church in which they are taught, there can be no reason why they should not be tolerated. . . .

That we may draw toward a conclusion. The sum of all we drive at is that every man may enjoy the same rights that are granted to others. Is it permitted to worship God in the Roman manner? Let it be permitted to do it in the Geneva form also. Is it permitted to speak Latin in the market place? Let those that have a mind to it be permitted to do it also in the church. Is it lawful for any man in his own house to kneel, stand, sit, or use any other posture, and to clothe himself in white or black, in short or in long garments? Let it not be made unlawful to eat bread, drink wine, or wash with water in the church. In a word, whatsoever things are left free by law in the common occasions of life, let them remain free unto every church in divine worship. Let no man's life or body or house or estate suffer any manner of prejudice upon these accounts. . . .

Ecclesiastical assemblies and sermons are justified by daily experience and public allowance. These are allowed to people of some one persuasion, why not to all? . . . Thus if solemn assemblies, observations of festivals, public worship be permitted to any sort of professors, all these things ought to be permitted to the Presbyterians, Independents, Anabaptists, Arminians, Quakers, and others, with the same liberty. Nay, if we may openly speak the truth, and as becomes one man to another, neither pagan nor Mahometan nor Jew ought to be excluded from the civil rights of the commonwealth because of his religion. The Gospel commands no such thing. The church which "judgeth not those that are without" [1 Cor. 5:12, 13] wants it not. And the commonwealth, which embraces indifferently all men that are honest, peaceable, and industrious, requires it not. Shall we suffer a pagan to deal and trade with us, and shall we not suffer him to pray unto and worship God? If we allow the Jews to have private houses and dwellings amongst us, why should we not allow them to have synagogues? Is their doctrine more false, their worship more abominable, or is the civil peace more endangered by their meeting in public than in their private houses? But if these things may be granted to Jews and pagans, surely the condition of any Christians ought not to be worse than theirs in a Christian commonwealth.

You will say, perhaps, Yes, it ought to be; because they are more inclinable to factions, tumults, and civil wars. I answer, Is this the fault of the Christian religion? If it be so, truly the Christian religion is the worst of all religions, and ought neither to be embraced by any particular person nor tolerated by any commonwealth. For if this be the genius, this the nature of the Christian religion, to be turbulent and destructive to the civil peace, that church itself which the magistrate indulges will not always be innocent. But far be it from us to say any such thing of that religion which carries the greatest opposition to covetousness, ambition, discord, contention, and all manner of inordinate desires; and is the most modest and peaceable religion that ever was. We must therefore seek another cause of those evils that are charged upon religion. And if we consider right, we shall find it to consist wholly in the subject that I am treating of. It is not the diversity of opinions (which cannot be avoided), but the refusal of toleration to those that are of different opinions (which might have been granted), that has produced all the bustles and wars that have been in the Christian world upon account of religion. The heads and leaders of the church, moved by avarice and insatiable desire of dominion, making use of the immoderate ambition of magistrates and the credulous superstition of the giddy multitude, have incensed and animated them against those that dissent from themselves, by preaching unto them, contrary to the laws of the Gospel and to the precepts of charity, that schismatics and heretics are to be outed of their possessions and destroyed. And thus have they mixed together and confounded two things that are in themselves most different, the church and the commonwealth. Now as it is very difficult for men patiently to suffer themselves to be stripped of the goods which they have got by their honest industry and, contrary to all the laws of equity, both human and divine, to be delivered up for a prey to other men's violence and rapine, especially when they are otherwise altogether blameless; and that the occasion for which they are thus treated does not at all belong to the jurisdiction of the magistrate, but entirely to the conscience of every particular man, for the conduct of which he is accountable to God only; what else can be expected but that these men, growing weary of the evils under which they labor, should in the end think it lawful for them to resist force with force, and to defend their natural rights (which are not forfeitable upon account of religion) with arms as well as they can? That this has been hitherto the ordinary course of things is abundantly evident in history, and that it will continue to be so hereafter is but too apparent in reason. It cannot, indeed, be otherwise so long as the principle of persecution for religion shall prevail, as it has done hitherto, with magistrate and people. . . . This is the unhappy agreement that we see between the church and state. Whereas if each of them would contain itself within its own bounds—the one attending to the worldly welfare of the commonwealth, the other to the salvation of souls—it is impossible that any discord should ever have happened between them. . . .

4. KANT

Enlightenment and Progress

Immanuel Kant (1724–1804) published the essay (from which this selection is taken) "What Is Enlightenment?"* in the *Berlinische Monatsschrift* in 1784. It was the first in a series of works on philosophy of history which Kant published in his later years; this series culminated with "Toward Perpetual Peace" in 1795 and "The Old Question Raised Again: Is the Human Race Constantly Progressing?" in 1798. Kant has been primarily known for his contributions to philosophical problems of knowledge, ethics, metaphysics, and religion, but he was passionately committed to the liberal political and social ideals of the Enlightenment. For example, in 1798 at the age of seventy-four, Kant defended the French Revolution after its violence had disillusioned many of its early enthusiasts:

The revolution of a gifted people which we have seen unfolding in our day may succeed or miscarry; it may be filled with misery and atrocities to the point that a sensible man, were he boldly to hope to execute it successfully the second time, would never resolve to make the experiment at such cost—this revolution, I say, nonetheless finds in the hearts of all spectators (who are not engaged in this game themselves) a wishful participation that borders closely on enthusiasm, the very expression of which is fraught with danger; this sympathy, therefore, can have no other cause than a moral predisposition in the human race.

* Translated by Lewis White Beck in *Kant on History.* (Indianapolis: The Bobbs-Merrill Company, Inc, © 1963.) Reprinted by permission.

He believed that the movement of history is teleological and that the goal of human development is "the achievement of the universal civic society", through reason. In this essay Kant outlined the promise and the permissible limitations to the free exercise of reason.

Enlightenment is man's release from his self-incurred tutelage. Tutelage is man's inability to make use of his understanding without direction from another. Self-incurred is this tutelage when its cause lies not in lack of reason but in lack of resolution and courage to use it without direction from another. *Sapere aude!* "Have courage to use your own reason!"—that is the motto of enlightenment.

Laziness and cowardice are the reasons why so great a portion of mankind, after nature has long since discharged them from external direction (*naturaliter maiorennes*), nevertheless remains under lifelong tutelage, and why it is so easy for others to set themselves up as their guardians. It is so easy not to be of age. If I have a book which understands for me, a pastor who has a conscience for me, a physician who decides my diet, and so forth, I need not trouble myself. I need not think, if I can only pay—others will readily undertake the irksome work for me.

That the step to competence is held to be very dangerous by the far greater portion of mankind (and by the entire fair sex)—quite apart from its being arduous—is seen to by those guardians who have so kindly assumed superintendence over them. After the guardians have first made their domestic cattle dumb and have made sure that these placid creatures will not dare take a single step without the harness of the cart to which they are tethered, the guardians then show them the danger which threatens if they try to go alone. Actually, however, this danger is not so great, for by falling a few times they would finally learn to walk alone. But an example of this failure makes them timid and ordinarily frightens them away from all further trials.

For any single individual to work himself out of the life under tutelage which has become almost his nature is very difficult. He has come to be fond of this state, and he is for the present really incapable of making use of his reason, for no one has ever let him try it out. Statutes and formulas, those mechanical tools of the rational employment or rather misemployment of his natural gifts, are the fetters of an ever-lasting tutelage. Whoever throws them off makes only an uncertain leap over the narrowest ditch because he is not accustomed to that kind of free motion. Therefore, there are few who have succeeded by their own exercise of mind both in freeing themselves from incompetence and in achieving a steady pace.

But that the public should enlighten itself is more possible; indeed, if only freedom is granted, enlightenment is almost sure to follow. For there will always be some independent thinkers, even among the established guardians of the great masses, who, after throwing off the yoke of tutelage from their own shoulders, will disseminate the spirit of the rational appreciation of both their own worth and every man's vocation for thinking for himself. But be it noted that the public, which has first been brought under this yoke by their guardians, forces the guardians themselves to remain bound when it is incited to do so by some of the guardians who are themselves capable of some enlightenment—so harmful is it to implant prejudices, for they later take vengeance on their cultivators or on their descendants. Thus the public can only slowly attain enlightenment. Perhaps a fall of personal despotism or of avaricious or tyrannical oppression may be accomplished by revolution, but never a true reform in ways of thinking. Rather, new prejudices will serve as well as old ones to harness the great unthinking masses.

For this enlightenment, however, nothing is required but freedom, and indeed the most harmless among all the things to which this term can properly be applied. It is the freedom to make public use of one's reason at every point. But I hear on all sides, "Do not argue!" The officer says: "Do not argue but drill!" The tax collector: "Do not argue but pay!" The cleric: "Do not argue but believe!" Only one prince in the world says, "Argue as much as you will, and about what you will, but obey!" Everywhere there is restriction on freedom.

Which restriction is an obstacle to enlightenment, and which is not an obstacle but a promoter of it? I answer: The public use of one's reason must always be free, and it alone can bring about enlightenment among men. The private use of reason, on the other hand, may often be very narrowly restricted without particularly hindering the progress of enlightenment. By the public use of one's reason I understand the use which a person makes of it as a scholar before the reading public. Private use I call that which one may make of it in a particular civil post or office which is entrusted to him. Many affairs which are conducted in the interest of the community require a certain mechanism through which some members of the community must passively conduct themselves with an artificial unanimity, so that the government may direct them to public ends, or at least prevent them from destroying those ends. Here argument is certainly not allowed—one must obey. But so far as a part of the mechanism regards himself at the same time as a member of the whole community or of a society of world citizens, and thus in the role of a scholar who addresses the public (in the proper sense of the word) through his writings, he certainly can argue without hurting the affairs for which he is in part responsible as a passive member. Thus it would be ruinous for an officer in service to debate about the suitability or utility of a command given to him by his superior; he must obey. But the right to make remarks on errors in the military service and to lay them before the public for judgment cannot equitably be refused him as a scholar. The citizen cannot refuse to pay the taxes imposed on him; indeed, an impudent complaint at those levied on him can be punished as a scandal (as it could occasion general refractoriness). But the same person nevertheless does not act contrary to his duty as a citizen when, as a scholar, he publicly expresses his thoughts on the inappropriateness or even the injustice of these levies. Similarly a clergyman is obligated to make his sermon to his pupils in catechism and his congregation conform to the symbol of the church which he serves, for he has been accepted on his condition. But as a scholar he has complete freedom, even the calling, to communicate to the public all his carefully tested and well-meaning thoughts on that which is erroneous in the symbol and to make suggestions for the better organization of the religious body and church. In doing this there is nothing that could be laid as a burden on his conscience. For what he teaches as a consequence of his office as a representative of the church, this he considers something about which he has no freedom to teach according to his own lights; it is something which he is appointed to propound at the dictation of and in the name of another. He will say, "Our church teaches this or that; those are the proofs which it adduces." He thus extracts all practical uses for his congregation from statutes to which he himself would not subscribe with full conviction but to the enunciation of which he can very well pledge himself because it is not impossible that truth lies hidden in them, and, in any case, there is at least nothing in them contradictory to inner religion. For if he believed he had found such in them, he could not conscientiously discharge the duties of his office; he would have to give it up. The use, therefore, which an appointed teacher makes of his reason before his congregation is merely private, because this congregation is only a domestic one (even if it be a large gathering); with respect to it, as a priest, he is not free, nor can he be free, because he carries out the orders of another. But as a scholar, whose writings speak to his public, the world, the clergyman in the public use of his reason enjoys an unlimited freedom to use his own reason and to speak in his own person. That the guardians of the people (in spiritual things) should themselves be incompetent is an absurdity which amounts to the eternalization of absurdities.

But would not a society of clergymen, perhaps a church conference or a venerable classis (as they call themselves among the Dutch), be justified in obligating itself by oath to a certain unchangeable symbol in order to enjoy an unceasing guardianship over each of its members and thereby over the people as a whole, and even to make it eternal? I answer that this is altogether impossible. Such a contract, made to shut off all further enlightenment from the human race, is absolutely null and void even if confirmed by the supreme power, by parliaments, and by the most ceremonious of peace treaties. An age cannot bind itself and ordain to put the succeeding one into such a condition that it cannot extend its (at best very occasional) knowledge, purify itself of errors, and progress in general enlightenment. That would be a crime against human nature, the proper destination of which lies precisely in this progress; and the descendants would be fully justified in rejecting those decrees as having been made in an unwarranted and malicious manner.

The touchstone of everything that can be concluded as a law for a people lies in the question whether the people could have imposed such a law on itself. Now such a religious compact might be possible for a short and definitely limited time, as it were, in expectation of a better. . . . But to unite in a permanent religious institution which is not to be subject to doubt before the public even in the lifetime of one man, and thereby to make a period of time fruitless in the progress of mankind toward improvement, thus working to the disadvantage of posterity—that is absolutely forbidden. For himself (and only for a short time) a man may postpone enlightenment in what he ought to know, but to renounce it for himself and even more to renounce it for posterity is to injure and trample on the rights of mankind.

And what a people may not decree for itself can even less be decreed for them by a monarch, for his law-giving authority rests on his uniting the general public will in his own. If he only sees to it that all true or alleged improvement stands together with civil order, he can leave it to his subjects to do what they find necessary for their spiritual welfare. This is not his concern, though it is incumbent on him to prevent one of them from violently hindering another in determining and promoting this welfare to the best of his ability. To meddle in these matters lowers his own majesty, since by the writings in which his subjects seek to present their views he may evaluate his own governance. He can do this when, with deepest understanding, he lays upon himself the reproach, "Caesar non est supra grammaticos" ["The emperor is not above the grammarians"]. Far more does he injure his own majesty when he degrades his supreme power by supporting the ecclesiastical despotism of some tyrants in his state over his other subjects.

If we are asked, "Do we now live in an *enlightened age?*" the answer is, "No," but we do live in an *age of enlightenment*. As things now stand, much is lacking which prevents men from being, or easily becoming, capable of correctly using their own reason in religious matters with assurance and free from outside direction. But, on the other hand, we have clear indications that the field has now been opened wherein men may freely deal with these things and that the obstacles to general enlightenment or the release from self-imposed tutelage are gradually being reduced. In this respect, this is the age of enlightenment, or the century of Frederick. . . .

I have placed the main point of enlightenment—the escape of men from their self-incurred tutelage—chiefly in matters of religion because our rulers have no interest in playing the guardian with respect to the arts and sciences and also because religious incompetence is not only the most harmful but also the most degrading of all. But the manner of thinking of the head of a state who favors religious enlightenment goes further, and he sees that there is no danger to his law-giving in allowing his subjects to make public use of their reason and to publish their thoughts on a better formulation of his legislation and even their open-minded criticisms of the laws already made. . . .

As nature has uncovered the seed for which she most tenderly cares —the propensity and vocation to free thinking—this gradually works back upon the character of the people, who thereby gradually become capable of managing freedom; finally, it affects the principles of government, which finds it to its advantage to treat men, who are now more than machines, in accordance with their dignity.

5. VON HUMBOLDT
The Positive and the Negative State

Wilhelm von Humboldt (1767–1835) served as Minister of Worship and Public Instruction in Prussia and was a founder of the University of Berlin, now called Humboldt University. Humboldt's political career which began in 1801 followed an earlier ten year period of travel, writing, and retirement. During that time he wrote many works including *Ideas for a Proposed Definition of the Limits of the Legality of the State*, which was published in 1792. The selection is taken from this work.*

I consider the following maxim as amply demonstrated: *That true reason cannot desire for man any condition other than that in which not only every individual enjoys the most absolute, unbounded freedom to develop himself out of himself, in true individuality, but in which physical nature, as well, need receive no other shaping by human hands than that which is given to her voluntarily by each individual, according to the measure of his wants and his inclinations, restricted only by the limits of his energy and his rights.* From this maxim, in my estimation, reason may never yield more than is essential for its own preservation. It must therefore be at the foundations of . . . every political policy.

Expressed in a completely general formula, one might call the true extent of state operations all those things which the government may do for the well-being of society, without violating the above maxim; and from this maxim we may derive the even more definite restriction that any state interference in the private affairs of its citizens is to be condemned, wherever it is not, strictly occasioned by the interference with one citizen's rights by another. Meanwhile it will be necessary, in order to solve our entire problem; to examine carefully the various aspects of the state's usual or possible activity.

* From *Humanist Without Portfolio*; translated by Marianne Cowan. (Detroit: Wayne State University Press, 1963.) Used by permission.

The aims of a state may be twofold: it may promote happiness or it may merely prevent evil, and, in the latter case, either evils of nature or evils of mankind. If it restricts itself to the latter, it aims merely at security. This security I wish to oppose to all other possible aims that are considered under the name of positive state welfare. The variety of the means employed by the state, moreover, affects the extension of its activities. It either seeks to attain its aims directly, either by coercion —laws and punishment—or else by encouragement and example; or it may work indirectly, by an attempt to shape the citizens' external lives in such a way that they fall in with its desires, or it prevents them from acting otherwise. Finally, it may actually seek to sway their preferences by exercising an influence upon their thoughts and feelings. In the first case, it supervises only single actions; in the second, the citizen's whole way of life, and in the third, their character and modes of thinking. Likewise, the effect of the state's restriction is least in the first case, greater in the second, and greatest in the third, partly because it affects the source of a number of actions, partly because the very possibility of such influence means that a number of separate agencies must be at work. However separate the various aspects of governmental operations look, there is hardly an institution of government which does not pertain to several at once, since for example security and welfare are very much dependent on one another, and since even single acts lead to habits which in turn influence character. It is therefore extremely difficult to find a proper systematic division of our subject. It will probably be best, first of all, regardless of whether the state is to promote the positive social welfare of the nation, or merely maintain its security, to look at all its institutions in line with what is their main object or their main consequence, and to examine in connection with each aim those means which the state may allow itself.

I shall speak here, then, of the entire effort of the state to elevate the positive social welfare of the nation, its solicitude for population, for the subsistence of its inhabitants, whether manifested directly through its poor laws, or indirectly through the encouragement of agriculture, industry, and commerce, for all its finance and currency regulations, trade regulations, etc. (insofar as they have the above aim); finally for all its measures for the preventing or remedying of natural catastrophes—in short, for every arrangement and institution of the state which has as its purpose the maintenance or promotion of the physical well-being of the nation. . . .

Now all of these aforementioned social institutions, I assert, have disadvantageous consequences and are inappropriate to true political policy which proceeds from the highest but always human points of view.

1. The spirit of the government pervades every institution of this kind, and—regardless of how wise and salutary this spirit may happen to be—it produces monotony, uniformity, and alienates people's actions from their own character. Instead of human beings socializing themselves in order to sharpen their energies, even at a loss of some part of their exclusive possessions and enjoyments, they now attain *goods* at the cost of *energy*. The very diversity which is the result of the communion of men is the highest good that society can offer; it is sure to get lost in the same degree that the state intervenes. It is now no longer the individual members of a nation who live in communion with one another, but instead the isolated subjects of a state which stand in a certain relation to the spirit which rules it, a relationship which is predetermined by the greater power which the state exerts over the free play of individual energies. Like causes produce like effects. The more the state cooperates, the more uniform grow not only the operators, but the materials they operate with. And this of course, coincides with the state's purposes. The state desires well-being and tranquillity. These are always to be had where there is least contention between individuals. But what human beings are after, and should be after, is diversity and activity. Only they will yield many-faceted and strong characters, and surely we human beings have not sunk so low that we actually prefer welfare and happiness to greatness for ourselves, as individuals. But if we reason that we want them for others, not for ourselves, then we ought justly to be suspected of failing to recognize human nature for what it is and of wishing to turn men into machines.

2. The second disadvantage, then, is that the social institutions of a state weaken the energies of the nation. For material substance is annihilated by externally imposed form, though strengthened in fullness and beauty by that form which grows out of itself. For what is matter other than the union of opposites, a union which constantly requires the finding of new combinations, hence whole new series of discoveries, which constantly increase the tension between themselves and those that have gone before. But if external form is superimposed upon matter, a something is being suppressed in favor of a nothing. Everything intrinsically human means organization, organic life. What is to flourish, must first be sown. All energy presupposes enthusiasm,

and only a few things so nourish enthusiasm, as to consider its object as a present or future possession.

Now man does not so much regard what he *has* as his property as that what he *does*, and the worker who plants a garden is its owner in a truer sense than the idle consumer who enjoys it. Perhaps such a line of reasoning seems too general to permit of specific application. Perhaps it will even seem that the extension and propagation of many sciences which we owe to these and other social institutions of the state, which is the only agency able to carry on vast experimentation, actually increases our intellectual powers and thereby culture and human character in general. But we must remember that not every enrichment of knowledge signifies refinement, not even of the intellectual energies as such, and whenever such refinement does as a matter of fact take place through state agency, it does not take place in the nation as a whole but only in those members who have directly to do with governmental operations. Man's understanding, like all his other energies, is cultivated only by each human being's own activity, his own inventiveness, or his own utilization of the inventions of others. Governmental regulations all carry coercion to some degree and even where they don't, they habituate man to expect teaching, guidance and help outside himself, instead of formulating his own.

The only method of instruction that the government has available is that it declares certain procedures to be best, as the result of its investigations, and then orders them to be followed either by law or by some other institution binding upon its citizens, or else stimulates them by the backing of its own prestige, or reward, or other means of encouragement, or even only recommends them by argumentation. But whatever method the government chooses, it will be very far from a good method of instruction. For sound instruction undoubtedly consists of spreading out before the person to be instructed various solutions, and then preparing him to choose the most appropriate, or, even better, to invent his own solution by simply arranging before him all the difficulties to be conquered. This method of instruction can be followed by the state, in connection with its adult citizens, only negatively, namely by allowing them complete freedom, permitting obstacles to rise which in turn produce strength and skill for their removal, or positively in connection with its youthful citizens alone, who are partaking of a genuine national [public] education. . . .

6. BENTHAM
The Legislation of Morals

Jeremy Bentham (1748–1832) wrote his most important work, *Introduction to the Principles of Morals and Legislation*, in 1789. The opening sections, excerpted below, were a concise formulation of the principle of utility as governing all moral and legislative actions. In the concluding sections of the work, Bentham developed his criticism of legislative intervention on moral issues as the consequence of the application of the principle of utility. Unlike Bentham's hostility to governmental intervention in economic processes, his views on legislation of morality have continued to receive almost universal support among liberals.

OF THE PRINCIPLE OF UTILITY

Nature has placed mankind under the governance of two sovereign masters, *pain* and *pleasure*. It is for them alone to point out what we ought to do, as well as to determine what we shall do. On the one hand the standard of right and wrong, on the other the chain of causes and effects, are fastened to their throne. They govern us in all we do, in all we say, in all we think: every effort we can make to throw off our subjection, will serve but to demonstrate and confirm it. In words a man may pretend to abjure their empire: but in reality he will remain subject to it all the while. The *principle of utility* recognises this subjection, and assumes it for the foundation of that system, the object of which is to rear the fabric of felicity by the hands of reason and of law. . . .

The principle of utility is the foundation of the present work: it will be proper therefore at the outset to give an explicit and determinate account of what is meant by it. By the principle of utility is meant that principle which approves or disapproves of every action whatsoever, according to the tendency which it appears to have to augment or diminish the happiness of the party whose interest is in question: or, what is the same thing in other words, to promote or to oppose that happiness. I say of every action whatsoever; and therefore not only of every action of a private individual, but of every measure of government.

By utility is meant that property in any object, whereby it tends to produce benefit, advantage, pleasure, good, or happiness (all this in the present case comes to the same thing), or (what comes again to the same thing) to prevent the happening of mischief, pain, evil, or unhappiness to the party whose interest is considered: if that party be the community in general, then the happiness of the community: if a particular individual, then the happiness of that individual.

The interest of the community is one of the most general expressions that can occur in the phraseology of morals: no wonder that the meaning of it is often lost. When it has a meaning, it is this. The community is a fictitious *body*, composed of the individual persons who are considered as constituting as it were its *members*. The interest of the community then is, what?—the sum of the interests of the several members who compose it.

It is in vain to talk of the interest of the community, without understanding what is the interest of the individual. A thing is said to promote the interest, or to be *for* the interest, of an individual, when it tends to add to the sum total of his pleasures: or, what comes to the same thing, to diminish the sum total of his pains.

An action then may be said to be conformable to the principle of utility, or, for shortness sake, to utility (meaning with respect to the community at large), when the tendency it has to augment the happiness of the community is greater than any it has to diminish it. . . .

OF THE CASES UNMEET FOR PUNISHMENT

The general object which all laws have, or ought to have, in common, is to augment the total happiness of the community; and therefore, in the first place, to exclude, as far as may be, everything that tends to subtract from that happiness: in other words, to exclude mischief.

But all punishment is mischief: all punishment in itself is evil. Upon the principle of utility, if it ought at all to be admitted, it ought only to be admitted in as far as it promises to exclude some greater evil. . . .

It is plain, therefore, that in the following cases punishment ought not to be inflicted.

1. Where it is *groundless:* where there is no mischief for it to prevent; the act not being mischievous upon the whole.

2. Where it must be *inefficacious:* where it cannot act so as to prevent the mischief.

3. Where it is *unprofitable*, or too *expensive:* where the mischief it would produce would be greater than what is prevented.

4. Where it is *needless:* where the mischief may be prevented, or cease of itself, without it: that is, at a cheaper rate.

Cases in which punishment is groundless.

These are,

1. Where there has never been any mischief: where no mischief has been produced to anybody by the act in question. Of this number are those in which the act was such as might, on some occasions, be mischievous or disagreeable, but the person whose interest it concerns gave his *consent* to the performance of it. This consent, provided it be free, and fairly obtained, is the best proof that can be produced, that, to the person who gives it, no mischief, at least no immediate mischief, upon the whole, is done. For no man can be so good a judge as the man himself, what it is gives him pleasure or displeasure. . . .

Cases where punishment is needless.

These are,

1. Where the purpose of putting an end to the practice may be attained as effectually at a cheaper rate: by instruction, for instance, as well as by terror: by informing the understanding, as well as by exercising an immediate influence on the will. This seems to be the case with respect to all those offences which consist in the disseminating pernicious principles in matters of *duty;* of whatever kind the duty be; whether political, or moral, or religious. And this, whether such principles be disseminated *under*, or even *without*, a sincere persuasion of their being beneficial. I say, even *without:* for though in such a case it is not instruction that can prevent the writer from endeavouring to inculcate his principles, yet it may the readers from adopting them: without which, his endeavouring to inculcate them will do no harm. In such a case, the sovereign will commonly have little need to take an active part: if it be the interest of *one* individual to inculcate principles that are pernicious, it will as surely be

the interest of *other* individuals to expose them. But if the sovereign must needs take a part in the controversy, the pen is the proper weapon to combat error with, not the sword.

OF THE LIMITS OF THE PENAL BRANCH
OF JURISPRUDENCE

. . . Ethics at large may be defined, the art of directing men's actions to the production of the greatest possible quantity of happiness, on the part of those whose interest is in view.

What then are the actions which it can be in a man's power to direct? They must be either his own actions, or those of other agents. Ethics, in as far as it is the art of directing a man's own actions, may be styled the *art of self-government,* or *private ethics.*

What other agents then are there, which, at the same time that they are under the influence of man's direction, are susceptible of happiness? They are of two sorts: 1. Other human beings who are styled persons. 2. Other animals, which, on account of their interests having been neglected by the insensibility of the ancient jurists, stand degraded into the class of *things.* As to other human beings, the art of directing their actions to the above end is what we mean, or at least the only thing which, upon the principle of utility, we *ought* to mean, by the art of government: which, in as far as the measures it displays itself in are of a permanent nature, is generally distinguished by the name of *legislation:* as it is by that of *administration,* when they are of a temporary nature, determined by the occurrences of the day. . . .

As to ethics in general, a man's happiness will depend, in the first place, upon such parts of his behaviour as none but himself are interested in; in the next place, upon such parts of it as may affect the happiness of those about him. In as far as his happiness depends upon the first-mentioned part of his behaviour, it is said to depend upon his *duty to himself.* Ethics then, in as far as it is the art of directing a man's actions in this respect, may be termed the art of discharging one's duty to one's self: and the quality which a man manifests by the discharge of this branch of duty (if duty it is to be called) is that of *prudence.* In as far as his happiness, and that of any other person or persons whose interests are considered, depends upon such parts of his behaviour as may affect the interests of those about him, it may be said to depend upon his *duty to others;* or, to use a phrase now somewhat antiquated, his *duty to his neighbour.* Ethics then, in as far as it is the art of directing a man's actions in this respect, may be termed the art of discharging one's duty to one's neighbour. Now the happiness of one's neighbour may be consulted in two ways: 1. In a negative way, by forbearing to diminish it. 2. In a positive way, by studying to increase it. A man's duty to his neighbour is accordingly partly negative and partly positive: to discharge the negative branch of it, is *probity:* to discharge the positive branch, *beneficence.*

It may here be asked, How it is that upon the principle of private ethics, legislation and religion out of the question, a man's happiness depends upon such parts of his conduct as affect, immediately at least, the happiness of no one but himself: this is as much as to ask, What motives (independent of such as legislation and religion may chance to furnish) can one man have to consult the happiness of another? by what motives, or, which comes to the same thing, by what obligations, can he be bound to obey the dictates of *probity* and *beneficence?* In answer to this, it cannot but be admitted, that the only interests which a man at all times and upon all occasions is sure to find *adequate* motives for consulting, are his own. Notwithstanding this, there are no occasions in which a man has not some motives for consulting the happiness of other men. In the first place, he has, on all occasions, the purely social motive of sympathy or benevolence: in the next place, he has, on most occasions, the semi-social motives of love of amity and love of reputation. The motive of sympathy will act upon him with more or less effect, according to the *bias* of his sensibility: the two other motives, according to a variety of circumstances, principally according to the strength of his intellectual powers, the firmness and steadiness of his mind, the quantum of his moral sensibility, and the characters of the people he has to deal with.

Now private ethics has happiness for its end: and legislation can have no other. Private ethics concerns every member, that is, the happiness and the actions of every member, of any community that can be proposed; and legislation can concern no more. Thus far, then, private ethics and the art of legislation go hand in hand. The end they have, or ought to have, in view, is of the same nature. The persons whose happiness they ought to have in view, as also the persons whose conduct they ought to be occupied in directing, are precisely the same. The very acts they ought to be conversant about, are even in a *great measure* the same. Where then lies the difference? In that the acts which they ought to be conversant about, though in a great measure, are not *perfectly and throughout* the same. There is no case in which a private man ought not to direct his own conduct to the production of his own happiness, and of that of his fellow-creatures: but there are cases in which the legislator ought not (in a direct way at least, and by means of punishment applied immediately to particular *individual* acts) to attempt to direct the conduct of the several other members of the community. Every act which promises to be beneficial upon the whole to the community (himself included) each individual ought to perform of himself: but it is not every such act that the legislator ought to compel him to perform. Every act which promises to be pernicious upon the whole to the community (himself included) each individual ought to abstain from of himself: but it is not every such act that the legislator ought to compel him to abstain from. . . .

For the sake of obtaining the clearer idea of the limits between the art of legislation and private ethics, it may now be time to call to mind the distinctions above established with regard to ethics in general. The degree in which private ethics stands in need of the assistance of legislation, is different in the three branches of duty above distinguished. Of the rules of moral duty, those which seem to stand least in need of the assistance of legislation are the rules of *prudence*. It can only be through some defect on the part of the understanding, if a man be ever deficient in point of duty to himself. If he does wrong, there is nothing else that it can be owing to but either some *inadvertence* or some *mis-supposal* with regard to the circumstances on which his happiness depends. It is a standing topic of complaint, that a man knows too little of himself. Be it so: but is it so certain that the legislator must know more? It is plain, that of individuals the legislator can know nothing: concerning those points of conduct which depend upon the particular circumstances of each individual, it is plain, therefore, that he can determine nothing to advantage. It is only with respect to those broad lines of conduct in which all persons, or very large and permanent descriptions of persons, may be in a way to engage, that he can have any pretence for interfering; and even here the propriety of his interference will, in most instances, lie very open to dispute. At any rate, he must never expect to produce a perfect compliance by the mere force of the sanction of which he is himself the author. All he can hope to do, is to increase the efficacy of private ethics, by giving strength and direction to the influence of the moral sanction. With what chance of success, for example, would a legislator go about to extirpate drunkenness and fornication by dint of legal punishment? Not all the tortures which ingenuity could invent would compass it:

and, before he had made any progress worth regarding, such a mass of evil would be produced by the punishment, as would exceed, a thousand-fold, the utmost possible mischief of the offence. The great difficulty would be in the procuring evidence; an object which could not be attempted, with any probability of success, without spreading dismay through every family, tearing the bonds of sympathy asunder, and rooting out the influence of all the social motives. All that he can do then, against offences of this nature, with any prospect of advantage, in the way of direct legislation, is to subject them, in cases of notoriety, to a slight censure, so as thereby to cover them with a slight shade of artificial disrepute.

It may be observed, that with regard to this branch of duty, legislators have, in general, been disposed to carry their interference full as far as is expedient. The great difficulty here is, to persuade them to confine themselves within bounds. A thousand little passions and prejudices have led them to narrow the liberty of the subject in this line, in cases in which the punishment is either attended with no profit at all, or with none that will make up for the expense.

The mischief of this sort of interference is more particularly conspicuous in the article of religion. The reasoning, in this case, is of the following stamp. There are certain errors, in matters of belief, to which all mankind are prone: and for these errors in judgment, it is the determination of a Being of infinite benevolence, to punish them with an infinity of torments. But from these errors the legislator himself is necessarily free: for the men, who happen to be at hand for him to consult with, being men perfectly enlightened, unfettered, and unbiassed, have such advantages over all the rest of the world, that when they sit down to enquire out the truth relative to points so plain and so familiar as those in question, they cannot fail to find it. This being the case, when the sovereign sees his people ready to plunge headlong into an abyss of fire, shall he not stretch out a hand to save them? Such, for example, seems to have been the train of reasoning and such the motives, which led Louis the XIVth into those coercive measures which he took for the conversion of heretics and the confirmation of true believers. The ground-work, pure sympathy and loving-kindness: the superstructure, all the miseries which the most determined malevolence could have devised. . . .

To conclude this section, let us recapitulate and bring to a point the difference between private ethics, considered as an art or science, on the one hand, and that branch of jurisprudence which contains the art or science of legislation, on the other. Private ethics teaches how each man may dispose himself to pursue the course most conducive to his own happiness, by means of such motives as offer of themselves: the art of legislation (which may be considered as one branch of the science of jurisprudence) teaches how a multitude of men, composing a community, may be disposed to pursue that course which upon the whole is the most conducive to the happiness of the whole community, by means of motives to be applied by the legislator. . . .

7. J. S. MILL
Liberty and Utility

John Stuart Mill (1806–73) worked on his most famous essay, *On Liberty*, together with his wife Harriet for several years. Conceived in 1854, it was published in 1859. *On Liberty* was, Mill wrote, "more directly and literally our joint production than anything else which bears my name." The selection is taken from this essay which was recognized, soon after publication, as the classic statement of British liberalism.

INTRODUCTORY

. . . The struggle between liberty and authority is the most conspicuous feature in the portions of history with which we are earliest familiar, particularly in that of Greece, Rome, and England. But in old times this contest was between subjects, or some classes of subjects, and the government. By liberty was meant protection against the tyranny of the political rulers. . . .

The aim, therefore, of patriots was to set limits to the power which the ruler should be suffered to exercise over the community; and this limitation was what they meant by liberty. It was attempted in two ways. First, by obtaining a recognition of certain immunities, called political liberties or rights, which it was to be regarded as a breach of duty in the ruler to infringe, and which if he did infringe, specific resistance or general rebellion was held to be justifiable. A second, and generally a later, expedient was the establishment of constitutional checks by which the consent of the community, or of a body of some sort, supposed to represent its interests, was made a necessary condition to some of the more important acts of the governing power. To the first of these modes of limitation, the ruling power, in most European countries, was compelled, more or less, to submit. It was not so with the second; and, to attain this, or, when already in some degree possessed, to attain it more completely, became everywhere the principal object of the lovers of liberty. And so long as mankind were content to combat one enemy by another, and to be ruled by a master on condition of being guaranteed more or less efficaciously against his tyranny, they did not carry their aspirations beyond this point.

A time, however, came, in the progress of human affairs, when men ceased to think it a necessity of nature that their governors should be an independent power opposed in interest to themselves. It appeared to them much better that the various magistrates of the state should be their tenants or delegates, revocable at their pleasure. In that way alone, it seemed, could they have complete security that the powers of government would never be abused to their disadvantage. By degrees this new demand for elective and temporary rulers became the prominent object of the exertions of the popular party wherever any such party existed, and superseded, to a considerable extent, the previous efforts to limit the power of rulers. As the struggle proceeded for making the ruling power emanate from the periodical choice of the ruled, some persons began to think that too much importance had been attached to the limitation of the power itself. *That* (it might seem) was a resource against rulers whose interests were habitually opposed to those of the people. What was now wanted was that the rulers should be identified with the people, that their interest and will should be the interest and will of the nation. The nation did not need to be protected against its own will. There was no fear of its tyrannizing over itself. Let the rulers be effectually responsible to it, promptly removable by it, and it could afford to trust them with power of which it could itself dictate the use to be made. Their power was but the nation's own power, concentrated and in a form convenient for exercise. This mode of thought, or rather perhaps of feeling, was common among the last generation of European liberalism, in the Continental section of which it still apparently predominates. Those who admit any limit to what a government may do, except in the case of such governments as they think ought not to exist, stand out as brilliant exceptions among the political thinkers of the Continent. A similar tone of sentiment might by this time have been prevalent in our own country if the circumstances which for a time encouraged it had continued unaltered.

But, in political and philosophical theories as well as in persons, success discloses faults and infirmities which failure might have concealed from observation. The notion that the people have no need to limit their power over themselves might seem axiomatic, when popular government was a thing only dreamed about, or read of as having existed at some distant period of the past. Neither was that notion necessarily disturbed by such temporary aberrations as those of the French Revolution, the worst of which were the work of a usurping few, and which, in any case, belonged, not to the permanent working of popular institutions, but to a sudden and convulsive outbreak against monarchical and aristocratic despotism. In time, however, a democratic republic came to occupy a large portion of the earth's surface and made itself felt as one of the most powerful members of the community of nations; and elective and responsible government became subject to the observations and criticisms which wait upon a great existing fact. It was now perceived that such phrases as "self-government," and "the power of the people over themselves," do not express the true state of the case. The "people" who exercise the power are not always the same people with those over whom it is exercised; and the "self-government" spoken of is not the government of each by himself, but of each by all the rest. The will of the people, moreover, practically means the will of the most numerous or the most active *part* of the people—the majority, or those who succeed in making themselves accepted as the majority; the people, consequently, *may* desire to oppress a part of their number, and precautions are as much needed against this as against any other abuse of power. The limitation, therefore, of the power of government over individuals loses none of its importance when the holders of power are regularly accountable to the community, that is, to the strongest party therein. This view of things, recommending itself equally to the intelligence of thinkers and to the inclination of those important classes in European society to whose real or supposed interests democracy is adverse, has had no difficulty in establishing itself; and in political speculations "the tyranny of the majority" is now generally included among the evils against which society requires to be on its guard.

Like other tyrannies, the tyranny of the majority was at first, and is still vulgarly, held in dread, chiefly as operating through the acts of the public authorities. But reflecting persons perceived that when society is itself the tyrant—society collectively over the separate individuals who compose it—its means of tyrannizing are not restricted to the acts which it may do by the hands of its political functionaries. Society can and does execute its own mandates; and if it issues wrong mandates instead of right, or any mandates at all in things with which it ought not to meddle, it practices a social tyranny more formidable than many kinds of political oppression, since, though not usually upheld by such extreme penalties, it leaves fewer means of escape, penetrating much more deeply into the details of life, and enslaving the soul itself. Protection, therefore, against the tyranny of the magistrate is not enough; there needs protection also against the tyranny of the prevailing opinion and feeling, against the tendency of society to impose, by other means than civil penalties, its own ideas and practices as rules of conduct on those who dissent from them; to fetter the development and, if possible, prevent the formation of any individuality not in harmony with its ways, and compel all characters to fashion themselves upon the model of its own. There is a limit to the legitimate interference of collective opinion with individual independence; and to find that limit, and maintain it against encroachment, is as indispensable to a good condition of human affairs as protection against political despotism.

But though this proposition is not likely to be contested in general terms, the practical question where to place the limit—how to make the fitting adjustment between individual independence and social control —is a subject on which nearly everything remains to be done. . . .

The object of this essay is to assert one very simple principle, as entitled to govern absolutely the dealings of society with the individual in the way of compulsion and control, whether the means used be physical force in the form of legal penalties or the moral coercion of public opinion. That principle is that the sole end for which mankind are warranted, individually or collectively, in interfering with the liberty of action of any of their number is self-protection. That the only purpose for which power can be rightfully exercised over any member of a civilized community, against his will, is to prevent harm to others. His own good, either physical or moral, is not a sufficient warrant. He cannot rightfully be compelled to do or forbear because it will be better for him to do so, because it will make him happier, because, in the opinions of others, to do so would be wise or even right. These are good reasons for remonstrating with him, or reasoning with him, or persuading him, or entreating him, but not for compelling him or visiting him with any evil in case he do otherwise. To justify that, the conduct from which it is desired to deter him must be calculated to produce evil to someone else. The only part of the conduct of anyone for which he is amenable to society is that which concerns others. In the part which merely concerns himself, his independence is, of right, absolute. Over himself, over his own body and mind, the individual is sovereign.

It is, perhaps, hardly necessary to say that this doctrine is meant to apply only to human beings in the maturity of their faculties. We are not speaking of children or of young persons below the age which the law may fix as that of manhood or womanhood. Those who are still in a state to require being taken care of by others must be protected against their own actions as well as against external injury. For the same reason we may leave out of consideration those backward states of society in which the race itself may be considered as in its nonage. The early difficulties in the way of spontaneous progress are so great that there is seldom any choice of means for overcoming them; and a ruler full of the spirit of improvement is warranted in the use of any expedients that will attain an end perhaps otherwise unattainable. Despotism is a legitimate mode of government in dealing with barbarians, provided the end be their improvement and the means justified by actually effecting that end. Liberty, as a principle, has no application to any state of things anterior to the time when mankind have become capable of being improved by free and equal discussion. . . .

It is proper to state that I forego any advantage which could be derived to my argument from the idea of abstract right as a thing independent of utility. I regard utility as the ultimate appeal on all ethical questions; but it must be utility in the largest sense, grounded on the permanent interests of man as a progressive being. Those interests, I contend, authorize the subjection of individual spontaneity to external control only in respect to those actions of each which concern the interest of other people. If anyone does an act hurtful to others, there is a *prima facie* case for punishing him by law or, where legal penalties are not safely applicable, by general disapprobation. There are also many positive acts for the benefit of others which he may rightfully be compelled to perform, such as to give evidence in a court of justice, to bear his fair share in the common defense or in any other joint work necessary to the interest of the society of which he enjoys the protection, and to perform certain acts of individual beneficence, such as saving a fellow creature's life or interposing to protect the defenseless against ill usage—things which whenever it is obviously a man's duty to do he may rightfully be made responsible to society for not doing. . . .

But there is a sphere of action in which society, as distinguished from the individual, has, if any, only an indirect interest: comprehending all that portion of a person's life and conduct which affects only himself, or, if it also affects others, only with their free, voluntary, and undeceived consent and participation. When I say only himself, I mean directly and in the first instance; for whatever affects himself may affect others through himself; and the objection which may be grounded on this contingency will receive consideration in the sequel. This, then, is the appropriate region of human liberty. It comprises, first, the inward domain of consciousness, demanding liberty of conscience in the most comprehensive sense, liberty of thought and feeling, absolute freedom of opinion and sentiment on all subjects, practical or speculative, scientific, moral, or theological. The liberty of expressing and publishing opinions may seem to fall under a different principle, since it belongs to that part of the conduct of an individual which concerns other people, but, being almost of as much importance as the liberty of thought itself and resting in great part on the same reasons, is practically inseparable from it. Secondly, the principle requires liberty of tastes and pursuits, of framing the plan of our life to suit our own character, of doing as we like, subject to such consequences as may follow, without impediment from our fellow creatures, so long as what we do does not harm them, even though they should think our conduct foolish, perverse, or wrong. Thirdly, from this liberty of each individual follows the liberty, within the same limits, of combination among individuals; freedom to unite for any purpose not involving harm to others: the persons combining being supposed to be of full age and not forced or deceived.

No society in which these liberties are not, on the whole, respected is free, whatever may be its form of government; and none is completely free in which they do not exist absolute and unqualified. The only freedom which deserves the name is that of pursuing our own good in our own way, so long as we do not attempt to deprive others of theirs or impede their efforts to obtain it. Each is the proper guardian of his own health, whether bodily *or* mental and spiritual. Mankind are greater gainers by suffering each other to live as seems good to themselves than by compelling each to live as seems good to the rest. . . .

It will be convenient for the argument if, instead of at once entering upon the general thesis, we confine ourselves in the first instance to a single branch of it on which the principle here stated is, if not fully, yet to a certain point, recognized by the current opinions. This one branch is the Liberty of Thought, from which it is impossible to separate the cognate liberty of speaking and of writing. Although these liberties, to some considerable amount, form part of the political morality of all countries which profess religious toleration and free institutions, the grounds, both philosophical and practical, on which they rest are perhaps not so familiar to the general mind, nor so thoroughly appreciated by many, even of the leaders of opinion, as might have been expected. Those grounds, when rightly understood, are of much wider application than to only one division of the subject, and a thorough consideration of this part of the question will be found the best introduction to the remainder. . . .

OF THE LIBERTY OF THOUGHT AND DISCUSSION

The time, it is to be hoped, is gone by when any defense would be necessary of the "liberty of the press" as one of the securities against corrupt or tyrannical government. No argument, we may suppose, can now be needed against permitting a legislature or an executive, not identified in interest with the people, to prescribe opinions to them and determine what doctrines or what arguments they shall be allowed to hear. . . . Let us suppose, therefore, that the government is entirely at one with the people, and never thinks of exerting any power of coercion unless in agreement with what it conceives to be their voice. But I deny the right of the people to exercise such coercion, either by themselves or by their government. The power itself is illegitimate. The best government has no more title to it than the worst. It is as noxious, or more noxious, when exerted in accordance with public opinion than when in opposition to it. If all mankind minus one were of one opinion, mankind would be no more justified in silencing that one person than he, if he had the power, would be justified in silencing mankind. Were an opinion a personal possession of no value except to the owner, if to be obstructed in the enjoyment of it were simply a private injury, it would make some difference whether the injury was inflicted only on a few persons or on many. But the peculiar evil of silencing the expression of an opinion is that it is robbing the human race, posterity as well as the existing generation—those who dissent from the opinion, still more than those who hold it. If the opinion is right, they are deprived of the opportunity of exchanging error for truth; if wrong, they lose, what is almost as great a benefit, the clearer perception and livelier impression of truth produced by its collision with error.

It is necessary to consider separately these two hypotheses, each of which has a distinct branch of the argument corresponding to it. We can never be sure that the opinion we are endeavoring to stifle is a false opinion; and if we were sure, stifling it would be an evil still.

First, the opinion which it is attempted to suppress by authority may possibly be true. Those who desire to suppress it, of course, deny its truth; but they are not infallible. They have no authority to decide the question for all mankind and exclude every other person from the means of judging. To refuse a hearing to an opinion because they are sure that it is false is to assume that *their* certainty is the same thing as *absolute* certainty. All silencing of discussion is an assumption of infallibility. Its condemnation may be allowed to rest on this common argument, not the worse for being common.

Unfortunately for the good sense of mankind, the fact of their fallibility is far from carrying the weight in their practical judgment which is always allowed to it in theory; for while every one well knows himself to be fallible, few think it necessary to take any precautions against their own fallibility, or admit the supposition that any opinion, of which they feel very certain, may be one of the examples of the error to which they acknowledge themselves to be liable. Absolute princes, or others who are accustomed to unlimited deference, usually feel this complete confidence in their own opinions on nearly all subjects. People more happily situated, who sometimes hear their opinions disputed, and are not wholly unused to be set right when they are wrong, place the same unbounded reliance only on such of their opinions as are shared by all who surround them, or to whom they habitually defer; for in proportion to a man's want of confidence in his own solitary judgment, does he usually repose, with implicit trust, on the infallibility of "the world" in general. And the world, to each individual, means the part of it with which he comes in contact: his party, his sect, his church, his class of society; the man may be called, by comparison, almost liberal and large-minded to whom it means anything so comprehensive as his own country or his own age. Nor is his faith in this collective authority at all shaken by his being aware that other ages, countries, sects, churches, classes, and parties have thought, and even now think, the exact reverse. He devolves upon his own world the responsibility of being in the right against the dissentient worlds of other people; and it never troubles him that mere accident has decided which of these numerous worlds is the object of his reliance, and that the same causes which make him a Churchman in London, would have made him a Buddhist or a Confucian in Pekin. Yet it is as evident in itself, as any amount of argument can make it, that ages are no more infallible than individuals; every age having held many opinions which subsequent ages have deemed not only false but absurd; and it is as certain that many opinions now general will be rejected by future ages, as it is that many, once general, are rejected by the present.

The objection likely to be made to this argument would probably take some such form as the following. There is no greater assumption of infallibility in forbidding the propagation of error than in any other thing which is done by public authority on its own judgment and responsibility. Judgment is given to men that they may use it. Because it may be used erroneously, are men to be told that they ought not to use it at all? To prohibit what they think pernicious is not claiming exemption from error, but fulfilling the duty incumbent on them, although fallible, of acting on their conscientious conviction. If we were never to act on our opinions, because those opinions may be wrong, we should leave all our interests uncared for, and all our duties unperformed. An objection which applies to all conduct can be no valid objection to any conduct in particular. It is the duty of governments, and of individuals, to form the truest opinions they can; to form them carefully, and never impose them upon others unless they are quite sure of being right. But when they are sure (such reasoners may say), it is not conscientiousness but cowardice to shrink from acting on their opinions and allow doctrines which they honestly think dangerous to the welfare of mankind, either in this life or in another, to be scattered abroad without restraint, because other people, in less enlightened times, have persecuted opinions now believed to be true. Let us take care, it may be said, not to make the same mistake; but governments and nations have made mistakes in other things which are not denied to be fit subjects for the exercise of authority: they have laid on bad taxes, made unjust wars. Ought we therefore to lay on no taxes and, under whatever provocation, make no wars?

Men and governments must act to the best of their ability. There is no such thing as absolute certainty, but there is assurance sufficient for the purposes of human life. We may, and must, assume our opinion to be true for the guidance of our own conduct; and it is assuming no more when we forbid bad men to pervert society by the propagation of opinions which we regard as false and pernicious.

I answer, that it is assuming very much more. There is the greatest difference between presuming an opinion to be true because, with every opportunity for contesting it, it has not been refuted, and assuming its truth for the purpose of not permitting its refutation. Complete liberty of contradicting and disproving our opinion is the very condition which justifies us in assuming its truth for purposes of action; and on no other terms can a being with human faculties have any rational assurance of being right. . . .

Let us now pass to the second division of the argument, and dismissing the supposition that any of the received opinions may be false, let us assume them to be true, and examine into the worth of the manner in which they are likely to be held, when their truth is not freely and openly canvassed. However unwillingly a person who has a strong opinion may admit the possibility that his opinion may be false, he ought to be moved by the consideration that, however true it may be, if it is not fully, frequently, and fearlessly discussed, it will be held as a dead dogma, not a living truth.

There is a class of persons (happily not quite so numerous as formerly) who think it enough if a person assents undoubtingly to what they think true, though he has no knowledge whatever of the grounds of the opinion, and could not make a tenable defense of it against the most superficial objections. Such persons, if they can once get their creed taught from authority, naturally think that no good, and some harm, comes of its being allowed to be questioned. Where their influence prevails, they make it nearly impossible for the received opinion to be rejected wisely and considerately, though it may still be rejected rashly and ignorantly; for to shut out discussion entirely is seldom possible, and when it once gets in, beliefs not grounded on convictions are apt to give way before the slightest semblance of an argument. Waiving, however, this possibility—assuming that the true opinion abides in the mind, but abides as a prejudice, a belief independent of, and proof against, argument—this is not the way in which truth ought to be held by a rational being. This is not knowing the truth. Truth, thus held, is but one superstition the more, accidently clinging to the words which enunciate a truth.

It still remains to speak of one of the principal causes which make diversity of opinion advantageous, and will continue to do so until mankind shall have entered a stage of intellectual advancement which at present seems at an incalculable distance. We have hitherto considered only two possibilities: that the received opinion may be false, and some other opinion, consequently, true; or that, the received opinion being true, a conflict with the opposite error is essential to a clear apprehension and deep feeling of its truth. But there is a commoner case than either of these: when the conflicting doctrines, instead of being one true and the other false, share the truth between them, and the nonconforming opinion is needed to supply the remainder of the truth of which the received doctrine embodies only a part. Popular opinions, on subjects not palpable to sense, are often true, but seldom or never the whole truth. They are a part of the truth, sometimes a greater, sometimes a smaller part, but exaggerated, distorted, and disjointed from the truths by which they ought to be accompanied and limited. Heretical opinions, on the other hand, are generally some of these suppressed and neglected truths, bursting the bonds which kept them down, and either seeking reconciliation with the truth contained in the common opinion, or fronting it as enemies, and setting themselves up, with similar exclusiveness, as the whole truth. The latter case is hitherto the most frequent, as, in the human mind, one-sidedness has always been the rule, and many-sidedness the exception. Hence, even in revolutions of opinion, one part of the truth usually sets while another rises. Even progress, which ought to superadd, for the most part only substitutes one partial and incomplete truth for another; improvement consisting chiefly in this, that the new fragment of truth is more wanted, more adapted to the needs of the time than that which it displaces. Such being the partial character of prevailing opinions, even when resting on a true foundation, every opinion which embodies somewhat of the portion of truth which the common opinion omits ought to be considered precious, with whatever amount of error and confusion that truth may be blended. No sober judge of human affairs will feel bound to be indignant because those who force on our notice truths which we should otherwise have overlooked, overlook some of those which we see. Rather, he will think that so long as popular truth is one-sided, it is more desirable than otherwise that unpopular truth should have one-sided assertors, too, such being usually the most energetic and the most likely to compel reluctant attention to the fragment of wisdom which they proclaim as if it were the whole. . . .

When there are persons to be found who form an exception to the apparent unanimity of the world on any subject, even if the world is in the right, it is always probable that dissentients have something worth hearing to say for themselves, and that truth would lose something by their silence. . . .

We have now recognized the necessity to the mental well-being of mankind (on which all their other well-being depends) of freedom of opinion, and freedom of the expression of opinion, on four distinct grounds, which we will now briefly recapitulate:

First, if any opinion is compelled to silence, that opinion may, for aught we can certainly know, be true. To deny this is to assume our own infallibility.

Secondly, though the silenced opinion be an error, it may, and very commonly does, contain a portion of truth; and since the general or prevailing opinion on any subject is rarely or never the whole truth, it is only by the collision of adverse opinions that the remainder of the truth has any chance of being supplied.

Thirdly, even if the received opinion be not only true, but the whole truth; unless it is suffered to be, and actually is, vigorously and earnestly contested, it will, by most of those who receive it, be held in the manner of a prejudice, with little comprehension or feeling of its rational grounds. And not only this, but, fourthly, the meaning of the doctrine itself will be in danger of being lost or enfeebled, and deprived of its vital effect on the character and conduct: the dogma becoming a mere formal profession, inefficacious for good, but cumbering the ground and preventing the growth of any real and heartfelt conviction from reason or personal experience. . . .

OF INDIVIDUALITY, AS ONE OF THE ELEMENTS OF WELL-BEING

Such being the reasons which make it imperative that human beings should be free to form opinions and to express their opinions without reserve; and such the baneful consequences to the intellectual, and through that to the moral nature of man, unless this liberty is either conceded or asserted in spite of prohibition; let us next examine whether the same reasons do not require that men should be free to act upon their opinions—to carry these out in their lives without hindrance, either physical or moral, from their fellow men, so long as it is at their own risk and peril. This last proviso is of course indispensable. No one pretends that actions should be as free as opinions. On the contrary, even opinions lose their immunity when the circumstances in which they are expressed are such as to constitute their expression a positive instigation to some mischievous act. An opinion that corn dealers are starvers of the poor, or that private property is robbery, ought to be unmolested when simply circulated through the press, but may justly incur punishment when delivered orally to an excited mob assembled before the house of a corn dealer, or when handed about among the same mob in the form of a placard. Acts, of whatever kind, which without justifiable cause do harm to others may be, and in the more important cases absolutely require to be, controlled by the unfavorable sentiments, and, when needful, by the active interference of mankind. The liberty of the individual must be thus far limited; he must not make himself a nuisance to other people. But if he refrains from molesting others in what concerns them, and merely acts according to his own inclination and judgment in things which concern himself, the same reasons which show that opinion should be free prove also that he should be allowed, without molestation, to carry his opinions into practice at his own cost. That mankind are not infallible; that their truths, for the most part, are only half-truths; that unity of opinion, unless resulting from the fullest and freest comparison of opposite opinions, is not desirable, and diversity not an evil, but a good, until mankind are much more capable than at present of recognizing all sides of the truth, are principles applicable to men's modes of action not less than to their opinions. As it is useful that while mankind are imperfect there should be different opinions, so it is that there should be different experiments of living; that free scope should be given to varieties of character, short of injury to others; and that the worth of different modes of life should be proved practically, when anyone thinks fit to try them. It is desirable, in short, that in things which do not primarily concern others individuality should assert itself. Where not the person's own character but the traditions or customs of other people are the rule of conduct, there is wanting one of the principal ingredients of human happiness, and quite the chief ingredient of individual and social progress. . . .

The despotism of custom is everywhere the standing hindrance to human advancement, being unceasing antagonism to that disposition to aim at something better than customary, which is called, according to circumstances, the spirit of liberty, or that of progress or improvement. The spirit of improvement is not always a spirit of liberty, for it may aim at forcing improvements on an unwilling people; and the spirit of liberty, in so far as it resists such attempts, may ally itself locally and temporarily with the opponents of improvement; but the only unfailing and permanent source of improvement is liberty, since by it there are as many possible independent centres of improvement as there are individuals.

OF THE LIMITS TO THE AUTHORITY OF SOCIETY OVER THE INDIVIDUAL

What, then, is the rightful limit to the sovereignty of the individual over himself? Where does the authority of society begin? How much of human life should be assigned to individuality, and how much to society?

Each will receive its proper share if each has that which more particularly concerns it. To individuality should belong the part of life in which it is chiefly the individual that is interested; to society, the part which chiefly interests society. . . .

The distinction here pointed out between the part of a person's life which concerns only himself and that which concerns others, many persons will refuse to admit. How (it may be asked) can any part of the conduct of a member of society be a matter of indifference to the other members? No person is an entirely isolated being; it is impossible for a person to do anything seriously or permanently hurtful to himself without mischief reaching at least to his near connections, and often far beyond them. If he injures his property, he does harm to those who directly or indirectly derived support from it, and usually diminishes, by a greater or less amount, the general resources of the community. If he deteriorates his bodily or mental faculties, he not only brings evil upon all who depended on him for any portion of their happiness, but disqualifies himself for rendering the services which he owes to his fellow creatures generally, perhaps becomes a burden on their affection or benevolence; and if such conduct were very frequent hardly any offense that is committed would detract more from the general sum of good. Finally, if by his vices or follies a person does no direct harm to others, he is nevertheless (it may be said) injurious by his example, and ought to be compelled to control himself for the sake of those whom the sight or knowledge of his conduct might corrupt or mislead.

And even (it will be added) if the consequences of misconduct could be confined to the vicious or thoughtless individual, ought society to abandon to their own guidance those who are manifestly unfit for it? If protection against themselves is confessedly due to children and persons under age, is not society equally bound to afford it to persons of mature years who are equally incapable of self-government? If gambling, or drunkenness, or incontinence, or idleness, or uncleanliness are as injurious to happiness, and as great a hindrance to improvement, as many or most of the acts prohibited by law, why (it may be asked) should not law, so far as is consistent with practicability and social convenience, endeavor to repress these also? And as a supplement to the unavoidable imperfections of law, ought not opinion at least to organize a powerful police against these vices and visit rigidly with social penalties those who are known to practice them? There is no question here (it may be said) about restricting individuality, or impeding the trial of new and original experiments in living. The only things it is sought to prevent are things which have been tried and condemned from the beginning of the world until now—things which experience has shown not to be useful or suitable to any person's individuality. There must be some length of time and amount of experience after which a moral or prudential truth may be regarded as established; and it is merely desired to prevent generation after generation from falling over the same precipice which has been fatal to their predecessors.

I fully admit that the mischief which a person does to himself may seriously affect, both through their sympathies and their interests, those nearly connected with him and, in a minor degree, society at large. When, by conduct of this sort, a person is led to violate a distinct and assignable obligation to any other person or persons, the case is taken out of the self-regarding class and becomes amenable to moral disapprobation in the proper sense of the term. If, for example, a man, through intemperance or extravagance, becomes unable to pay his debts, or, having undertaken the moral responsibility of a family, becomes from the same cause incapable of supporting or educating them, he is deservedly reprobated and might be justly punished; but it is for the breach of duty to his family or creditors, not for the extravagance. . . . In like manner, when a person disables himself, by conduct purely self-regarding, from the performance of some definite duty incumbent on him to the public, he is guilty of a social offense. No person ought to be punished simply for being drunk; but a soldier or a policeman should be punished for being drunk on duty. Whenever, in short, there is a definite damage, or a definite risk of damage, either to an individual or to the public, the case is taken out of the province of liberty and placed in that of morality or law.

But with regard to the merely contingent or, as it may be called, constructive injury which a person causes to society by conduct which neither violates any specific duty to the public, nor occasions perceptible hurt to any assignable individual except himself, the inconvenience is one which society can afford to bear, for the sake of the greater good of human freedom. If grown persons are to be punished for not taking proper care of themselves, I would rather it were for their own sake than under pretense of preventing them from impairing their capacity or rendering to society benefits which society does not pretend it has a right to exact. But I cannot consent to argue the point as if society had no means of bringing its weaker members up to its ordinary standard of rational conduct, except waiting till they do something irrational, and then punishing them, legally or morally, for it. Society has had absolute power over them during all the early portion of their existence; it has had the whole period of childhood and nonage in which to try whether it could make them capable of rational conduct in life. The existing generation is master both of the training and the entire circumstances of the generation to come; it cannot indeed make them perfectly wise and good, because it is itself so lamentably deficient in goodness and wisdom; and its best efforts are not always, in individual cases, its most successful ones; but it is perfectly well able to make the rising generation, as a whole, as good as, and a little better than, itself. If society lets any considerable number of its members grow up mere children, incapable of being acted on by rational consideration of distant motives, society has itself to blame for the consequences. Armed not only with all the powers of education, but with the ascendancy which the authority of a received opinion always exercises over the minds who are least fitted to judge for themselves, and aided by the *natural* penalties which cannot be prevented from falling on those who incur the distaste or the contempt of those who know them—let not society pretend that it needs, besides all this, the power to issue commands and enforce obedience in the personal concerns of individuals in which, on all principles of justice and policy, the decision ought to rest with those who are to abide the consequences.

Nor is there anything which tends more to discredit and frustrate the better means of influencing conduct than a resort to the worse. If there be among those whom it is attempted to coerce into prudence or temperance any of the material of which vigorous and independent characters are made, they will infallibly rebel against the yoke. No such person will ever feel that others have a right to control him in his concerns, such as they have to prevent him from injuring them in theirs; and it easily comes to be considered a mark of spirit and courage to fly in the face of such usurped authority and do with ostentation the exact opposite of what it enjoins, as in the fashion of grossness which succeeded, in the time of Charles II, to the fanatical moral intolerance of the Puritans. With respect to what is said of the necessity of protecting society from the bad example set to others by the vicious or the self-indulgent, it is true that bad example may have a pernicious effect, especially the example of doing wrong to others with impunity to the wrongdoer. But we are now speaking of conduct which, while it does no wrong to others, is supposed to do great harm to the agent himself; and I do not see how those who believe this can think otherwise than that the example, on the whole, must be more salutary than hurtful, since, if it displays the misconduct, it displays also the painful or degrading consequences which, if the conduct is justly censured, must be supposed to be in all or most cases attendant on it.

But the strongest of all the arguments against the interference of the public with purely personal conduct is that, when it does interfere, the odds are that it interferes wrongly and in the wrong place. On questions of social morality, of duty to others, the opinion of the public, that is, of an over-ruling majority, though often wrong, is likely to be still oftener right, because on such questions they are only required to judge of their own interests, of the manner in which some mode of conduct, if allowed to be practiced, would affect themselves. But the opinion of a similar majority, imposed as a law on the minority, on questions of self-regarding conduct is quite as likely to be wrong as right, for in these cases public opinion means, at the best, some people's opinion of what is good or bad for other people, while very often it does not even mean that—the public, with the most perfect indifference, passing over the pleasure or convenience of those whose conduct they censure and considering only their own preference. There are many who consider as an injury to themselves any conduct which they have a distaste for, and resent it as an outrage to their feelings; as a religious bigot, when charged with disregarding the religious feelings of others, has been known to retort that they disregard his feelings by persisting in their abominable worship or creed. But there is no parity between the feeling of a person for his own opinion and the feeling of another who is offended at his holding it, no more than between the desire of a thief to take a purse and the desire of the right owner to keep it. And a person's taste is as much his own peculiar concern as his opinion or his purse. . . .

The worth of a State, in the long run, is the worth of the individuals composing it . . . a State which dwarfs its men, in order that they may be more docile instruments in its hands even for beneficial purposes— will find that with small men no great thing can really be accomplished; and that the perfection of machinery to which it has sacrificed every- thing will in the end avail it nothing, for want of the vital power which, in order that the machine might work more smoothly, it has preferred to banish.

8. HOBHOUSE
Individuality and Social Control

Leonard Hobhouse (1864–1929), the first professor of sociology at the University of London, had been editorial writer of the leading liberal newspaper, the Manchester *Guardian*, and had previously taught philosophy at Oxford. *Liberalism* by Hobhouse is both a characteristic work of British liberalism in the period just before World War I and a representative statement of the way in which liberals of many European countries were redefining their political outlook in the light of their rejection of laissez-faire economics and Millian liberalism.

The selection is taken from Chapters VI and VII of *Liberalism*.*

*Published, with an Introduction by Alan P. Grimes, by Oxford University Press, New York, © 1964. Used by permission.

THE HEART OF LIBERALISM

The teaching of Mill brings us close to the heart of Liberalism. We learn from him, in the first place, that liberty is no mere formula of law, or of the restriction of law. There may be a tyranny of custom, a tyranny of opinion, even a tyranny of circumstance, as real as any tyranny of government and more pervasive. Nor does liberty rest on the self-assertion of the individual. There is scope abundant for Liberalism and illiberalism in personal conduct. Nor is liberty opposed to discipline, to organization, to strenuous conviction as to what is true and just. Nor is it to be identified with tolerance of opposed opinions. The Liberal does not meet opinions which he conceives to be false with toleration, as though they did not matter. He meets them with justice, and exacts for them a fair hearing as though they mattered just as much as his own. He is always ready to put his own convictions to the proof, not because he doubts them, but because he believes in them. For, both as to that which he holds for true and as to that which he holds for false, he believes that one final test applies. Let error have free play, and one of two things will happen. Either as it develops, as its implications and consequences become clear, some elements of truth will appear within it. They will separate themselves out; they will go to enrich the stock of human ideas; they will add something to the truth which he himself mistakenly took as final; they will serve to explain the root of the error; for error itself is generally a truth misconceived, and it is only when it is explained that it is finally and satisfactorily confuted. Or, in the alternative, no element of truth will appear. In that case the more fully the error is understood, the more patiently it is followed up in all the windings of its implications and consequences, the more thoroughly will it refute itself. The cancerous growth cannot be extirpated by the knife. The root is always left, and it is only the evolution of the self-protecting anti-toxin that works the final cure. Exactly parallel is the logic of truth. The more the truth is developed in all its implications, the greater is the opportunity of detecting any element of error that it may contain; and, conversely, if no error appears, the more completely does it establish itself as the whole truth and nothing but the truth. Liberalism applies the wisdom of Gamaliel in no spirit of indifference, but in the full conviction of the potency of truth. If this thing be of man, *i.e.* if it is not rooted in actual verity, it will come to nought. If it be of God, let us take care that we be not found fighting against God.

Divergencies of opinion, of character, of conduct are not unimportant

matters. They may be most serious matters, and no one is called on in
the name of Liberalism to overlook their seriousness. There are, for
example, certain disqualifications inherent in the profession of certain
opinions. It is not illiberal to recognize such disqualifications. It is not
illiberal for a Protestant in choosing a tutor for his son to reject a
conscientious Roman Catholic who avows that all his teaching is
centred on the doctrine of his Church. It would be illiberal to reject the
same man for the specific purpose of teaching arithmetic, if he avowed
that he had no intention of using his position for the purpose of religious
propagandism. For the former purpose the divergence of religious
opinion is an inherent disqualification. It negates the object propounded,
which is the general education of the boy on lines in which the father
believes. For the latter purpose the opinion is no disqualification. The
devout Catholic accepts the multiplication table, and can impart his
knowledge without reference to the infallibility of the Pope. To refuse
to employ him is to impose an extraneous penalty on his convictions.
It is not illiberal for an editor to decline the services of a member of the
opposite party as a leader writer, or even as a political reviewer or in
any capacity in which his opinions would affect his work. It is illiberal
to reject him as a compositor or as a clerk, or in any capacity in which
his opinions would not affect his work for the paper. It is not illiberal
to refuse a position of trust to the man whose record shows that he
is likely to abuse such a trust. It is illiberal—and this the "moralist"
has yet to learn—to punish a man who has done a wrong in one relation
by excluding him from the performance of useful social functions for
which he is perfectly fitted, by which he could at once serve society
and re-establish his own self-respect. There may, however, yet come
a time when Liberalism, already recognized as a duty in religion and
in politics, will take its true place at the centre of our ethical conceptions,
and will be seen to have its application not only to him whom we
conceive to be the teacher of false opinions, but to the man whom we
hold a sinner.

The ground of Liberalism so understood is certainly not the view
that a man's personal opinions are socially indifferent, nor that his
personal morality matters nothing to others. So far as Mill rested his
case on the distinction between self-regarding actions and actions
that affect others, he was still dominated by the older individualism.
We should frankly recognize that there is no side of a man's life which
is unimportant to society, for whatever he is, does, or thinks may
affect his own well-being, which is and ought to be matter of common

concern, and may also directly or indirectly affect the thought, action, and character of those with whom he comes in contact. The underlying principle may be put in two ways. In the first place, the man is much more than his opinions and his actions. . . . The real man is something more than is ever adequately expressed in terms which his fellows can understand; and just as his essential humanity lies deeper than all distinctions of rank, and class, and colour, and even, though in a different sense, of sex, so also it goes far below those comparatively external events which make one man figure as a saint and another as a criminal. This sense of ultimate oneness is the real meaning of equality, as it is the foundation of social solidarity and the bond which, if genuinely experienced, resists the disruptive force of all conflict, intellectual, religious, and ethical.

But, further, while personal opinions and social institutions are like crystallized results, achievements that have been won by certain definite processes of individual or collective effort, human personality is that within which lives and grows, which can be destroyed but cannot be made, which cannot be taken to pieces and repaired, but can be placed under conditions in which it will flourish and expand, or, if it is diseased, under conditions in which it will heal itself by its own re- cuperative powers. The foundation of liberty is the idea of growth. Life is learning, but whether in theory or practice what a man genuinely learns is what he absorbs, and what he absorbs depends on the energy which he himself puts forth in response to his surroundings. Thus, to come at once to the real crux, the question of moral discipline, it is of course possible to reduce a man to order and prevent him from being a nuisance to his neighbours by arbitrary control and harsh punishment. This may be to the comfort of the neighbours, as is admitted, but regarded as a moral discipline it is a contradiction in terms. It is doing less than nothing for the character of the man himself. It is merely crushing him, and unless his will is killed the effect will be seen if ever the superincumbent pressure is by chance removed. It is also possible, though it takes a much higher skill, to teach the same man to discipline himself, and this is to foster the development of will, of personality, of self-control, or whatever we please to call that central harmonizing power which makes us capable of directing our own lives. Liberalism is the belief that society can safely be founded on this self- directing power of personality, that it is only on this foundation that a true community can be built, and that so established its foundations are so deep and so wide that there is no limit that we can place to the extent of the building. Liberty then becomes not so much a right of the individual as a necessity of society. It rests not on the claim of A to be let alone by B, but on the duty of B to treat A as a rational being. It is not right to let crime alone or to let error alone, but it is imperative to treat the criminal or the mistaken or the ignorant as beings capable of right and truth, and to lead them on instead of merely beating them down. The rule of liberty is just the application of rational method. It is the opening of the door to the appeal of reason, of imagination, of social feeling; and except through the response to this appeal there is no assured progress of society.

Now, I am not contending that these principles are free from difficulty in application. At many points they suggest difficulties both in theory and in practice, with some of which I shall try to deal later on. Nor, again, am I contending that freedom is the universal solvent, or the idea of liberty the sole foundation on which a true social philosophy can be based. On the contrary, freedom is only one side of social life. Mutual aid is not less important than mutual forbearance, the theory of collective action no less fundamental than the theory of personal freedom. But, in an inquiry where all the elements are so closely interwoven as they are in the field of social life, the point of departure becomes almost indifferent. Wherever we start we shall, if we are quite frank and consistent, be led on to look at the whole from some central point, and this, I think, has happened to us in working with the conception of "liberty." For, beginning with the right of the individual, and the antithesis between personal freedom and social control, we have been led on to a point at which we regard liberty as primarily a matter of social interest, as something flowing from the necessities of continuous advance in those regions of truth and of ethics which constitute the matters of highest social concern. At the same time, we have come to look for the effect of liberty in the firmer establishment of social solidarity, as the only foundation on which such solidarity can securely rest. . . .

THE STATE AND THE INDIVIDUAL

We have seen something of the principle underlying the Liberal idea and of its various applications. We have now to put the test question. Are these different applications compatible? Will they work together to make that harmonious whole of which it is easy enough to talk in abstract terms? Are they themselves really harmonious in theory and in practice? Does scope for individual development, for example, consort with the idea of equality? Is popular sovereignty a practicable basis of personal freedom, or does it open an avenue to the tyranny of the mob? Will the sentiment of nationality dwell in unison with the ideal of peace? Is the love of liberty compatible with the full realization of the common will? If reconcilable in theory, may not these ideals collide in practice? Are there not clearly occasions demonstrable in history when development in one direction involves retrogression in another? If so, how are we to strike the balance of gain and loss? Does political progress offer us nothing but a choice of evils, or may we have some confidence that, in solving the most pressing problem of the moment, we shall in the end be in a better position for grappling with the obstacles that come next in turn?

I shall deal with these questions as far as limits of space allow, and I will take first the question of liberty and the common will upon which everything turns. Enough has already been said on this topic to enable us to shorten the discussion. We have seen that social liberty rests on restraint. A man can be free to direct his own life only in so far as others are prevented from molesting and interfering with him. So far there is no real departure from the strictest tenets of individualism. We have, indeed, had occasion to examine the application of the doctrine to freedom of contract on the one hand, and to the action of combinations on the other, and have seen reason to think that in either case nominal freedom, that is to say, the absence of legal restraint, might have the effect of impairing real freedom, that is to say, would allow the stronger party to coerce the weaker. We have also seen that the effect of combination may be double edged, that it may restrict freedom on one side and enlarge it on the other. In all these cases our contention has been simply that we should be guided by real and not by verbal considerations,—that we should ask in every case what policy will yield effective freedom—and we have found a close connection in each instance between freedom and equality. In these cases, however, we were dealing with the relations of one man with another, or of one body of men with another, and we could regard the community as an arbiter between them whose business it was to see justice done and prevent the abuse of coercive power. Hence we could treat a very large part of the modern development of social control as motived by the desire for a more effective liberty. The case is not so clear when we find the will of the individual in conflict with the will of the community as a whole. When such conflict occurs, it would seem that we must be prepared for one of two things. Either we must admit the legitimacy of coercion, avowedly not in the interests of freedom but in furtherance, without regard to freedom, of other ends which the community deems good. Or we must admit limitations which may cramp the development of the general will, and perchance prove a serious obstacle to collective progress. Is there any means of avoiding this conflict? Must we leave the question to be fought out in each case by a balance of advantages and disadvantages, or are there any general considerations which help us to determine the true sphere of collective and of private action?

Let us first observe that, as Mill pointed out long ago, there are many forms of collective action which do not involve coercion. The State may provide for certain objects which it deems good without compelling anyone to make use of them. Thus it may maintain hospitals, though anyone who can pay for them remains free to employ his own doctors and nurses. It may and does maintain a great educational system, while leaving everyone free to maintain or to attend a private school. It maintains parks and picture galleries without driving anyone into them. There is a municipal tramway service, which does not prevent private people from running motor 'buses along the same streets, and so on. It is true that for the support of these objects rates and taxes are compulsorily levied, but this form of compulsion raises a set of questions of which we shall have to speak in another connection, and does not concern us here. For the moment we have to deal only with those actions of State which compel all citizens, or all whom they concern, to fall in with them and allow of no divergence. This kind of coercion tends to increase. Is its extension necessarily an encroachment upon liberty, or are the elements of value secured by collective control distinct from the elements of value secured by individual choice, so that within due limits each may develop side by side?

We have already declined to solve the problem by applying Mill's distinction between self-regarding and other-regarding actions, first because there are no actions which may not directly or indirectly affect others, secondly because even if there were they would not cease to be matter of concern to others. The common good includes the good of every member of the community, and the injury which a man inflicts upon himself is matter of common concern, even apart from any ulterior effect upon others. If we refrain from coercing a man for his own good, it is not because his good is indifferent to us, but because it cannot be furthered by coercion. The difficulty is founded on the nature of the good itself, which on its personal side depends on the spontaneous flow of feeling checked and guided not by external restraint but by rational self-control. To try to form character by coercion is to destroy it in the making. Personality is not built up from without but grows from within, and the function of the outer order is not to create it, but to provide for it the most suitable conditions of growth. Thus, to the common question whether it is possible to make men good by Act of Parliament, the reply is that it is not possible to compel morality because morality is the act or character of a free agent, but that it is possible to create the conditions under which morality can develop, and among these not the least important is freedom from compulsion by others.

The argument suggests that compulsion is limited not by indifference —how could the character of its members be matter of indifference to the community?—but by its own incapacity to achieve its ends. The spirit cannot be forced. Nor, conversely, can it prevail by force. It may require social expression. It may build up an association, a church for example, to carry out the common objects and maintain the common life of all who are like-minded. But the association must be free, because spiritually everything depends not on what is done but on the will with which it is done. The limit to the value of coercion thus lies not in the restriction of social purpose, but in the conditions of personal life. No force can compel growth. Whatever elements of social value depend on the accord of feeling, on comprehension of meaning, on the assent of will, must come through liberty. Here is the sphere and function of liberty in the social harmony.

Where, then, is the sphere of compulsion, and what is its value? The reply is that compulsion is of value where outward conformity is of value, and this may be in any case where the nonconformity of one wrecks the purpose of others. We have already remarked that liberty itself only rests upon restraint. Thus a religious body is not, properly speaking, free to march in procession through the streets unless people of a different religion are restrained from pelting the procession with stones and pursuing it with insolence. We restrain them from disorder not to teach them the genuine spirit of religion, which they will not learn in the police court, but to secure to the other party the right of worship unmolested. The enforced restraint has its value in the action that it sets free. But we may not only restrain one man from obstructing another—and the extent to which we do this is the measure of the freedom that we maintain—but we may also restrain him from obstructing the general will; and this we have to do whenever uniformity is necessary to the end which the general will has in view. The majority of employers in a trade we may suppose would be willing to adopt certain precautions for the health or safety of their workers, to lower hours or to raise the rate of wages. They are unable to do so, however, as long as a minority, perhaps as long as a single employer, stands out. He would beat them in competition if they were voluntarily to undertake expenses from which he is free. In this case, the will of a minority, possibly the will of one man, thwarts that of the remainder. It coerces them, indirectly, but quite as effectively as if he were their master. If they, by combination, can coerce him no principle of liberty is violated. It is coercion against coercion, differing possibly in form and method, but not in principle or in spirit. Further, if the community as a whole sympathizes with the one side rather than the other, it can reasonably bring the law into play. Its object is not the moral education of the recusant individuals. Its object is to secure certain conditions which it believes necessary for the welfare of its members, and which can only be secured by an enforced uniformity.

It appears, then, that the true distinction is not between self-regarding and other-regarding actions, but between coercive and non-coercive actions. The function of State coercion is to override individual coercion, and, of course, coercion exercised by any association of individuals within the State. It is by this means that it maintains liberty of expression, security of person and property, genuine freedom of contract, the rights of public meeting and association, and finally its own power to carry out common objects undefeated by the recalcitrance of individual members. Undoubtedly it endows both individuals and associations with powers as well as with rights. But over these powers it must exercise supervision in the interests of equal justice. Just as compulsion failed in the sphere of liberty, the sphere of spiritual growth, so liberty fails in the external order wherever, by the mere absence of supervisory restriction, men are able directly or indirectly to put constraint on one another. This is why there is no intrinsic and inevitable conflict between liberty and compulsion, but at bottom a mutual need. The object of compulsion is to secure the most favourable external conditions of inward growth and happiness so far as these conditions depend on combined action and uniform observance. The sphere of liberty is the sphere of growth itself. There is no true opposition between liberty as such and control as such, for every liberty rests on a corresponding act of control. The true opposition is between the control that cramps the personal life and the spiritual order, and the control that is aimed at securing the external and material conditions of their free and unimpeded development.

I do not pretend that this delimitation solves all problems. The "inward" life will seek to express itself in outward acts. A religious ordinance may bid the devout refuse military service, or withhold the payment of a tax, or decline to submit a building to inspection. Here are external matters where conscience and the State come into direct conflict, and where is the court of appeal that is to decide between them? In any given case the right, as judged by the ultimate effect on human welfare, may, of course, be on the one side, or on the other, or between the two. But is there anything to guide the two parties as long as each believes itself to be in the right and sees no ground for waiving its opinion? To begin with, clearly the State does well to avoid such conflicts by substituting alternatives. Other duties than that of military service may be found for a follower of Tolstoy, and as long as he is willing to take his full share of burdens the difficulty is fairly met. Again, the mere convenience of the majority cannot be fairly weighed against the religious convictions of the few. It might be convenient that certain public work should be done on Saturday, but mere convenience would be an insufficient ground for compelling Jews to participate in it. Religious and ethical conviction must be weighed against religious and ethical conviction. It is not number that counts morally, but the belief that is reasoned out according to the best of one's lights as to the necessities of the common good. But the conscience of the community has its rights just as much as the conscience of the individual. If we are convinced that the inspection of a convent laundry is required in the interest, not of mere official routine, but of justice and humanity, we can do nothing but insist upon it, and when all has been done that can be done to save the individual conscience the common conviction of the common good must have its way. In the end the external order belongs to the community, and the right of protest to the individual.

On the other side, the individual owes more to the community than is always recognized. Under modern conditions he is too much inclined to take for granted what the State does for him and to use the personal security and liberty of speech which it affords him as a vantage ground from which he can in safety denounce its works and repudiate its authority. He assumes the right to be in or out of the social system as he chooses. He relies on the general law which protects him, and emancipates himself from some particular law which he finds oppressive to his conscience. He forgets or does not take the trouble to reflect that, if everyone were to act as he does, the social machine would come to a stop. He certainly fails to make it clear how a society would subsist in which every man should claim the right of unrestricted disobedience to a law which he happens to think wrong. In fact, it is possible for an over-tender conscience to consort with an insufficient sense of social responsibility. The combination is unfortunate; and we may fairly say that, if the State owes the utmost consideration to the conscience, its owner owes a corresponding debt to the State. With such mutual consideration, and with the development of the civic sense, conflicts between law and conscience are capable of being brought within very narrow limits, though their complete reconciliaton will always remain a problem until men are generally agreed as to the fundamental conditions of the social harmony.

It may be asked, on the other hand, whether in insisting on the free development of personality we have not understated the duty of society to its members. We all admit a collective responsibility for children. Are there not grown-up people who stand just as much in need of care? What of the idiot, the imbecile, the feeble-minded or the drunkard? What does rational self-determination mean for these classes? They may injure no one but themselves except by the contagion of bad example. But have we no duty towards them, having in view their own good alone and leaving every other consideration aside? Have we not the right to take the feeble-minded under our care and to keep the drunkard from drink, purely for their own good and apart from every ulterior consideration? And, if so, must we not extend the whole sphere of permissible coercion, and admit that a man may for his own sake and with no ulterior object, be compelled to do what we think right and avoid what we think wrong?

The reply is that the argument is weak just where it seeks to generalize. We are compelled to put the insane under restraint for social reasons apart from their own benefit. But their own benefit would be a fully sufficient reason if no other existed. To them, by their misfortune, liberty, as we understand the term, has no application, because they are incapable of rational choice and therefore of the kind of growth for the sake of which freedom is valuable. The same thing is true of the feeble-minded, and if they are not yet treated on the same principle it is merely because the recognition of their type as a type is relatively modern. But the same thing is also in its degree true of the drunkard, so far as he is the victim of an impulse which he has allowed to grow beyond his own control; and the question whether he should be regarded as a fit object for tutelage or not is to be decided in each case by asking whether such capacity of self-control as he retains would be impaired or repaired by a period of tutelar restraint. There is nothing in all this to touch the essential of liberty which is the value of the power of self-governance where it exists. All that is proved is that where it does not exist it is right to save men from suffering, and if the case admits to put them under conditions in which the normal balance of impulse is most likely to be restored. It may be added that, in the case of the drunkard—and I think the argument applies to all cases where overwhelming impulse is apt to master the will—it is a still more obvious and elementary duty to remove the sources of temptation, and to treat as anti-social in the highest degree every attempt to make profit out of human weakness, misery, and wrong-doing. The case is not unlike that of a very unequal contract. The tempter is coolly seeking his profit, and the sufferer is beset with a fiend within. There is a form of coercion here which the genuine spirit of liberty will not fail to recognize as its enemy, and a form of injury to another which is not the less real because its weapon is an impulse which forces that other to the consent which he yields.

I conclude that there is nothing in the doctrine of liberty to hinder the movement of general will in the sphere in which it is really efficient, and nothing in a just conception of the objects and methods of the general will to curtail liberty, in the performance of the functions, social and personal, in which its value lies. Liberty and compulsion have complementary functions, and the self-governing State is at once the product and the condition of the self-governing individual. . . .

II

Constitutionalism and Democracy

The political organization usually advanced by liberals is some form of political democracy defended by a constitutional arrangement which sets limits to governmental power. An early statement of liberal constitutional doctrine is Locke's *Two Treatises of Government*, written in the 1680's, about a hundred and thirty years before the word "liberal" was introduced as the name for a political party concerned with democratic government. The final selection, that of the Austrian economist Joseph Schumpeter, was published in the United States in 1940, several years after the eclipse of all liberal parties on the continent of Europe. Locke's *Treatise* is directly related to the extension of parliamentary rights in Britain against the British monarchy. Schumpeter's work, although in great measure a criticism of eighteenth-century theories of democracy, reflects the rise of totalitarian mass movements in Central Europe and the consequent need for new revision of democratic theory. Between these two points of reference, the seven selections show the direction of liberal political thought in the major transformation of modern European political institutions.

The inextricable relationship between political theory and institutional practice suggests that the tracing of a single line of development for European liberalism is artificial. One central point of reference for European political liberalism is the French Revolution. The French *Declaration of the Rights of Man and of the Citizen* formulated the justification of political revolution by reference to the natural rights of all men. To a significant degree, liberals were identified by their attitude to "Liberty, Equality, and Fraternity," where "Liberty" meant civic rights for all in a republican society; "Equality" was often interpreted as equality before the law or as equality of opportunity in a market economy; and "Fraternity" referred to the integrated ideal provided by the national community where civic participation was afforded through representative institutions. Those, such as Montesquieu, who were interpreted as stressing the virtue of judiciary or executive restraints on popular control, were viewed as conservative liberals; those, such as Rousseau, who were interpreted as champions of the popular will, were the source of radical liberalism. Kant developed the conception of the rule of law as the safeguard of freedom in the new republican order. After the Reign of Terror, liberal Parliamentarians, like Constant or Tocqueville, reasserted the primacy of freedom of press or assembly for a free society in an era of popular dictatorship.

If theories of the natural rights of man were one source for liberal democracy, theories of maximizing the greatest good for the greatest number were another. The utilitarians, following Bentham, rejected doctrines of natural rights, yet justified representative democracy as providing protection for each person's interests. Bentham's utilitarian point of view was developed by James Mill and John Stuart Mill. These arguments were advanced in the context of the extension of suffrage and the nineteenth-century reform of British political institutions.

European liberal democracy, for a variety of reasons including periods of economic depression as well as two great wars for European dominance, was unable to develop a democratic structure which integrated the masses of population into its civic institutions. Since the debacle of totalitarianism and of the Second World War, the institutions of the democratic state have been restored through most of Western Europe. The heritage of political liberalism has become part of the institutional fabric of Western Europe defended by conservatives, liberals, and socialists. In part, presumably for Spain, Greece, or Eastern Europe, the agenda of liberalism would be in the introduction of parliamentary regimes with free press, free trade unions, competing political parties, and universal suffrage.

But in the face of new postwar conditions European liberals also must develop a new agenda. Three items may suggest the scope of the challenge for any new European liberalism. First, the experience of European economic integration suggests the need for new federal European institutions of political control. Second, there is the integration into the body politic of the alienated "proletarian" constituencies which have not yet found in democratic and liberal institutions the vehicle for expressing their social or political will. Third, there is a gap between the multinational corporate structures which introduce the new technologies reshaping the environment and the national instruments of political and social organization through representative institutions. The context for all these problems is the intense dynamism of the nations of Western Europe, in the twentieth century, when for the first time their political decisions are overshadowed by the decisions of non-European powers.

9. LOCKE

Consent and Revolution

It had long been believed that John Locke wrote two *Treatises of Government* after the Glorious Revolution of 1688. However, on the basis of the discovery of new manuscripts, it has recently been argued that most of the work was written ten years earlier.

Important as this controversy may be for the interpretation of the relation of political theory to practice, there can be no doubt of the enormous subsequent significance of this work for political liberalism. Locke's defense of property rights and his doctrine of separation of powers, for example, were continuously appealed to by conservative liberals. His belief in the supremacy of the legislature and his justification of revolution were a major source for radical liberals.

The selection is taken from the *Second Treatise* which Locke had originally entitled "An Essay Concerning the True Original, Extent, and End of Civil Government."

OF THE STATE OF NATURE

4. To understand political power right, and derive it from its original, we must consider what state all men are naturally in, and that is a state of perfect freedom to order their actions and dispose of their possessions and persons as they think fit, within the bounds of the law of nature, without asking leave or depending upon the will of any other man.

A state also of equality, wherein all the power and jurisdiction is reciprocal, no one having more than another; there being nothing more evident than that creatures of the same species and rank, promiscuously born to all the same advantages of nature and the use of the same faculties, should also be equal one amongst another without subordination or subjection . . . .

6. But though this be a state of liberty, yet it is not a state of licence; though man in that state have an uncontrollable liberty to dispose of

his person or possessions, yet he has not liberty to destroy himself, or so much as any creature in his possession, but where some nobler use than its bare preservation calls for it. The state of nature has a law of nature to govern it which obliges everyone; and reason, which is that law, teaches all mankind who will but consult it that, being all equal and independent, no one ought to harm another in his life, health, liberty, or possessions . . . .

7. And that all men may be restrained from invading others' rights and from doing hurt to one another, and the law of nature be observed which willeth the peace and preservation of all mankind, the execution of the law of nature is, in that state, put into every man's hands, whereby everyone has a right to punish the transgressors of that law to such a degree as may hinder its violation; for the law of nature would, as all other laws that concern men in this world, be in vain, if there were nobody that in the state of nature had a power to execute that law and thereby preserve the innocent and restrain offenders. And if any one in the state of nature may punish another for any evil he has done, everyone may do so; for in that state of perfect equality where naturally there is no superiority or jurisdiction of one over another, what any may do in prosecution of that law, every one must needs have a right to do. . . .

OF THE BEGINNING OF POLITICAL SOCIETIES

95. Men being, as has been said, by nature all free, equal, and independent, no one can be put out of this estate and subjected to the political power of another without his own consent. The only way whereby anyone divests himself of his natural liberty, and puts on the bonds of civil society, is by agreeing with other men to join and unite into a community for their comfortable, safe, and peaceable living one amongst another, in a secure enjoyment of their properties and a greater security against any that are not of it. This any number of men may do, because it injures not the freedom of the rest; they are left as they were in the liberty of the state of nature. When any number of men have so consented to make one community or government, they are thereby presently incorporated and make one body politic wherein the majority have a right to act and conclude the rest.

96. For when any number of men have, by the consent of every individual, made a community, they have thereby made that community one body, with a power to act as one body, which is only by the will and determination of the majority; for that which acts any community

being only the consent of the individuals of it, and it being necessary to that which is one body to move one way, it is necessary the body should move that way whither the greater force carries it, which is the consent of the majority; or else it is impossible it should act or continue one body, one community, which the consent of every individual that united into it agreed that it should; and so everyone is bound by that consent to be concluded by the majority. And therefore we see that in assemblies impowered to act by positive laws, where no number is set by that positive law which impowers them, the act of the majority passes for the act of the whole, and, of course, determines, as having by the law of nature and reason the power of the whole.

97. And thus every man, by consenting with others to make one body politic under one government, puts himself under an obligation to everyone of that society to submit to the determination of the majority, and to be concluded by it; or else this original compact, whereby he with others incorporates into one society, would signify nothing, and be no compact, if he be left free and under no other ties than he was in before the state of nature. For what appearance would there be of any compact? What new engagement if he were no farther tied by any decrees of the society than he himself thought fit and did actually consent to? This would be still as great a liberty as he himself had before his compact, or anyone else in the state of nature hath who may submit himself and consent to any acts of it if he thinks fit . . . .

99. Whosoever, therefore, out of a state of nature unite into a community must be understood to give up all the power necessary to the ends for which they unite into society to the majority of the community, unless they expressly agreed in any number greater than the majority. And this is done by barely agreeing to unite into one political society, which is all the compact that is, or needs be, between the individuals that enter into or make up a commonwealth. And thus that which begins and actually constitutes any political society is nothing but the consent of any number of freemen capable of a majority to unite and incorporate into such a society. And this is that, and that only, which did or could give beginning to any lawful government in the world. . . .

119. Every man being, as has been shown, naturally free, and nothing being able to put him into subjection to any earthly power but only his own consent, it is to be considered what shall be understood to be a sufficient declaration of a man's consent to make him subject to the laws of any government. There is a common distinction of an express and a tacit consent which will concern our present case. Nobody doubts but

an express consent of any man entering into any society makes him a perfect member of that society, a subject of that government. The difficulty is, what ought to be looked upon as a tacit consent, and how far it binds,—*i.e.*, how far any one shall be looked upon to have consented and thereby submitted to any government, where he has made no expressions of it at all. And to this I say that every man that hath any possessions or enjoyment of any part of the dominions of any government doth thereby give his tacit consent and is as far forth obliged to obedience to the laws of that government, during such enjoyment, as anyone under it; whether this his possession be of land to him and his heirs for ever, or a lodging only for a week, or whether it be barely travelling freely on the highway; and, in effect, it reaches as far as the very being of anyone within the territories of that government.

120. To understand this the better, it is fit to consider that every man, when he at first incorporates himself into any commonwealth, he, by his uniting himself thereunto, annexes also, and submits to the community, those possessions which he has or shall acquire that do not already belong to any other government; for it would be a direct contradiction for anyone to enter into society with others for the securing and regulating of property, and yet to suppose his land, whose property is to be regulated by the laws of the society, should be exempt from the jurisdiction of that government to which he himself, the proprietor of the land, is a subject. By the same act, therefore, whereby anyone unites his person, which was before free, to any commonwealth, by the same he unites his possessions, which were before free, to it also; and they become, both of them, person and possession, subject to the government and dominion of that commonwealth as long as it hath a being. Whoever, therefore, from thenceforth by inheritance, purchase, permission, or otherwise, enjoys any part of the land so annexed to, and under the government of that commonwealth, must take it with the condition it is under—that is, of submitting to the government of the commonwealth under whose jurisdiction it is as far forth as any subject of it.

121. But since the government has a direct jurisdiction only over the land, and reaches the possessor of it—before he has actually incorporated himself in the society—only as he dwells upon and enjoys that, the obligation anyone is under by virtue of such enjoyment, to submit to the government, begins and ends with the enjoyment; so that whenever the owner, who has given nothing but such a tacit consent to the government, will, by donation, sale, or otherwise, quit the said posses-

sion, he is at liberty to go and incorporate himself into any other commonwealth, or to agree with others to begin a new one *in vacuis locis*, in any part of the world they can find free and unpossessed. Whereas he that has once, by actual agreement and any express declaration, given his consent to be of any commonwealth is perpetually and indispensably obliged to be and remain unalterably a subject to it, and can never be again in the liberty of the state of nature, unless by any calamity the government he was under comes to be dissolved, or else by some public act cuts him off from being any longer a member of it.

122. But submitting to the laws of any country, living quietly and enjoying privileges and protection under them, makes not a man a member of that society; this is only a local protection and homage due to and from all those who, not being in a state of war, come within the territories belonging to any government, to all parts whereof the force of its laws extends. But this no more makes a man a member of that society, a perpetual subject of that commonwealth, than it would make a man a subject to another in whose family he found it convenient to abide for some time, though, whilst he continued in it, he were obliged to comply with the laws, and submit to the government he found there. And thus we see that foreigners, by living all their lives under another government and enjoying the privileges and protection of it, though they are bound, even in conscience, to submit to its administration as far forth as any denizen, yet do not thereby come to be subjects or members of that commonwealth. Nothing can make any man so but his actually entering into it by positive engagement and express promise and compact. This is that which I think concerning the beginning of political societies and that consent which makes anyone a member of any commonwealth.

OF THE ENDS OF POLITICAL SOCIETY
AND GOVERNMENT

123. If man in the state of nature be so free, as has been said, if he be absolute lord of his own person and possessions, equal to the greatest, and subject to nobody, why will he part with his freedom, why will he give up his empire and subject himself to the dominion and control of any other power? To which it is obvious to answer that though in the state of nature he hath such a right, yet the enjoyment of it is very uncertain and constantly exposed to the invasion of others; for all being kings as much as he, every man his equal, and the greater part no strict

observers of equity and justice, the enjoyment of the property he has in this state is very unsafe, very unsecure. This makes him willing to quit a condition which, however free, is full of fears and continual dangers; and it is not without reason that he seeks out and is willing to join in society with others who are already united, or have a mind to unite, for the mutual preservation of their lives, liberties, and estates, which I call by the general name "property."

124. The great and chief end, therefore, of men's uniting into commonwealths and putting themselves under government is the preservation of their property. To which in the state of nature there are many things wanting:

First, There wants an established, settled, known law, received and allowed by common consent to be the standard of right and wrong and the common measure to decide all controversies between them; for though the law of nature be plain and intelligible to all rational creatures, yet men, being biased by their interest as well as ignorant for want of studying it, are not apt to allow of it as a law binding to them in the application of it to their particular cases.

125. Secondly, In the state of nature there wants a known and indifferent judge with authority to determine all differences according to the established law; for every one in that state being both judge and executioner of the law of nature, men being partial to themselves, passion and revenge is very apt to carry them too far and with too much heat in their own cases, as well as negligence and unconcernedness to make them too remiss in other men's.

126. Thirdly, In the state of nature, there often wants power to back and support the sentence when right, and to give it due execution. They who by any injustice offend will seldom fail, where they are able, by force, to make good their injustice; such resistance many times makes the punishment dangerous and frequently destructive to those who attempt it.

127. Thus mankind, notwithstanding all the privileges of the state of nature, being but in an ill condition while they remain in it, are quickly driven into society. Hence it comes to pass that we seldom find any number of men live any time together in this state. The inconveniences that they are therein exposed to by the irregular and uncertain exercise of the power every man has of punishing the transgressions of others make them take sanctuary under the established laws of government and therein seek the preservation of their property. It is this makes them so willingly give up every one his single power of punishing, to

be exercised by such alone as shall be appointed to it amongst them; and by such rules as the community, or those authorized by them to that purpose, shall agree on. And in this we have the original right of both the legislative and executive power, as well as of the governments and societies themselves.

128. For in the state of nature, to omit the liberty he has of innocent delights, a man has two powers:

The first is to do whatsoever he thinks fit for the preservation of himself and others within the permission of the law of nature, by which law, common to them all, he and all the rest of mankind are one community, make up one society, distinct from all other creatures. And, were it not for the corruption and viciousness of degenerate men, there would be no need of any other, no necessity that men should separate from this great and natural community and by postive agreements combine into smaller and divided associations.

The other power a man has in the state of nature is the power to punish the crimes committed against that law. Both these he gives up when he joins in a private, if I may so call it, or particular politic society and incorporates into any commonwealth separate from the rest of mankind.

129. The first power, viz., of doing whatsoever he thought fit for the preservation of himself and the rest of mankind, he gives up to be regulated by laws made by the society, so far forth as the preservation of himself and the rest of that society shall require; which laws of the society in many things confine the liberty he had by the law of nature.

130. Secondly, The power of punishing he wholly gives up, and engages his natural force—which he might before employ in the execution of the law of nature by his own single authority, as he thought fit—to assist the executive power of the society, as the law thereof shall require; for being now in a new state, wherein he is to enjoy many conveniences from the labour, assistance, and society of others in the same community as well as protection from its whole strength, he is to part also with as much of his natural liberty, in providing for himself, as the good, prosperity, and safety of the society shall require, which is not only necessary, but just, since the other members of the society do the like.

131. But though men when they enter into society give up the equality, liberty, and executive power they had in the state of nature into the hands of the society, to be so far disposed of by the legislative as the good of the society shall require, yet it being only with an inten-

tion in everyone the better to preserve himself, his liberty and property—for no rational creature can be supposed to change his condition with an intention to be worse—the power of the society, or legislative constituted by them, can never be supposed to extend farther than the common good, but is obliged to secure everyone's property by providing against those three defects above-mentioned that made the state of nature so unsafe and uneasy. And so whoever has the legislative or supreme power of any commonwealth is bound to govern by established standing laws, promulgated and known to the people, and not by extemporary decrees; by indifferent and upright judges who are to decide controversies by those laws; and to employ the force of the community at home only in the execution of such laws, or abroad to prevent or redress foreign injuries, and secure the community from inroads and invasion. And all this to be directed to no other end but the peace, safety, and public good of the people. . . .

OF THE EXTENT OF THE LEGISLATIVE POWER

134. The great end of men's entering into society being the enjoyment of their properties in peace and safety, and the great instrument and means of that being the laws established in that society, the first and fundamental positive law of all commonwealths is the establishing of the legislative power; as the first and fundamental natural law which is to govern even the legislative itself is the preservation of the society and, as far as will consist with the public good, of every person in it. This legislative is not only the supreme power of the commonwealth, but sacred and unalterable in the hands where the community have once placed it; nor can any edict of anybody else, in what form soever conceived or by what power soever backed, have the force and obligation of a law which has not its sanction from that legislative which the public has chosen and appointed; for without this the law could not have that which is absolutely necessary to its being a law; the consent of the society over whom nobody can have a power to make laws, but by their own consent and by authority received from them. And therefore all the obedience, which by the most solemn ties anyone can be obliged to pay, ultimately terminates in this supreme power and is directed by those laws which it enacts; nor can any oaths to any foreign power whatsoever, or any domestic subordinate power, discharge any member of the society from his obedience to the legislative acting pursuant to their trust, nor oblige him to any obedience contrary to the

laws so enacted, or farther than they do allow; it being ridiculous to imagine one can be tied ultimately to obey any power in the society which is not supreme.

135. Though the legislative, whether placed in one or more, whether it be always in being, or only by intervals, though it be the supreme power in every commonwealth; yet:

First, It is not, nor can possibly be, absolutely arbitrary over the lives and fortunes of the people; for it being but the joint power of every member of the society given up to that person or assembly which is legislator, it can be no more than those persons had in a state of nature before they entered into society and gave up to the community; for nobody can transfer to another more power than he has in himself, and nobody has an absolute arbitrary power over himself, or over any other, to destroy his own life, or take away the life or property of another. A man, as has been proved, cannot subject himself to the arbitrary power of another; and having in the state of nature no arbitrary power over the life, liberty, or possession of another, but only so much as the law of nature gave him for the preservation of himself and the rest of mankind, this is all he doth or can give up to the commonwealth, and by it to the legislative power, so that the legislative can have no more than this. Their power, in the utmost bounds of it, is limited to the public good of the society. It is a power that hath no other end but preservation, and therefore can never have a right to destroy, enslave, or designedly to impoverish the subjects. The obligations of the law of nature cease not in society but only in many cases are drawn closer and have by human laws known penalties annexed to them to enforce their observation. Thus the law of nature stands as an eternal rule to all men, legislators as well as others. The rules that they make for other men's actions must, as well as their own and other men's actions, be conformable to the law of nature—i.e., to the will of God, of which that is a declaration—and the fundamental law of nature being the preservation of mankind, no human sanction can be good or valid against it.

136. Secondly, The legislative or supreme authority cannot assume to itself a power to rule by extemporary, arbitrary decrees, but is bound to dispense justice and to decide the rights of the subject by promulgated, standing laws, and known authorized judges. For the law of nature being unwritten, and so nowhere to be found but in the minds of men, they who through passion or interest shall miscite or misapply it, cannot so easily be convinced of their mistake where there is no established judge; and so it serves not, as it ought, to determine the

rights and fence the properties of those that live under it, especially where everyone is judge, interpreter, and executioner of it, too, and that in his own case; and he that has right on his side, having ordinarily but his own single strength, hath not force enough to defend himself from injuries, or to punish delinquents. To avoid these inconveniences which disorder men's properties in the state of nature, men unite into societies that they may have the united strength of the whole society to secure and defend their properties, and may have standing rules to bound it by which everyone may know what is his. To this end it is that men give up all their natural power to the society which they enter into, and the community put the legislative power into such hands as they think fit with this trust, that they shall be governed by declared laws, or else their peace, quiet, and property will still be at the same uncertainty as it was in the state of nature.

137. Absolute arbitrary power, or governing without settled standing laws, can neither of them consist with the ends of society and government which men would not quit the freedom of the state of nature for, and tie themselves up under, were it not to preserve their lives, liberties, and fortunes, and by stated rules of right and property to secure their peace and quiet. It cannot be supposed that they should intend, had they a power so to do, to give to any one or more an absolute arbitrary power over their persons and estates and put a force into the magistrate's hand to execute his unlimited will arbitrarily upon them. This were to put themselves into a worse condition than the state of nature wherein they had a liberty to defend their right against the injuries of others and were upon equal terms of force to maintain it, whether invaded by a single man or many in combination. Whereas, by supposing they have given up themselves to the absolute arbitrary power and will of a legislator, they have disarmed themselves and armed him to make a prey of them when he pleases . . . .

138. Thirdly, The supreme power cannot take from any man part of his property without his own consent; for the preservation of property being the end of government and that for which men enter into society, it necessarily supposes and requires that the people should have property, without which they must be supposed to lose that, by entering into society, which was the end for which they entered into it—too gross an absurdity for any man to own. Men, therefore, in society having property, they have such right to the goods which by the law of the community are theirs, that nobody hath a right to take their substance or any part of it from them without their own consent; without this,

they have no property at all, for I have truly no property in that which another can by right take from me when he pleases, against my consent. Hence it is a mistake to think that the supreme or legislative power of any commonwealth can do what it will, and dispose of the estates of the subject arbitrarily, or take any part of them at pleasure. . . .

139. But government, into whatsoever hands it is put, being, as I have before shown, entrusted with this condition, and for this end, that men might have and secure their properties, the prince, or senate, however it may have power to make laws for the regulating of property between the subjects one amongst another, yet can never have a power to take to themselves the whole or any part of the subjects' property without their own consent; for this would be in effect to leave them no property at all. And to let us see that even absolute power, where it is necessary, is not arbitrary by being absolute, but is still limited by that reason and confined to those ends which required it in some cases to be absolute, we need look no farther than the common practice of martial discipline; for the preservation of the army, and in it of the whole commonwealth, requires an absolute obedience to the command of every superior officer, and it is justly death to disobey or dispute the most dangerous or unreasonable of them; but yet we see that neither the sergeant, that could command a soldier to march up to the mouth of a cannon or stand in a breach where he is almost sure to perish, can command that soldier to give him one penny of his money; nor the general, that can condemn him to death for deserting his post, or for not obeying the most desperate orders, can yet, with all his absolute power of life and death, dispose of one farthing of that soldier's estate or seize one jot of his goods, whom yet he can command anything, anp hang for the least disobedience. Because such a blind obedience is necessary to that end for which the commander has his power, viz., the preservation of the rest; but the disposing of his goods has nothing to do with it.

140. It is true, governments cannot be supported without great charge, and it is fit everyone who enjoys his share of the protection should pay out of his estate his proportion for the maintenance of it. But still it must be with his own consent—*i.e.*, the consent of the majority, giving it either by themselves or their representatives chosen by them. For if any one shall claim a power to lay and levy taxes on the people, by his own authority and without such consent of the people, he thereby invades the fundamental law of property and subverts the

end of government; for what property have I in that which another may by right take, when he please, to himself?

141. Fourthly, The legislative cannot transfer the power of making laws to any other hands; for it being but a delegated power from the people, they who have it cannot pass it over to others. The people alone can appoint the form of the commonwealth, which is by constituting the legislative and appointing in whose hands that shall be. And when the people have said, we will submit to rules and be governed by laws made by such men, and in such forms, nobody else can say other men shall make laws for them; nor can the people be bound by any laws but such as are enacted by those whom they have chosen and authorized to make laws for them. The power of the legislative, being derived from the people by a positive voluntary grant and institution, can be no other than what that positive grant conveyed, which being only to make laws, and not to make legislators, the legislative can have no power to transfer their authority of making laws and place it in other hands.

142. These are the bounds which the trust that is put in them by the society and the law of God and nature have set to the legislative power of every commonwealth, in all forms of government:

First, They are to govern by promulgated established laws, not to be varied in particular cases, but to have one rule for rich and poor, for the favourite at court and the countryman at plough.

Secondly, These laws also ought to be designed for no other end ultimately but the good of the people.

Thirdly, They must not raise taxes on the property of the people without the consent of the people, given by themselves or their deputies. And this properly concerns only such governments where the legislative is always in being, or at least where the people have not reserved any part of the legislative to deputies to be from time to time chosen by themselves.

Fourthly, The legislative neither must nor can transfer the power of making laws to anybody else, or place it anywhere but where the people have.

OF THE DISSOLUTION OF GOVERNMENT

211. He that will with any clearness speak of the dissolution of government ought in the first place to distinguish between the dissolution of the society and the dissolution of the government. That which makes the community and brings men out of the loose state of nature into one politic society is the agreement which everybody has

with the rest to incorporate and act as one body, and so be one distinct commonwealth. The usual and almost only way whereby this union is dissolved is the inroad of foreign force making a conquest upon them; for in that case, not being able to maintain and support themselves as one entire and independent body, the union belonging to that body which consisted therein must necessarily cease, and so every one return to the state he was in before, with a liberty to shift for himself and provide for his own safety, as he thinks fit, in some other society. Whenever the society is dissolved, it is certain the government of that society cannot remain. Thus conquerors' swords often cut up governments by the roots and mangle societies to pieces, separating the subdued or scattered multitude from the protection of and dependence on that society which ought to have preserved them from violence. . . .

212. Besides this overturning from without, governments are dissolved from within.

First, When the legislative is altered. Civil society being a state of peace amongst those who are of it, from whom the state of war is excluded by the umpirage which they have provided in their legislative for the ending all differences that may arise amongst any of them, it is in their legislative that the members of a commonwealth are united and combined together into one coherent living body. This is the soul that gives form, life, and unity to the commonwealth; from hence the several members have their mutual influence, sympathy, and connexion; and, therefore, when the legislative is broken or dissolved, dissolution and death follows; for the essence and union of the society consisting in having one will, the legislative, when once established by the majority, has the declaring and, as it were, keeping of that will. The constitution of the legislative is the first and fundamental act of society, whereby provision is made for the continuation of their union under the direction of persons and bonds of laws made by persons authorized thereunto by the consent and appointment of the people, without which no one man or number of men amongst them can have authority of making laws that shall be binding to the rest. When any one or more shall take upon them to make laws, whom the people have not appointed so to do, they make laws without authority, which the people are not therefore bound to obey; by which means they come again to be out of subjection and may constitute to themselves a new legislative as they think best, being in full liberty to resist the force of those who without authority would impose anything upon them. Every one is at the disposure of his own will when those who had by the delegation of the society the declaring of the public will are excluded from it, and others usurp the place who have no such authority or delegation. . . .

220. . . . when the government is dissolved, the people are at liberty to provide for themselves by erecting a new legislative, differing from the other by the change of persons or form, or both, as they shall find it most for their safety and good; for the society can never by the fault of another lose the native and original right it has to preserve itself, which can only be done by a settled legislative, and a fair and impartial execution of the laws made by it. But the state of mankind is not so miserable that they are not capable of using this remedy till it be too late to look for any. To tell people they may provide for themselves by erecting a new legislative, when by oppression, artifice, or being delivered over to a foreign power, their old one is gone, is only to tell them they may expect relief when it is too late and the evil is past cure. This is in effect no more than to bid them first be slaves, and then to take care of their liberty; and when their chains are on, tell them they may act like freemen. This, if barely so, is rather mockery than relief; and men can never be secure from tyranny if there be no means to escape it till they are perfectly under it; and therefore it is that they have not only a right to get out of it, but to prevent it.

221. There is . . . another way whereby governments are dissolved, and that is when the legislative or the prince, either of them act contrary to their trust.

First, The legislative acts against the trust reposed in them when they endeavour to invade the property of the subject, and to make themselves or any part of the community masters or arbitrary disposers of the lives, liberties, or fortunes of the people.

222. The reason why men enter into society is the preservation of their property; and the end why they choose and authorize a legislative is that there may be laws made and rules set as guards and fences to the properties of all the members of the society, to limit the power and moderate the dominion of every part and member of the society; for since it can never be supposed to be the will of the society that the legislative should have a power to destroy that which every one designs to secure by entering into society, and for which the people submitted themselves to legislators of their own making. Whenever the legislators endeavour to take away and destroy the property of the people, or to reduce them to slavery under arbitrary power, they put themselves into a state of war with the people who are thereupon absolved from any further obedience, and are left to the common refuge which God hath

provided for all men against force and violence. Whensoever, therefore, the legislative shall transgress this fundamental rule of society, and either by ambition, fear, folly, or corruption, endeavour to grasp themselves, or put into the hands of any other, an absolute power over the lives, liberties, and estates of the people, by this breach of trust they forfeit the power the people had put into their hands for quite contrary ends, and it devolves to the people who have a right to resume their original liberty, and by the establishment of a new legislative, such as they shall think fit, provide for their own safety and security, which is the end for which they are in society. . . .

223. To this perhaps it will be said that the people being ignorant and always discontented, to lay the foundation of government in the unsteady opinion and uncertain humour of the people is to expose it to certain ruin; and no government will be able long to subsist, if the people may set up a new legislative whenever they take offence at the old one. To this I answer: Quite the contrary. People are not so easily got out of their old forms as some are apt to suggest. They are hardly to be prevailed with to amend the acknowledged faults in the frame they have been accustomed to. And if there be any original defects, or adventitious ones introduced by time or corruption it is not an easy thing to get them changed, even when all the world sees there is an opportunity for it. . . .

224. But it will be said this hypothesis lays a ferment for frequent rebellion. To which I answer:

First, No more than any other hypothesis; for when the people are made miserable, and find themselves exposed to the ill-usage of arbitrary power, cry up their governors as much as you will for sons of Jupiter, let them be sacred or divine, descended, or authorized from heaven, give them out for whom or what you please, the same will happen. The people generally ill-treated, and contrary to right, will be ready upon any occasion to ease themselves of a burden that sits heavy upon them. They will wish and seek for the opportunity, which in the change, weakness, and accidents of human affairs seldom delays long to offer itself. . . .

225. Secondly, I answer, such revolutions happen not upon every little mismanagement in public affairs. Great mistakes in the ruling part, many wrong and inconvenient laws, and all the slips of human frailty will be borne by the people without mutiny or murmur. But if a long train of abuses, prevarications, and artifices, all tending the same way, make the design visible to the people, and they cannot but feel what

they lie under and see whither they are going, it is not to be wondered that they should then rouse themselves and endeavour to put the rule into such hands which may secure to them the ends for which government was at first erected, and without which ancient names and specious forms are so far from being better that they are much worse than the state of nature or pure anarchy—the inconveniences being all as great and as near, but the remedy farther off and more difficult. . . .

226. Thirdly, I answer that this doctrine of a power in the people of providing for their safety anew by a new legislative, when their legislators have acted contrary to their trust by invading their property, is the best fence against rebellion, and the most probable means to hinder it; for rebellion being an opposition, not to persons, but authority which is founded only in the constitutions and laws of the government, those, whoever they be, who by force break through, and by force justify their violation of them, are truly and properly rebels; for when men, by entering into society and civil government, have excluded force and introduced laws for the preservation of property, peace, and unity amongst themselves, those who set up force again in opposition to the laws do *rebellare*—that is, bring back again the state of war—and are properly rebels; which they who are in power, by the pretence they have to authority, the temptation of force they have in their hands and the flattery of those about them, being likeliest to do, the properest way to prevent the evil is to show them the danger and injustice of it who are under the greatest temptation to run into it.

228. But if they who say "it lays a foundation for rebellion" mean that it may occasion civil wars or intestine broils, to tell the people they are absolved from obedience when illegal attempts are made upon their liberties or properties, and may oppose the unlawful violence of those who were their magistrates when they invade their properties contrary to the trust put in them, and that therefore this doctrine is not to be allowed, being so destructive to the peace of the world: they may as well say, upon the same ground, that honest men may not oppose robbers or pirates, because this may occasion disorder or bloodshed. If any mischief come in such cases, it is not to be charged upon him who defends his own right, but on him that invades his neighbour's. If the innocent honest man must quietly quit all he has, for peace's sake, to him who will lay violent hands upon it, I desire it may be considered what a kind of peace there will be in the world, which consists only in violence and rapine, and which is to be maintained only for the benefit of robbers and oppressors. Who would not think it an

admirable peace betwixt the mighty and the mean when the lamb without resistance yielded his throat to be torn by the imperious wolf? . . .

229. The end of government is the good of mankind. And which is best for mankind? That the people should be always exposed to the boundless will of tyranny, or that the rulers should be sometimes liable to be opposed when they grow exorbitant in the use of their power and employ it for the destruction and not the preservation of the properties of their people? . . .

231. That subjects or foreigners attempting by force on the properties of any people may be resisted with force, is agreed on all hands. But that magistrates doing the same thing may be resisted, hath of late been denied; as if those who had the greatest privileges and advantages by the law had thereby a power to break those laws by which alone they were set in a better place than their brethren; whereas their offence is thereby the greater, both as being ungrateful for the greater share they have by the law, and breaking also that trust which is put into their hands by their brethren.

232. Whosoever uses force without right, as every one does in society who does it without law, puts himself into a state of war with those against whom he so uses it; and in that state all former ties are cancelled, all other rights cease, and every one has a right to defend himself and to resist the aggressor. . . .

240. Here, it is like, the common question will be made: "Who shall be judge whether the prince or legislative act contrary to their trust?" This, perhaps, ill-affected and factious men may spread amongst the people, when the prince only makes use of his due prerogative. To this I reply: The people shall be judge; for who shall be judge whether his trustee or deputy acts well and according to the trust reposed in him but he who deputes him and must, by having deputed him, have still a power to discard him when he fails in his trust? If this be reasonable in particular cases of private men, why should it be otherwise in that of the greatest moment where the welfare of millions is concerned, and also where the evil, if not prevented, is greater and the redress very difficult, dear, and dangerous? . . .

242. If a controversy arise betwixt a prince and some of the people in a matter where the law is silent or doubtful, and the thing be of great consequence, I should think the proper umpire in such a case should be the body of the people; for in cases where the prince hath a trust reposed in him and is dispensed from the common ordinary rules of the law, there, if any men find themselves aggrieved and think the

prince acts contrary to or beyond that trust, who so proper to judge as the body of the people—who, at first, lodged that trust in him—how far they meant it should extend? But if the prince, or whoever they be in the administration, decline that way of determination, the appeal then lies nowhere but to heaven; force between either persons who have no known superior on earth, or which permits no appeal to a judge on earth, being properly a state of war wherein the appeal lies only to heaven; and in that state the injured party must judge for himself when he will think fit to make use of that appeal and put himself upon it.

243. To conclude, the power that every individual gave the society when he entered into it can never revert to the individuals again as long as the society lasts, but will always remain in the community, because without this there can be no community, no commonwealth, which is contrary to the original agreement; so also when the society hath placed the legislative in any assembly of men, to continue in them and their successors with direction and authority for providing such successors, the legislative can never revert to the people whilst that government lasts, because having provided a legislative with power to continue for ever, they have given up their political power to the legislative and cannot resume it. But if they have set limits to the duration of their legislative and made this supreme power in any person or assembly only temporary, or else when by the miscarriages of those in authority it is forfeited, upon the forfeiture, or at the determination of the time set, it reverts to the society, and the people have a right to act as supreme and continue the legislative in themselves, or erect a new form, or under the old form place it in new hands, as they think good.

10.   MONTESQUIEU
Separation of Powers

By virtue of its scope and method, *The Spirit of the Laws* is generally considered the first modern systematic treatise on politics. The work was published in 1748 and met with immediate success—it apparently had twenty-two editions—as well as with controversy. Voltaire and Helvetius criticized it as pro-aristocratic; the Sorbonne and the Assembly of the Bishops threatened to ban it as radical. Although the impact of the writings and political activity of Charles Louis de Secondat, the Baron de Montesquieu (1689–1755), within the French political scene of his time was to reinforce the defense of the aristocracy against revolutionary or royalist tendencies, his significance for constitutional liberalism has been enormous. In particular, Montesquieu's version of the doctrine of separation of powers, which was formulated in Book XI of *The Spirit of the Laws*, had great influence on English jurists, on the authors of the American Constitution, and on German liberalism.

The following selection is a slightly abridged text of Chapter XI in the translation of Thomas Nugent.

OF THE LAWS WHICH ESTABLISH POLITICAL LIBERTY WITH REGARD TO THE CONSTITUTION

Different Significations of the word Liberty

There is no word that admits of more various significations, and has made more varied impressions on the human mind, than that of liberty. Some have taken it as a means of deposing a person on whom they had conferred a tyrannical authority; others for the power of choosing a superior whom they are obliged to obey; others for the right of bearing arms, and of being thereby enabled to use violence; others, in fine, for the privilege of being governed by a native of their own country, or by their own laws. A certain nation for a long time thought liberty consisted in the privilege of wearing a long beard. Some have annexed this name to one form of government exclusive of others: those who had a republican taste applied it to this species of polity; those who liked a monarchical state gave it to monarchy. Thus they have all applied the name of liberty to the government most suitable to their own customs and inclinations: and as in republics the people have not so constant and so present a view of the causes of their misery, and as the magistrates seem to act only in conformity to the laws, hence liberty is generally said to reside in republics, and to be banished from monarchies. In fine, as in democracies the people seem to act almost as they please, this sort of government has been deemed the most free, and the power of the people has been confounded with their liberty.

In what Liberty consists

It is true that in democracies the people seem to act as they please;

but political liberty does not consist in an unlimited freedom. In governments, that is, in societies directed by laws, liberty can consist only in the power of doing what we ought to will, and in not being constrained to do what we ought not to will.

We must have continually present to our minds the difference between independence and liberty. Liberty is a right of doing whatever the laws permit, and if a citizen could do what they forbid he would be no longer possessed of liberty, because all his fellow-citizens would have the same power.

The same Subject continued

Democratic and aristocratic states are not in their own nature free. Political liberty is to be found only in moderate governments; and even in these it is not always found. It is there only when there is no abuse of power. But constant experience shows us that every man invested with power is apt to abuse it, and to carry his authority as far as it will go. Is it not strange, though true, to say that virtue itself has need of limits?

To prevent this abuse, it is necessary from the very nature of things that power should be a check to power. A government may be so constituted, as no man shall be compelled to do things to which the law does not oblige him, nor forced to abstain from things which the law permits.

Of the End or View of different Governments

Though all governments have the same general end, which is that of preservation, yet each has another particular object. Increase of dominion was the object of Rome; war, that of Sparta; religion, that of the Jewish laws; commerce, that of Marseilles; public tranquillity, that of the laws of China; navigation, that of the laws of Rhodes; natural liberty, that of the policy of the Savages; in general, the pleasures of the prince, that of despotic states; that of monarchies, the prince's and the kingdom's glory; the independence of individuals is the end aimed at by the laws of Poland, thence results the oppression of the whole.

One nation there is also in the world that has for the direct end of its constitution political liberty. We shall presently examine the principles on which this liberty is founded; if they are sound, liberty will appear in its highest perfection.

To discover political liberty in a constitution, no great labor is requisite. If we are capable of seeing it where it exists, it is soon found, and we need not go far in search of it.

Of the Constitution of England

In every government there are three sorts of power: the legislative; the executive in respect of things dependent on the law of nations; and the executive in regard to matters that depend on the civil law.

By virtue of the first, the prince or magistrate enacts temporary or perpetual laws, and amends or abrogates those that have been already enacted. By the second, he makes peace or war, sends or receives embassies, establishes the public security, and provides against invasions. By the third, he punishes criminals, or determines the disputes that arise between individuals. The latter we shall call the judiciary power, and the other simply the executive power of the state.

The political liberty of the subject is a tranquillity of mind arising from the opinion each person has of his safety. In order to have this liberty, it is requisite the government be so constituted as one man need not be afraid of another.

When the legislative and executive powers are united in the same person, or in the same body of magistrates, there can be no liberty; because apprehensions may arise, lest the same monarch or senate should enact tyrannical laws, to execute them in a tyrannical manner.

Again, there is no liberty, if the judiciary power be not separated from the legislative and executive. Were it joined with the legislative, the life and liberty of the subject would be exposed to arbitrary control; for the judge would be then the legislator. Were it joined to the executive power, the judge might behave with violence and oppression.

There would be an end of everything, were the same man or the same body, whether of the nobles or of the people, to exercise those three powers, that of enacting laws, that of executing the public resolutions, and of trying the causes of individuals. . . .

If the legislature leaves the executive power in possession of a right to imprison those subjects who can give security for their good behavior, there is an end of liberty; unless they are taken up, in order to answer without delay to a captial crime, in which case they are really free, being subject only to the power of the law.

But should the legislature think itself in danger by some secret conspiracy against the state, or by a correspondence with a foreign enemy, it might authorize the executive power, for a short and limited time, to imprison suspected persons, who in that case would lose their liberty only for a while, to preserve it forever. . . .

As in a country of liberty, every man who is supposed a free agent ought to be his own governor; the legislative power should reside in the whole body of the people. But since this is impossible in large states, and in small ones is subject to many inconveniences, it is fit the people should transact by their representatives what they cannot transact by themselves.

The inhabitants of a particular town are much better acquainted with its wants and interests than with those of other places; and are better judges of the capacity of their neighbors than of that of the rest of their countrymen. The members, therefore, of the legislature should not be chosen from the general body of the nation; but it is proper that in every considerable place a representative should be elected by the inhabitants.

The great advantage of representatives is, their capacity of discussing public affairs. For this the people collectively are extremely unfit, which is one of the chief inconveniences of a democracy. . . .

All the inhabitants of the several districts ought to have a right of voting at the election of a representative, except such as are in so mean a situation as to be deemed to have no will of their own.

One great fault there was in most of the ancient republics, that the people had a right to active resolutions, such as require some execution, a thing of which they are absolutely incapable. They ought to have no share in the government but for the choosing of representatives, which is within their reach. For though few can tell the exact degree of men's capacities, yet there are none but are capable of knowing in general whether the person they choose is better qualified than most of his neighbors.

Neither ought the representative body to be chosen for the executive part of government, for which it is not so fit; but for the enacting of laws, or to see whether the laws in being are duly executed, a thing suited to their abilities, and which none indeed but themselves can properly perform.

In such a state there are always persons distinguished by their birth, riches, or honors: but were they to be confounded with the common people, and to have only the weight of a single vote like the rest, the common liberty would be their slavery, and they would have no interest in supporting it, as most of the popular resolutions would be against them. The share they have, therefore, in the legislature ought to be proportioned to their other advantages in the state; which happens only when they form a body that has a right to check the licentiousness of the people, as the people have a right to oppose any encroachment of theirs. . . .

The executive power ought to be in the hands of a monarch, because this branch of government, having need of despatch, is better administered by one than by many: on the other hand, whatever depends on the legislative power is oftentimes better regulated by many than by a single person.

But if there were no monarch, and the executive power should be committed to a certain number of persons selected from the legislative body, there would be an end then of liberty; by reason the two powers would be united, as the same persons would sometimes possess, and would be always able to possess, a share in both.

Were the legislative body to be a considerable time without meeting, this would likewise put an end to liberty. For of two things one would naturally follow: either that there would be no longer any legislative resolutions, and then the state would fall into anarchy; or that these resolutions would be taken by the executive power, which would render it absolute.

It would be needless for the legislative body to continue always assembled. This would be troublesome to the representatives, and, moreover, would cut out too much work for the executive power, so as to take off its attention to its office, and oblige it to think only of defending its own prerogatives, and the right it has to execute. . . .

Were the executive power not to have a right of restraining the encroachments of the legislative body, the latter would become despotic; for as it might arrogate to itself what authority it pleased, it would soon destroy all the other powers.

But it is not proper, on the other hand, that the legislative power should have a right to stay the executive. For as the execution has its natural limits, it is useless to confine it; besides, the executive power is generally employed in momentary operations. The power, therefore, of the Roman tribunes was faulty, as it put a stop not only to the legislation, but likewise to the executive part of government; which was attended with infinite mischief.

But if the legislative power in a free state has no right to stay the executive, it has a right and ought to have the means of examining in what manner its laws have been executed; an advantage which this government has over that of Crete and Sparta, where the Cosmi and the Ephori gave no account of their administration.

But whatever may be the issue of that examination, the legislative body ought not to have a power of arraigning the person, nor, of course, the conduct, of him who is intrusted with the executive power. His person should be sacred, because as it is necessary for the good of the state to prevent the legislative body from rendering themselves arbitrary, the moment he is accused or tried there is an end of liberty.

In this case the state would be no longer a monarchy, but a kind of republic, though not a free government. But as the person intrusted with the executive power cannot abuse it without bad counsellors, and such as have the laws as ministers, though the laws protect them as subjects, these men may be examined and punished . . . .

Here, then, is the fundamental constitution of the government we are treating of. The legislative body being composed of two parts, they check one another by the mutual privilege of rejecting. They are both restrained by the executive power, as the executive is by the legislative.

These three powers should naturally form a state of repose or inaction. But as there is a necessity for movement in the course of human affairs, they are forced to move, but still in concert.

As the executive power has no other part in the legislative than the privilege of rejecting, it can have no share in the public debates. It is not even necessary that it should propose, because as it may always disapprove of the resolutions that shall be taken, it may likewise reject the decisions on those proposals which were made against its will.

In some ancient commonwealths, where public debates were carried on by the people in a body, it was natural for the executive power to propose a debate in conjunction with the people, otherwise their resolutions must have been attended with a strange confusion.

Were the executive power to determine the raising of public money, otherwise than by giving its consent, liberty would be at an end; because it would become legislative in the most important point of legislation.

If the legislative power was to settle the subsidies, not from year to year, but forever, it would run the risk of losing its liberty, because the executive power would be no longer dependent; and when once it was possessed of such a perpetual right, it would be a matter of indifference whether it held it of itself or of another. The same may be said if it should come to a resolution of intrusting, not an annual, but a perpetual command of the fleets and armies to the executive power.

To prevent the executive power from being able to oppress, it is requisite that the armies with which it is intrusted should consist of the people, and have the same spirit as the people, as was the case at Rome till the time of Marius. To obtain this end, there are only two ways, either that the persons employed in the army should have sufficient property to answer for their conduct to their fellow-subjects, and be enlisted only for a year, as was customary at Rome; or if there should be a standing army, composed chiefly of the most despicable part of the nation, the legislative power should have a right to disband them as soon as it pleased; the soldiers should live in common with the rest of the people; and no separate camp, barracks, or fortress should be suffered.

When once an army is established, it ought not to depend immediately on the legislative, but on the executive power; and this from the very nature of the thing, its business consisting more in action than in deliberation. . . .

As all human things have an end, the state we are speaking of will lose its liberty, will perish. Have not Rome, Sparta, and Carthage perished? It will perish when the legislative power shall be more corrupt than the executive.

It is not my business to examine whether the English actually enjoy this liberty or not. Sufficient it is for my purpose to observe that it is established by their laws; and I inquire no further.

Neither do I pretend by this to undervalue other governments, nor to say that this extreme political liberty ought to give uneasiness to those who have only a moderate share of it. How should I have any such design, I who think that even the highest refinement of reason is not always desirable, and that mankind generally find their account better in mediums than in extremes? . . .

11. ROUSSEAU

The Social Contract

Jean-Jacques Rousseau (1712–78) published *The Social Contract* in Holland in 1762. The book was immediately condemned at Paris, and Rousseau sought refuge in Switzerland. His native city, Geneva, however, issued a warrant for his arrest upon arrival. The censorship of that city condemned *The Social Contract* as a work whose author considers "all forms of government to be only provisional, experiments that can always be changed," and those who govern to be "instruments that the people can always change or crush at will." Rousseau found refuge in England on the invitation of David Hume; he returned to Paris in 1770.

In 1794 the new French Republic honored Rousseau as an intellectual precursor of the revolution and removed his body to a national shrine. The selection is taken from the Tozer translation with corrections.

BOOK ONE

INTRODUCTORY NOTE

I wish to enquire whether, taking men as they are and laws as they can be made, it is possible to establish some just and legitimate rule of administration in civil affairs. In this investigation I shall always strive to reconcile what right permits with what interest prescribes, so that justice and utility may not be severed.

I enter upon this enquiry without demonstrating the importance of my subject. I shall be asked whether I am a prince or a legislator that I write on politics. I reply that I am not; and that it is for this very reason that I write on politics. If I were a prince or a legislator, I should not waste my time in saying what ought to be done; I should do it or remain silent.

Having been born a citizen of a free State, and a member of the sovereign body, however feeble an influence my voice may have in public affairs, the right to vote upon them is sufficient to impose on me the duty of informing myself about them; and I feel happy, whenever I meditate on governments, always to discover in my researches new reasons for loving that of my own country.

SUBJECT OF THE FIRST BOOK

Man is born free, and everywhere he is in chains. Many a one believes himself the master of others, and yet he is a greater slave than they. How has this change come about? I do not know. What can render it legitimate? I believe that I can answer this question.

If I considered only force and the results that proceed from it, I should say that so long as a people is compelled to obey and does obey, it does well; but that, so soon as it can shake off the yoke and does shake it off, it does better; for, if men recover their freedom by virtue of the same right by which it was taken away, either they are justified in resuming it, or there was no justification for depriving them of it. But the social order is a sacred right which serves as a foundation for all others. This right, however, does not come from nature. It is therefore based on conventions. The question is to know what these conventions are. . . .

THE SOCIAL COMPACT

I assume that men have reached a point at which the obstacles that endanger their preservation in the state of nature overcome by their resistance the forces which each individual can exert with a view to maintaining himself in that state. Then this primitive condition can no longer subsist, and the human race would perish unless it changed its mode of existence.

Now, as men cannot create any new forces, but only combine and direct those that exist, they have no other means of self-preservation than to form by aggregation a sum of forces which may overcome the resistance, to put them in action by a single motive power, and to make them work in concert.

This sum of forces can be produced only by the combination of many; but the strength and freedom of each man being the chief instruments of his preservation, how can he pledge them without injuring himself, and without neglecting the cares which he owes to himself? This difficulty, applied to my subject, may be expressed in these terms:—

"To find a form of association which may defend and protect with the whole force of the community the person and property of every associate, and by means of which each, coalescing with all may, nevertheless obey only himself, and remain as free as before." Such is the fundamental problem of which *The Social Contract* furnishes the solution.

The clauses of this contract are so determined by the nature of the act that the slightest modification would render them vain and ineffectual; so that, although they have never perhaps been formally enunciated, they are everywhere the same, everywhere tacitly admitted and recognised, until, the social compact being violated, each man regains his original rights and recovers his natural liberty, whilst losing the conventional liberty for which he renounced it.

These clauses, rightly understood, are reducible to one only, viz., the total alienation to the whole community of each associate with all his rights; for, in the first place, since each gives himself up entirely, the conditions are equal for all; and, the conditions being equal for all, no one has any interest in making them burdensome to others.

Further, the alienation being made without reserve, the union is as perfect as it can be, and an individual associate can no longer claim anything; for, if any rights were left to individuals, since there would be no common superior who could judge between them and the public, each, being on some point his own judge, would soon claim to be so on all; the state of nature would still subsist, and the association would necessarily become tyrannical or useless.

In short, each giving himself to all, gives himself to nobody; and as there is not one associate over whom we do not acquire the same right which we concede to him over ourselves, we gain the equivalent of all that we lose, and more power to preserve what we have.

If, then, we set aside what is not of the essence of the social contract, we shall find that is is reducible to the following terms: *Each of us puts in common his person and his whole power under the supreme direction of the general will; and in return we receive every member as an indivisible part of the whole. . . .*

THE SOVEREIGN

Now, the sovereign, being formed only of the individuals that compose it, neither has nor can have any interest contrary to theirs; consequently the sovereign power needs no guarantee towards its subjects, because it is impossible that the body should wish to injure all its members; and we shall see hereafter that it can injure no one as an individual. The sovereign, for the simple reason that it is so, is always everything that it ought to be.

But this is not the case as regards the relation of subjects to the sovereign, which, notwithstanding the common interest, would have no security for the performance of their engagements, unless it found means to ensure their fidelity.

Indeed, every individual may, as a man, have a particular will contrary to, or divergent from, the general will which he has as a citizen; his private interest may prompt him quite differently from the common interest; his absolute and naturally independent existence may make him regard what he owes to the common cause as a gratuitous contribution, the loss of which will be less harmful to others than the payment of it will be burdensome to him; and, regarding the moral person that constitutes the State as an imaginary being because it is not a man, he would be willing to enjoy the rights of a citizen without being willing to fulfil the duties of a subject. The progress of such injustice would bring about the ruin of the body politic.

In order, then, that the social compact may not be a vain formulary, it tacitly includes this engagement, which can alone give force to the others,—that whoever refuses to obey the general will shall be constrained to do so by the whole body; which means nothing else than that he shall be forced to be free; for such is the condition which, uniting every citizen to his native land, guarantees him from all personal dependence, a condition that ensures the control and working of the political machine, and alone renders legitimate civil engagements, which, without it, would be absurd and tyrannical, and subject to the most enormous abuses.

THE CIVIL STATE

The passage from the state of nature to the civil state produces in man a very remarkable change, by substituting in his conduct justice for instinct, and by giving his actions the moral quality that they previously lacked. It is only when the voice of duty replaces physical impulse, and right replaces appetite, that man, who till then had regarded only himself, sees that he is obliged to act on other principles, and to consult his reason before listening to his inclinations. Although, in this state, he is deprived of many advantages that he derives from nature, he acquires equally great ones in return; his faculties are exercised and developed; his ideas are expanded; his feelings are ennobled; his whole soul is exalted to such a degree that, if the abuses of this new condition did not often degrade him below that from which he has emerged, he ought to bless without ceasing the happy moment that released him from it for ever, and transformed him from a stupid and ignorant animal into an intelligent being and a man.

Let us reduce this whole balance to terms easy to compare. What man loses by the social contract is his natural liberty and an unlimited right to anything which tempts him and which he is able to attain; what he gains is civil liberty and property in all that he possesses. In order that we may not be mistaken about these compensations, we must clearly distinguish natural liberty, which is limited only by the powers of the individual, from civil liberty, which is limited by the general will; and possession, which is nothing but the result of force or the right of first occupancy, from property, which can be based only on a positive title.

Besides the preceding, we might add to the acquisitions of the civil state moral freedom, which alone renders man truly master of himself; for the impulse of mere appetite is slavery, while obedience to a self-prescribed law is liberty. But I have already said too much on this head, and the philosophical meaning of the term *liberty* does not belong to my present subject.

REAL PROPERTY

Every member of the community at the moment of its formation gives himself up to it, just as he actually is, himself and all his powers, of which the property that he possesses forms part. . . .

The peculiarity of this alienation is that the community, in receiving the property of individuals, so far from robbing them of it, only assures them lawful possession, and changes usurpation into true right, enjoyment into ownership. Also, the possessors being considered as depositaries of the public property, and their rights being respected by all the members of the State, as well as maintained by all its power against foreigners, they have, as it were, by a transfer advantageous to the public and still more to themselves, acquired all that they have given up—a paradox which is easily explained by distinguishing between the rights which the sovereign and the proprietor have over the same property . . . .

It may also happen that men begin to unite before they possess anything, and that afterwards occupying territory sufficient for all, they enjoy it in common, or share it among themselves, either equally or in proportions fixed by the sovereign. In whatever way this acquisition is made, the right which every individual has over his own property is always subordinate to the right which the community has over all; otherwise there would be no stability in the social union, and no real force in the exercise of sovereignty.

I shall close this chapter and this book with a remark which ought to serve as a basis for the whole social system; it is that instead of destroying natural equality, the fundamental compact, on the contrary, substitutes a moral and lawful equality for the physical inequality which nature imposed upon men, so that, although unequal in strength or intellect, they all become equal by convention and legal right.

BOOK TWO

THAT SOVEREIGNTY IS INALIENABLE

The first and most important consequence of the principles above established is that the general will alone can direct the forces of the State according to the object of its institution, which is the common good; for if the opposition of private interests has rendered necessary the establishment of societies, the agreement of these same interests has rendered it possible. That which is common to these different interests forms the social bond; and unless there were some point in which all interests agree, no society could exist. Now, it is solely with regard to this common interest that the society should be governed.

I say, then, that sovereignty, being nothing but the exercise of the general will, can never be alienated, and that the sovereign power, which is only a collective being, can be represented by itself alone; power indeed can be transmitted, but not will.

In fact, if it is not impossible that a particular will should agree on some point with the general will, it is at least impossible that this agreement should be lasting and constant; for the particular will naturally tends to preferences, and the general will to equality. It is still more impossible to have a security for this agreement; even though it should always exist, it would not be a result of art, but of chance. The sovereign may indeed say: "I will now what a certain man wills, or at least what he says that he wills;" but he cannot say: "What that man wills tomorrow, I shall also will," since it is absurd that the will should bind itself as regards the future, and since it is not incumbent on any will to consent to anything contrary to the welfare of the being that wills. If, then, the nation simply promises to obey, it dissolves itself by that act and loses its character as a people; the moment there is a master, there is no longer a sovereign, and forthwith the body politic is destroyed.

This does not imply that the orders of the chiefs cannot pass for decisions of the general will, so long as the sovereign, free to oppose them, refrains from doing so. In such a case the consent of the people should be inferred from the universal silence. . . .

WHETHER THE GENERAL WILL CAN ERR

It follows from what precedes that the general will is always right and always tends to the public advantage; but it does not follow that the resolutions of the people have always the same rectitude. Men always desire their own good, but do not always discern it; the people are never corrupted, though often deceived, and it is only then that they seem to will what is evil.

There is often a great deal of difference between the will of all and the general will; the latter regards only the common interest, while the former has regard to private interests, and is merely a sum of particular wills; but take away from these same wills the pluses and minuses which cancel one another, and the general will remains as the sum of the differences.

If the people came to a resolution when adequately informed and without any communication among the citizens, the general will would always result from the great number of slight differences, and the resolutions would always be good. But when factions, partial associations, are formed to the detriment of the whole society, the will of each of these associations becomes general with reference to its members, and particular with reference to the State; it may then be said that there are no longer as many voters as there are men, but only as many voters as there are associations. The differences become less numerous and yield a less general result. Lastly, when one of these associations becomes so great that it predominates over all the rest, you no longer have as the result a sum of small differences, but a single difference; there is then no longer a general will, and the opinion which prevails is only a particular opinion.

It is important, then, in order to have a clear declaration of the general will, that there should be no partial association in the State, and that every citizen should express only his own opinion. Such was the unique and sublime institution of the great Lycurgus. But if there are partial associations, it is necessary to multiply their number and prevent inequality, as Solon, Numa, and Servius did. These are the only proper precautions for ensuring that the general will may always be enlightened, and that the people may not be deceived.

THE LIMITS OF THE SOVEREIGN POWER

If the State or city is nothing but a moral person, the life of which consists in the union of its members, and if the most important of its cares is that of self-preservation, it needs a universal and compulsive force to move and dispose every part in the manner most expedient for the whole. As nature gives every man an absolute power over all his limbs, the social compact gives the body politic an absolute power over all its members; and it is this same power which, when directed by the general will, bears, as I said, the name of sovereignty.

But besides the public person, we have to consider the private persons who compose it, and whose life and liberty are naturally independent of it. The question, then, is to distinguish clearly between the respective rights of the citizens and of the sovereign, as well as between the duties which the former have to fulfil in their capacity as subjects and the natural rights which they ought to enjoy in their character as men.

It is admitted that whatever part of his power, property, and liberty each one alienates by the social compact is only that part of the whole of which the use is important to the community; but we must also admit that the sovereign alone is judge of what is important.

All the services that a citizen can render to the State he owes to it as soon as the sovereign demands them; but the sovereign, on its part, cannot impose on its subjects any burden which is useless to the community; it cannot even wish to do so, for, by the law of reason, just as by the law of nature, nothing is done without a cause.

The engagements which bind us to the social body are obligatory only because they are mutual; and their nature is such that in fulfilling them we cannot work for others without also working for ourselves. Why is the general will always right, and why do all invariably desire the prosperity of each, unless it is because there is no one but appropriates to himself this word *each* and thinks of himself in voting on behalf of all? This proves that equality of rights and the notion of justice that it produces are derived from the preference which each gives to himself, and consequently from man's nature; that the general will, to be truly such, should be so in its object as well as in its essence; that it ought to proceed from all in order to be applicable to all; and that it loses its natural rectitude when it tends to some individual and determinate object, because in that case, judging of what is unknown to us, we have no true principle of equity to guide us. . . .

From this we must understand that what generalizes the will is not so much the number of voices as the common interest which unites them; for, under this system, each necessarily submits to the conditions which he imposes on others—an admirable union of interest and justice, which gives to the deliberations of the community a spirit of equity that seems to disappear in the discussion of any private affair, for want of a common interest to unite and identify the ruling principle of the judge with that of the party.

By whatever path we return to our principle we always arrive at the same conclusions, viz. that the social compact establishes among the citizens such an equality that they all pledge themselves under the same conditions and ought all to enjoy the same rights. Thus, by the nature of the compact, every act of sovereignty, that is, every authentic act of the general will, binds or favours equally all the citizens; so that the sovereign knows only the body of the nation, and distinguishes none of those that compose it.

What, then, is an act of sovereignty properly so called? It is not an agreement between a superior and an inferior, but an agreement of the body with each of its members; a lawful agreement, because it has the social contract as its foundation; equitable, because it is common to all; useful, because it can have no other object than the general welfare; and stable because it has the public force and the supreme power as a guarantee. So long as the subjects submit only to such conventions, they obey no one, but simply their own will; and to ask how far the respective rights of the sovereign and citizens extend is to ask up to what point the latter can make engagements among themselves, each with all and all with each.

Thus we see that the sovereign power, wholly absolute, wholly sacred, and wholly inviolable as it is, does not, and cannot, pass the limits of general conventions, and that every man can fully dispose of what is left to him of his property and liberty by these conventions; so that the sovereign never has a right to burden one subject more than another, because then the matter becomes particular and his power is no longer competent.

These distinctions once admitted, so untrue is it that in the social contract there is on the part of individuals any real renunciation, that their situation, as a result of this contract, is in reality preferable to what it was before, and that, instead of an alienation, they have only made an advantageous exchange of an uncertain and precarious mode of existence for a better and more assured one, of natural independence for liberty, of the power to injure others for their own safety, and of their strength, which others might overcome, for a right which the social union renders inviolable. Their lives, also, which they have devoted to the State, are continually protected by it; and in exposing their lives for its defence, what do they do but restore what they have received from it? What do they do but what they would do more frequently and with more risk in the state of nature, when, engaging in inevitable struggles, they would defend at the peril of their lives their means of preservation? All have to fight for their country in case of need, it is true; but then no one ever has to fight for himself. Do we not gain, moreover, by incurring, for what ensures our safety, a part of the risks that we should have to incur for ourselves individually, as soon as we were deprived of it?

THE RIGHT OF LIFE AND DEATH

It may be asked how individuals who have no right to dispose of their own lives can transmit to the sovereign this right which they do not possess. The question appears hard to solve only because it is badly stated. Every man has a right to risk his own life in order to preserve it. Has it ever been said that one who throws himself out of a window to escape from a fire is guilty of suicide? Has this crime, indeed, ever been imputed to a man who perishes in a storm, although, on embarking, he was not ignorant of the danger?

The social treaty has as its end the preservation of the contracting parties. He who desires the end desires also the means and some risks, even some losses, are inseparable from these means. He who is willing to preserve his life at the expense of others ought also to give it up for them when necessary. . . .

THE LAW

By the social compact we have given existence and life to the body politic; the question now is to endow it with movement and will by legislation. For the original act by which this body is formed and consolidated determines nothing in addition as to what it must do for its own preservation.

What is right and conformable to order is such by the nature of things, and independently of human conventions. All justice comes from God, he alone is the source of it; but could we receive it direct from so lofty a source, we should need neither government nor laws. Without doubt there is a universal justice emanating from reason alone; but this justice, in order to be admitted among us, should be reciprocal. Regarding things from a human standpoint, the laws of justice are inoperative among men for want of a natural sanction; they only bring good to the wicked and evil to the just when the latter observe them with every one, and no one observes them in return. Conventions and laws, then, are necessary to couple rights with duties and apply justice to its object. In the state of nature, where everything is in common, I owe nothing to those to whom I have promised nothing; I recognize as belonging to others only what is useless to me. This is not the case in the civil state, in which all rights are determined by law.

But then, finally, what is a law? . . .

I have already said that there is no general will with reference to a particular object. . . .

But when the whole people decree concerning the whole people, they consider themselves alone. . . . Then the matter respecting which they decree is general like the will that decrees. It is this act that I call a law.

When I say that the object of the laws is always general, I mean that the law considers subjects collectively, and actions as abstract, never a man as an individual nor a particular action. Thus the law may indeed decree that there shall be privileges, but cannot confer them on any person by name; the law can create several classes of citizens, and even assign the qualifications which shall entitle them to rank in these classes, but it cannot nominate such and such persons to be admitted to them; it can establish a royal government and a hereditary succession, but cannot elect a king or appoint a royal family; in a word, no function which has reference to an individual object appertains to the legislative power.

From this standpoint we see immediately that it is no longer necessary to ask whose office it is to make laws, since they are acts of the general will; nor whether the prince is above the laws, since he is a member of the State; nor whether the law can be unjust, since no one is unjust to himself; nor how we are free and yet subject to the laws, since the laws are only registers of our wills.

We see, further, that since the law combines the universality of the will with the universality of the object, whatever any man prescribes on his own authority is not a law; and whatever the sovereign itself prescribes respecting a particular object is not a law, but a decree, not an act of sovereignty, but of magistracy.

I therefore call any State a republic which is governed by laws, under whatever form of administration it may be; for then only does the public interest predominate and the commonwealth count for something. Every legitimate government is republican. . . .

Laws are properly only the conditions of civil association. The people, being subjected to the laws, should be the authors of them; it concerns only the associates to determine the conditions of association. But how will they be determined? Will it be by a common agreement, by a sudden inspiration? Has the body politic an organ for expressing its will? Who will give it the foresight necessary to frame its acts and publish them at the outset? Or how shall it declare them in the hour of need? How would a blind multitude, which often knows not what it wishes because it rarely knows what is good for it, execute of itself an enterprise so great, so difficult, as a system of legislation? Of themselves, the people always desire what is good, but do not always discern it. The general will is always right, but the judgment which guides it is not always enlightened. It must be made to see objects as they are, sometimes as they ought to appear; it must be shown the good path that it is seeking, and guarded from the seduction of private interests; it must be made to observe closely times and places, and to balance the attraction of immediate and palpable advantages against the danger of remote and concealed evils. Individuals see the good which they reject; the public desire the good which they do not see. All alike have need of guides. The former must be compelled to conform their wills to their reason; the people must be taught to know what they require. Then from the public enlightenment results the union of the understanding and the will in the social body; and from that the close cooperation of the parts, and, lastly, the maximum power of the whole. Hence arises the need of a legislator.

BOOK FOUR

THAT THE GENERAL WILL IS INDESTRUCTIBLE

So long as a number of men in combination are considered as a single body, they have but one will, which relates to the common preservation and to the general well-being. In such a case all the forces of the State are vigorous and simple, and its principles are clear and luminous; it has no confused and conflicting interests; the common good is everywhere plainly manifest and only good sense is required to perceive it. Peace, union, and equality are foes to political subtleties. Upright and simple-minded men are hard to deceive because of their simplicity; allurements and refined pretexts do not impose upon them; they are not even cunning enough to be dupes. When, in the happiest nation in the world, we see troops of peasants regulating the affairs of the State under an oak and always acting wisely, can we refrain from despising the refinements of other nations, who make themselves illustrious and wretched with so much art and mystery?

A State thus governed needs very few laws; and in so far as it becomes necessary to promulgate new ones, this necessity is universally recognized. The first man to propose them only gives expression to what all have previously felt, and neither factions nor eloquence will be needed to pass into law what every one has already resolved to do, so soon as he is sure that the rest will act as he does.

What deceives reasoners is that, seeing only States that are ill-constituted from the beginning, they are impressed with the impossibility of maintaining such a policy in those States; they laugh to think of all the follies to which a cunning knave, an insinuating speaker, can persuade the people of Paris or London. They know not that Cromwell would have been put in irons by the people of Berne, and the Duke of Beaufort imprisoned by the Genevese.

But when the social bond begins to be relaxed and the State weakened, when private interests begin to make themselves felt and small associations to exercise influence on the State, the common interest is injuriously affected and finds adversaries; unanimity no longer reigns in the voting; the general will is no longer the will of all; opposition and disputes arise, and the best counsel does not pass uncontested.

Lastly, when the State, on the verge of ruin, no longer subsists except in a vain and illusory form, when the social bond is broken in all hearts, when the basest interest shelters itself impudently under the sacred name of the public welfare, the general will becomes dumb; all, under the guidance of secret motives, no more express their opinions as citizens than if the State had never existed; and, under the name of laws, they deceitfully pass unjust decrees which have only private interest as their end.

Does it follow from this that the general will is destroyed or corrupted? No; it is always constant, unalterable, and pure; but it is subordinated to others which get the better of it. Each, detaching his own interest from the common interest, sees clearly that he cannot completely separate it; but his share in the injury done to the State appears to him as nothing in comparison with the exclusive advantage which he aims at appropriating to himself. This particular advantage being excepted, he desires the general welfare for his own interests quite as strongly as any other. Even in selling his vote for money, he does not extinguish in himself the general will, but eludes it. The fault that he commits is to change the state of the question, and to answer something different from what he was asked; so that, instead of saying by a vote: "It is beneficial to the State," he says: "It is beneficial to a certain man or a certain party that such or such a motion should pass." Thus the law of public order in assemblies is not so much to maintain in them the general will as to ensure that it shall always be consulted and always respond.

I might in this place make many reflections on the simple right of voting in every act of sovereignty—a right which nothing can take away from the citizens—and on that of speaking, proposing, dividing, and discussing, which the government is always very careful to leave to its members only; but this important matter would require a separate treatise, and I cannot say everything in this one.

VOTING

We see from the previous chapter that the manner in which public affairs are managed may give a sufficiently trustworthy indication of the character and health of the body politic. The more that harmony reigns in the assemblies, that is, the more the voting approaches unanimity, the more also is the general will predominant; but long discussions, dissensions, and uproar proclaim the ascendency of private interests and the decline of the State. . . .

There is but one law which by its nature requires unanimous consent, that is, the social compact; for civil association is the most voluntary act in the world; every man being born free and master of himself, no one can, under any pretext whatever, enslave him without his assent. To decide that the son of a slave is born a slave is to decide that he is not born a man.

If, then, at the time of the social compact, there are opponents of it, their opposition does not invalidate the contract, but only prevents them from being included in it; they are foreigners among citizens. When the State is established, consent lies in residence; to dwell in the territory is to submit to the sovereignty.

Excepting this original contract, the vote of the majority always binds all the rest, this being a result of the contract itself. But it will be asked how a man can be free and yet forced to conform to wills which are not his own. How are opponents free and yet subject to laws they have not consented to?

I reply that the question is wrongly put. The citizen consents to all the laws, even to those which are passed in spite of him, and even to those which punish him when he dares to violate any of them. The unvarying will of all the members of the State is the general will; it is through that that they are citizens and free. When a law is proposed in the assembly of the people, what is asked of them is not exactly whether they approve the proposition or reject it, but whether it is conformable or not to the general will, which is their own; each one in giving his vote expresses his opinion thereupon; and from the counting of the votes is obtained the declaration of the general will. When, therefore, the opinion opposed to my own prevails, that simply shows that I was mistaken, and that what I considered to be the general will was not so. Had my private opinion prevailed, I should have done something other than I wished; and in that case I should not have been free.

This supposes, it is true, that all the marks of the general will are still in the majority; when they cease to be so, whatever side we take, there is no longer any liberty.

In showing before how particular wills were substituted for general wills in public resolutions, I have sufficiently indicated the means practicable for preventing this abuse; I will speak of it again hereafter. With regard to the proportional number of votes for declaring this will, I have also laid down the principles according to which it may be determined. The difference of a single vote destroys unanimity; but between unanimity and equality there are many unequal divisions, at each of which this number can be fixed according to the condition and requirements of the body politic.

Two general principles may serve to regulate these proportions: the one, that the more important and weighty the resolutions, the nearer should the opinion which prevails approach unanimity; the other, that the greater the despatch requisite in the matter under discussion, the more should we restrict the prescribed difference in the division of opinions; in resolutions which must be come to immediately the majority of a single vote should suffice. The first of these principles appears more suitable to laws, the second to affairs. Be that as it may, it is by their combination that are established the best proportions which can be assigned for the decision of a majority.

12. KANT
Liberty, Equality, Interdependence

Immanuel Kant wrote *The Principles of Political Right* in 1793. In this work Kant developed his "model" of political society from his conception of moral freedom as obedience to laws one prescribes for oneself. In so doing, Kant emerged as the architect of the ideal of liberal state as state governed by rule of law, whose attainment became one of the main political goals of nineteenth-century German liberalism.

The selection is from the W. Hastie translation.

The establishment of a civil constitution in society is one of the most important facts in human history. In the principle on which it is founded this institution differs from all the other forms of social union among mankind. Viewed as a compact, and compared with other modes of compact by which numbers of men are united into one society, the formation of a civil constitution has much in common with all other forms of social union in respect of the mode in which it is carried out in practice. But while all such compacts are established for the purpose of promoting in common some chosen end, the civil union is essentially distinguished from all others by the principle on which it is based. In all social contracts we find a union of a number of persons for the purpose of carrying out some one end which they all have in common. But a union of a multitude of men, viewed as an end in itself that every person ought to carry out, and which consequently is a primary and unconditional duty amid all the external relations of men who cannot help exercising a mutual influence on one another,—is at once peculiar and unique of its kind. Such a union is only to be found in a society which, by being formed into a civil state, constitutes a commonwealth. Now the end which in such external relations is itself a duty and even the highest formal condition—the *conditio sine qua non*—of all other external duties, is the realization of the rights of men under public compulsory laws, by which every individual can have what is his own assigned to him and secured against the encroachments or assaults of others.

The idea of an external law generally arises wholly out of the idea of human freedom, or liberty, in the external relations of men to one another. As such, it has nothing specially to do with the realization of happiness as a purpose which all men naturally have, or with prescribing the means of attaining it; so that therefore such a prescription in any statute must not be confounded with the motive behind the law itself. Law in general may be defined as the limitation of the freedom of any individual to the extent of its agreement with the freedom of all other individuals, in so far as this is possible by a universal law. Public law, again, is the sum of the external laws which make such a complete agreement of freedom in society possible. Now as all limitation of freedom by external acts of the will of another is a mode of coercion or compulsion, it follows that the civil constitution is a relation of free men who live under coercive laws, without otherwise prejudicing their liberty in the whole of their connection with others. . . .

The civil state, then, regarded merely as a social state that is regulated by righteous laws, is founded upon the following rational principles:

1. The liberty of every member of the society as a man;

2. The equality of every member of the society with every other, as a subject;

3. The self-dependency of every member of the commonwealth, as a citizen.

These principles are not so much laws given by the State when it is established as they are fundamental conditions according to which alone the institution of a State is possible, in conformity with the purely rational principles of external human right generally.

1. The liberty of every member of the State as a man is the first

principle in the constitution of a rational commonwealth. I would express this principle in the following form: "No one has a right to compel me to be happy in the peculiar way in which he may think of the well-being of other men; but every one is entitled to seek his own happiness in the way that seems to him best, if it does not infringe the liberty of others in striving after a similar end for themselves when their liberty is capable of consisting with the right of liberty in all others according to possible universal laws." A government founded upon the principle of benevolence toward the people—after the analogy of a father to his children, and therefore called a paternal government—would be one in which the subjects would be regarded as children or minors unable to distinguish what is beneficial or injurious to them. These subjects would be thus compelled to act in a merely passive way; and they would be trained to expect all that ought to make them happy, solely from the judgment of the sovereign and just as he might will it, merely out of his goodness. Such a government would be the greatest conceivable despotism; for it would present a constitution that would abolish all liberty in the subjects and leave them no rights. It is not a paternal government, but only a patriotic government that is adapted for men who are capable of rights, and at the same time fitted to give scope to the good-will of the ruler. By 'patriotic' is meant that condition of mind in which every one in the State—the head of it not excepted—regards the commonwealth as the maternal bosom, and the country as the paternal soil out of and on which he himself has sprung into being, and which he also must leave to others as a dear inheritance. Thus, and thus only, can he hold himself entitled to protect the rights of his fatherland by laws of the common will, but not to subject it to an unconditional purpose of his own at pleasure.

This right of liberty thus belongs to him as a man, while he is a member of the commonwealth; or, in point of fact, so far as he is a being capable of rights generally.

2. The equality of every member of the State as a subject is the second principle in the constitution of a rational commonwealth. The formula of this principle may be put thus: "Every member of the commonwealth has rights against every other that may be enforced by compulsory laws, from which only the sovereign or supreme ruler of the State is excepted, because he is regarded not as a mere member of the commonwealth, but as its creator or maintainer; and he alone has the right to compel without being himself subject to compulsory law." All, however, who live under laws in a State are its subjects; and, con-

sequently, they are subjected to the compulsory law, like all other members of the commonwealth, one only, whether an individual sovereign or a collective body, constituting the supreme head of the State and as such being accepted as the medium through which alone all rightful coercion or compulsion can be exercised. For, should the head of the State also be subject to compulsion, there would no longer be a supreme head, and the series of members subordinate and super-ordinate would go on upward *ad infinitum*. Again, were there in the State two such powers as persons exempt from legal compulsion, neither of them would be subject to compulsory laws, and as such the one could do no wrong to the other; which is impossible.

This thoroughgoing equality of the individual men in a State as its subjects is, however, quite compatible with the greatest inequality in the extent and degrees of their possessions, whether consisting in cor-poreal or spiritual superiority over others, or in the external gifts of fortune, or in rights generally—of which there may be many—in relation to others. Thus the prosperity of the one may greatly depend on the will of another, as in the case of the poor in relation to the rich. One may even have of necessity to obey and another to command, as in the relation of children to parents and of wife to husband. Again, one may have to work and another to pay, as in the case of a day laborer; and so on. But in relation to the involved law of right, which as the expression of the universal will of the State can be only one, and which regards the form of the right, and not the matter or object to which the right refers; in all cases, the persons as subjects are to be regarded as all equal to one another. For no one has a right to compel or coerce any one whomsoever in the State, otherwise than by the public law and through the sovereign or ruler executing it; and any one may resist another thus far, and through the same medium. On the other hand, no one can lose this right, as a title to proceed by legal compulsion against others, except by his own fault or a criminal act. Nor can any one divest himself of it voluntarily, or by a compact, so as to bring it about by a supposed act of right, that he should have no rights but only duties towards others; for in so doing he would be depriving himself of the right of making a compact, and consequently the act would annul itself.

Out of this idea of the equality of men as subjects in the common-wealth, there arises the following formula: "Every member of the State should have it made possible for him to attain to any position or rank that may belong to any subject to which his talent, his industry or his fortune may be capable of raising him; and his fellow subjects are not entitled to stand in the way by any hereditary prerogative, forming the exclusive privilege of a certain class, in order to keep him and his posterity forever below them."

For all law consists merely in restriction of the liberty of another to the condition that is consistent with my liberty according to a universal law; and national law in a commonwealth is only the product of actual legislation conformable to this principle and conjoined with power, in virtue of which all who belong to a nation as its subjects find themselves in a condition constituted and regulated by law. And, as such, this condition is in fact a condition of equality inasmuch as it is determined by the action and reaction of free wills limiting one another, according to the universal law of freedom; and it thus constitutes the civil state of human society. Hence the inborn right of all individuals in this sphere (that is, considered as being prior to their having actually entered upon juridical action) to bring compulsion to bear upon any others is entirely identical and equal throughout, on the assumption that they are always to remain within the bounds of unanimity and concord in the mutual use of their liberty. Now birth is not an act on the part of him who is born, and consequently it does not entail upon him any inequality in the state of law, nor any subjection under laws of compulsion other than what is common to him with all others as a subject of the one supreme legislative power; and, therefore, there can be no inborn privilege by way of law in any member of the commonwealth as a subject before another fellow subject. Nor, consequently, has any one a right to transmit the privilege or prerogative of the rank which he holds in the commonwealth to his posterity so that they should be, as it were, qualified by birth for the rank of nobility; nor should they be prevented from attaining by their own merit to the highest stages in the gradations of social rank. Everything else that partakes of the nature of a thing and does not relate to personality may be bequeathed; and, since such things may be acquired as property, they may also be alienated or conveyed. Hence after a number of generations a considerable inequality in external circumstances may arise among the members of a commonwealth, producing such relations as those of master and servant, landlord and tenant, etc. These circumstances and relations, however, ought not to hinder any of the subjects of the State from rising to such positions as their talent, their industry and their fortune may make it possible for them to fill. For otherwise such a one would be qualified to coerce without being liable to be coerced by the counter action of others in return; and he would rise above the stage of being a fellow subject. Further, no man who lives under the legalized conditions of a commonwealth can fall out of this equality otherwise than by his own crime, and never either by compact or through any military occupancy. For he cannot by any legal act, whether of himself or of another, cease to be the owner of himself, or enter into the class of domestic cattle, which are used for all sorts of services at will and are maintained in this condition without their consent as long as there is a will to do it, although under the limitation—which is sometimes sanctioned even by religion, as among the Hindus—that they are not to be mutilated or slain. Under any conditions, he is to be regarded as happy who is conscious that it depends only on himself—that is, on his faculty or earnest will—or on circumstances which he cannot impute to any other, and not on the irresistible will of others, that he does not rise to a stage of equality with others who as his fellow subjects have no advantage over him as far as law is concerned.

3. The self-dependency of a member of the commonwealth as a citizen, or fellow legislator, is the third principle or condition of law in the State. In the matter of the legislation itself, all are to be regarded as free and equal under the already-existing public laws; but they are not to be regarded as equal in relation to the right to give or enact these laws. Those who are not capable of this right are, notwithstanding, subjected to the observance of the laws as members of the commonwealth, and thereby they participate in the protection which is in accordance therewith; they are, however, not to be regarded as citizens but as protected fellow subjects.

All right, in fact, depends on laws. A public law, however, which determines for all what is to be legally allowed or not allowed in their regard is the act of a public will, from which all law proceeds and which therefore itself can do no wrong to any one. For this, however, there is no other will competent than that of the whole people, as it is only when all determine about all that each one in consequence determines about himself. For it is only to himself that one can do no wrong. But if it be another will that is in question, then the mere will of any one different from it could determine nothing for it which might not be wrong; and consequently the law of such a will would require another law to limit its legislation. And thus no particular will can be legislative for a commonwealth. Properly speaking, in order to make out this, the ideas of the external liberty, equality and unity of the will of all are to be taken into account; and for the last of these self-dependency is the condition, since the exercising of a vote is required when the former two ideas are taken along with it. The fundamental law thus indicated, which can only arise out of the universal united will of the people, is what is called the *original contract*.

Now any one who has the right of voting in this system of legislation is a citizen as distinguished from a burgess; he is a *citoyen* as distinguished from a *bourgeois*. The quality requisite for this status, in addition to the natural one of not being a child or a woman, is solely this, that the individual is his own master by right; and, consequently, that he has some property that supports him, under which may be reckoned any art or handicraft, or any fine art or science. Otherwise put, the condition in those cases in which the citizen must acquire from others in order to live is that he acquires it only by alienation of what is his own, and not by a consent given to others to make use of his powers; and consequently that he serves no one but the commonwealth, in the proper sense of the term. In this relation those skilled in the arts and large or small proprietors are all equal to one another as, in fact, each one is entitled to only one vote. . . . The great possessor of an estate does in fact annihilate as many smaller owners, and their voices, as might occupy the place he takes up; he does not vote in their name, and he has consequently only one vote. It thus must be left to depend merely on the means, the industry and the fortune of each member of the commonwealth that each one may acquire a part of it, and all of its members the whole. But these distinctions cannot be brought into consideration in connection with a universal legislation; and hence the number of those qualified to have a voice in the legislation must be reckoned by the heads of those who are in possession and not according to the extent of their possessions.

Furthermore, all who have this right of voting must agree in order to realize the laws of public justice, for otherwise there would arise a conflict of right between those who were not in agreement with it and the others who were; and this would give rise to the need of a higher principle of right that the conflict might be decided. A universal agreement cannot be expected from a whole people; and consequently it is only a plurality of voices, and not even of those who immediately vote in a large nation, but only of their delegates as representative of the people that can alone be foreseen as practically attainable. And hence even the principle of making the majority of votes suffice as representing the general consent will have to be taken as by compact; and it must thus be regarded as the ultimate basis of the establishment of any civil constitution.

13.   The Declaration of the Rights of Man and of the Citizen

"The Declaration of the Rights of Man and of the Citizen" was adopted by the French National Assembly on August 26, 1789. It has been suggested that the idea of listing rights in series was borrowed from American bills of rights, particularly since there is significant parallelism between the French Declaration and the Virginian Declaration of 1776. The text was developed by a committee of leaders of the National Assembly from a draft proposed by Mounier. The Declaration was added to the French Constitution of 1793 and became a model for liberal European constitutions. R. R. Palmer in tracing the influence of the idea of the French Revolution for European history writes "The Declaration of 1789, by laying down the principles of the modern democratic state, remains the chief single document of the Revolution of the Western World."

The selection is the translation which appears in Thomas Paine's *Rights of Man* (1790).

DECLARATION OF THE RIGHTS OF MAN
AND OF THE CITIZEN

The representatives of the people of France, formed into a National Assembly, considering that ignorance, neglect, or contempt of human rights, are the sole causes of public misfortunes and corruptions of Government, have resolved to set forth in a solemn declaration, these natural, imprescriptible, and inalienable rights: that this declaration being constantly present to the minds of the members of the body social, they may for ever kept attentive to their rights and their duties; that the acts of the legislative and executive powers of government, being capable of being every moment compared with the end of political institutions, may be more respected; and also, that the future claims of the citizens, being directed by simple and incontestable principles, may always tend to the maintenance of the Constitution, and the general happiness.

For these reasons, the National Assembly doth recognize and declare, in the presence of the Supreme Being, and with the hope of his blessing and favour, the following *sacred* rights of men and of citizens:

I. Men are born, and always continue, free and equal in respect of their rights. Civil distinctions, therefore, can be founded only on public utility.

II. The end of all political associations, is the preservation of the natural and imprescriptible rights of man; and these rights are liberty, property, security, and resistance of oppression.

III. The nation is essentially the source of all sovereignty; nor can any individual, or any body of men, be entitled to any authority which is not expressly derived from it.

IV. Political liberty consists in the power of doing whatever does not injure another. The exercise of the natural rights of every man, has no other limits than those which are necessary to secure to every *other* man the free exercise of the same rights; and these limits are determinable only by the law.

V. The law ought to prohibit only actions hurtful to society. What is not prohibited by the law, should not be hindered; nor should any one be compelled to that which the law does not require.

VI. The law is an expression of the will of the community. All citizens have a right to concur, either personally, or by their representatives, in its formation. It should be the same to all, whether it protects or punishes; and all being equal in its sight, are equally eligible to all honours, places, and employments, according to their different abilities, without any other distinction than that created by their virtues and talents.

VII. No man should be accused, arrested, or held in confinement, except in cases determined by the law, and according to the forms which it has prescribed. All who promote, solicit, execute, or cause to be executed, arbitrary orders, ought to be punished, and every citizen called upon, or apprehended by virtue of the law, ought immediately to obey, and renders himself culpable by resistance.

VIII. The law ought to impose no other penalties but such as are absolutely and evidently necessary; and no one ought to be punished, but in virtue of a law promulgated before the offence, and legally applied.

IX. Every man being presumed innocent till he has been convicted, whenever his detention becomes indispensable, all rigour to him, more than is necessary to secure his person, ought to be provided against by the law.

X. No man ought to be molested on account of his opinions, not even on account of his *religious* opinions, provided his avowal of them does not disturb the public order established by the law.

XI. The unrestrained communication of thoughts and opinions being one of the most precious rights of man, every citizen may speak, write, and publish freely, provided he is responsible for the abuse of this liberty, in cases determined by the law.

XII. A public force being necessary to give security to the rights of men and of citizens, that force is instituted for the benefit of the community and not for the particular benefit of the persons to whom it is intrusted.

XIII. A common contribution being necessary for the support of the public force, and for defraying the other expenses of government, it ought to be divided equally among the members of the community, according to their abilities.

XIV. Every citizen has a right, either by himself or his representative, to a free voice in determining the necessity of public contributions, the appropriation of them, and their amount, mode of assessment, and duration.

XV. Every community has had a right to demand of all its agents an account of their conduct.

XVI. Every community in which a separation of powers and a security of rights is not provided for, wants a constitution.

XVII. The right to property being inviolable and sacred, no one ought to be deprived of it, except in cases of evident public necessity, legally ascertained, and on condition of a previous just indemnity.

14.   JAMES MILL
Interests and Representation

James Mill (1773–1836) wrote *An Essay on Government*, from which the selection is taken, in 1819. It was one of a series of articles which he wrote for the *Encyclopaedia Britannica*. The essay was subsequently reprinted and became recognized as the classic statement of the political theory of the British utilitarians.

The work had a direct impact on the passage of the British Reform Act of 1832, the first of several acts of extension of suffrage which reshaped British political institutions in the nineteenth century. Mill justified representative democracy on the ground that any disenfranchised group will suffer neglect of its interests. At the same time he argued that the inability of the poorer classes to discern their own interests required severe limitation of suffrage.

James Mill is a major figure in the development of the British liberal tradition, both because of his works in political and economic theory and because he became the major propagandist for the philosophical writings of Bentham.

THE END OF GOVERNMENT; VIZ., THE GOOD OR BENEFIT FOR THE SAKE OF WHICH IT EXISTS

The question with respect to government is a question about the adaptation of means to an end. . . .

The end of government has been described in a great variety of expressions. By Locke it was said to be "the public good"; by others it has been described as being "the greatest happiness of the greatest number. . . ."

It is immediately obvious that a wide and difficult field is presented, and that the whole science of human nature must be explored to lay a foundation for the science of government. To understand what is included in the happiness of the greatest number, we must understand what is included in the happiness of the individuals of whom it is composed. That dissection of human nature which would be necessary for exhibiting, on proper evidence, the primary elements into which human happiness may be resolved, it is not compatible with the present design to undertake. We must content ourselves with assuming certain results.

We may allow, for example, in general terms that the lot of every human being is determined by his pains and pleasures, and that his happiness corresponds with the degree in which his pleasures are great and his pains are small. Human pains and pleasures are derived from two sources: they are produced either by our fellow men or by causes independent of other men. We may assume it as another principle that the concern of government is with the former of these two sources: that its business is to increase to the utmost the pleasures, and diminish to the utmost the pains, which men derive from one another.

Of the laws of nature on which the condition of man depends, that which is attended with the greatest number of consequences is the necessity of labor for obtaining the means of subsistence as well as the means of the greatest part of our pleasures. This is no doubt the primary cause of government; for if nature had produced spontaneously all the objects which we desire, and in sufficient abundance for the desires of all, there would have been no source of dispute or of injury among men, nor would any man have possessed the means of ever acquiring authority over another.

The results are exceedingly different when nature produces the objects of desire not in sufficient abundance for all. The source of dispute is then exhaustless, and every man has the means of acquiring authority over others in proportion to the quantity of those objects which he is able to possess. In this case the end to be obtained through government as the means is to make that distribution of the scanty materials of happiness which would insure the greatest sum of it in the members of the community taken altogether, preventing every individual or combination of individuals from interfering with that distribution or making any man to have less than his share.

When it is considered that most of the objects of desire and even the means of subsistence are the product of labor, it is evident that the means of insuring labor must be provided for as the foundation of all. The means for the insuring of labor are of two sorts: the one made out of the matter of evil, the other made out of the matter of good. The first sort is commonly denominated "force," and under its application the laborers are slaves. This mode of procuring labor we need not consider, for if the end of government be to produce the greatest happiness of the greatest number, that end cannot be attained by making the greatest number slaves.

The other mode of obtaining labor is by allurement, or the advantage which it brings. To obtain all the objects of desire in the greatest possible quantity, we must obtain labor in the greatest possible quantity; and to obtain labor in the greatest possible quantity, we must raise to the greatest possible height the advantage attached to labor. It is impossible to attach to labor a greater degree of advantage than the whole of the product of labor. Why so? Because if you give more to one man than the produce of his labor, you can do so only by taking it away from the produce of some other man's labor. The greatest possible happiness of society is, therefore, attained by insuring to every man the greatest possible quantity of the produce of his labor.

How is this to be accomplished? For it is obvious that every man who has not all the objects of his desire has inducement to take them from any other man who is weaker than himself: and how is he to be prevented? One mode is sufficiently obvious, and it does not appear that there is any other: the union of a certain number of men to protect one another. The object, it is plain, can best be attained when a great number of men combine and delegate to a small number the power necessary for protecting them all. This is government.

With respect to the end of government, or that for the sake of which it exists, it is not conceived to be necessary on the present occasion that the analysis should be carried any further. What follows is an attempt to analyze the means.

THE MEANS OF ATTAINING THE END OF GOVERNMENT; VIZ., POWER, AND SECURITIES AGAINST THE ABUSE OF THAT POWER

Two things are here to be considered: the power with which the small number are entrusted, and the use which they are to make of it. With respect to the first there is no difficulty. The elements out of which the power of coercing others is fabricated are obvious to all. Of these we shall therefore not lengthen this article by any explanation. All the difficult questions of government relate to the means of restraining those in whose hands are lodged the powers necessary for the protection of all from making bad use of it.

Whatever would be the temptations under which individuals would lie if there was no government, to take the objects of desire from others weaker than themselves, under the same temptations the members of government lie to take the objects of desire from the members of the community if they are not prevented from doing so. Whatever, then, are the reasons for establishing government, the very same exactly are the reasons for establishing securities that those entrusted with the powers necessary for protecting others make use of them for that purpose solely, and not for the purpose of taking from the members of the community the objects of desire.

THAT THE REQUISITE SECURITIES AGAINST THE ABUSE OF POWER ARE NOT FOUND IN ANY OF THE SIMPLE FORMS OF GOVERNMENT

There are three modes in which it may be supposed that the powers for the protection of the community are capable of being exercised. The community may undertake the protection of itself and of its members. The powers of protection may be placed in the hands of a few. And, lastly, they may be placed in the hands of an individual. The many, the few, the one: these varieties appear to exhaust the subject. It is not possible to conceive any hands or combination of hands in which the powers of protection can be lodged, which will not fall under one or other of those descriptions. And these varieties correspond to the three forms of government: the democratical, the aristocratical, and the monarchical. It will be necessary to look somewhat closely at each of these forms in their order.

(1) *The democratical.* It is obviously impossible that the community in a body can be present to afford protection to each of its members. It must employ individuals for that purpose. Employing individuals, it must choose them; it must lay down the rules under which they are to act; and it must punish them if they act in disconformity to those rules. In these functions are included the three great operations of government: administration, legislation, and judicature. The community, to perform any of these operations, must be assembled. This circumstance alone seems to form a conclusive objection against the democratical form. To assemble the whole of a community as often as the business of government requires performance would almost preclude the existence of labor, hence that of property, and hence the existence of the community itself.

There is another objection, not less conclusive. A whole community would form a numerous assembly. But all numerous assemblies are essentially incapable of business. It is unnecessary to be tedious in the proof of this proposition. In an assembly everything must be done by speaking and assenting. But where the assembly is numerous, so many persons desire to speak, and feelings by mutual inflammation become so violent, that calm and effectual deliberation is impossible.

It may be taken, therefore, as a position from which there will be no dissent, that a community in mass is ill-adapted for the business of government. There is no principle more in conformity with the sentiments and the practice of the people than this. The management of the joint affairs of any considerable body of the people they never undertake for themselves. What they uniformly do is to choose a certain number of themselves to be the actors in their stead. Even in the case of a common benefit club, the members choose a committee of management and content themselves with a general control.

(2) *The aristocratical.* This term applies to all those cases in which the powers of government are held by any number of persons intermediate between a single person and the majority. When the number is small, it is common to call the government an oligarchy; when it is considerable, to call it an aristocracy. The cases are essentially the same, because the motives which operate in both are the same. This is a proposition which carries, we think, its own evidence along with it. We, therefore, assume it as a point which will not be disputed.

The source of evil is radically different in the case of aristocracy from what it is in that of democracy.

The community cannot have an interest opposite to its interest. To affirm this would be a contradiction in terms. The community within itself, and with respect to itself, can have no sinister interest. One community may intend the evil of another; never its own. This is an indubitable proposition, and one of great importance. The community may act wrong from mistake. To suppose that it could from design, would be to suppose that human beings can wish their own misery.

The circumstances from which the inaptitude of the community, as a body, for the business of government arises—namely, the inconvenience of assembling them, and the inconvenience of their numbers when assembled—do not necessarily exist in the case of aristocracy. If the number of those who hold among them the powers of government is so great as to make it inconvenient to assemble them, or impossible for them to deliberate calmly when assembled, this is only an objection to so extended an aristocracy and has no application to an aristocracy not too numerous, when assembled, for the best exercise of deliberation.

The question is whether such an aristocracy may be trusted to make that use of the powers of government which is most conducive to the end for which government exists?

There may be a strong presumption that any aristocracy monopolizing the powers of government would not possess intellectual powers in any very high perfection. Intellectual powers are the offspring of labor. But a hereditary artistocracy are deprived of the strongest motives to labor. The greater part of them will, therefore, be defective in those mental powers. This is one objection, and an important one, though not the greatest.

We have already observed that the reason for which government exists is that one man, if stronger than another, will take from him whatever that other possesses and he desires. But if one man will do this, so will several. And if powers are put into the hands of a comparatively small number, called an aristocracy—powers which make them stronger than the rest of the community—they will take from the rest of the community as much as they please of the objects of desire. They will thus defeat the very end for which government was instituted. The unfitness, therefore, of an aristocracy to be entrusted with the powers of government rests on demonstration.

(3) *The monarchical.* It will be seen, and therefore words to make it manifest are unnecessary, that in most respects the monarchical form of government agrees with the aristocratical and is liable to the same objections. If government is founded upon this, as a law of human nature, that a man if able will take from others anything which they have and he desires, it is sufficiently evident that when a man is called a king it does not change his nature; so that when he has got power to enable him to take from every man what he pleases, he will take whatever he pleases. To suppose that he will not is to affirm that government is unnecessary and that human beings will abstain from injuring one another of their own accord.

It is very evident that this reasoning extends to every modification of the smaller number. Whenever the powers of government are placed in any hands other than those of the community—whether those of one man, of a few, or of several—those principles of human nature which imply that government is at all necessary imply that those persons will make use of them to defeat the very end for which government exists. . . .

IN THE REPRESENTATIVE SYSTEM ALONE THE SECURITIES FOR GOOD GOVERNMENT ARE TO BE FOUND

What, then, is to be done? For according to this reasoning we may be told that good government appears to be impossible. The people as a body cannot perform the business of government for themselves. If the powers of government are entrusted to one man or a few men, and a monarchy or governing aristocracy is formed, the results are fatal; and it appears that a combination of the simple forms is impossible.

Notwithstanding the truth of these propositions, it is not yet proved that good government in unattainable. For though the people, who cannot exercise the powers of government themselves, must entrust them to some one individual or set of individuals, and such individuals will infallibly have the strongest motives to make a bad use of them, it is possible that checks may be found sufficient to prevent them. The next subject of inquiry, then, is the doctrine of checks. It is sufficiently conformable to the established and fashionable opinions to say that upon the right constitution of checks all goodness of government depends. To this proposition we fully subscribe. Nothing, therefore, can exceed the importance of correct conclusions upon this subject. After the developments already made, it is hoped that the inquiry will be neither intricate nor unsatisfactory.

In the grand discovery of modern times, the system of representation, the solution of all the difficulties both speculative and practical will perhaps be found. If it cannot, we seem to be forced upon the extraordinary conclusion that good government is impossible. For as there is no individual or combination of individuals, except the community itself, who would not have an interest in bad government if entrusted with its powers, and as the community itself is incapable of exercising those powers and must entrust them to some individual or combination of individuals, the conclusion is obvious: the community itself must check those individuals, else they will follow their interest and produce bad government.

But how is it the community can check? The community can act only when assembled; and then it is incapable of acting. The community, however, can choose representatives, and the question is whether the representatives of the community can operate as a check.

WHAT IS REQUIRED IN A REPRESENTATIVE BODY TO MAKE IT A SECURITY FOR GOOD GOVERNMENT?

We may begin by laying down two propositions which appear to involve a great portion of the inquiry, and about which it is unlikely that there will be any dispute.

1. The checking body must have a degree of power sufficient for the business of checking.

2. It must have an identity of interest with the community, otherwise it will make a mischievous use of its power.

1. To measure the degree of power which is requisite upon any occasion, we must consider the degree of power which is necessary to be overcome. Just as much as suffices for that purpose is requisite, and no more. We have then to inquire what power it is which the representatives of the community, acting as a check, need power to overcome. The answer here is easily given. It is all that power, wheresoever lodged, which they in whose hands it is lodged have an interest in misusing. We have already seen that to whomsoever the community entrusts the powers of government, whether one or a few, they have an interest in misusing them. All the power, therefore, which the one or the few, or which the one and the few combined, can apply to insure the accomplishment of their sinister ends, the checking body must have power to overcome otherwise its check will be unavailing. In other words, there will be no check.

This is so exceedingly evident that we hardly think it necessary to say another word in illustration of it. If a king is prompted by the inherent principles of human nature to seek the gratification of his will, and if he finds an obstacle in that pursuit, he removes it, of course, if he can. If any man or any set of men oppose him, he overcomes them if he is able; and to prevent him they must, at the least, have equal power with himself.

The same is the case with an aristocracy. To oppose them with success in pursuing their interest at the expense of the community, the checking body must have power successfully to resist whatever power they possess. If there is both a king and an aristocracy, and if they would combine to put down the checking force and to pursue their mutual interest at the expense of the community, the checking body must have sufficient power successfully to resist the united power of both king and aristocracy.

These conclusions are not only indisputable, but the very theory of the British constitution is erected upon them. The House of Commons, according to that theory, is the checking body. It is also an admitted doctrine that if the King had the power of bearing down any opposition to his will that could be made by the House of Commons, or if the King and the House of Lords combined had the power of bearing down its opposition to their joint will, it would cease to have the power of checking them; it must, therefore, have a power sufficient to overcome the united power of both.

2. All the questions which relate to the degree of power necessary to be given to that checking body, on the perfection of whose operations all the goodness of governments depends, are thus pretty easily solved. The grand difficulty consists in finding the means of constituting a checking body the power of which shall not be turned against the community for whose protection it is created.

There can be no doubt that if power is granted to a body of men, called representatives, they, like any other men, will use their power, not for the advantage of the community, but for their own advantage, if they can. The only question is, therefore, how they can be prevented; in other words, how are the interests of the representatives to be identified with those of the community?

Each representative may be considered in two capacities: in his capacity of representative, in which he has the exercise of power over others, and in his capacity of member of the community, in which others have the exercise of power over him.

If things were so arranged that, in his capacity of representative, it would be impossible for him to do himself so much good by misgovernment as he would do himself harm in his capacity of member of the community, the object would be accomplished. We have already seen that the amount of power assigned to the checking body cannot be diminished beyond a certain amount. It must be sufficient to overcome all resistance on the part of all those in whose hands the powers of government are lodged. But if the power assigned to the representative cannot be diminished in amount, there is only one other way in which it can be diminished, and that is in duration.

This, then, is the instrument: lessening of duration is the instrument by which, if by anything, the object is to be attained. The smaller the period of time during which any man retains his capacity of representative, as compared with the time in which he is simply a member of the community, the more difficult it will be to compensate the sacrifice of the interests of the longer period by the profits of misgovernment during the shorter.

This is an old and approved method of identifying as nearly as possible the interests of those who rule with the interests of those who are ruled. It is in pursuance of this advantage that the members of the British House of Commons have always been chosen for a limited period. If the members were hereditary, or even if they were chosen for life, every inquirer would immediately pronounce that they would employ for their own advantage, the powers entrusted to them, and that they would go just as far in abusing the persons and properties of the people as their estimate of the powers and spirit of the people to resist them would allow them to contemplate as safe.

As it thus appears, by the consent of all men, from the time when the Romans made their consuls annual down to the present day, that the end is to be attained by limiting the duration either of the acting or (which is better) of the checking power, the next question is, to what degree should the limitation proceed?

The general answer is plain. It should proceed till met by over-balancing inconveniences on the other side. What, then, are the inconveniences which are likely to flow from a too-limited duration?

They are of two sorts: those which affect the performance of the service for which the individuals are chosen, and those which arise from the trouble of election. It is sufficiently obvious that the business of government requires time to perform it. The matter must be proposed and deliberated upon; a resolution must be taken and executed. If the powers of government were to be shifted from one set of hands to another every day, the business of government could not proceed. Two conclusions, then, we may adopt with perfect certainty: that whatsoever time is necessary to perform the periodical round of the stated operations of government should be allotted to those who are invested with the checking powers; and, secondly, that no time which is not necessary for that purpose should by any means be allotted to them. With respect to the inconvenience arising from frequency of election, though it is evident that the trouble of election, which is always something, should not be repeated oftener than is necessary, no great allowance will need to be made for it, because it may easily be reduced to an inconsiderable amount.

As it thus appears that limiting the duration of their power is a security against the sinister interest of the people's representatives, so it appears that it is the only security of which the nature of the case admits. The only other means which could be employed to that end would be punishment on account of abuse. It is easy, however, to see that punishment could not be effectually applied. Previous to punishment, definition is required of the punishable acts, and proof must be established of the commission. But abuses of power may be carried to a great extent without allowing the means of proving a determinate offense. No part of political experience is more perfect than this.

If the limiting of duration be the only security, it is unnecessary to speak of the importance which ought to be attached to it.

In the principle of limiting the duration of the power delegated to the representatives of the people is not included the idea of changing them. The same individual may be chosen any number of times. The check of the short period for which he is chosen, and during which he can promote his sinister interest, is the same upon the man who has been chosen and rechosen twenty times as upon the man who has been chosen for the first time. And there is good reason for always re-electing the man who has done his duty, because the longer he serves, the better acquainted he becomes with the business of the service. Upon this principle of rechoosing, or of the permanency of the individual, united with the power of change, has been recommended the plan of permanent service with perpetual power of removal. This, it has been said, reduces the period within which the representative can promote his sinister interest to the narrowest possible limits; because the moment when his constituents begin to suspect him, that moment they may turn him out. On the other hand, if he continues faithful, the trouble of election is performed once for all, and the man serves as long as he lives. Some disadvantages, on the other hand, would accompany this plan. The present, however, is not the occasion on which the balance of different plans is capable of being adjusted.

15. J. S. MILL
Participatory Democracy

John Stuart Mill published *Considerations on Representative Government* in 1861. The work exemplifies the continuous growth among nineteenth-century utilitarians and liberals of faith in democracy. Mill asserts the classic view that politics should be an expression of the active and involved life and that political education is accomplished by the exercise of political responsibility. The dilemma for Mill, and for the other democratic liberals, was the reconciliation of this democratic faith with the beginning of the mass culture that has developed since the last half of the nineteenth century.

The selection is from Chapter III of *Considerations on Representative Government*, entitled "That the Ideally Best Form of Government is Representative Government."

THAT THE IDEALLY BEST FORM OF GOVERNMENT IS REPRESENTATIVE GOVERNMENT

There is no difficulty is showing that the ideally best form of government is that in which the sovereignty, or supreme controlling power in the last resort, is vested in the entire aggregate of the community, every citizen not only having a voice in the exercise of that ultimate sovereignty, but being, at least occasionally, called on to take an actual part in the government by the personal discharge of some public function, local or general.

To test this proposition, it has to be examined in reference to the two branches into which . . . the inquiry into the goodness of a government conveniently divides itself—namely, how far it promotes the good management of the affairs of society by means of the existing faculties, moral, intellectual, and active, of its various members, and what is its effect in improving or deteriorating those faculties.

The ideally best form of government, it is scarcely necessary to say, does not mean one which is practicable or eligible in all states of civilization, but the one which, in the circumstances in which it is practicable and eligible, is attended with the greatest amount of beneficial consequences, immediate and prospective. A completely popular government is the only polity which can make out any claim to this character. It is pre-eminent in both the departments between which the excellence of a political constitution is divided. It is both more favorable to present good government and promotes a better and higher form of national character than any other polity whatsoever.

Its superiority in reference to present well-being rests upon two principles of as universal truth and applicability as any general propositions which can be laid down respecting human affairs. The first is that the rights and interests of every or any person are only secure from being disregarded when the person interested is himself able, and habitually disposed, to stand up for them. The second is that the general prosperity attains a greater height and is more widely diffused in proportion to the amount and variety of the personal energies enlisted in promoting it.

Putting these two propositions into a shape more special to their present application: human beings are only secure from evil at the hands of others in proportion as they have the power of being, and are, self-*protecting;* and they only achieve a high degree of success in their struggle with nature in proportion as they are self-*dependent,* relying on what they themselves can do, either separately or in concert, rather than on what others do for them.

The former proposition—that each is the only safe guardian of his own rights and interests—is one of those elementary maxims of prudence which every person capable of conducting his own affairs implicitly acts upon wherever he himself is interested. Many, indeed, have a great dislike to it as a political doctrine and are fond of holding it up to obloquy as a doctrine of universal selfishness. To which we may answer that whenever it ceases to be true that mankind, as a rule, prefer themselves to others, and those nearest to them to those more remote, from that moment Communism is not only practicable but the only defensible form of society, and will, when that time arrives, be assuredly carried into effect. For my own part, not believing in universal selfishness, I have no difficulty in admitting that Communism would even now be practicable among the *élite* of mankind, and may become so among the rest. But as this opinion is anything but popular with those defenders of existing institutions who find fault with the doctrine of the general predominance of self-interest, I am inclined to think they do in reality believe that most men consider themselves before other people. It is not, however, necessary to affirm even thus much in order to support the claim of all to participate in the sovereign power. We need not suppose that when power resides in an exclusive class, that class will knowingly and deliberately sacrifice the other classes to themselves; it suffices that, in the absence of its natural defenders, the interest of the excluded is always in danger of being overlooked, and, when looked at, is seen with very different eyes from those of the persons whom it directly concerns. In this country, for example, what are called the working classes may be considered as excluded from all direct participation in the government. I do not believe that the classes who do participate in it have in general any intention of sacrificing the working classes to themselves. They once had that intention—witness the persevering attempts so long made to keep down wages by law. But in the present day their ordinary disposition is the very opposite: they willingly make considerable sacrifices, especially of their pecuniary interest, for the benefit of the working classes, and err rather by too lavish and indiscriminating beneficence; nor do I believe that any rulers in history have been actuated by a more sincere desire to do their duty toward the poorer portion of their countrymen. Yet does Parliament, or almost any of the members composing it, ever for an instant look at any question with the eyes of a workingman? When a subject arises in which the laborers as such have an interest, is it regarded from any point of view but that of the employers of labor? I do not say that the workingmen's view of these questions is in general nearer to the truth than the other, but it is sometimes quite as near; and in any case it ought to be respectfully listened to instead of being, as it is, not merely turned away from, but ignored. On the question of strikes, for instance, it is doubtful if there is so much as one among the leading members of either House who is not firmly convinced that the reason of the matter is unqualifiedly on the side of the masters, and that the men's view of it is simply absurd. Those who have studied the question know well how far this is from being the case, and in how different and how infinitely less superficial a manner the point would have to be argued if the classes who strike were able to make themselves heard in Parliament.

It is an adherent condition of human affairs that no intention, however sincere, of protecting the interests of others can make it safe or salutary to tie up their own hands. Still more obviously true is it that by their own hands only can any positive and durable improvement of their circumstances in life be worked out. Through the joint influence of these two principles, all free communities have both been more exempt from social injustice and crime, and have attained more brilliant prosperity, than any others, or than they themselves after they lost their freedom. Contrast the free states of the world, while their freedom lasted, with the contemporary subjects of mqnarchical or oligarchical despotism: the Greek cities with the Persian satrapies; the Italian republics and the free towns of Flanders and Germany with the feudal monarchies of Europe; Switzerland, Holland, and England with Austria or ante-revolutionary France. Their superior prosperity was too obvious ever to have been gainsaid, while their superiority in good government and social relations is proved by the prosperity, and is manifest besides in every page of history. If we compare, not one age with another, but the different governments which coexisted in the same age, no amount of disorder which exaggeration itself can pretend to have existed amidst the publicity of the free states can be compared for a moment with the contemptuous trampling upon the mass of the people which pervaded the whole life of the monarchical countries, or the disgusting individual tyranny which was of more than daily occurrence under the systems of plunder which they called fiscal arrangements and in the secrecy of their frightful courts of justice.

It must be acknowledged that the benefits of freedom, so far as they have hitherto been enjoyed, were obtained by the extension of its privileges to a part only of the community; and that a government in which they are extended impartially to all is a desideratum still unrealized. But though every approach to this has an independent value, and in many cases more than an approach could not, in the existing state of general improvement, be made, the participation of all in these benefits is the ideally perfect conception of free government. In proportion as any, no matter who, are excluded from it, the interests of the excluded are left without the guaranty accorded to the rest, and they themselves have less scope and encouragement than they might otherwise have to that exertion of their energies for the good of themselves and of the community, to which the general prosperity is always proportioned.

Thus stands the case as regards present well-being; the good management of the affairs of the existing generation. If we now pass to the influence of the form of government upon character, we shall find the superiority of popular government over every other to be, if possible, still more decided and indisputable.

This question really depends upon a still more fundamental one, viz., which of two common types of character, for the general good of humanity, it is most desirable should predominate—the active or the passive type: that which struggles against evils or that which endures them; that which bends to circumstances or that which endeavors to make circumstances bend to itself.

The commonplaces of moralists, and the general sympathies of mankind, are in favor of the passive type. Energetic characters may be admired, but the acquiescent and submissive are those which most men personally prefer. The passiveness of our neighbors increases our own sense of security and plays into the hands of our willfulness. Passive characters, if we do not happen to need their activity, seem an obstruction the less in our own path. A contented character is not a dangerous rival. Yet nothing is more certain than that improvement in human affairs is wholly the work of the uncontented characters, and, moreover, that it is much easier for an active mind to acquire the virtues of patience than for a passive one to assume those of energy. . . .

Now there can be no kind of doubt that the passive type of character is favored by the government of one or a few, and the active self-helping type by that of the many. Irresponsible rulers need the quiescence of the ruled more than they need any activity but that which they can compel. Submissiveness to the prescriptions of men as necessities of nature is the lesson inculcated by all governments upon those who are wholly without participation in them. The will of superiors, and the law as the will of superiors, must be passively yielded to. But no men are mere instruments or materials in the hands of their rulers who have will or spirit or a spring of internal activity in the rest of their proceedings; and any manifestation of these qualities, instead of receiving encouragement from despots, has to get itself forgiven by them. Even when irresponsible rulers are not sufficiently conscious of danger from the mental activity of their subjects to be desirous of repressing it, the position itself is a repression. Endeavour is even more effectually restrained by the certainty of its impotence than by any positive discouragement. Between subjection to the will of others and the virtues of self-help and self-government, there is a natural incompatibility. This is more or less complete, according as the bondage is strained or relaxed. Rulers differ very much in the length to which they carry the control of the free agency of their subjects or the supersession of it by managing their business for them. But the difference is in degree, not in principle; and the best despots often go the greatest lengths in chaining up the free agency of their subjects. A bad despot, when his own personal indulgences have been provided for, may sometimes be willing to let the people alone; but a good despot insists on doing them good, by making them do their own business in a better way than they themselves know of. The regulations which restricted to fixed processes all the leading branches of French manufacturers were the work of the great Colbert.

Very different is the state of the human faculties where a human being feels himself under no other external restraint than the necessities of nature, or mandates of society which he has his share in imposing, and which it is open to him, if he thinks them wrong, publicly to dissent from and exert himself actively to get altered. No doubt, under a government partially popular, this freedom may be exercised even by those who are not partakers in the full privileges of citizenship. But it is a great additional stimulus to anyone's self-help and self-reliance when he starts from even ground and has not to feel that his success depends on the impression he can make upon the sentiments and dispositions of a body of whom he is not one. It is a great discouragement to an individual, and a still greater one to a class, to be left out of the constitution—to be reduced to plead from outside the door to the arbiters of their destiny, not taken into consultation within. The maximum of the invigorating effect of freedom upon the character is only obtained when the person acted on either is, or is looking forward to becoming, a citizen as fully privileged as any other. What is still more important than even this matter of feeling is the practical discipline which the character obtains from the occasional demand made upon the citizens to exercise, for a time and in their turn, some social function. It is not sufficiently considered how little there is in most men's ordinary life to give any largeness either to their conceptions or to their sentiments. Their work is routine; not a labor of love, but of self-interest in the most elementary form, the satisfaction of daily wants; neither the thing done nor the process of doing it introduces the mind to thoughts or feelings extending beyond individuals; if instructive books are within their reach, there is no stimulus to read them; and in most cases the individual has no access to any person of cultivation much superior to his own. Giving him something to do for the public supplies, in a measure, all these deficiencies. If circumstances allow the amount of public duty assigned him to be considerable, it makes him an educated man. Notwithstanding the defects of the social system and moral ideas of antiquity, the practice of the dicastery and the ecclesia* raised the intellectual standard of an average Athenian citizen far beyond anything of which there is yet an example in any other mass of men, ancient or modern. The proofs of this are apparent in every page of our great historian of Greece; but we need scarcely look further than to the high quality of the addresses which their great orators deemed best calculated to act with effect on their understanding and will. A benefit of the same kind, though far less in degree, is produced on Englishmen of the lower middle class by their liability to be placed on juries and to serve parish offices; which though it does not occur to so many, nor is so continuous, nor introduces them to so great a variety of elevated considerations as to admit of comparison with the public education which every citizen of Athens

* [The popular court and assembly, respectively, in which all Athenian citizens could participate.]

obtained from her democratic institutions, must make them nevertheless very different beings, in range of ideas and development of faculties,
from those who have done nothing in their lives but drive a quill or
sell goods over a counter. Still more salutary is the moral part of the
instruction afforded by the participation of the private citizen, if even
rarely, in public functions. He is called upon, while so engaged, to weigh
interests not his own; to be guided, in case of conflicting claims, by
another rule than his private partialities; to apply, at every turn,
principles and maxims which have for their reason of existence the
common good; and he usually finds associated with him in the same
work minds more familiarized than his own with these ideas and operations, whose study it will be to supply reason to his understanding, and
stimulation to his feeling for the general interest. He is made to feel
himself one of the public, and whatever is for their benefit to be for his
benefit. Where this school of public spirit does not exist, scarcely any
sense is entertained that private persons, in no eminent social situation,
owe any duties to society, except to obey the laws and submit to the
government. There is no unselfish sentiment of identification with the
public. Every thought or feeling, either of interest or of duty, is absorbed
in the individual and in the family. The man never thinks of any collective interest, of any objects to be pursued jointly with others, but only
in competition with them, and in some measure at their expense. A
neighbor, not being an ally or an associate, since he is never engaged
in any common undertaking for joint benefit, is therefore only a rival.
Thus even private morality suffers, while public is actually extinct.
Were this the universal and only possible state of things, the utmost
aspirations of the lawgiver or the moralist could only stretch to make
the bulk of the community a flock of sheep innocently nibbling the
grass side by side.

From these accumulated considerations it is evident that the only
government which can fully satisfy all the exigencies of the social state
is one in which the whole people participate; that any participation,
even in the smallest public function, is useful; that the participation
should everywhere be as great as the general degree of improvement of
the community will allow; and that nothing less can be ultimately
desirable than the admission of all to a share in the sovereign power of
the state. But since all cannot, in a community exceeding a single small
town, participate personally in any but some very minor portions of the
public business, it follows that the ideal type of a perfect government
must be representative.

16. CONSTANT
Liberty and Popular Despotism

The political activity of Benjamin Constant de Rebecque (1767–1830) reflects the crosscurrents of postrevolutionary French politics. Constant lived in exile during most of Napoleon's regime which he severely criticized. Yet he became a member of the French Council of State, after Napoleon's return from Elba, in an effort to liberalize the restored empire. He was a member of the Chamber of Deputies during the 1820's yet supported King Louis-Philippe in the revolution of 1830.

Constant's political writing, however, is remarkably consistent. His preference was for a parliamentary monarchy. In his two major works, *The Principles of Politics* and *The Spirit of Conquest*, as well as in his numerous pamphlets and speeches, he is concerned with safeguards for individual liberties. In particular, he stressed the new potential for abuse of freedom inherent in revolutionary zeal and popular sovereignty.

The first selection is taken from the first chapter of *Principles of Politics** which Constant published in 1815, three weeks before Waterloo. The other selections are from *The Spirit of Conquest,** first published in Paris in 1814.

THE PRINCIPLES OF POLITICS

Of the Sovereignty of the People

The error of those who, sincere in their love of freedom, have attributed unlimited power to the sovereign people, comes of the manner in which their ideas about politics have been formed. They have seen in history a few men, or even one man alone, possessed of immense and very harmful power; and their anger has turned against the possessors of power and not against power itself. Instead of destroying it, they dreamt only of displacing it. It was a scourge, but they looked

* From *Readings from Liberal Writers*, translated by John Plamenatz. (London: George Allen & Unwin, 1965.) Used by permission.

upon it as something to be conquered. They endowed society as a whole with it. And it passed perforce from the whole to the majority, and from the majority into the hands of a few men, and often of one man alone; and it has done as much harm as before. Manifold examples, objections, arguments and facts have been used to condemn all political institutions.

Certainly, in a society where the people's sovereignty is accepted as a basic principle, no man and no class may subject the others to his or their particular will; but it is not true that society as a whole possesses over its members an unlimited sovereignty.

The generality of citizens constitute the sovereign in the sense that no individual, no fraction, no partial association can assume the sovereignty unless it has been delegated to him or them. But it does not follow that the citizens generally, or those in whom they have vested the sovereignty, may dispose absolutely of the lives of individuals. On the contrary, there is a part of life which necessarily remains personal and independent, which of right is beyond the competence of society. Sovereignty can be only limited and relative. At the point where personal independence and life begin, the jurisdiction of the sovereign ceases. If society goes beyond this point, it is as guilty as the despot whose only title is the sword of the destroyer; society cannot pass beyond the sphere of its competence without usurpation, nor the majority without factiousness. The assent of the majority is not always enought to make its acts legitimate: there are some which nothing can justify. When authority commits such actions, it matters little from what source the authority is alleged to come, or whether it belongs to an individual or a nation; even when it is exercised by the whole nation, except for the citizen oppressed, it is not the more legitimate for that.

Rousseau failed to recognize this truth, and his error has made of his *Social Contract*, so often invoked in favour of liberty, the most terrible support of all kinds of despotism. He defines the contract made by society with its members as the complete and unreserved alienation of each individual with all his rights to the community. To reassure us about the consequences of so absolute a surrender of all aspects of our life to an abstract being, he tells us that the sovereign, that is to say the social body, cannot injure either its members in general or any one of them in particular; that, since each gives himself entire, the condition is the same for all, and none has an interest in making it burdensome to others; that each in giving himself to all gives himself to nobody, that each acquires over all his associates the rights which he grants to them, and gains the equivalent of all that he loses together with greater power to preserve what he has. But he forgets that all these preservative attributes which he confers on the abstract being he calls the sovereign derive from its including within it all individuals without exception. But, as soon as the sovereign has to make use of the power belonging to him—that is to say, as soon as authority has to be organized for practical purposes—the sovereign, since he cannot himself exercise it, must delegate it; and all these attributes disappear. Since the action taken in the name of all is willy nilly done by one person or by a few, it is not true that in giving oneself to all one gives oneself to no one; on the contrary, one gives oneself to those who act in the name of all. Whence it follows that, in giving oneself entire, one does not enter a condition which is equal for all, because there are some who alone benefit from the sacrifice of the others. It is not true that no one has an interest in making the condition a burden to others, since there are associates to whom the condition does not apply. It is not true that all the associates acquire over others the rights which they grant to them over themselves; they do not all gain the equivalent of what they lose, and what results from their sacrifice is, or may be, the establishment of a power which takes from them what they have.

Rousseau himself took fright at these consequences. Appalled by the immensity of the social power he had created, he did not know in what hands to place that monstrous power, and could find as a safeguard against the danger inseparable from sovereignty thus conceived only an expedient which made its exercise impossible. He declared that sovereignty could not be alienated or delegated or represented; which amounted to saying that it could not be exercised. This was to annihilate the principle he had just proclaimed. . . .

Where sovereignty is unlimited, there is no way of protecting the individual against the government. It is in vain that you claim to subject governments to the general will. It is they who give utterance to that will, and all precautions become illusory.

The people, says Rousseau, are sovereign in one respect, and subjects in another: but in practice these two respects merge into one another. Authority can easily oppress the people taken as subjects in order to compel them in their sovereign capacity to express a will prescribed to them by authority.

No political organization can remove this danger. It is in vain that you separate the powers: if the sum total of power is unlimited, the separate powers have only to make an alliance, and there is despotism without a remedy. What matters is not that our rights should be inviolable by one power without the approval of another, but that the violation be forbidden to all the powers. It is not enough that executive agents should have to invoke a grant of authority by the legislator; the legislator must be able to grant them authority to act only within a legitimate sphere. It is of little moment that the executive power should not have the right to act without the backing of the law, if limits are not set to that backing; if it is not laid down that there are matters about which the lawmaker may not make law—or, in other words, that sovereignty is limited, and there are decisions which neither the people nor their delegates have the right to make.

It is this that must be proclaimed; this, the important truth, the essential principle, to be established.

No authority on earth is unlimited; whether it resides in the people, or in the men who claim to be their representatives, or in kings, whatever their title to rule, or in the law, which, being only the expression of the people's or the prince's will (depending on the form of government), must be confined within the same limits as that will.

Citizens possess rights independently of all social or political authority, and every authority which violates these rights becomes illegitimate. These rights are freedom of person, of religious worship, and of opinion (including its publication), the enjoyment of property, and security against arbitrary power. No one in authority can infringe these rights without destroying his own title to authority. . . .

We owe to public tranquillity many sacrifices; and we should be morally to blame if, by holding inflexibly to our rights, we resisted all laws which appeared to us to impair them; but no duty binds us to those pretended laws whose corrupting influence threatens the noblest aspects of life, to the laws which not only restrict our legitimate rights but require of us actions contrary to the eternal principles of justice and compassion which man cannot cease to observe without degrading and belying his nature.

So long as a law, though a bad one, does not tend to deprave us, so long as the encroachments of authority require only sacrifices which do not make us vile or cruel, we can submit. We then make compromises which affect only ourselves. But if the law should require us to tread underfoot our affections or our duties; if, on the pretext of an extraordinary and factitious sacrifice, in favour either of the monarchy or the republic (as the case may be), it should forbid loyalty to friends in misfortune; if it should require us to betray our allies, or even to persecute vanquished enemies, anathema upon the promotion of injustices and crimes thus covered with the name of law!

Whenever a law appears unjust, it is a positive, general unrestricted duty not to become an executor of it. This force of inertia entails neither upheavals, nor revolutions, nor disorders.

Nothing justifies the man who gives his support to a law which he believes is iniquitous. . . .

OF THE SPIRIT OF CONQUEST

Of Uniformity

It is remarkable that uniformity should never have been more in favour than during a revolution made in the name of the rights and the liberty of men. At first, lovers of system were enraptured by symmetry. Then lovers of power discovered the immense advantage procured to them by this symmetry. Though patriotism is maintained by a lively attachment to local interests, manners and customs, our self-styled patriots have declared war on all that. They have dried up this natural source of patriotism, and have wanted to put in its place a factitious passion towards an abstract being, a general idea, stripped of everything that strikes the imagination and speaks to the memory. Before putting up the building, they pounded and reduced to powder the materials they had to use. It almost came to their designating cities and provinces by numbers, as they did legions and army corps, so great their apparent fear that some moral sentiment might attach itself to what they were setting up!

Despotism, which has taken the place of demagogy and made itself the heir of all its achievements, has kept skilfully to the road marked out for it. The two extremes found themselves at one on this point because, at bottom, there was in both of them a will to tyranny. Interests and memories born of local habits have in them a seed of resistance which authority suffers with reluctance and is eager to uproot. In this way it makes shorter work of individuals; and without effort rolls its enormous weight over them as over sand.

Today, admiration for uniformity, real in some limited minds and affected by many servile ones, is received as a religious dogma and is echoed again and again, assiduously, as becomes a favoured opinion. . . .

But every generation, says a foreigner among those who best foresaw our errors from the beginning, *every generation inherits from its ancestors a store of moral rights, an invisible and precious treasure which it leaves to its descendants.* For a people to lose this treasure is an incalculable evil. In depriving them of it, you take away from them all sense of their peculiar worth and dignity. Though what you put in its place may be of greater value, yet, since what you take away was respectable in their eyes and your improvements are imposed by force, your operation results only in their committing an act of cowardice which debases and demoralizes them. . . .

Nothing is more absurd than to do violence to men's habits on the pretext of serving their interests. Their prime interest is to be happy, and habits make up an essential part of happiness.

Clearly, peoples differently situated, raised to different customs, inhabiting dissimilar places, are not to be brought over to forms, usages, practices and laws that are completely alike except by a constraint which is more costly than profitable to them. The sequence of ideas gradually forming their moral being from the time of their birth cannot be altered by a purely nominal and external arrangement, independent of their will. Devotion to local customs is closely connected with all the disinterested, noble and pious sentiments. How deplorable the policy which makes rebellion of this devotion! For what then happens? In all States where vitality is destroyed in the parts, there forms a small state at the centre, and all interests are concentrated in the capital. There all ambitions are astir, but elsewhere nothing moves. Individuals, lost in unnatural isolation, strangers to the place of their birth, out of touch with the past, living in a hurried present, thrown like atoms on an immense and level plain, are detached from a fatherland nowhere visible to them, from the whole to which they grow indifferent because their affection can settle on none of its parts.

Variety is organic, and uniformity mechanical. Variety is life, uniformity is death. . . .

One cannot but regret the times when the earth was côvered with small peoples, numerous and full of life; when the human species was active and enterprising in all kinds of ways but always within a sphere proportionate to its strength. Authority did not then need to be harsh to get itself obeyed; liberty could be stormy without being anarchic; eloquence dominated men's minds and stirred their hearts; glory was within reach of talent, which, in its fight against mediocrity, was not submerged by wave upon wave of a heavy and numberless multitude;

morality found a support in a public made up of close neighbours, a public that was spectator and judge of all actions in their smallest details and most delicate shades of difference.

Those times are no more, and regrets are useless. But, at least, since we have to renounce all these advantages, we cannot too often repeat to the masters of the earth: that in their vast empires they leave in being as much variety as those empires allow of, the variety that nature calls for and experience consecrates. A rule is perverted when it is applied to cases too dissimilar; the yoke weighs heavy merely for being kept the same in too different circumstances.

Of the Means Employed to Give to the Moderns the Liberty of the Ancients

"To have tyranny," says Machiavelli, "one must change everything." It can also be said that to change everything, one must have tyranny. Our legislators felt it was so, and proclaimed that despotism is indispensable to lay the foundations of liberty.

There are axioms which seem clear because they are short. Artful men throw them as fodder to the crowd; fools take hold of them to save themselves the trouble of thinking, and repeat them to give the impression of understanding them. Propositions whose absurdity astonishes us, when they are analysed, slide in this way into a thousand heads, are rehearsed by a thousand mouths, and one is reduced to endlessly proving the obvious.

Of these is the axiom we have just cited; for ten years it has resounded on all the platforms of France. What then does it mean? Freedom is of an inestimable price only because it gives sound judgment to the mind, strength to the character, elevation to the soul. But do not these benefits come of having freedom? If, to bring in freedom, you resort to despotism, what do you establish? Mere empty forms. The substance eludes you always.

What must one say to a people to bring home to them the advantages of freedom?—You were oppressed by a privileged minority: the great majority were sacrificed to the ambition of a few; unequal laws supported the strong against the weak; you had only precarious enjoyments, which arbitrary power threatened to take from you at any moment; you took no part in making your laws or electing your magistrates. All these abuses will disappear, all your rights will be restored to you.

As for those who claim to establish freedom by means of despotism, what can they say?—There will be no privileges bearing heavily upon the citizens, but each day suspects will be struck down without being heard; virtue will be the first or the sole distinction, but the most violent persecutors will set themselves up as a patrician order of tyrants maintained by terror; the laws will protect property, but expropriation will be the lot of suspect individuals and classes; the people will elect their magistrates, but if they do not elect in the way prescribed in advance, their votes will be declared invalid; opinions will be free, but every opinion opposed, not only to the system, but to any chance measure, will be punished as an outrage.

Such was the language and such the practice of the reformers of France during long years.

They gained seeming victories, but victories contrary to the spirit of what they wanted to establish; and, since these victories did not persuade the vanquished, they failed to reassure the victors. That they might be formed for liberty, men were held close by fear of drastic punishments; the attempts of the old authority to restrict freedom of thought were traduced, while the enslavement of thought was the mark of the new authority; tyrannical governments were denounced, and there was organized the most tyrannical of governments.

Liberty was adjourned, it was said, until the factions should have calmed down; but factions grow calmer only when liberty is not adjourned. Violent measures taken dictatorially while the birth of a public spirit is awaited prevent that birth; there is movement in a vicious circle; a period is appointed which assuredly can never be reached, for the means chosen to reach it do not allow of its coming. Force makes force always more necessary, anger thrives on anger, laws are made to be used as weapons, and codes become declarations of war; and the blind friends of liberty, who thought to impose it by despotism, raise up against them all free souls, and to support them have only the basest flatterers of power.

In the front rank of the enemies whom our demagogues had to fight were the classes that used to benefit from the social order now destroyed, and whose privileges, though perhaps unjustified, had yet been means to leisure, improvement and enlightenment. A large independent fortune is security against several forms of baseness and vice. To be sure of respect is to be preserved from the anxious and susceptible vanity which everywhere sees insults and suspects disdain; an implacable passion which takes vengeance in the evil it does for the pain it endures. Gentle manners and the habit of fine discrimination give to the soul a delicate sensibility and make the mind quick and supple.

These precious qualities should have been put to good use, and the spirit of chivalry bridled but given its head in the courses which nature makes common to us all. The Greeks spared the prisoners who recited the verses of Euripides. The least flicker of light, germ of thought, gentle feeling, elegant form, must be carefully protected. They are so many elements indispensable to the happiness of society; they must be preserved from the storm; they must be so, both for the sake of justice and for the sake of freedom; for all these things converge upon freedom by ways more or less direct. . . .

In all violent encounters, interests come hurrying in the wake of impassioned beliefs, as birds of prey follow armies prepared for battle. Hatred, vengeance, cupidity, ingratitude impudently parodied the noblest examples, held up crudely for imitation. The perfidious friend, the defaulting debtor, the obscure informer, the prevaricating judge found their apologies written out in advance in conventional phrases. Patriotism came to be the trite excuse made ready for all crimes. The great sacrifices, the acts of devotion, the victories over natural inclination of the austere republicans of antiquity served as a pretext for giving a loose to selfish passions. Because, long ago, inexorable but just fathers had condemned their guilty sons, their modern imitators delivered innocent enemies to the executioner. There was no safety even in being obscure, in keeping quiet, in having an unknown name. Inaction was taken for crime, the domestic affections for indifference to the fatherland and happiness for suspect desire. The crowd, corrupted by both danger and example, tremulously repeated the slogan required of them, and took fright at the sound of their own voice. Everyone formed part of the multitude, and was afraid of the multitude he helped to enlarge. It was then that there spread over France the unaccountable lightheadedness which has been called the reign of terror. Who can be surprised that the people have turned away from the goal to which it was intended to lead them by such a road?

Not only do extremes touch, but they follow one another. An excess always produces its opposite. When certain ideas have come to be associated with certain words, it is in vain that we prove the association to be an abuse of language; the repeated words long recall the same ideas. In the name of liberty there were brought to us prisons, scaffolds and innumerable vexations; this name, calling to mind a thousand odious and tyrannical measures, could not but awaken hatred and fear.

But are we to conclude from this that the peoples of today are inclined to resign themselves to despotism? What was it then that moved them to resist stubbornly what was offered to them for liberty? It was their resolve not to sacrifice their repose or their habits or their enjoyments. And, since despotism is the irreconcilable enemy of all repose and all enjoyments, does it not follow that these peoples, believing that liberty was abhorrent to them, have abhorred only despotism?

Of the Effects of Arbitrary Power on Diverse Parts of Human Life

Arbitrary power, whether exercised in the name of one person or of all, reaches to all that makes for human tranquility and happiness.

It destroys morality, for there is no morality without security; there are no gentle affections without assurance that their objects rest secure, made safe by their innocence. When arbitrary power strikes without scruple at men who are suspect to it, it does not persecute one man alone; it rouses a whole people to indignation and afterwards degrades them. Men incline always to free themselves from pain. When what they love is threatened, they either detach themselves from it or defend it. Morals, says M. de Paw, are corrupted suddenly in towns attacked by the plague; men steal from one another as they die. Arbitrary power is to morals what the plague is to the body. Everyone repels the companion in misfortune who wishes to cling to him; everyone abjures the ties of his past. He stands aloof the better to defend himself, and sees in entreaties inspired by weakness or friendship only obstacles to his own safety. One thing alone keeps its price: it is not public opinion, for there is no more glory for the powerful and no respect for victims; it is not justice, for its laws are disregarded and its forms profaned: it is wealth. Wealth can disarm tyranny; it can seduce some of its agents, appease the proscriber, make flight easier, and add a few passing pleasures to a life that is always threatened. Men accumulate in order to enjoy; they enjoy in order to forget inevitable dangers. Faced with the misfortunes of others they are hard, and are careless of their own; they see blood flow in the neighbourhood of festivals; they stifle sympathy with Stoical ferocity; they snatch eagerly at pleasure like voluptuous sybarites.

When a people look indifferently on one act of tyranny after another, when without a murmur they see the prisons filled to overflowing, and letters of exile multiplied, are we to believe that, in such hateful circumstances, a few trite phrases will be enough to bring honest and generous sentiments back to life? Men speak of the need for paternal authority but the first duty of a son is to defend his father who is oppressed. And when you take a father away from his children, and impose a cowardly silence on them, what then is the effect of your maxims and your codes, your pronouncements and your laws? Men pay homage to the sanctity of marriage, but on a secret denunciation or a bare suspicion, by what is called a police measure, a husband is parted from his wife, a wife from her husband! Are we to believe that conjugal love dies and is reborn, as it suits authority? Men speak highly of domestic ties; but the confirmation of these ties is personal liberty, the well-grounded hope of living together, of living in freedom, in the asylum which justice secures to the citizen. If domestic ties really existed, would fathers, children, husbands, wives, friends, would the persons close to those oppressed by arbitrary power, submit to that power? Men speak of credit, of commerce, of industry; but the man arrested has creditors whose fortunes depend on his, associates with an interest in his enterprises. His detention does not merely deprive him of liberty for a time, but interrupts his business operations, and perhaps ruins him. This ruin extends to all who have a part in his interests. It extends even further; it strikes at all opinions, and makes everyone feel less secure. When anyone is made to suffer without having been found guilty, everyone not bereft of intelligence feels himself threatened, and with good reason, for the guarantee is destroyed. Men keep silent because they are afraid; but all dealings between them are affected thereby. The earth shakes and men walk upon it fearfully.

17. DE TOCQUEVILLE

Equality and Liberty

Alexis de Tocqueville (1805–59) visited America in 1831 for about one year. *Democracy in America* was published in 1835 and upon publication was ranked with Montesquieu's *Spirit of the Laws* as a major contribution to the study of politics. There is a suggestive parallel with *Spirit of the Laws*. Montesquieu had visited England and on the basis of his interpretation of

British political institutions formulated for Continental liberalism a continuing concern with separation of powers. De Tocqueville visited America and from his essentially favorable view of democratic development there formulated for liberalism a forceful argument on the compatibility of democracy with freedom.

In particular, there are three special claims of de Tocqueville for European liberalism. *Democracy in America* was the first work to focus on the significance of the American Revolution, and especially Jacksonian democracy for European political theory. Second, like Constant's work, it was especially prophetic about the dangers of democratic despotism. Finally, in a period in which French politics oscillated intensely between dictatorship, revolution, and monarchy, it suggested the program of bourgeois liberalism.

De Tocqueville's political career, subsequent to publication of *Democracy in America*, was consistent with the political views developed there. He was a member of the Chamber of Deputies in opposition to the government of Louis-Philippe, was elected to the legislative Assembly of the Second Republic in 1849, and withdrew from political life with the emergence of the dictatorship of Napoleon III, which he denounced as a regime of military terror.

The selection is from *Democracy in America*, in the Henry Reeve translation.

THAT EQUALITY NATURALLY GIVES MEN A TASTE FOR FREE INSTITUTIONS

The principle of equality, which makes men independent of each other, gives them a habit and a taste for following, in their private actions, no other guide but their own will. This complete independence, which they constantly enjoy towards their equals and in the intercourse of private life, tends to make them look upon all authority with a jealous eye, and speedily suggests to them the notion and the love of political freedom. Men living at such times have a natural bias to free institutions. Take any one of them at a venture, and search if you can his most deep-seated instincts; you will find that of all governments he will soonest conceive and most highly value that government, whose head he has himself elected, and whose administration he may control.

Of all the political effects produced by the equality of conditions, this love of independence is the first to strike the observing, and to alarm the timid; nor can it be said that their alarm is wholly misplaced, for anarchy has a more formidable aspect in democratic countries than elsewhere. As the citizens have no direct influence on each other, as soon as the supreme power of the nation fails, which kept them all in their several stations, it would seem that disorder must instantly reach its utmost pitch, and that, every man drawing aside in a different direction, the fabric of society must at once crumble away.

I am however persuaded that anarchy is not the principal evil which democratic ages have to fear, but the least. For the principle of equality begets two tendencies; the one leads men straight to independence, and may suddenly drive them into anarchy; the other conducts them by a longer, more secret, but more certain road, to servitude. Nations readily discern the former tendency, and are prepared to resist it; they are led away by the latter, without perceiving its drift; hence it is peculiarly important to point it out.

For myself, I am so far from urging as a reproach to the principle of equality that it renders men untractable, that this very circumstance principally calls forth my approbation. I admire to see how it deposits in the mind and heart of man the dim conception and instinctive love of political independence, thus preparing the remedy for the evil which it engenders: it is on this very account that I am attached to it.

THAT THE NOTIONS OF DEMOCRATIC NATIONS ON GOVERNMENT ARE NATURALLY FAVOURABLE TO THE CONCENTRATION OF POWER

The notion of secondary powers, placed between the sovereign and his subjects, occurred naturally to the imagination of aristocratic nations, because those communities contained individuals or families raised above the common level, and apparently destined to command by their birth, their education, and their wealth. This same notion is naturally wanting in the minds of men in democratic ages, for converse reasons; it can only be introduced artificially, it can only be kept there with difficulty; whereas they conceive, as it were without thinking upon the subject, the notion of a sole and central power which governs the whole community by its direct influence. . . .

The very next notion to that of a sole and central power, which presents itself to the minds of men in the ages of equality, is the notion of uniformity of legislation. As every man sees that he differs but little from those about him, he cannot understand why a rule which is applicable to one man should not be equally applicable to all others. Hence the slightest privileges are repugnant to his reason; the faintest dissimilarities in the political institutions of the same people offend him, and uniformity of legislation appears to him to be the first condition of good government. . . .

As the conditions of men become equal amongst a people, individuals seem of less importance, and society of greater dimensions; or rather, every citizen, being assimilated to all the rest, is lost in the crowd, and nothing stands conspicuous but the great and imposing image of the people at large. This naturally gives the men of democratic periods a lofty opinion of the privileges of society, and a very humble notion of the rights of individuals; they are ready to admit that the interests of the former are everything, and those of the latter nothing. They are willing to acknowledge that the power which represents the community has far more information and wisdom than any of the members of that community; and that it is the duty, as well as the right of that power to guide as well as govern each private citizen. . . .

The unity, the ubiquity, the omnipotence of the supreme power, and the uniformity of its rules, constitute the principal characteristics of all the political systems which have been put forward in our age. They recur even in the wildest visions of political regeneration: the human mind pursues them in its dreams. . . .

Our contemporaries are therefore much less divided than is commonly supposed; they are constantly disputing as to the hands in which supremacy is to be vested, but they readily agree upon the duties and the rights of that supremacy. The notion they all form of government is that of a sole, simple, providential, and creative power. . . .

OF CERTAIN PECULIAR AND ACCIDENTAL CAUSES WHICH EITHER LEAD A PEOPLE TO COMPLETE CENTRALIZATION OF GOVERNMENT, OR WHICH DIVERT THEM FROM IT

. . . I have said that amongst democratic nations the notion of government naturally presents itself to the mind under the form of a sole and central power, and that the notion of intermediate powers is not familiar to them. This is peculiarly applicable to the democratic nations which have witnessed the triumph of the principle of equality by means of a violent revolution. As the classes which managed local affairs have been suddenly swept away by the storm, and as the confused mass which remains has as yet neither the organization nor the habits which fit it to assume the administration of these same affairs, the State alone seems capable of taking upon itself all the details of government, and centralization becomes, as it were, the unavoidable state of the country. . . .

. . . If at all times education enables men to defend their independence, this is most especially true in democratic ages. When all men are alike, it is easy to found a sole and all-powerful government, by the aid of mere instinct. But men require much intelligence, knowledge, and art to organize and to maintain secondary powers under similar circumstances, and to create amidst the independence and individual weakness of the citizens such free associations as may be in a condition to struggle against tyranny without destroying public order.

Hence the concentration of power and the subjection of individuals will increase amongst democratic nations, not only in the same proportion as their equality, but in the same proportion as their ignorance. It is true, that in ages of imperfect civilization the government is frequently as wanting in the knowledge required to impose a despotism upon the people as the people are wanting in the knowledge required to shake it off; but the effect is not the same on both sides. However rude a democratic people may be, the central power which rules it is never completely devoid of cultivation, because it readily draws to its own uses what little cultivation is to be found in the country, and, if necessary, may seek assistance elsewhere. Hence, amongst a nation which is ignorant as well as democratic, an amazing difference cannot fail speedily to arise between the intellectual capacity of the ruler and that of each of his subjects. This completes the easy concentration of all power in his hands: the administrative function of the State is perpetually extended, because the State alone is competent to administer the affairs of the country. . . .

I think that extreme centralization of government ultimately enervates society, and thus after a length of time weakens the government itself; but I do not deny that a centralized social power may be able to execute great undertakings with facility in a given time and on a particular point. This is more especially true of war, in which success depends much more on the means of transferring all the resources of a nation to one single point, than on the extent of those resources. Hence it is chiefly in war that nations desire and frequently require to increase the powers of the central government. All men of military genius are fond of centralization, which increases their strength; and all men of centralizing genius are fond of war, which compels nations to combine all their powers in the hands of the government. Thus the democratic tendency which leads men unceasingly to multiply the privileges of the state, and to circumscribe the rights of private persons, is much more rapid and constant amongst those democratic nations which are exposed by their position to great and frequent wars, than amongst all others.

I have shown how the dread of disturbance and the love of well-being insensibly lead democratic nations to increase the functions of central government, as the only power which appears to be intrinsically sufficiently strong, enlightened, and secure, to protect them from anarchy. I would now add, that all the particular circumstances which tend to make the state of a democratic community agitated and precarious, enhance this general propensity, and lead private persons more and more to sacrifice their rights to their tranquillity.

A people is therefore never so disposed to increase the functions of central government as at the close of a long and bloody revolution, which, after having wrested property from the hands of its former possessors, has shaken all belief, and filled the nation with fierce hatreds, conflicting interests, and contending factions. The love of public tranquillity becomes at such times an indiscriminating passion, and the members of the community are apt to conceive a most inordinate devotion to order. . . .

A revolution which overthrows an ancient regal family, in order to place men of more recent growth at the head of a democratic people, may temporarily weaken the central power; but however anarchical such a revolution may appear at first, we need not hesitate to predict that its final and certain consequence will be to extend and to secure the prerogatives of that power.

The foremost or indeed the sole condition which is required in order to succeed in centralizing the supreme power in a democratic community, is to love equality, or to get men to believe you love it. Thus the science of despotism, which was once so complex, is simplified, and reduced as it were to a single principle. . . .

THAT AMONGST THE EUROPEAN NATIONS OF OUR TIME THE POWER OF GOVERNMENTS IS INCREASING, ALTHOUGH THE PERSONS WHO GOVERN ARE LESS STABLE

. . . Europe has endured, in the course of the last half-century, many revolutions and counter-revolutions which have agitated it in opposite directions: but all these perturbations resemble each other in one respect,—they have all shaken or destroyed the secondary powers of government. . . .

My object is to remark, that all these various rights, which have been successively wrested, in our time, from classes, corporations, and individuals, have not served to raise new secondary powers on a more democratic basis, but have uniformly been concentrated in the hands of the sovereign. Everywhere the State acquires more and more direct control over the humblest members of the community, and a more exclusive power of governing each of them in his smallest concerns.

Almost all the charitable establishments of Europe were formerly in the hands of private persons or of corporations; they are now almost all dependent on the supreme government, and in many countries are actually administered by that power. The State almost exclusively undertakes to supply bread to the hungry, assistance and shelter to the sick, work to the idle, and to act as the sole reliever of all kinds of misery.

Education, as well as charity, is become in most countries at the present day a national concern. The State receives, and often takes, the child from the arms of the mother, to hand it over to official agents: the State undertakes to train the heart and to instruct the mind of each generation. Uniformity prevails in the courses of public instruction as in everything else; diversity, as well as freedom, are disappearing day by day. . . .

But this is as yet only one side of the picture. The authority of government has not only spread, as we have just seen, throughout the sphere of all existing powers, till that sphere can no longer contain it, but it goes further, and invades the domain heretofore reserved to private independence. A multitude of actions, which were formerly entirely beyond the control of the public administration, have been subjected to that control in our time, and the number of them is constantly increasing. . . .

I assert that there is no country in Europe in which the public administration has not become, not only more centralized, but more inquisitive and more minute: it everywhere interferes in private concerns more than it did; it regulates more undertakings, and undertakings of a lesser kind; and it gains a firmer footing every day about, above, and around all private persons, to assist, to advise, and to coerce them. . . .

If the reader, after having investigated these details of human affairs, will seek to survey the wide prospect as a whole, he will be struck by the result. On the one hand the most settled dynasties shaken or over-thrown;—the people everywhere escaping by violence from the sway of their laws,—abolishing or limiting the authority of their rulers or their princes;—the nations, which are not in open revolution, restless at least, and excited,—all of them animated by the same spirit of revolt: and on the other hand, at this very period of anarchy, and amongst these untractable nations, the incessant increase of the prerogative of the supreme government, becoming more centralized, more adventurous, more absolute, more extensive:—the people perpetually falling under the control of the public administration,—led insensibly to surrender to it some further portion of their individual independence, till the very men, who from time to time upset a throne and trample on a race of kings, bend more and more obsequiously to the slightest dictate of a clerk. Thus, two contrary revolutions appear, in our days, to be going on; the one continually weakening the supreme power, the other as continually strengthening it: at no other period in our history has it appeared so weak or so strong.

But upon a more attentive examination of the state of the world, it appears that these two revolutions are intimately connected together, that they originate in the same source, and that after having followed a separate course, they lead men at last to the same result. . . .

All the old political powers of Europe, the greatest as well as the least, were founded in ages of aristocracy, and they more or less represented or defended the principles of inequality and of privilege. To make the novel wants and interests, which the growing principle of equality introduced, preponderate in government, our contemporaries had to overturn or to coerce the established powers. This led them to make revolutions, and breathed into many of them, that fierce love of dis-turbance and independence, which all revolutions, whatever be their object, always engender.

I do not believe that there is a single country in Europe in which the progress of equality has not been preceded or followed by some violent changes in the state of property and persons; and almost all these changes have been attended with much anarchy and licence, because they have been made by the least civilized portion of the nation against that which is most civilized.

Hence proceeded the twofold contrary tendencies which I have just pointed out. As long as the democratic revolution was glowing with heat, the men who were bent upon the destruction of old aristocratic powers hostile to that revolution, displayed a strong spirit of independence; but as the victory or the principle of equality became more complete, they gradually surrendered themselves to the propensities natural to that condition of equality, and they strengthened and centralized their governments. They had sought to be free in order to make themselves equal; but in proportion as equality was more established by the aid of freedom, freedom itself was thereby rendered of more difficult attainment.

These two states of a nation have sometimes been contemporaneous: the last generation in France showed how a people might organize a stupendous tyranny in the community, at the very time when they were baffling the authority of the nobility and braving the power of all kings,—at once teaching the world the way to win freedom, and the way to lose it.

In our days men see that constituted powers are dilapidated on every side—they see all ancient authority gasping away, all ancient barriers tottering to their fall, and the judgment of the wisest is troubled at the sight: they attend only to the amazing revolution which is taking place before their eyes, and they imagine that mankind is about to fall into perpetual anarchy: if they looked to the final consequences of this revolution, their fears would perhaps assume a different shape. For myself, I confess that I put no trust in the spirit of freedom which appears to animate my contemporaries. I see well enough that the nations of this age are turbulent, but I do not clearly perceive that they are liberal; and I fear lest, at the close of those perturbations which rock the base of thrones, the domination of sovereigns may prove more powerful than it ever was before.

WHAT SORT OF DESPOTISM DEMOCRATIC NATIONS HAVE TO FEAR

No sovereign ever lived in former ages so absolute or so powerful as to undertake to administer by his own agency, and without the assistance of intermediate powers, all the parts of a great empire: none ever attempted to subject all his subjects indiscriminately to strict uniformity of regulation, and personally to tutor and direct every member of the community. The notion of such an undertaking never occurred to the human mind; and if any man had conceived it, the want of information, the imperfection of the administrative system, and above all, the natural obstacles caused by the inequality of conditions, would speedily have checked the execution of so vast a design.

When the Roman emperors were at the height of their power, the different nations of the empire still preserved manners and customs of great diversity; although they were subject to the same monarch, most of the provinces were separately administered; they abounded in powerful and active municipalities; and although the whole government of the empire was centred in the hands of the emperor alone, and he always remained, upon occasions, the supreme arbiter in all matters, yet the details of social life and private occupations lay for the most part beyond his control. The emperors possessed, it is true, an immense and unchecked power, which allowed them to gratify all their whimsical tastes, and to employ for that purpose the whole strength of the State. They frequently abused that power arbitrarily to deprive their subjects of property or of life: their tyranny was extremely onerous to the few, but it did not reach the greater number; it was fixed to some few main objects, and neglected the rest; it was violent, but its range was limited.

But it would seem that if despotism were to be established amongst the democratic nations of our days, it might assume a different character; it would be more extensive and more mild; it could degrade men without tormenting them. I do not question, that in an age of instruction and equality like our own, sovereigns might more easily succeed in collecting all political power into their own hands, and might interfere more habitually and decidedly within the circle of private interests, than any sovereign of antiquity could ever do. But this same principle of equality which facilitates despotism, tempers its rigour. We have seen how the manners of society become more humane and gentle in proportion as men become more equal and alike. When no member of the community has much power or much wealth, tyranny is, as it were, without opportunities and a field of action. As all fortunes are scanty, the passions of men are naturally circumscribed—their imagination limited, their pleasures simple. This universal moderation moderates the sovereign himself, and checks within certain limits the inordinate stretch of his desires. . . .

I think then that the species of oppression by which democratic nations are menaced is unlike anything which ever before existed in the world; our contemporaries will find no prototype of it in their memories. I am trying myself to choose an expression which will accurately convey the whole of the idea I have formed of it, but in vain; the old words despotism and tyranny are inappropriate: the thing itself is new; and since I cannot name it, I must attempt to define it.

I seek to trace the novel features under which despotism may appear in the world. The first thing that strikes the observation is an innumerable multitude of men all equal and alike, incessantly endeavouring to procure the petty and paltry pleasures with which they glut their lives. Each of them, living apart, is as a stranger to the fate of all the rest,— his children and his private friends constitute to him the whole of mankind; as for the rest of his fellow-citizens, he is close to them, but he sees them not;—he touches them, but he feels. them not; he exists but in himself and for himself alone; and if his kindred still remain to him, he may be said at any rate to have lost his country.

Above this race of men stands an immense and tutelary power, which takes upon itself alone to secure their gratifications, and to watch over their fate. That power is absolute, minute, regular, provident, and mild. It would be like the authority of a parent, if, like that authority, its object was to prepare men for manhood; but it seeks on the contrary to keep them in perpetual childhood; it is well content that the people should rejoice, provided they think of nothing but rejoicing. For their happiness such a government willingly labours, but it chooses to be the sole agent and the only arbiter of that happiness: it provides for their security, foresees and supplies their necessities, facilitates their pleasures, manages their principal concerns, directs their industry, regulates the descent of property, and subdivides their inheritances—what remains, but to spare them all the care of thinking and all the trouble of living?

Thus it every day renders the exercise of the free agency of man less useful and less frequent; it circumscribes the will within a narrower range, and gradually robs a man of all the uses of himself. The principle of equality has prepared men for these things: it has predisposed men to endure them, and oftentimes to look on them as benefits.

After having thus successively taken each member of the community in its powerful grasp, and fashioned them at will, the supreme power then extends its arm over the whole community. It covers the surface of society with a network of small complicated rules, minute and uniform, through which the most original minds and the most energetic characters cannot penetrate, to rise above the crowd. The will of man is not shattered, but softened, bent, and guided: men are seldom forced by it to act, but they are constantly restrained from acting: such a power does not destroy, but it prevents existence; it does not tyrannize, but it compresses, enervates, extinguishes, and stupefies a people, till each nation is reduced to be nothing better than a flock of timid and industrious animals, of which the government is the shepherd.

I have always thought that servitude of the regular, quiet and gentle kind which I have just described, might be combined more easily than is commonly believed with some of the outward forms of freedom; and that it might even establish itself under the wing of the sovereignty of the people.

Our contemporaries are constantly excited by two conflicting passions; they want to be led, and they wish to remain free: as they cannot destroy either one or the other of these contrary propensities, they strive to satisfy them both at once. They devise a sole, tutelary, and all-powerful form of government, but elected by the people. They combine the principle of centralization and that of popular sovereignty; this gives them a respite: they console themselves for being in tutelage by the reflection that they have chosen their own guardians. Every man allows himself to be put in leading-strings, because he sees that it is not a person or a class of persons, but the people at large that holds the end of his chain.

By this system the people shake off their state of dependence just long enough to select their master, and then relapse into it again. A great many persons at the present day are quite contented with this sort of compromise between administrative despotism and the sovereignty of the people; and they think they have done enough for the protection of individual freedom when they have surrendered it to the power of the nation at large. This does not satisfy me: the nature of him I am to obey signifies less to me than the fact of extorted obedience.

I do not however deny that a constitution of this kind appears to me to be infinitely preferable to one, which, after having concentrated all the powers of government, should vest them in the hands of an irresponsible person or body of persons. Of all the forms which democratic despotism could assume, the latter would assuredly be the worst.

When the sovereign is elective, or narrowly watched by a legislature which is really elective and independent, the oppression which he exercises over individuals is sometimes greater, but it is always less degrading; because every man, when he is oppressed and disarmed, may still imagine, that whilst he yields obedience it is to himself he yields it, and that it is to one of his own inclinations that all the rest give way. In like manner I can understand that when the sovereign represents the nation, and is dependent upon the people, the rights and the power of which every citizen is deprived, not only serve the head of the state, but the state itself; and that private persons derive some return from the sacrifice of their independence which they have made to the public. To create a representation of the people in every centralized country is, therefore, to diminish the evil which extreme centralization may produce, but not to get rid of it.

I admit that by this means room is left for the intervention of individuals in the more important affairs; but it is not the less suppressed in the smaller and more private ones. It must not be forgotten that it is especially dangerous to enslave men in the minor details of life. For my own part, I should be inclined to think freedom less necessary in great things than in little ones, if it were possible to be secure of the one without possessing the other.

Subjection in minor affairs breaks out every day, and is felt by the whole community indiscriminately. It does not drive men to resistance, but it crosses them at every turn, till they are led to surrender the exercise of their will. Thus their spirit is gradually broken and their character enervated; whereas that obedience, which is exacted on a few important but rare occasions, only exhibits servitude at certain intervals, and throws the burden of it upon a small number of men. It is in vain to summon a people, which has been rendered so dependent on the central power, to choose from time to time the representatives of that power; this rare and brief exercise of their free choice, however important it may be, will not prevent them from gradually losing the faculties of thinking, feeling, and acting for themselves, and thus gradually falling below the level of humanity.

I add that they will soon become incapable of exercising the great and only privilege which remains to them. The democratic nations which have introduced freedom into their political constitution, at the very time when they were augmenting the despotism of their administrative constitution, have been led into strange paradoxes. To manage those minor affairs in which good sense is all that is wanted,—the people are held to be unequal to the task; but when the government of the country is at stake, the people are invested with immense powers; they are alternately made the playthings of their ruler, and his masters— more than kings, and less than men. After having exhausted all the different modes of election, without finding one to suit their purpose, they are still amazed, and still bent on seeking further; as if the evil they remark did not originate in the constitution of the country far more than in that of the electoral body.

It is, indeed, difficult to conceive how men who have entirely given up the habit of self-government should succeed in making a proper choice of those by whom they are to be governed; and no one will ever believe that a liberal, wise, and energetic government can spring from the suffrages of a subservient people.

A constitution, which should be republican in its head and ultra-monarchical in all its other parts, has ever appeared to me to be a short-lived monster. The vices of rulers and the ineptitude of the people would speedily bring about its ruin; and the nation, weary of its representatives and of itself, would create freer institutions, or soon return to stretch itself at the feet of a single master.

CONTINUATION OF THE PRECEDING CHAPTERS

I believe that it is easier to establish an absolute and despotic government amongst a people in which the conditions of society are equal, than amongst any other; and I think that if such a government were once established amongst such a people, it would not only oppress men, but would eventually strip each of them of several of the highest qualities of humanity. Despotism therefore appears to me peculiarly to be dreaded in democratic ages. I should have loved freedom, I believe, at all times, but in the time in which we live I am ready to worship it.

On the other hand, I am persuaded that all who shall attempt, in the ages upon which we are entering, to base freedom upon aristocratic privilege, will fail;—that all who shall attempt to draw and to retain authority within a single class, will fail. . . . Thus the question is not how to reconstruct aristocratic society, but how to make liberty proceed out of that democratic state of society in which God has placed us.

These two truths appear to me simple, clear, and fertile in consequences; and they naturally lead me to consider what kind of free government can be established amongst a people in which social conditions are equal.

It results from the very constitution of democratic nations and from their necessities, that the power of government amongst them must be more uniform, more centralized, more extensive, more searching, and more efficient than in other countries. Society at large is naturally stronger and more active, individuals more subordinate and weak; the former does more, the latter less; and this is inevitably the case.

It is not therefore to be expected that the range of private independence will ever be as extensive in democratic as in aristocratic countries;—nor is this to be desired; for, amongst aristocratic nations, the mass is often sacrificed to the individual, and the prosperity of the greater number to the greatness of the few. It is both necessary and desirable that the government of a democratic people should be active and powerful: and our object should not be to render it weak or indolent, but solely to prevent it from abusing its aptitude and its strength.

The circumstance which most contributed to secure the independence of private persons in aristocratic ages, was, that the supreme power did not affect to take upon itself alone the government and administration of the community; those functions were necessarily partially left to the members of the aristocracy: so that as the supreme power was always divided, it never weighed with its whole weight and in the same manner on each individual. . . .

I readily admit that recourse cannot be had to the same means at the present time: but I discover certain democratic expedients which may be substituted for them. Instead of vesting in the government alone all the administrative powers of which corporations and nobles have been deprived, a portion of them may be entrusted to secondary public bodies, temporarily composed of private citizens: thus the liberty of private persons will be more secure, and their equality will not be diminished. . . .

Aristocratic countries abound in wealthy and influential persons who are competent to provide for themselves, and who cannot be easily or secretly oppressed: such persons restrain a government within general habits of moderation and reserve. I am very well aware that democratic countries contain no such persons naturally; but something analogous to them may be created by artificial means. I firmly believe that an aristocracy cannot again be founded in the world; but I think that private citizens, by combining together, may constitute bodies of great wealth, influence, and strength, corresponding to the persons of an aristocracy. By this means many of the greatest political advantages of aristocracy would be obtained without its injustice or its dangers. An association for political, commercial, or manufacturing purposes, or even for those of science and literature, is a powerful and enlightened member of the community, which cannot be disposed of at pleasure, or oppressed without remonstrance: and which, by defending its own rights against the encroachments of the government, saves the common liberties of the country. . . .

Men living in democratic ages do not readily comprehend the utility of forms: they feel an instinctive contempt for them—I have elsewhere shown for what reasons. Forms excite their contempt and often their hatred; as they commonly aspire to none but easy and present gratifications, they rush onwards to the object of their desires, and the slightest delay exasperates them. This same temper, carried with them into

political life, renders them hostile to forms, which perpetually retard
or arrest them in some of their projects.

Yet this objection which the men of democracies make to forms is the
very thing which renders forms so useful to freedom; for their chief
merit is to serve as a barrier between the strong and the weak, the ruler
and the people, to retard the one, and give the other time to look about
him. Forms become more necessary in proportion as the government
becomes more active and more powerful, whilst private persons are
becoming more indolent and more feeble. Thus democratic nations
stand more in need of forms than other nations, and they naturally
respect them less. . . .

Another tendency, which is extremely natural to democratic nations
and extremely dangerous, is that which leads them to despise and undervalue the rights of private persons. The attachment which men feel to
a right, and the respect which they display for it, is generally proportioned to its importance, or to the length of time during which they
have enjoyed it. The rights of private persons amongst democratic
nations are commonly of small importance, of recent growth, and
extremely precarious,—the consequence is that they are often sacrificed
without regret, and almost always violated without remorse.

But it happens that at the same period and amongst the same nations
in which men conceive a natural contempt for the rights of private
persons, the rights of society at large are naturally extended and consolidated: in other words, men become less attached to private rights
at the very time at which it would be most necessary to retain and to
defend what little remains of them. It is therefore most especially in
the present democratic ages, that the true friends of the liberty and the
greatness of man ought constantly to be on the alert to prevent the
power of government from lightly sacrificing the private rights of
individuals to the general execution of its designs. At such times no
citizen is so obscure that it is not very dangerous to allow him to be
oppressed—no private rights are so unimportant that they can be surrendered with impunity to the caprices of a government. The reason is
plain:—if the private right of an individual is violated at a time when
the human mind is fully impressed with the importance and the sanctity
of such rights, the injury done is confined to the individual whose right
is infringed; but to violate such a right, at the present day, is deeply to
corrupt the manners of the nation and to put the whole community in
jeopardy, because the very notion of this kind of right constantly tends
amongst us to be impaired and lost. . . .

I shall conclude by one general idea, which comprises not only all the particular ideas which have been expressed in the present chapter, but also most of those which it is the object of this book to treat of. In the ages of aristocracy which preceded our own, there were private persons of great power, and a social authority of extreme weakness. The outline of society itself was not easily discernible, and constantly confounded with the different powers by which the community was ruled. The principal efforts of the men of those times were required to strengthen, aggrandise, and secure the supreme power; and on the other hand, to circumscribe individual independence within narrower limits, and to subject private interests to the interests of the public. Other perils and other cares await the men of our age. Amongst the greater part of modern nations, the government, whatever may be its origin, its constitution, or its name, has become almost omnipotent, and private persons are falling, more and more, into the lowest stage of weakness and dependence.

In olden society everything was different; unity and uniformity were nowhere to be met with. In modern society everything threatens to become so much alike, that the peculiar characteristics of each individual will soon be entirely lost in the general aspect of the world. Our forefathers were ever prone to make an improper use of the notion, that private rights ought to be respected; and we are naturally prone on the other hand to exaggerate the idea that the interest of a private individual ought always to bend to the interest of the many.

The political world is metamorphosed: new remedies must henceforth be sought for new disorders. To lay down extensive, but distinct and settled limits, to the action of the government; to confer certain rights on private persons, and to secure to them the undisputed enjoyment of those rights; to enable individual man to maintain whatever independence, strength, and original power he still possesses; to raise him by the side of society at large, and uphold him in that position,—these appear to me the main objects of legislators in the ages upon which we are now entering.

It would seem as if the rulers of our time sought only to use men in order to make things great; I wish that they would try a little more to make great men; that they would set less value on the work, and more upon the workman; that they would never forget that a nation cannot long remain strong when every man belonging to it is individually weak, and that no form or combination of social polity has yet been devised, to make an energetic people out of a community of pusillanimous and enfeebled citizens.

I trace amongst our contemporaries two contrary notions which are equally injurious. One set of men can perceive nothing in the principle of equality but the anarchical tendencies which it engenders: they dread their own free agency—they fear themselves. Other thinkers, less numerous but more enlightened, take a different view: beside that track which starts from the principle of equality to terminate in anarchy, they have at last discovered the road which seems to lead men to inevitable servitude. They shape their souls beforehand to this necessary condition; and, despairing of remaining free, they already do obeisance in their hearts to the master who is soon to appear. The former abandon freedom, because they think it dangerous; the latter, because they hold it to be impossible.

If I had entertained the latter conviction, I should not have written this book, but I should have confined myself to deploring in secret the destiny of mankind. I have sought to point out the dangers to which the principle of equality exposes the independence of man, because I firmly believe that these dangers are the most formidable, as well as the least foreseen, of all those which futurity holds in store: but I do not think that they are insurmountable.

The men who live in the democratic ages upon which we are entering have naturally a taste for independence: they are naturally impatient of regulation, and they are wearied by the permanence even of the condition they themselves prefer. They are fond of power; but they are prone to despise and hate those who wield it, and they easily elude its grasp by their own mobility and insignificance.

These propensities will always manifest themselves, because they originate in the groundwork of society, which will undergo no change: for a long time they will prevent the establishment of any despotism, and they will furnish fresh weapons to each succeeding generation which shall struggle in favour of the liberty of mankind. Let us then look forward to the future with that salutary fear which makes men keep watch and ward for freedom, not with that faint and idle terror which depresses and enervates the heart.

18. SCHUMPETER

Pluralist Democracy

Joseph Alois Schumpeter (1883–1950) was trained as an economist and had been Austrian Minister of Finance in 1919–20. He then served as professor of economics at the University of Bonn until 1932 when he emigrated to the United States, where he taught at Harvard. Schumpeter wrote several works in which he analyzed the implications of current social and economic development for the ideals of democracy. In *Capitalism, Socialism and Democracy*, Schumpeter outlined that "model" of democratic society which he regarded as possible and perhaps desirable in contemporary society.

The selection is taken from Chapters XXI and XXII of this work.*

THE CLASSICAL DOCTRINE OF DEMOCRACY

I. The Common Good and the Will of the People

The eighteenth-century philosophy of democracy may be couched in the following definition: the democratic method is that institutional arrangement for arriving at political decisions which realizes the common good by making the people itself decide issues through the election of individuals who are to assemble in order to carry out its will. Let us develop the implications of this.

It is held, then, that there exists a Common Good, the obvious beacon light of policy, which is always simple to define and which every normal person can be made to see by means of rational argument. There is hence no excuse for not seeing it and in fact no explanation for the presence of people who do not see it except ignorance—which can be removed—stupidity and anti-social interest. Moreover, this common good implies definite answers to all questions so that every social fact and every measure taken or to be taken can unequivocally be classed

* From *Capitalism, Socialism and Democracy*. (New York: Harper & Row, Publishers, 1942.) Used by permission.

as "good" or "bad." All people having therefore to agree, in principle at least, there is also a Common Will of the people (= will of all reasonable individuals) that is exactly coterminous with the common good or interest or welfare or happiness. The only thing, barring stupidity and sinister interests, that can possibly bring in disagreement and account for the presence of an opposition is a difference of opinion as to the speed with which the goal, itself common to nearly all, is to be approached. Thus every member of the community, conscious of that goal, knowing his or her mind, discerning what is good and what is bad, takes part, actively and responsibly, in furthering the former and fighting the latter and all the members taken together control their public affairs.

It is true that the management of some of these affairs requires special aptitudes and techniques and will therefore have to be entrusted to specialists who have them. This does not affect the principle, however, because these specialists simply act in order to carry out the will of the people exactly as a doctor acts in order to carry out the will of the patient to get well. It is also true that in a community of any size, especially if it displays the phenomenon of division of labor, it would be highly inconvenient for every individual citizen to have to get into contact with all the other citizens on every issue in order to do his part in ruling or governing. It will be more convenient to reserve only the most important decisions for the individual citizens to pronounce upon—say by referendum—and to deal with the rest through a committee appointed by them—an assembly or parliament whose members will be elected by popular vote. This committee or body of delegates, as we have seen, will not represent the people in a legal sense but it will do so in a less technical one—it will voice, reflect or represent the will of the electorate. Again as a matter of convenience, this committee being large, may resolve itself into smaller ones for the various departments of public affairs. Finally, among these smaller committees there will be a general-purpose committee, mainly for dealing with current administration, called cabinet or government, possibly with a general secretary or scapegoat at its head, a so-called prime minister.

As soon as we accept all the assumptions that are being made by this theory of the polity—or implied by it—democracy indeed acquires a perfectly unambiguous meaning and there is no problem in connection with it except how to bring it about. Moreover we need only forget a few logical qualms in order to be able to add that in this case the democratic arrangement would not only be the best of all conceivable ones, but that few people would care to consider any other. It is no less obvious however that these assumptions are so many statements of fact every one of which would have to be proved if we are to arrive at that conclusion. And it is much easier to disprove them.

There is, first, no such thing as a uniquely determined common good that all people could agree on or be made to agree on by the force of rational argument. This is due not primarily to the fact that some people may want things other than the common good but to the much more fundamental fact that to different individuals and groups the common good is bound to mean different things. This fact, hidden from the utilitarian by the narrowness of his outlook on the world of human valuations, will introduce rifts on questions of principle which cannot be reconciled by rational argument because ultimate values—our conceptions of what life and what society should be—are beyond the range of mere logic. They may be bridged by compromise in some cases but not in others. Americans who say, "We want this country to arm to its teeth and then to fight for what we conceive to be right all over the globe" and Americans who say, "We want this country to work out its own problems which is the only way it can serve humanity" are facing irreducible differences of ultimate values which compromise could only maim and degrade.

Secondly, even if a sufficiently definite common good—such as for instance the utilitarian's maximum of economic satisfaction—proved acceptable to all, this would not imply equally definite answers to individual issues. Opinions on these might differ to an extent important enough to produce most of the effects of "fundamental" dissension about ends themselves. The problems centering in the evaluation of present versus future satisfactions, even the case of socialism versus capitalism, would be left still open, for instance, after the conversion of every individual citizen to utilitarianism. "Health" might be desired by all, yet people would still disagree on vaccination and vasectomy. And so on.

The utilitarian fathers of democratic doctrine failed to see the full importance of this simply because none of them seriously considered any substantial change in the economic framework and the habits of bourgeois society. They saw little beyond the world of an eighteenth-century ironmonger.

But, third, as a consequence of both preceding propositions, the particular concept of the will of the people or the *volonté générale* that the utilitarians made their own vanishes into thin air. For that concept

presupposes the existence of a uniquely determined common good discernible to all. Unlike the romanticists the utilitarians had no notion
of that semi-mystic entity endowed with a will of its own—that "soul
of the people" which the historical school of jurisprudence made so
much of. They frankly derived their will of the people from the wills of
individuals. And unless there is a center, the common good, toward
which, in the long run at least, *all* individual wills gravitate, we shall
not get that particular type of "natural" *volonté générale*. The utilitarian
center of gravity, on the one hand, unifies individual wills, tends to
weld them by means of rational discussion into the will of the people
and, on the other hand, confers upon the latter the exclusive ethical
dignity claimed by the classic democratic creed. *This creed does not
consist simply in worshiping the will of the people as such* but rests on
certain assumptions about the "natural" object of that will which
object is sanctioned by utilitarian reason. Both the existence and the
dignity of this kind of *volonté générale* are gone as soon as the idea of
the common good fails us. And both the pillars of the classical doctrine
inevitably crumble into dust.

ANOTHER THEORY OF DEMOCRACY

I. Competition for Political Leadership

I think that most students of politics have by now come to accept
the criticisms leveled at the classical doctrine of democracy in the
preceding chapter. I also think that most of them agree, or will agree
before long, in accepting another theory which is much truer to life
and at the same time salvages much of what sponsors of the democratic method really mean by this term. Like the classical theory, it
may be put into the nutshell of a definition.

It will be remembered that our chief troubles about the classical
theory centered in the proposition that "the people" hold a definite
and rational opinion about every individual question and that they
give effect to this opinion—in a democracy—by choosing "representatives" who will see to it that that opinion is carried out. Thus
the selection of the representatives is made secondary to the primary
purpose of the democratic arrangement which is to vest the power of
deciding political issues in the electorate. Suppose we reverse the roles
of these two elements and make the deciding of issues by the electorate

secondary to the election of the men who are to do the deciding. To put it differently, we now take the view that the role of the people is to produce a government, or else an intermediate body which in turn will produce a national executive or government. And we define: the democratic method is that institutional arrangement for arriving at political decisions in which individuals acquire the power to decide by means of a competitive struggle for the people's vote.

Defense and explanation of this idea will speedily show that, as to both plausibility of assumptions and tenability of propositions, it greatly improves the theory of the democratic process.

First of all, we are provided with a reasonably efficient criterion by which to distinguish democratic governments from others. We have seen that the classical theory meets with difficulties on that score because both the will and the good of the people may be, and in many historical instances have been, served just as well or better by governments that cannot be described as democratic according to any accepted usage of the term. Now we are in a somewhat better position partly because we are resolved to stress a *modus procedendi* the presence or absence of which it is in most cases easy to verify.

For instance, a parliamentary monarchy like the English one fulfills the requirements of the democratic method because the monarch is practically constrained to appoint to cabinet office the same people as parliament would elect. A "constitutional" monarchy does not qualify to be called democratic because electorates and parliaments, while having all the other rights that electorates and parliaments have in parliamentary monarchies, lack the power to impose their choice as to the governing committee: the cabinet ministers are in this case servants of the monarch, in substance as well as in name, and can in principle be dismissed as well as appointed by him. Such an arrangement may satisfy the people. The electorate may reaffirm this fact by voting against any proposal for change. The monarch may be so popular as to be able to defeat any competition for the supreme office. But since no machinery is provided for making this competition effective the case does not come within our definition.

Second, the theory embodied in this definition leaves all the room we may wish to have for a proper recognition of the vital fact of leadership. The classical theory did not do this but, as we have seen, attributed to the electorate an altogether unrealistic degree of initiative which practically amounted to ignoring leadership. But collectives act almost exclusively by accepting leadership—this is the dominant mechanism of practically any collective action which is more than a reflex. Propositions about the working and the results of the democratic method that take account of this are bound to be infinitely more realistic than propositions which do not. They will not stop at the execution of a *volonté générale* but will go some way toward showing how it emerges or how it is substituted or faked. What we have termed Manufactured Will is no longer outside the theory, an aberration for the absence of which we piously pray; it enters on the ground floor as it should.

Third, however, so far as there are genuine group-wise volitions at all—for instance the will of the unemployed to receive unemployment benefit or the will of other groups to help—our theory does not neglect them. On the contrary we are now able to insert them in exactly the role they actually play. Such volitions do not as a rule assert themselves directly. Even if strong and definite they remain latent, often for decades, until they are called to life by some political leader who turns them into political factors. This he does, or else his agents do it for him, by organizing these volitions, by working them up and by including eventually appropriate items in his competitive offering. The interaction between sectional interests and public opinion and the way in which they produce the pattern we call the political situation appear from this angle in a new and much clearer light.

Fourth, our theory is of course no more definite than is the concept of competition for leadership. This concept presents similar difficulties as the concept of competition in the economic sphere, with which it may be usefully compared. In economic life competition is never completely lacking, but hardly ever is it perfect. Similarly, in political life there is always some competition, though perhaps only a potential one, for the allegiance of the people. To simplify matters we have restricted the kind of competition for leadership which is to define democracy, to free competition for a free vote. The justification for this is that democracy seems to imply a recognized method by which to conduct the competitive struggle, and that the electoral method is practically the only one available for communities of any size. But though this excludes many ways of securing leadership which should be excluded, such as competition by military insurrection, it does not exclude the cases that are strikingly analogous to the economic phenomena we label "unfair" or "fraudulent" competition or restraint of competition. And we cannot exclude them because if we did we should be left with a completely unrealistic ideal. Between this ideal case which does not exist and the cases in which all competition with the established leader is prevented by force, there is a continuous range of variation within which the democratic method of government shades off into the autocratic one by imperceptible steps. But if we wish to understand and not to philosophize, this is as it should be. The value of our criterion is not seriously impaired thereby.

Fifth, our theory seems to clarify the relation that subsists between democracy and individual freedom. If by the latter we mean the existence of a sphere of individual self-government the boundaries of which are historically variable—*no* society tolerates absolute freedom even of conscience and of speech, *no* society reduces that sphere to zero—the question clearly becomes a matter of degree. We have seen that the democratic method does not necessarily guarantee a greater amount of individual freedom than another political method would permit in similar circumstances. It may well be the other way round. But there is still a relation between the two. If, on principle at least, everyone is free to compete for political leadership by presenting himself to the electorate, this will in most cases though not in all mean a considerable amount of freedom of discussion *for all*. In particular it will normally mean a considerable amount of freedom of the press. This relation between democracy and freedom is not absolutely stringent and can be tampered with. But, from the standpoint of the intellectual, it is nevertheless very important. At the same time, it is all there is to that relation.

Sixth, it should be observed that in making it the primary function of the electorate to produce a government (directly or through an intermediate body) I intended to include in this phrase also the function of evicting it. The one means simply the acceptance of a leader or a group of leaders, the other means simply the withdrawal of this acceptance. This takes care of an element the reader may have missed. He may have thought that the electorate controls as well as installs. But since electorates normally do not control their political leaders in any way except by refusing to reelect them or the parliamentary majorities that support them, it seems well to reduce our ideas about this control in the way indicated by our definition. Occasionally, spontaneous revulsions occur which upset a government or an individual minister directly or else enforce a certain course of action. But they are not only exceptional, they are, as we shall see, contrary to the spirit of the democratic method.

Seventh, our theory sheds much-needed light on an old controversy. Whoever accepts the classical doctrine of democracy and in consequence believes that the democratic method is to guarantee that issues be decided and policies framed according to the will of the people must be struck by the fact that, even if that will were undeniably real and definite, decision by simple majorities would in many cases distort it rather than give effect to it. Evidently the will of the majority is the will of the majority and not the will of "the people." The latter is a mosaic that the former completely fails to "represent." To equate both by definition is not to solve the problem. Attempts at real solutions have however been made by the authors of the various plans for Proportional Representation.

These plans have met with adverse criticism on practical grounds. It is in fact obvious not only that proportional representation will offer opportunities for all sorts of idiosyncrasies to assert themselves but also that it may prevent democracy from producing efficient governments and thus prove a danger in times of stress. But before concluding that democracy becomes unworkable if its principle is carried out consistently it is just as well to ask ourselves whether this principle really implies proportional representation. As a matter of fact it does not. If acceptance of leadership is the true function of the electorate's vote, the case for proportional representation collapses because its premises are no longer binding. The principle of democracy then merely means that the reins of government should be handed to those who command more support than do any of the competing individuals or teams. And this in turn seems to assure the standing of the majority system within the logic of the democratic method, although we might still condemn it on grounds that lie outside of that logic.

III

Progress, Economic Liberalism, and Social Democracy

A central liberal theme has been the belief that progress has been achieved through the application of scientific intelligence to the social and economic problems of the society. As the three concluding selections of this section—those by von Hayek, Bernstein, and Keynes—show, this theme has received divergent interpretation in the twentieth century.

Traditionally, for European liberalism, the major social science which could be applied for human betterment was economic theory. Since classical economic theory seemed to limit state intervention in economic affairs, liberalism became identified with laissez-faire policy. In America, liberals shifted their position in the twentieth century and became advocates of state planning and control. To a marked degree, European liberalism retained the older tradition, and von Hayek provides one of the most reasoned statements for some necessary connection between the ideal of personal liberty and the operation of a free market.

The ideals of liberalism were both political and economic. They were characteristically justified on the ground that each individual ought to determine the political decisions that affected him through the political mechanism of free consent and elections; and that he should determine the economic decisions that affected him through the economic mechanism of free consent—the market. In this view, if the economic framework of society was coercing the choice of the individual, it was an extension of the political ideal of liberty to allow democratic governments to intervene in economic decision making. The form of political democracy would be given concrete significance in economic democracy. This line of reasoning led many liberals to argue the compatibility of the ideal of liberalism with the economics of socialism. This outlook, which can be found among the English Fabians and many Continental social democrats, received an early and interesting formulation, in the selection here presented from *Evolutionary Socialism* by Eduard Bernstein.

Many liberals, however, have sought a redefinition of liberal theory which would allow for governmental controls in a free economy. The most persuasive defense of this position in the twentieth century derives from criticism of the assumptions governing classical economic theory provided by the new and influential economic theory of J. M. Keynes.

In his lecture *An End to Laissez-Faire* Keynes masterfully traces the relations of liberalism with the ideology of laissez-faire. The economics of Adam Smith, the utilitarianism of Bentham, and the population of Malthus were crucial aspects in this development. Keynes suggests a new agenda for liberalism which will interpret the historical tradition in the light of the new economic and social situation. Thus, the Malthusian concern with population growth is transposed by Keynes into the need for national population policy which will deal with environmental quality and human resources.

To a significant degree, the issues that distinguish the economic policies of a socialist, a classical liberal, or a Keynesian interventionist have become controversies within the discipline of economics. To that degree, they approximate the St.Simonian view that in the future, scientific moralists would not debate issues but would jointly calculate optimal policies. As the struggles within the developing countries show, however, these policies still relate to questions of ideology or world-view and fundamentally to choices of priorities among values.

These three spokesmen for the contemporary interpretation of liberalism, share, however, the secular faith in progressive amelioration through the exercise of rational choice, individual, group, or governmental. Their classic source within the liberal tradition had been Condorcet. Condorcet's own economic theory was directed against state intervention—his wife had translated some of Adam Smith's writings into French—but his argument for perfectibility transcended his economics and offered a general vision of man's redemption in history through reason. The combination of modern scientific methods with irrational ends has, in the period just prior to the Second World War and since, therefore generated the most profound of all crises of modern liberalism. It is only if liberalism can respond to the significance of this phenomenon that there can be a viable European liberalism in the years ahead.

19. CONDORCET

Reason and History

Marie Jean Antoine Nicholas de Caritat, Marquis de Condorcet (1743–94), wrote his major work *A Sketch for the Historical Picture of the Progress of the Human Mind* while he was in hiding from Robespierre's police between July, 1793, and March, 1794. A warrant had been issued for his arrest by the revolutionary Jacobins when he attacked the Jacobin Constitution of 1793. He was discovered, taken to prison, and died in the detention room. The work has therefore had the aura of the last testament and declaration of faith of the visionary liberal during a reign of revolutionary terror.

Condorcet was a gifted mathematician who had been elected Secretary of the Academy of Sciences in 1785. In the early years of the French Revolution he was President of the Legislative Assembly.

The selection is from Condorcet's description of the ninth and tenth stages of human history in *A Sketch for the Historical Picture of the Progress of the Human Mind.**

THE NINTH STAGE

From Descartes to the foundation of the French Republic

. . . This sketch of the progress of philosophy and of the dissemination of enlightenment . . . brings us up to the stage when the influence of progress upon public opinion, of public opinion upon nations or their leaders, suddenly ceases to be a slow, imperceptible affair, and produces a revolution in the whole order of several nations, a certain earnest of the revolution that must one day include in its scope the whole of the human race.

After long periods of error, after being led astray by vague or incomplete theories, publicists have at last discovered the true rights

* Translated by June Barraclough. (London: Weidenfeld & Nicolson, 1955.) Used by permission.

of man and how they can all be deduced from the single truth, that *man is a sentient being, capable of reasoning and of acquiring moral ideas.*

They have seen that the maintenance of these rights was the sole object of men's coming together in political societies, and that the social art is the art of guaranteeing the preservation of these rights and their distribution in the most equal fashion over the largest area. It was felt that in every society the means of assuring the rights of the individual should be submitted to certain common rules, but that the authority to choose these means and to determine these rules could belong only to the majority of the members of the society itself; for in making this choice the individual cannot follow his own reason without subjecting others to it, and the will of the majority is the only mark of truth that can be accepted by all without loss of equality.

Each man can in fact genuinely bind himself in advance to the will of the majority which then becomes unanimous; but he can bind only himself; and he cannot engage even himself towards this majority when it fails to respect the rights of the individual, after having once recognized them. . . .

Nor did men any longer dare to divide humanity into two races, the one fated to rule, the other to obey, the one to deceive, the other to be deceived. They had to recognize that all men have an equal right to be informed on all that concerns them, and that none of the authorities established by men over themselves has the right to hide from them one single truth. . . .

Man has certain needs and also certain faculties with which to satisfy them; from these faculties and from their products, modified and distributed in different ways, there results an accumulation of wealth out of which must be met the common needs of mankind. But what are the laws according to which this wealth is produced or distributed, accumulated or consumed, increased or dissipated? What, too, are the laws governing that general tendency towards an equilibrium between supply and demand from which it follows that, with any increase in wealth, life becomes easier and men are happier, until a point is reached when no further increase is possible; or that, again, with any decrease in wealth, life becomes harder, suffering increases, until the consequent fall in population restores the balance? How, with all the astonishing multifariousness of labour and production, supply and demand, with all the frightening complexity of conflicting interests that link the survival and well-being of one individual to the general organization of societies, that make his well-being dependent on every accident of nature and every political event, his pain and pleasure on what is happening in the remotest corner of the globe, how, with all this seeming chaos, is it that, by a universal moral law, the efforts made by each individual on his own behalf minister to the welfare of all, and that the interests of society demand that everyone should understand where his own interests lie, and should be able to follow them without hindrance?

Men, therefore, should be able to use their faculties, dispose of their wealth and provide for their needs in complete freedom. The common interest of any society, far from demanding that they should restrain such activity, on the contrary, forbids any interference with it; and as far as this aspect of public order is concerned, the guaranteeing to each man his natural rights is at once the whole of social utility, the sole duty of the social power, the only right that the general will can legitimately exercise over the individual.

But it is not enough merely that this principle should be acknowledged by society; the public authority has specific duties to fulfil. It must establish by law recognized measures for the determination of the weight, volume, size and length of all articles of trade; it must create a coinage to serve as a common measure of value and so to facilitate comparison between the value of one article of trade and that of another, so that having a value itself, it can be exchanged against anything else that can be given one; for without this common measure trade must remain confined to barter, and can acquire very little activity or scope.

The wealth produced each year provides a portion for disposal which is not required to pay for either the labour that has produced it or the labour required to ensure its replacement by an equal or greater production of wealth. The owner of this disposable portion does not owe it directly to his work; he possesses it independently of the use to which he puts his faculties in order to provide for his needs. Hence it is out of this available portion of the annual wealth that the public authority, without violating anyone's rights, can establish the funds required for the security of the State, the preservation of peace within its borders, the protection of individual rights, the exercise of those powers established for the formulation or execution of the law, and, finally, the maintenance of public prosperity.

There are certain undertakings and institutions which are beneficial to society in general, and which it therefore ought to initiate, control and supervise; these provide services which the wishes and interests of individuals cannot provide by themselves, and which advance the progress of agriculture, industry or trade or the prevention or alleviation of inevitable natural hardships or unforeseen accidents. . . .

Thus, an understanding of the natural rights of man, the belief that these rights are inalienable and indefeasible, a strongly expressed desire for liberty of thought and letters, of trade and industry, and for the alleviation of the people's suffering, for the proscription of all penal laws against religious dissenters and the abolition of torture and barbarous punishments, the desire for a milder system of criminal legislation and jurisprudence which should give complete security to the innocent, and for a simpler civil code, more in conformance with reason and nature, indifference in all matters of religion which now were relegated to the status of superstitions and political impostures, a hatred of hypocrisy and fanaticism, a contempt for prejudice, zeal for the propagation of enlightenment: all these principles, gradually filtering down from philosophical works to every class of society whose education went beyond the catechism and the alphabet, became the common faith, the badges of all those who were neither Machiavellians nor fools. In some countries these principles formed a public opinion sufficiently widespread for even the mass of the people to show a willingness to be guided by it and to obey it. For a feeling of humanity, a tender and active compassion for all the misfortunes that afflict the human race and a horror of anything that in the actions of public institutions, or governments, or individuals, adds new pains to those that are natural and inevitable, were the natural consequences of those principles; and this feeling exhaled from all the writings and all the speeches of the time, and already its happy influence had been felt in the laws and the public institutions, even of those nations still subject to despotism.

The philosophers of different nations who considered the interests of the whole of humanity without distinction of country, race, or creed, formed a solid phalanx banded together against all forms of error, against all manifestations of tyranny, despite their differences in matters of theory. Activated by feelings of universal philanthropy, they fought injustice even when it occurred in countries other than their own and could not harm them personally; they fought injustice even when it was their own country that was guilty of acts against others; they raised an outcry in Europe against the crimes of greed that sullied the shores of America, Africa, and Asia. English and French philosophers considered themselves honoured to be called the *friends* of the black races whom their foolish tyrants disdained to consider as members of the human race. In France writers lavished encomiums on the new-won tolerance accorded in Russia and Sweden: whilst in Italy Beccaria denounced the barbarous tenets of French jurisprudence. In France writers sought to free England from her commercial prejudices and her superstitious respect for the vices of her constitution and her laws, whilst the worthy Howard denounced to the French the callous indifference which was causing the death of so many human victims in their prison-cells and hospitals. . . .

Force or persuasion on the part of governments, priestly intolerance, and even national prejudices, had all lost their deadly power to smother the voice of truth, and nothing could now protect the enemies of reason or the oppressors of freedom from a sentence to which the whole of Europe would soon subscribe.

Finally, we see the rise of a new doctrine which was to deal the final blow to the already tottering structure of prejudice—the doctrine of the indefinite perfectibility of the human race of which Turgot, Price and Priestley were the first and the most brilliant apostles. . . .

A comparison of the attitude of mind I have already described with the forms of government prevalent at that time would have made it easy to foresee that a great revolution was inevitable, and that there were only two ways in which it could come about; either the people themselves would establish the reasonable and natural principles that philosophy had taught them to admire, or governments would hasten to anticipate them and carry out what was required by public opinion. If the revolution should come about in the former way it would be swifter and more thorough, but more violent; if it should come about in the latter way, it would be less swift and less thorough, but also less violent: if in the former way, then freedom and happiness would be purchased at the price of transient evils; if in the latter, then these evils would be avoided but, it might be, at the price of long delaying the harvest of the fruits that the revolution must, nevertheless, inevitably bear. The ignorance and corruption of the governments of the time saw that it came about in the former way, and the human race was avenged by the swift triumph of liberty and reason. . . .

From the moment when the genius of Descartes gave men's minds that general impetus which is the first principle of a revolution in the destinies of the human race, to the happy time of complete and pure social liberty when man was able to regain his natural independence only after having lived through a long series of centuries of slavery and misery, the picture of the progress of the mathematical and physical sciences reveals an immense horizon whose different parts must be distributed and ordered if we wish to grasp the significance of the whole and properly observe its relations. . . .

If we were to confine ourselves to showing the benefits that we have derived from the sciences in their immediate uses or in their applications to the arts, either for the well-being of individuals or for the prosperity of nations, we should display only a very small portion of their blessings.

The most important of these, perhaps, is to have destroyed prejudices and to have redirected the human intelligence, which had been obliged to follow the false directions imposed on it by the absurd beliefs that were implanted in each generation in infancy with the terrors of superstition and the fear of tyranny.

All errors in politics and morals are based on philosophical errors and these in turn are connected with scientific errors. There is not a religious system nor a supernatural extravagance that is not founded on ignorance of the laws of nature. The inventors, the defenders of these absurdities could not foresee the successive perfection of the human mind. Convinced that men in their day knew everything that they could ever know and would always believe what they then believed, they confidently supported their idle dreams on the current opinions of their country and their age. . . .

At the same time the habit of correct reasoning about the objects of these sciences, the precise ideas gained by their methods, and the means of recognizing or proving the truth of a belief should naturally lead us to compare the sentiment that forces us to accept well founded opinions credible for good reasons, with that which ties us to habitual prejudices or forces us to submit to authority. Such a comparison is enough to teach us to mistrust opinions of the latter kind, to convince us that we do not really believe them even when we boast of believing them, even when we profess them with the purest sincerity. This secret, once discovered, makes their destruction immediate and certain.

Finally this progress of the physical sciences which neither the passions nor self-interest can disturb, in which neither birth, nor profession, nor position are thought to confer on one the right to judge what one is not in a condition to understand, this inexorable progress cannot be contemplated by men of enlightenment without their wishing to make the other sciences follow the same path. . . .

Up to this stage, the sciences had been the birthright of very few;

they were now becoming common property and the time was at hand when their elements, their principles, and their simpler methods would become truly popular. For it was then, at last, that their application to the arts and their influence on men's judgment would become of truly universal utility. . . .

We shall show how the printing press multiplies and spreads abroad even those works primarily intended to be performed or read aloud in public, and so allows them to reach incomparably more people as readers than they ever could as mere listeners; we shall show how, as a consequence of the way that any important decision taken in a large assembly is now determined by what the members of that assembly have learnt through the written word, a new art of persuasion has arisen amongst the moderns, different from that practised by the ancients, a difference that is analogous to the differences in the effects produced, in the means employed between this modern art and that of the ancients . . . .

Turning now our attention to the human race in general, we shall show how the discovery of the correct method of procedure in the sciences, the growth of scientific theories, their application to every part of the natural world, to the subject of every human need, the lines of communication established between one science and another, the great number of men who cultivate the sciences, and most important of all, the spread of printing, how together all these advances ensure that no science will ever fall below the point it has reached. We shall point out that the principles of philosophy, the slogans of liberty, the recognition of the true rights of man and his real interests, have spread through far too great a number of nations, and now direct in each of them the opinions of far too great a number of enlightened men, for us to fear that they will ever be allowed to relapse into oblivion. And indeed what reason could we have for fear, when we consider that the languages most widely spoken are the languages of the two peoples who enjoy liberty to the fullest extent and who best understand its principles, and that no league of tyrants, no political intrigues, could prevent the resolute defence, in these two languages, of the rights of reason and of liberty?

But although everything tells us that the human race will never relapse into its former state of barbarism, although everything combines to reassure us against that corrupt and cowardly political theory which would condemn it to oscillate forever between truth and error, liberty and servitude, nevertheless we still see the forces of enlightenment in possession of no more than a very small portion of the globe, and the truly enlightened vastly outnumbered by the great mass of men who are still given over to ignorance and prejudice. We still see vast areas in which men groan in slavery, vast areas offering the spectacle of nations either degraded by the vices of a civilization whose progress is impeded by corruption, or still vegetating in the infant condition of early times. We observe that the labours of recent ages have done much for the progress of the human mind, but little for the perfection of the human race; that they have done much for the honour of man, something for his liberty, but so far almost nothing for his happiness. At a few points our eyes are dazzled with a brilliant light; but thick darkness still covers an immense stretch of the horizon. There are a few circumstances from which the philosopher can take consolation; but he is still afflicted by the spectacle of the stupidity, slavery, barbarism and extravagance of mankind; and the friend of humanity can find unmixed pleasure only in tasting the sweet delights of hope for the future. . . .

THE TENTH STAGE

The future progress of the human mind

. . . Our hopes for the future condition of the human race can be subsumed under three important heads: the abolition of inequality between nations, the progress of equality within each nation, and the true perfection of mankind. Will all nations one day attain that state of civilization which the most enlightened, the freest and the least burdened by prejudices, such as the French and the Anglo-Americans, have attained already? Will the vast gulf that separates these peoples from the slavery of nations under the rule of monarchs, from the barbarism of African tribes, from the ignorance of savages, little by little disappear? . . .

We shall find in the experience of the past, in the observation of the progress that the sciences and civilization have already made, in the analysis of the progress of the human mind and of the development of its faculties, the strongest reasons for believing that nature has set no limit to the realization of our hopes.

If we glance at the state of the world today we see first of all that in Europe the principles of the French constitution are already those of all enlightened men. We see them too widely propagated, too seriously professed, for priests and despots to prevent their gradual penetration even into the hovels of their slaves; there they will soon awaken in these slaves the remnants of their common sense and inspire them with that smouldering indignation which not even constant humiliation and fear can smother in the soul of the oppressed. . . .

Can we doubt that either common sense or the senseless discords of European nations will add to the effects of the slow but inexorable progress of their colonies, and will soon bring about the independence of the New World? And then will not the European population in these colonies, spreading rapidly over that enormous land, either civilize or peacefully remove the savage nations who still inhabit vast tracts of its land? . . .

The time will therefore come when the sun will shine only on free men who know no other master but their reason; when tyrants and slaves, priests and their stupid or hypocritical instruments will exist only in works of history and on the stage; and when we shall think of them only to pity their victims and their dupes; to maintain ourselves in a state of vigilance by thinking on their excesses; and to learn how to recognize and so to destroy, by force of reason, the first seeds of tyranny and superstition, should they ever dare to reappear amongst us.

In looking at the history of societies we shall have had occasion to observe that there is often a great difference between the rights that the law allows its citizens and the rights that they actually enjoy, and, again, between the equality established by political codes and that which in fact exists amongst individuals: and we shall have noticed that these differences were one of the principal causes of the destruction of freedom in the ancient republics, of the storms that troubled them, and of the weakness that delivered them over to foreign tyrants.

These differences have three main causes: inequality in wealth; inequality in status between the man whose means of subsistence are hereditary and the man whose means are dependent on the length of his life, or, rather, on that part of his life in which he is capable of work; and, finally, inequality in education.

. . . These three sorts of real inequality must constantly diminish without however disappearing altogether: for they are the result of natural and necessary causes which it would be foolish and dangerous to wish to eradicate; and one could not even attempt to bring about the entire disappearance of their effects without introducing even more fecund sources of inequality, without striking more direct and more fatal blows at the rights of man. . . .

[One] necessary cause of inequality, of dependence and even of misery, which ceaselessly threatens the most numerous and most active class in our society. . . . can be in great part eradicated by guaranteeing people in old age a means of livelihood produced partly by their own savings and partly by the savings of others who make the same outlay, but who die before they need to reap the reward; or, again, on the same principle of compensation, by securing for widows and orphans an income which is the same and costs the same for those families which suffer an early loss and for those which suffer it later; or again by providing all children with the capital necessary for the full use of their labour, available at the age when they start work and found a family, a capital which increases at the expense of those whom premature death prevents from reaching this age. It is to the application of the calculus to the probabilities of life and the investment of money that we owe the idea of these methods which have already been successful, although they have not been applied in a sufficiently comprehensive and exhaustive fashion to render them really useful, not merely to a few individuals, but to society as a whole, by making it possible to prevent those periodic disasters which strike at so many families and which are such a recurrent source of misery and suffering.

We shall point out that schemes of this nature, which can be organized in the name of the social authority and become one of its greatest benefits, can also be the work of private associations, which will be formed without any real risk, once the principles for the proper working of these schemes have been widely diffused and the mistakes which have been the undoing of a large number of these associations no longer hold terrors for us. . . .

The degree of equality in education that we can reasonably hope to attain, but that should be adequate, is that which excludes all dependence, either forced or voluntary. We shall show how this condition can be easily attained in the present state of human knowledge even by those who can study only for a small number of years in childhood, and then during the rest of their life in their few hours of leisure. We shall prove that, by a suitable choice of syllabus and of methods of education, we can teach the citizen everything that he needs to know in order to be able to manage his household, administer his affairs and employ his labour and his faculties in freedom; to know his rights and to be able to exercise them; to be acquainted with his duties and fulfil them satisfactorily; to judge his own and other men's actions according to his own lights and to be a stranger to none of the high

and delicate feelings which honour human nature; not to be in a state
of blind dependence upon those to whom he must entrust his affairs or
the exercise of his rights; to be in a proper condition to choose and
supervise them; to be no longer the dupe of those popular errors
which torment man with superstitious fears and chimerical hopes; to
defend himself against prejudice by the strength of his reason alone;
and, finally, to escape the deceits of charlatans who would lay snares
for his fortune, his health, his freedom of thought and his conscience
under the pretext of granting him health, wealth and salvation. . . .

. . . various causes of equality do not act in isolation; they unite,
combine and support each other and so their cumulative effects are
stronger, surer and more constant. With greater equality of education
there will be greater equality in industry and so in wealth; equality in
wealth necessarily leads to equality in education: and equality between
the nations and equality within a single nation are mutually dependent.

So we might say that a well directed system of education rectifies
natural inequality in ability instead of strengthening it, just as good
laws remedy natural inequality in the means of subsistence, and just
as in societies where laws have brought about this same equality,
liberty, though subject to a regular constitution, will be more widespread, more complete than in the total independence of savage life.
Then the social art will have fulfilled its aim, that of assuring and
extending to all men enjoyment of the common rights to which they
are called by nature.

The real advantages that should result from this progress, of which
we can entertain a hope that is almost a certainty, can have no other
term than that of the absolute perfection of the human race; since, as
the various kinds of equality come to work in its favour by producing
ampler sources of supply, more extensive education, more complete
liberty, so equality will be more real and will embrace everything
which is really of importance for the happiness of human beings. . . .

Is there any vicious habit, any practice contrary to good faith, any
crime, whose origin and first cause cannot be traced back to the legislation, the institutions, the prejudices of the country wherein this habit,
this practice, this crime can be observed? In short will not the general
welfare that results from the progress of the useful arts once they are
grounded on solid theory, or from the progress of legislation once it is
rooted in the truths of political science, incline mankind to humanity,
benevolence and justice? In other words, do not all these observations
which I propose to develop further in my book, show that the moral

goodness of man, the necessary consequence of his constitution, is capable of indefinite perfection like all his other faculties, and that nature has linked together in an unbreakable chain truth, happiness and virtue?

Among the causes of the progress of the human mind that are of the utmost importance to the general happiness, we must number the complete annihilation of the prejudices that have brought about an inequality of rights between the sexes, an inequality fatal even to the party in whose favour it works. It is vain for us to look for a justification of this principle in any differences of physical organization, intellect or moral sensibility between men and women. This inequality has its origin solely in an abuse of strength, and all the later sophistical attempts that have been made to excuse it are vain. . . .

Once people are enlightened they will know that they have the right to dispose of their own life and wealth as they choose; they will gradually learn to regard war as the most dreadful of scourges, the most terrible of crimes. The first wars to disappear will be those into which usurpers have forced their subjects in defence of their pretended hereditary rights.

Nations will learn that they cannot conquer other nations without losing their own liberty; that permanent confederations are their only means of preserving their independence; and that they should seek not power but security. Gradually mercantile prejudices will fade away: and a false sense of commercial interest will lose the fearful power it once had of drenching the earth in blood and of ruining nations under pretext of enriching them. When at last the nations come to agree on the principles of politics and morality, when in their own better interests they invite foreigners to share equally in all the benefits men enjoy either through the bounty of nature or by their own industry, then all the causes that produce and perpetuate national animosities and poison national relations will disappear one by one; and nothing will remain to encourage or even to arouse the fury of war.

Organizations more intelligently conceived than those projects of eternal peace which have filled the leisure and consoled the hearts of certain philosophers, will hasten the progress of the brotherhood of nations, and wars between countries will rank with assassinations as freakish atrocities, humiliating and vile in the eyes of nature and staining with indelible opprobrium the country or the age whose annals record them. . . .

All the causes that contribute to the perfection of the human race, all the means that ensure it must by their very nature exercise a perpetual influence and always increase their sphere of action. . . . We may conclude then that the perfectibility of man is indefinite. Meanwhile we have considered him as possessing the natural faculties and organization that he has at present. How much greater would be the certainty, how much vaster the scheme of our hopes if we could believe that these natural faculties themselves and this organization could also be improved? This is the last question that remains for us to ask ourselves.

Organic perfectibility or deterioration amongst the various strains in the vegetable and animal kingdom can be regarded as one of the general laws of nature. This law also applies to the human race. No one can doubt that, as preventitive medicine improves and food and housing becomes healthier, as a way of life is established that develops our physical powers by exercise without ruining them by excess, as the two most virulent causes of deterioration, misery and excessive wealth, are eliminated, the average length of human life will be increased and a better health and a stronger physical constitution will be ensured. The improvement of medical practice, which will become more efficacious with the progress of reason and of the social order, will mean the end of infectious and hereditary diseases and illnesses brought on by climate, food, or working conditions. It is reasonable to hope that all other diseases may likewise disappear as their distant causes are discovered. Would it be absurd then to suppose that this perfection of the human species might be capable of indefinite progress; that the day will come when death will be due only to extraordinary accidents or to the decay of the vital forces, and that ultimately the average span between birth and decay will have no assignable value? Certainly man will not become immortal, but will not the interval between the first breath that he draws and the time when in the natural course of events, without disease or accident, he expires, increase indefinitely? . . .

Finally may we not extend such hopes to the intellectual and moral faculties? May not our parents, who transmit to us the benefits or disadvantages of their constitution, and from whom we receive our shape and features, as well as our tendencies to certain physical affections, hand on to us also that part of the physical organization which determines the intellect, the power of the brain, the ardour of the soul or the moral sensibility? Is it not probable that education, in perfecting these qualities, will at the same time influence, modify and perfect the organization itself? Analogy, investigation of the human faculties and the study of certain facts, all seem to give substance to such conjectures which would further push back the boundaries of our hopes.

These are the questions with which we shall conclude this final stage. How consoling for the philosopher who laments the errors, the crimes, the injustices which still pollute the earth and of which he is often the victim is this view of the human race, emancipated from its shackles, released from the empire of fate and from that of the enemies of its progress, advancing with a firm and sure step along the path of truth, virtue and happiness! It is the contemplation of this prospect that rewards him for all his efforts to assist the progress of reason and the defence of liberty. He dares to regard these strivings as part of the eternal chain of human destiny; and in this persuasion he is filled with the true delight of virtue and the pleasure of having done some lasting good which fate can never destroy by a sinister stroke of revenge, by calling back the reign of slavery and prejudice. Such contemplation is for him an asylum, in which the memory of his persecutors cannot pursue him; there he lives in thought with man restored to his natural rights and dignity, forgets man tormented and corrupted by greed, fear or envy; there he lives with his peers in an Elysium created by reason and graced by the purest pleasures known to the love of mankind.

20. MALTHUS

Population Growth and Perfectibility

Thomas Malthus (1766–1834) wrote the first essay on population in 1798, at the urging of his father, David Malthus. The elder Malthus, a personal friend of Rousseau's, argued in favor of the thesis of perfectibility as advanced by Condorcet and Godwin against his son's analysis of the implication of population growth upon schemes for social improvement. The selection from the first chapter of this first essay presents Malthus' argument against the thesis of Condorcet.

Five years after the publication of the first essay, Malthus prepared a revised and enlarged edition. The change of title suggests Malthus' change in emphasis. The pamphlet of 1798 had been called *An Essay on the Principle of Population as It Affects the Future Improvement of Society, with Remarks on the Speculation of Mr. Godwin, Mr. Condorcet and Other Writers.* The sub-title of the 1803 book was: *A View of Its Past and Present Affects on Human Happiness with an Inquiry into Our Prospects Representing the Future Removal or Mitigation of the Evils Which It Occasions.* The selections from the second book, taken from Chapter Two and Chapter Fourteen, show Malthus' derivation of policy proposals on poverty from his analysis of population growth. This aspect of Malthus' work had great influence in its day. The British Poor Laws of 1834 were shaped by his doctrine.

POPULATION: THE FIRST ESSAY

The great and unlooked for discoveries that have taken place of late years in natural philosophy, the increasing diffusion of general knowledge from the extension of the art of printing, the ardent and unshackled spirit of inquiry that prevails thoroughout the lettered and even unlettered world, the new and extraordinary lights that have been thrown on political subjects which dazzle and astonish the under-standing, and particularly that tremendous phenomenon in the political horizon, the French revolution, which, like a blazing comet, seems destined either to inspire with fresh life and vigour, or to scorch up and destroy the shrinking inhabitants of the earth, have all concurred to lead many able men into the opinion that we were touching on a period big with the most important changes, changes that would in some measure be decisive of the future fate of mankind.

It has been said that the great question is now at issue, whether man shall henceforth start forwards with accelerated velocity towards illimitable, and hitherto unconceived improvement, or be condemned to a perpetual oscillation between happiness and misery, and after every effort remain still at an immeasurable distance from the wished-for goal. . . .

I have read some of the speculations on the perfectibility of man and of society with great pleasure. I have been warmed and delighted with the enchanting picture which they hold forth. I ardently wish for such happy improvements. But I see great, and, to my understanding, unconquerable difficulties in the way to them. These difficulties it is my present purpose to state, declaring, at the same time, that so far from exulting in them, as a cause of triumph over the friends of inno-vation, nothing would give me greater pleasure than to see them completely removed. . . .

In entering upon the argument I must premise that I put out of the question, at present, all mere conjectures, that is, all suppositions, the probable realization of which cannot be inferred upon any just philosophical grounds. A writer may tell me that he thinks man will ultimately become an ostrich. I cannot properly contradict him. But before he can expect to bring any reasonable person over to his opinion, he ought to shew, that the necks of mankind have been gradually elongating, that the lips have grown harder and more prominent, that the legs and feet are daily altering their shape, and that the hair is beginning to change into stubs of feathers. And till the probability of so wonderful a conversion can be shewn, it is surely lost time and lost eloquence to expatiate on the happiness of man in such a state; to describe his powers, both of running and flying, to paint him in a condition where all narrow luxuries would be contemned, where he would be employed only in collecting the necessaries of life, and where, consequently, each man's share of labour would be light, and his portion of leisure ample.

I think I may fairly make two postulata.

First, That food is necessary to the existence of man.

Secondly, That the passion between the sexes is necessary and will remain nearly in its present state.

These two laws, ever since we have had any knowledge of mankind, appear to have been fixed laws of our nature, and, as we have not hitherto seen any alteration in them, we have no right to conclude that they will ever cease to be what they now are . . . .

I do not know that any writer has supposed that on this earth man will ultimately be able to live without food. But Mr. Godwin has conjectured that the passion between the sexes may in time be extinguished. As, however, he calls this part of his work a deviation into the land of conjecture, I will not dwell longer upon it at present than to say that the best arguments for the perfectibility of man are drawn from a contemplation of the great progress that he has already made from the savage state and the difficulty of saying where he is to stop. But towards the extinction of the passion between the sexes, no progress whatever has hitherto been made. It appears to exist in as much force at present as it did two thousand or four thousand years ago. . . .

Assuming then, my postulata as granted, I say, that the power of population is indefinitely greater than the power in the earth to produce subsistence for man.

Population, when unchecked, increases in a geometrical ratio.

Subsistence increases only in an arithmetical ratio. A slight acquaintance with numbers will shew the immensity of the first power in comparison of the second.

By that law of our nature which makes food necessary to the life of man, the effects of these two unequal powers must be kept equal.

This implies a strong and constantly operating check on population from the difficulty of subsistence. This difficulty must fall somewhere and must necessarily be severely felt by a large portion of mankind.

Through the animal and vegetable kingdoms, nature has scattered the seeds of life abroad with the most profuse and liberal hand. She has been comparatively sparing in the room and the nourishment necessary to rear them. The germs of existence contained in this spot of earth, with ample food, and ample room to expand in, would fill millions of worlds in the course of a few thousand years. Necessity, that imperious all pervading law of nature, restrains them within the prescribed bounds. The race of plants, and the race of animals shrink under this great restrictive law. And the race of man cannot, by any efforts of reason, escape from it. Among plants and animals its effects are waste of seed, sickness, and premature death. Among mankind, misery and vice. The former, misery, is an absolutely necessary consequence of it. Vice is a highly probable consequence, and we therefore see it abundantly prevail, but it ought not, perhaps, to be called an absolutely necessary consequence. The ordeal of virtue is to resist all temptation to evil.

This natural inequality of the two powers of population and of production in the earth and that great law of our nature which must constantly keep their effects equal form the great difficulty that to me appears insurmountable in the way to the perfectibility of society. All other arguments are of slight and subordinate consideration in comparison of this. I see no way by which man can escape from the weight of this law which pervades all animated nature. No fancied equality, no agrarian regulations in their utmost extent, could remove the pressure of it even for a single century. And it appears, therefore, to be decisive against the possible existence of a society, all the members of which should live in ease, happiness, and comparative leisure; and feel no anxiety about providing the means of subsistence for themselves and families.

Consequently, if the premises are just, the argument is conclusive against the perfectibility of the mass of mankind. . . .

AN ESSAY ON THE PRINCIPLE OF POPULATION

Of the general Checks to Population, and the Mode of
their Operation

The ultimate check to population appears . . . to be a want of food, arising necessarily from the different ratios according to which population and food increase. But this ultimate check is never the immediate check, except in cases of actual famine.

The immediate check may be stated to consist in all those customs, and all those diseases, which seem to be generated by a scarcity of the means of subsistence; and all those causes, independent of this scarcity, whether of a moral or physical nature, which tend prematurely to weaken and destroy the human frame.

These checks to population, which are constantly operating with more or less force in every society, and keep down the number to the level of the means of subsistence, may be classed under two general heads—the preventive, and the positive checks.

The preventive check, as far as it is voluntary, is peculiar to man, and arises from that distinctive superiority in his reasoning faculties, which enables him to calculate distant consequences. The checks to the indefinite increase of plants and irrational animals are all either positive, or, if preventive, involuntary. But man cannot look around him, and see the distress which frequently presses upon those who have large families; he cannot contemplate his present possessions or earnings, which he now nearly consumes himself, and calculate the amount of each share, when with very little addition they must be divided, perhaps, among seven or eight, without feeling a doubt whether, if he follow the bent of his inclinations, he may be able to support the offspring which he will probably bring into the world. . . .

These considerations are calculated to prevent, and certainly do prevent, a great number of persons in all civilised nations from pursuing the dictate of nature in an early attachment to one woman. . . .

The positive checks to population are extremely various, and include every cause, whether arising from vice or misery, which in any degree contributes to shorten the natural duration of human life. Under this head, therefore, may be enumerated all unwholesome occupations, severe labour and exposure to the seasons, extreme poverty, bad nursing of children, great towns, excesses of all kinds, the whole train of common diseases and epidemics, wars, plague, and famine. . . .

The sum of all these preventive and positive checks, taken together, forms the immediate check to population. . . .

In every country some of these checks are, with more or less force, in constant operation; yet, notwithstanding their general prevalence, there are few states in which there is not a constant effort in the population to increase beyond the means of subsistence. This constant effort as constantly tends to subject the lower classes of society to distress, and to prevent any great permanent melioration of their condition. . . .

Of Our Rational Expectations Respecting Future Improvements

If the principles which I have endeavoured to establish be false, I most sincerely hope to see them completely refuted; but if they be true, the subject is so important, and interests the question of human happiness so nearly, that it is impossible they should not in time be more fully known and more generally circulated, whether any particular efforts be made for the purpose or not.

Among the higher and middle classes of society, the effect of this knowledge will, I hope, be to direct without relaxing their efforts in bettering the condition of the poor; to shew them what they can and what they cannot do; and that, although much may be done by advice and instruction, by encouraging habits of prudence and cleanliness, by discriminate charity, and by any mode of bettering the present condition of the poor which is followed by an increase of the preventive check; yet that, without this last effect, all the former efforts would be futile; and that, in any old and well-peopled state, to assist the poor in such a manner as to enable them to marry as early as they please, and rear up large families, is a physical impossibility. This knowledge, by tending to prevent the rich from destroying the good effects of their own exertions, and wasting their efforts in a direction where success is unattainable, would confine their attention to the proper objects, and thus enable them to do more good.

Among the poor themselves, its effects would be still more important. That the principal and most permanent cause of poverty has little or no *direct* relation to forms of government, or the unequal division of property; and that, as the rich do not in reality possess the *power* of finding employment and maintenance for the poor, the poor cannot, in the nature of things, possess the *right* to demand them; are important truths flowing from the principle of population, which, when properly explained, would by no means be above the most ordinary comprehensions. And it is evident that every man in the lower classes of society, who became acquainted with these truths, would be disposed to bear the distresses in which he might be involved with more patience; would feel less discontent and irritation at the government and the higher classes of society, on account of his poverty; would be on all occasions less disposed to insubordination and turbulence; and if he received assistance, either from any public institution or from the hand of private charity, he would receive it with more thankfulness, and more justly appreciate its value.

If these truths were by degrees more generally known, (which in the course of time does not seen to be improbable from the natural effects of the mutual interchange of opinions,) the lower classes of people, as a body, would become more peaceable and orderly, would be less inclined to tumultuous proceedings in seasons of scarcity and would at all times be less influenced by inflammatory and seditious publications, from knowing how little the price of labour and the means of supporting a family depend upon a revolution. The mere knowledge of these truths, even if they did not operate sufficiently to produce any marked change in the prudential habits of the poor with regard to marriage, would still have a most beneficial effect on their conduct in a political light; and undoubtedly, one of the most valuable of these effects would be the power, that would result to the higher and middle classes of society, of gradually improving their governments, without the apprehension of those revolutionary excesses, the fear of which, at present, threatens to deprive Europe even of that degree of liberty, which she had before experienced to be practicable, and the salutary effects of which she had long enjoyed.

From a review of the state of society in former periods, compared with the present, I should certainly say that the evils resulting from the principle of population have rather diminished than increased, even under the disadvantage of an almost total ignorance of the real cause. And if we can indulge the hope that this ignorance will be gradually dissipated, it does not seem unreasonable to expect that they will be still further diminished. The increase of absolute population, which will of course take place, will evidently tend but little to weaken this expectation, as everything depends upon the relative proportion between population and food, and not on the absolute number of people. In the former part of this work it appeared that the countries, which possessed the fewest people, often suffered the most from the effects of the principle of population; and it can scarcely be doubted that, taking Europe throughout, fewer famines and fewer diseases arising from want have prevailed in the last century than in those which preceded it.

On the whole, therefore, though our future prospects respecting the mitigation of the evils arising from the principle of population may not be so bright as we could wish, yet they are far from being entirely disheartening, and by no means preclude that gradual and progressive improvement in human society, which, before the late wild speculations on this subject, was the object of rational expectation.

21. SMITH

System of Natural Liberty

Adam Smith (1723–90) published the first edition of *The Wealth of Nations* in 1776. Although the book grew out of Smith's classroom lectures in political economy at the University of Glasgow, he first began writing it in France in 1767. Accordingly, the book reflects Smith's extensive contacts over several years with the French economists, the Physiocrats, who also championed a "natural order of liberty" in economic policy.

The Wealth of Nations is generally recognized as the founding work of modern economic theory and as the pioneer effort at interpretation of early stages of British capitalism. It provides the major theoretical framework for the economic views of nineteenth-century liberalism.

The selection shows two major features of this framework. First, Smith's exposition of a "system of natural liberty" was crucial for the liberal position on limits of state intervention into the economy. Second, Smith's defense of free trade crystallized, on economic grounds, liberal cosmopolitanism and, particularly, its opposition to imperialism.*

* The two selections are from *The Wealth of Nations*, from Book IV, Chapter IX "The Agricultural System," and from Book IV, Chapter II "Of Restraints upon Importation of Goods."

NATURAL LIBERTY

The greatest and most important branch of the commerce of every nation . . . is that which is carried on between the inhabitants of the town and those of the country. The inhabitants of the town draw from the country the rude produce which constitutes both the materials of. their work and the fund of their subsistence; and they pay for this rude produce by sending back to the country a certain portion of it manufactured and prepared for immediate use. The trade which is carried on between these two different sets of people consists ultimately in a certain quantity of rude produce exchanged for a certain quantity of manufactured produce. The dearer the latter, therefore, the cheaper the former; and whatever tends in any country to raise the price of manufactured produce tends to lower that of the rude produce of the land, and thereby to discourage agriculture. The smaller the quantity of manufactured produce which any given quantity of rude produce, or, what comes to the same thing, which the price of any given quantity of rude produce is capable of purchasing, the smaller the exchangeable value of that given quantity of rude produce, the smaller the encouragement which either the landlord has to increase its quantity by improving or the farmer by cultivating the land. Whatever, besides, tends to diminish in any country the number of artificers and manufacturers, tends to diminish the home market, the most important of all markets for the rude produce of the land, and thereby still further to discourage agriculture.

Those systems, therefore, which, preferring agriculture to all other employments, in order to promote it, impose restraints upon manufacturers and foreign trade, act contrary to the very end which they propose, and indirectly discourage that very species of industry which they mean to promote. They are so far, perhaps, more inconsistent than even the mercantile system. That system, by encouraging manufactures and foreign trade more than agriculture, turns a certain portion of the capital of the society from supporting a more advantageous, to support a less advantageous species of industry. But still it really and in the end encourages that species of industry which it means to promote. Those agricultural systems, on the contrary, really and in the end discourage their own favourite species of industry.

It is thus that every system which endeavours, either by extraordinary encouragements to draw towards a particular species of industry a greater share of the capital of the society than what would naturally go to it, or, by extraordinary restraints, force from a particular species of industry some share of the capital which would otherwise be employed in it, is in reality subversive of the great purpose which it means to promote. It retards, instead of accelerating, the progress of the society towards real wealth and greatness; and diminishes, instead of increasing, the real value of the annual produce of its land and labour.

All systems either of preference or of restraint, therefore, being thus completely taken away, the obvious and simple system of natural liberty establishes itself of its own accord. Every man, as long as he does not violate the laws of justice, is left perfectly free to pursue his own interest his own way, and to bring both his industry and capital into competition with those of any other man, or order of men. The sovereign is completely discharged from a duty, in the attempting to perform which he must always be exposed to innumerable delusions, and for the proper performance of which no human wisdom or knowledge could ever be sufficient; the duty of superintending the industry of private people, and of directing it towards the employments most suitable to the interest of the society. According to the system of natural liberty, the sovereign has only three duties to attend to; three duties of great importance, indeed, but plain and intelligible to common understandings: first, the duty of protecting the society from the violence and invasion of other independent societies; secondly, the duty of protecting, as far as possible, every member of the society from the injustice or oppression of every other member of it, or the duty of establishing an exact administration of justice; and, thirdly, the duty of erecting and maintaining certain public works and certain public institutions which it can never be for the interest of any individual, or small number of individuals, to erect and maintain; because the profit could never repay the expense to any individual or small number of individuals, though it may frequently do much more than repay it to a great society. . . .

FREE TRADE

. . . As the number of workmen that can be kept in employment by any particular person must bear a certain proportion to his capital, so the number of those that can be continually employed by all the members of a great society must bear a certain proportion to the whole capital of that society, and never can exceed that proportion. No regulation of commerce can increase the quantity of industry in any society beyond what its capital can maintain. It can only divert a part of it into a direction into which it might not otherwise have gone; and it is by no means certain that this artificial direction is likely to be more advantageous to the society than that into which it would have gone of its own accord.

Every individual is continually exerting himself to find out the most advantageous employment for whatever capital he can command. It is his own advantage, indeed, and not that of the society, which he has in view. But the study of his own advantage naturally, or rather necessarily, leads him to prefer that employment which is most advantageous to the society.

First, every individual endeavours to employ his capital as near home as he can, and consequently as much as he can in the support of domestic industry; provided always that he can thereby obtain the ordinary, or not a great deal less than the ordinary profits of stock.

Thus, upon equal or nearly equal profits, every wholesale merchant naturally prefers the home trade to the foreign trade of consumption, and the foreign trade of consumption to the carrying trade. In the home trade his capital is never so long out of his sight as it frequently is in the foreign trade of consumption. He can know better the character and situation of the persons whom he trusts, and if he should happen to be deceived, he knows better the laws of the country from which he must seek redress. . . . Home is in this manner the centre, if I may say so, round which the capitals of the inhabitants of every country are continually circulating, and towards which they are always tending, though by particular causes they may sometimes be driven off and repelled from it towards more distant employments. But a capital employed in the home trade, it has already been shown, necessarily puts into motion a greater quantity of domestic industry, and gives revenue and employment to a greater number of the inhabitants of the country, than an equal capital employed in the foreign trade of consumption: and one employed in the foreign trade of consumption has the same advantage over an equal capital employed in the carrying trade. Upon equal, or only nearly equal profits, therefore, every individual naturally inclines to employ his capital in the manner in which it is likely to afford the greatest support to domestic industry, and to give revenue and employment to the greatest number of people of his own country.

Secondly, every individual who employs his capital in the support of domestic industry, necessarily endeavours so to direct that industry that its produce may be of the greatest possible value.

The produce of industry is what it adds to the subject or materials upon which it is employed. In proportion as the value of this produce is great or small, so will likewise be the profits of the employer. But it is only for the sake of profit that any man employs a capital in the support of industry; and he will always, therefore, endeavour to employ it in the support of that industry of which the produce is likely to be of the greatest value, or to exchange for the greatest quantity either of money or of other goods.

But the annual revenue of every society is always precisely equal to the exchangeable value of the whole annual produce of its industry, or rather is precisely the same thing with that exchangeable value. As every individual, therefore, endeavours as much as he can both to employ his capital in the support of domestic industry, and so to direct that industry that its produce may be of the greatest value; every individual necessarily labours to render the annual revenue of the society as great as he can. He generally, indeed, neither intends to promote the public interest, nor knows how much he is promoting it. By preferring the support of domestic to that of foreign industry, he intends only his own security; and by directing that industry in such a manner as its produce may be of the greatest value, he intends only his own gain, and he is in this, as in many other cases, led by an invisible hand to promote an end which was no part of his intention. Nor is it always the worse for the society that it was no part of it. By pursuing his own interest he frequently promotes that of the society more effectually than when he really intends to promote it. I have never known much good done by those who affected to trade for the public good. It is an affectation, indeed, not very common among merchants, and very few words need be employed in dissuading them from it.

What is the species of domestic industry which his capital can employ, and of which the produce is likely to be of the greatest value, every individual, it is evident, can, in his local situation, judge much better than any statesman or lawgiver can do for him. The statesman who should attempt to direct private people in what manner they ought to employ their capitals would not only load himself with a most unnecessary attention, but assume an authority which could safely be trusted, not only to no single person, but to no council or senate whatever, and which would nowhere be so dangerous as in the hands of a man who had folly and presumption enough to fancy himself fit to exercise it.

To give the monopoly of the home market to the produce of domestic industry, in any particular art or manufacture, is in some measure to direct private people in what manner they ought to employ their capitals, and must, in almost all cases, be either a useless or a hurtful regulation. If the produce of domestic can be brought there as cheap as that of foreign industry, the regulation is evidently useless. If it cannot, it must generally be hurtful. It is the maxim of every prudent master of a family never to attempt to make at home what it will cost him more to make than to buy. The tailor does not attempt to make his own shoes, but buys them of the shoemaker. The shoemaker does not attempt to make his own clothes, but employs a tailor. The farmer attempts to make neither the one nor the other, but employs those different artificers. All of them find it for their interest to employ their whole industry in a way in which they have some advantage over their neighbours, and to purchase with a part of its produce, or what is the same thing, with the price of a part of it, whatever else they have occasion for.

What is prudence in the conduct of every private family can scarce be folly in that of a great kingdom. If a foreign country can supply us with a commodity cheaper than we ourselves can make it, better buy it of them with some part of the produce of our own industry employed in a way in which we have some advantage. The general industry of the country, being always in proportion to the capital which employs it, will not thereby be diminished, no more than that of the above-mentioned artificers; but only left to find out the way in which it can be employed with the greatest advantage. It is certainly not employed to the greatest advantage when it is thus directed towards an object which it can buy cheaper than it can make. The value of its annual produce is certainly more or less diminished when it is thus turned away from producing commodities evidently of more value than the commodity which it is directed to produce. According to the supposition, that commodity could be purchased from foreign countries cheaper than it can be made at home. It could, therefore, have been purchased with a part only of the commodities, or, what is the same thing, with a part only of the price of the commodities, which the industry employed by an equal capital would have produced at home, had it been left to follow its natural course. The industry of the country, therefore, is thus turned away from a more to a less advantageous employment, and the exchangeable value of its annual produce, instead of being increased, according to the intention of the lawgiver, must necessarily be diminished by every such regulation. . . .

22. BENTHAM
The Defense of Usury

Jeremy Bentham wrote *The Defense of Usury* in the form of letters to a friend, including a letter to Adam Smith, while he was visiting Russia in 1787. Bentham viewed himself as a disciple of Smith's in economic theory; he sought to develop Smith's doctrines in order to show how economic freedom for the individual on questions of rates of interest would maximize utility for the community. The specific context of Bentham's *Defense* was the proposal of a law setting maximum interest rates, and Bentham's intervention was successful in opposing passage of the law.

INTRODUCTION

Among the various species or modifications of liberty, of which on different occasions we have heard so much in England, I do not recollect ever seeing anything yet offered in behalf of the *liberty of making one's own terms in money-bargains*. From so general and universal a neglect, it is an old notion of mine, as you well know, that this meek and unassuming species of liberty has been suffering much injustice.

A fancy has taken me, just now, to trouble you with my reasons: which, if you think them capable of answering any good purpose, you may forward to the press: or in the other case, what will give you less trouble, to the fire.

In a word, the proposition I have been accustomed to lay down to myself on this subject is the following one, viz. that *no man of ripe years and of sound mind, acting freely, and with his eyes open, ought to be hindered, with a view to his advantage, from making such bargain, in the way of obtaining money, as he thinks fit: nor,* (what is a necessary consequence) *anybody hindered from supplying him, upon any terms he thinks proper to accede to.*

This proposition, were it to be received, would level, you see, at one stroke, all the barriers which law, either statute or common, have in their united wisdom set up, either against the crying sin of Usury, or against the hard-named and little-heard-of practice of Champerty; to which we must also add a portion of the multifarious, and as little-heard-of offence, of Maintenance.

On this occasion, were it any individual antagonist I had to deal with, my part would be a smooth and easy one. "You, who fetter contracts; you, who lay restraints on the liberty of man, it is for you" (I should say) "to assign a reason for your doing so." That contracts in general ought to be observed, is a rule, the propriety of which, no man was ever yet found wrong-headed enough to deny: if this case is one of the exceptions (for some doubtless there are) which the safety and welfare of every society require should be taken out of that general rule, in this case, as in all those others, it lies upon him, who alleges the necessity of the exception, to produce a reason for it. . . .

REASONS FOR RESTRAINT—PREVENTION OF USURY

. . . A law punishing usury supposes a law fixing the allowed legal rate of interest: and the propriety of the penal law must depend upon the propriety of the simply-prohibitive, or, if you please, declaratory one.

One thing then is plain; that, antecedently to custom growing from convention, there can be no such thing as usury: for what rate of interest is there that can naturally be more proper than another? what natural fixed price can there be for the use of money more than for the use of any other thing? Were it not then for custom, usury, considered in a moral view, would not then so much as admit of a definition: so far from having existence, it would not so much as be conceivable: nor therefore could the law, in the definition it took upon itself to give of such offence, have so much as a guide to steer by. Custom therefore is the sole basis, which, either the moralist in his rules and precepts, or the legislator in his injunctions, can have to build upon. But what basis can be more weak or unwarrantable, as a ground for coercive measures, than custom resulting from free choice? My neighbours, being at liberty, have happened to concur among themselves in dealing at a certain rate of interest. I, who have money to lend, and Titius, who wants to borrow it of me, would be glad, the one of us to accept, the other to give, an interest somewhat higher than theirs: why is the liberty they exercise to be made a pretence for depriving me and Titius of ours?

Nor has blind custom, thus made the sole and arbitrary guide, anything of steadiness or uniformity in its decisions: it has varied, from age to age, in the same country: it varies, from country to country, in the same age: and the legal rate has varied along with it: and indeed, with regard to times past, it is from the legal rate, more readily than from any other source, that we collect the customary. . . . Now, of all these widely different rates, what one is there, that is intrinsically more proper than another? What is it that evidences this propriety in each instance? what but the mutual convenience of the parties, as manifested by their consent? It is convenience then that has produced whatever there has been of custom in the matter: What can there then be in custom, to make it a better guide than the convenience which gave it birth? and what is there in convenience, that should make it a worse guide in one case than in another? It would be convenient to me to give six per cent for money: I wish to do so. "No," (says the law) "you shan't."—Why so? "Because it is not convenient to your neighbour to give above five for it." Can anything be more absurd than such a reason?

Much has not been done, I think, by legislators as yet in the way of fixing the price of other commodities: and, in what little has been done, the probity of the intention has, I believe, in general, been rather more unquestionable than the rectitude of the principle, of the felicity of the result. Putting money out at interest, is exchanging present money for future: but why a policy, which, as applied to exchanges in general, would be generally deemed absurd and mischievous, should be deemed necessary in the instance of this particular kind of exchange, mankind are as yet to learn. For him who takes as much as he can get for the use of any other sort of thing, an house for instance, there is no particular appellation, nor any mark of disrepute: nobody is ashamed of doing so, nor is it usual so much as to profess to do otherwise. Why a man who takes as much as he can get, be it six, or seven, or eight, or ten per cent for the use of a sum of money, should be called usurer, should be loaded with an opprobrious name, any more than if he had bought an house with it, and made a proportionable profit by the house, is more than I can see.

Another thing I would also wish to learn, is, why the legislator should
be more anxious to limit the rate of interest one way, than the other?
why he should set his face against the owners of that species of property
more than of any other? why he should make it his business to prevent
their getting *more* than a certain price for the use of it, rather than to
prevent their getting *less?* why, in short, he should not take means
for making it penal to offer less, for example, than five per cent as
well as to accept more? Let anyone that can, find an answer to these
questions; it is more than I can do: I except always the distant and
imperceptible advantage, of sinking the price of goods of all kinds;
and, in that remote way, multiplying the future enjoyments of individuals. But this was a consideration by far too distant and refined, to
have been the original ground for confining the limitation to this side.

REASONS FOR RESTRAINT—PROTECTION OF
INDIGENCE

Besides prodigals, there are three other classes of persons, and but
three, for whose security I can conceive these restrictive laws to have
been designed. I mean the indigent, the rashly enterprizing, and the
simple: those whose pecuniary necessities may dispose them to give
an interest above the ordinary rate, rather than not have it, and those
who, from rashness, may be disposed to venture upon giving such a
rate, or from carelessness combined with ignorance, may be disposed
to acquiesce in it. . . .

A man is in one of these situations, suppose, in which it would be
for his advantage to borrow. But his circumstances are such, that it
would not be worth anybody's while to lend him, at the highest rate
which it is proposed the law should allow; in short, he cannot get it
at that rate. If he thought he *could* get it at that rate, most surely he
would not give a higher: he may be trusted for that: for by the supposition he has nothing defective in his understanding. But the fact is,
he cannot get it at that lower rate. At a higher rate, however, he could
get it: and at that rate, though higher, it would be worth his while to
get it: so he judges, who has nothing to hinder him from judging right;
who has every motive and every means for forming a right judgment;
who has every motive and every means for informing himself of the
circumstances, upon which rectitude of judgment, in the case in
question, depends. The legislator, who knows nothing, nor can know

anything, of any one of all these circumstances, who knows nothing at all about the matter, comes and says to him—"It signifies nothing; you shall not have the money: for it would be doing you a mischief to let you borrow it upon such terms."—And this out of prudence and loving-kindness!—There may be worse cruelty: but can there be greater folly?

The folly of those who persist, as is supposed, without reason, in not taking advice, has been much expatiated upon. But the folly of those who persist, without reason, in forcing their advice upon others, has been but little dwelt upon, though it is, perhaps, the more frequent, and the more flagrant of the two. It is not often that one man is a better judge for another, than that other is for himself, even in cases were the adviser will take the trouble to make himself master of as many of the materials for judging, as are within the reach of the person to be advised. But the legislator is not, cannot be, in the possession of any one of these materials.—What private, can be equal to such public folly? . . .

23. BERNSTEIN

Socialism and Liberalism

Eduard Bernstein (1850–1932) published *Evolutionary Socialism*, from which the selection is taken, in 1899.* In the preface to the first edition he wrote: "The present work is substantially devoted to the establishment of ideas which the writer unfolded in a letter to the German Social Democratic Party assembled at Stuttgart from October 3rd to October 8th, 1898." Bernstein had called upon the Social Democratic Party to accentuate the achievement of power through democratic and parliamentary methods rather than by preparation for revolution arising from the anticipated catastrophic collapse of capitalism. The subsequent Party Congress in Hannover in 1899 put the book on the agenda, debated it for three and a half days, and rejected Bernstein's views.

* Eduard Bernstein, *Evolutionary Socialism: A Criticism and Affirmation*, translated by Edith C. Harvey.

Bernstein's "revisionism," as this explicit effort to revise the socialist doctrine of Marx and Engels was called, has proved to be of continuing significance for democratic socialists and for liberals.

Eduard Bernstein was one of the founders of the German Social Democratic Party in 1875. He moved to Switzerland in 1878 where he edited the Social Democratic Party paper which was distributed secretly in Germany. After the Swiss banished him in 1888, he moved to London where he collaborated with Marx and Engels. Engels named him as his literary executor. Bernstein returned to Germany in 1901, was elected to the Reichstag, and became a Minister of the German government after the First World War.

> "Who speaks of universal suffrage utters a cry of reconciliation."
>
> LASSALLE, Workers' Programme.

. . . What is the principle of democracy?

The answer to this appears very simple. At first one would think it settled by the definition "government by the people." But even a little consideration tells us that by that only quite a superficial, purely formal definition is given, whilst nearly all who use the word democracy today understand by it more than a mere form of government. We shall come much nearer to the definition if we express ourselves negatively, and define democracy as an absence of class government, as the indication of a social condition where a political privilege belongs to no one class as opposed to the whole community. By that the explanation is already given as to why a monopolist corporation is in principle anti-democratic. This negative definition has, besides, the advantage that it gives less room than the phrase "government by the people" to the idea of the oppression of the individual by the majority which is absolutely repugnant to the modern mind. Today we find the oppression of the minority by the majority "undemocratic," although it was originally held to be quite consistent with government by the people. The idea of democracy includes, in the conception of the present day, a notion of justice—an equality of rights for all members of the community, and in that principle the rule of the majority, to which in every concrete case the rule of the people extends, finds its limits. The more it is adopted and governs the general consciousness, the more will democracy be equal in meaning to the highest possible degree of freedom for all.

Democracy is in principle the suppression of class government, though it is not yet the actual suppression of classes. They speak of the conservative character of the democracy, and to a certain degree rightly. Absolutism, or semi-absolutism, deceives its supporters as well as its opponents as to the extent of their power. Therefore in countries where it obtains, or where its traditions still exist, we have flitting plans, exaggerated language, zigzag politics, fear of revolution, hope in oppression. In a democracy the parties, and the classes standing behind them, soon learn to know the limits of their power, and to undertake each time only as much as they can reasonably hope to carry through under the existing circumstances. Even if they make their demands rather higher than they seriously mean in order to give way in the unavoidable compromise—and democracy is the high school of compromise—they must still be moderate. The right to vote in a democracy makes its members virtually partners in the community, and this virtual partnership must in the end lead to real partnership. With a working class undeveloped in numbers and culture the general right to vote may long appear as the right to choose "the butcher"; with the growing number and knowledge of the workers it is changed, however, into the implement by which to transform the representatives of the people from masters into real servants of the people. . . .

Universal franchise is, from two sides, the alternative to a violent revolution. But universal suffrage is only a part of democracy, although a part which in time must draw the other parts after it as the magnet attracts to itself the scattered portions of iron. It certainly proceeds more slowly than many would wish, but in spite of that it is at work. And social democracy cannot further this work better than by taking its stand unreservedly on the theory of democracy—on the ground of universal suffrage with all the consequences resulting therefrom to its tactics.

In practice—that is, in its actions—it has in Germany always done so. But in their explanations its literary advocates have often acted otherwise, and still often do so today. Phrases which were composed in a time when the political privilege of property ruled all over Europe, and which under these circumstances were explanatory, and to a certain degree also justified, but which today are only a dead weight, are treated with such reverence as though the progress of the movement depended on them and not on the understanding of what can be done, and what should be done. Is there any sense, for example, in maintaining the phrase of the "dictatorship of the proletariat" at a time when in all possible places representatives of social democracy have placed themselves practically in the arena of Parliamentary work, have declared for the proportional representation of the people, and for direct legislation—all of which is inconsistent with a dictatorship.

The phrase is today so antiquated that it is only to be reconciled with reality by stripping the word dictatorship of its actual meaning and attaching to it some kind of weakened interpretation. The whole practical activity of social democracy is directed towards creating circumstances and conditions which shall render possible and secure a transition (free from convulsive outbursts) of the modern social order into a higher one. From the consciousness of being the pioneers of a higher civilisation, its adherents are ever creating fresh inspiration and zeal. In this rests also, finally, the moral justification of the socialist expropriation towards which they aspire. But the "dictatorship of the classes" belongs to a lower civilisation, and apart from the question of the expediency and practicability of the thing, it is only to be looked upon as a reversion, as political atavism. . . .

Finally, it is to be recommended that some moderation should be kept in the declaration of war against "liberalism." It is true that the great liberal movement of modern times arose for the advantage of the capitalist bourgeoisie first of all, and the parties which assumed the names of liberals were, or became in due course, simple guardians of capitalism. Naturally, only opposition can reign between these parties and social democracy. But with respect to liberalism as a great historical movement, socialism is its legitimate heir, not only in chronological sequence, but also in its spiritual qualities, as is shown moreover in every question of principle in which social democracy has had to take up an attitude.

Wherever an economic advance of the socialist programme had to be carried out in a manner, or under circumstances, that appeared seriously to imperil the development of freedom, social democracy has never shunned taking up a position against it. The security of civil freedom has always seemed to it to stand higher than the fulfilment of some economic progress.

The aim of all socialist measures, even of those which appear outwardly as coercive measures, is the development and the securing of a free personality. Their more exact examination always shows that the coercion included will raise the sum total of liberty in society, and will give more freedom over a more extended area than it takes away. The legal day of a maximum number of hours' work, for example, is actually a fixing of a minimum of freedom, a prohibition to sell freedom longer than for a certain number of hours daily, and, in principle, therefore, stands on the same ground as the prohibition agreed to by all liberals against selling oneself into personal slavery. It is thus no accident that the first country where a maximum hours' day was carried out was Switzerland, the most democratically progressive country in Europe, and democracy is only the political form of liberalism. Being in its origin a counter-movement to the oppression of nations under institutions imposed from without or having a justification only in tradition, liberalism first sought its realisation as the principle of the sovereignty of the age and of the people, both of which principles formed the everlasting discussion of the philosophers of the rights of the state in the seventeenth and eighteenth centuries, until Rousseau set them up in his *Contrat Social* as the fundamental conditions of the legitimacy of every constitution, and the French Revolution proclaimed them— in the Democratic Constitution of 1793 permeated with Rousseau's spirit—as inalienable rights of men.

The Constitution of 1793 was the logical expression of the liberal ideas of the epoch, and a cursory glance over its contents shows how little it was, or is, an obstacle to socialism. Baboeuf, and the believers in absolute equality, saw in it an excellent starting point for the realisation of their communistic strivings, and accordingly wrote "The Restoration of the Constitution of 1793" at the head of their demands.

There is actually no really liberal thought which does not also belong to the elements of the ideas of socialism. Even the principle of economic personal responsibility which belongs apparently so entirely to the Manchester School cannot, in my judgment, be denied in theory by socialism nor be made inoperative under any conceivable circumstances. Without responsibility there is no freedom; we may think as we like theoretically about man's freedom of action, we must practically start from it as the foundation of the moral law, for only under this condition is social morality possible. And similarly, in our states which reckon with millions, a healthy social life is, in the age of traffic, impossible if the economic personal responsibility of all those capable of work is not assumed. The recognition of individual responsibility is the return of the individual to society for services rendered or offered him by society. . . .

Liberalism had historically the task of breaking the chains which the fettered economy and the corresponding organisations of law of the middle ages had imposed on the further development of society.

That it at first strictly maintained the form of bourgeois liberalism did not stop it from actually expressing a very much wider-reaching general principle of society whose completion will be socialism.

Socialism will create no new bondage of any kind whatever. The individual is to be free, not in the metaphysical sense, as the anarchists dreamed—i.e., free from all duties towards the community—but free from every economic compulsion in his action and choice of a calling. Such freedom is only possible for all by means of organisation. In this sense one might call socialism "organising liberalism," for when one examines more closely the organisations that socialism wants and how it wants them, he will find that what distinguishes them above all from the feudalistic organisations, outwardly like them, is just their liberalism, their democratic constitution, their accessibility. . . .

If democracy is not to excel centralised absolutism in the breeding of bureaucracies, it must be built up on an elaborately organised self-government with a corresponding economic, personal responsibility of all the units of administration as well as of the adult citizens of the state. Nothing is more injurious to its healthy development than enforced uniformity and a too abundant amount of protectionism or subventionism.

To create the organisations described—or, so far as they are already begun, to develop them further—is the indispensable preliminary to what we call socialism of production. Without them the so-called social appropriation of the means of production would only result presumably in reckless devastation of productive forces, insane experimentalising and aimless violence, and the political sovereignty of the working class would, in fact, only be carried out in the form of a dictatorial, revolutionary, central power, supported by the terrorist dictatorship of revolutionary clubs. . . .

Simple as democracy appears to be at the first glance, its problems in such a complicated society as ours are in no way easy to solve. Read only in the volumes of *Industrial Democracy* by Mr. and Mrs. Webb how many experiments the English trade unions had to make and are still making in order to find out the most serviceable forms of government and administration, and of what importance this question of constitution is to trade unions. The English trade unions have been able to develop in this respect for over seventy years in perfect freedom. They began with the most elementary form of self-government and have been forced to convince themselves that this form is only suited to the most elementary organisms, for quite small, local unions. As they grew they gradually learned to renounce as injurious to their successful development certain cherished ideas of doctrinaire democracy (the imperative mandate, the unpaid official, the powerless central representation), and to form instead of it a democracy capable of governing with representative assemblies, paid officials, and central government with full powers. This section of the history of the development of "trade union democracy" is extremely instructive. If all that concerns trade unions does not quite fit the units of national administration, yet much of it does. . . .

I am not concerned with what will happen in the more distant future, but with what can and ought to happen in the present, for the present and the nearest future. And so the conclusion of this exposition is the very banal statement that the conquest of the democracy, the formation of political and social organs of the democracy, is the indispensable preliminary condition to the realisation of socialism.

Feudalism, with its unbending organisations and corporations, had to be destroyed nearly everywhere by violence. The liberal organisations of modern society are distinguished from those exactly because they are flexible, and capable of change and development. They do not need to be destroyed, but only to be further developed. For that we need organisation and energetic action, but not necessarily a revolutionary dictatorship. "As the object of the class war is especially to destroy distinctions of class," wrote some time since (October, 1897) a social democratic Swiss organ, the *Vorwärts* of Basle, "a period must logically be agreed upon in which the realisation of this object, of this ideal, must be begun. This beginning, these periods following on one another, are already founded in our democratic development; they come to our help, to serve gradually as a substitute for the class war, to absorb it into themselves by the building up of the social democracy." "The bourgeoisie, of what ever shade of opinion it may be." declared lately the Spanish socialist, Pablo Iglesias, "must be convinced of this, that we do not wish to take possession of the Government by the same means that were once employed, by violence and bloodshed, but by lawful means which are suited to civilisation" (*Vorwärts*, October 16th, 1898). . . . And another organ of the English socialist working class democracy, the *Clarion*, accompanied an extract from my article on the theory of catastrophic evolution with the following commentary:

"The formation of a true democracy—I am quite convinced that that is the most pressing and most important duty which lies before

us. This is the lesson which the socialist campaign of the last ten years
has taught us. That is the doctrine which emerges out of all my knowledge and experiences of politics. We must build up a national of democrats before socialism is possible."

24. VON HAYEK
The Rule of Law

Friedrich August von Hayek (1899–   ) was born in Vienna,
where he was trained as an economist and became Director of the Austrian
Institute for Economic Research. He left Austria in the 1930's, has since
taught at London and Chicago, and is currently at the University of Freiburg
in Germany. In his book *The Constitution of Liberty*, published in 1960, von
Hayek reformulated the traditional conception of economic liberalism as
excluding various measures of state interventions on the ground that inter-
ventionism over the long run was incompatible with rule of law. The selection
is Chapter Fifteen of that work.*

ECONOMIC POLICY AND THE RULE OF LAW

The house of representatives . . . can make no law which will
not have its full operation on themselves and their friends, as
well as the great mass of society. This [circumstance] has always
been deemed one of the strongest bonds by which human policy
can connect the rulers and the people together. It creates between
them that communion of interest, and sympathy of sentiments,
of which few governments have furnished examples; but without
which every government degenerates into tyranny.

JAMES MADISON

1. The classical argument for freedom in economic affairs rests on
the tacit postulate that the rule of law should govern policy in this as

* From *The Constitution of Liberty*. (Chicago: University of Chicago Press, 1960.)
Used by permission.

in all other spheres. We cannot understand the nature of the opposition of men like Adam Smith or John Stuart Mill to government "intervention" unless we see it against this background. Their position was therefore often misunderstood by those who were not familiar with that basic conception; and confusion arose in England and America as soon as the conception of the rule of law ceased to be assumed by every reader. Freedom of economic activity had meant freedom under the law, not the absence of all government action. The "interference" or "intervention" of government which those writers opposed as a matter of principle therefore meant only the infringement of that private sphere which the general rules of law were intended to protect. They did not mean that government should never concern itself with any economic matters. But they did mean that there were certain kinds of governmental measures which should be precluded on principle and which could not be justified on any grounds of expediency.

To Adam Smith and his immediate successors the enforcement of the ordinary rules of common law would certainly not have appeared as government interference; nor would they ordinarily have applied this term to an alteration of these rules or the passing of a new rule by the legislature so long as it was intended to apply equally to all people for an indefinite period of time. Though they perhaps never explicitly said so, interference meant to them the exercise of the coercive power of government which was not regular enforcement of the general law and which was designed to achieve some specific purpose. The important criterion was not the aim pursued, however, but the method employed. There is perhaps no aim which they would not have regarded as legitimate if it was clear that the people wanted it; but they excluded as generally inadmissible in a free society the method of specific orders and prohibitions. Only indirectly, by depriving government of some means by which alone it might be able to attain certain ends, may this principle deprive government of the power to pursue those ends.

The later economists bear a good share of the responsibility for the confusion on these matters. True, there are good reasons why all governmental concern with economic matters is suspect and why, in particular, there is a strong presumption against government's actively participating in economic efforts. But these arguments are quite different from the general argument for economic freedom. They rest on the fact that the great majority of governmental measures which have been advocated in this field are, in fact, inexpedient, either because they will fail or because their costs will outweigh the advantages. This means that, so long as they are compatible with the rule of law, they cannot be rejected out of hand as government intervention but must be examined in each instance from the viewpoint of expediency. The habitual appeal to the principle of non-interference in the fight against all ill-considered or harmful measures has had the effect of blurring the fundamental distinction between the kinds of measures which are and those which are not compatible with a free system. And the opponents of free enterprise have been only too ready to help this confusion by insisting that the desirability or undesirability of a particular measure could never be a matter of principle but is always one of expediency.

In other words, it is the character rather than the volume of government activity that is important. A functioning market economy presupposes certain activities on the part of the state; there are some other such activities by which its functioning will be assisted; and it can tolerate many more, provided that they are of the kind which are compatible with a functioning market. But there are those which run counter to the very principle on which a free system rests and which must therefore be altogether excluded if such a system is to work. In consequence, a government that is comparatively inactive but does the wrong things may do much more to cripple the forces of a market economy than one that is more concerned with economic affairs but confines itself to actions which assist the spontaneous forces of the economy.

It is the purpose of this chapter to show that the rule of law provides the criterion which enables us to distinguish between those measures which are and those which are not compatible with a free system. Those that are may be examined further on the grounds of expediency. Many such measures will, of course, still be undesirable or even harmful. But those that are not must be rejected even if they provide an effective, or perhaps the only effective, means to a desirable end. We shall see that the observation of the rule of law is a necessary, but not yet a sufficient, condition for the satisfactory working of a free economy. But the important point is that all coercive action of government must be unambiguously determined by a permanent legal framework which enables the individual to plan with a degree of confidence and which reduces human uncertainty as much as possible.

2. Let us consider, first, the distinction between the coercive measures of government and those pure service activities where coercion does

not enter or does so only because of the need of financing them by taxation. In so far as the government merely undertakes to supply services which otherwise would not be supplied at all (usually because it is not possible to confine the benefits to those prepared to pay for them), the only question which arises is whether the benefits are worth the cost. Of course, if the government claimed for itself the exclusive right to provide particular services, they would cease to be strictly non-coercive. In general, a free society demands not only that the government have the monopoly of coercion but that it have the monopoly only of coercion and that in all other respects it operate on the same terms as everybody else.

A great many of the activities which governments have universally undertaken in this field and which fall within the limits described are those which facilitate the acquisition of reliable knowledge about facts of general significance. The most important function of this kind is the provision of a reliable and efficient monetary system. Others scarcely less important are the setting of standards of weights and measures; the providing of information gathered from surveying, land registration, statistics, etc.; and the support, if not also the organization, of some kind of education.

All these activities of government are part of its effort to provide a favorable framework for individual decisions; they supply means which individuals can use for their own purposes. Many other services of a more material kind fall into the same category. Though government must not use its power of coercion to reserve for itself activities which have nothing to do with the enforcement of the general rules of law, there is no violation of principle in its engaging in all sorts of activities on the same terms as the citizens. If in the majority of fields there is no good reason why it should do so, there are fields in which the desirability of government action can hardly be questioned.

To this latter group belong all those services which are clearly desirable but which will not be provided by competitive enterprise because it would be either impossible or difficult to charge the individual beneficiary for them. Such are most sanitary and health services, often the construction and maintenance of roads, and many of the amenities provided by municipalities for the inhabitants of cities. Included also are the activities which Adam Smith described as "those public works, which, though they may be in the highest degree advantageous to a great society, are, however, of such a nature, that the profit could never repay the expense to any individual or small number of individuals." And there are many other kinds of activity in which the government may legitimately wish to engage, in order perhaps to maintain secrecy in military preparations or to encourage the advancement of knowledge in certain fields. But though government may at any moment be best qualified to take the lead in such fields, this provides no justification for assuming that this will always be so and therefore for giving it exclusive responsibility. In most instances, moreover, it is by no means necessary that government engage in the actual management of such activities; the services in question can generally be provided, and more effectively provided, by the government's assuming some or all of the financial responsibility but leaving the conduct of the affairs to independent and in some measure competitive agencies.

There is considerable justification for the distrust with which business looks on all state enterprise. There is great difficulty in ensuring that such enterprise will be conducted on the same terms as private enterprise; and it is only if this condition is satisfied that it is not objectionable in principle. So long as government uses any of its coercive powers, and particularly its power of taxation, in order to assist its enterprises, it can always turn their position into one of actual monopoly. To prevent this, it would be necessary that any special advantages, including subsidies, which government gives to its own enterprises in any field, should also be made available to competing private agencies. There is no need to emphasize that it would be exceedingly difficult for government to satisfy these conditions and that the general presumption against state enterprise is thereby considerably strengthened. But this does not mean that all state enterprise must be excluded from a free system. Certainly it ought to be kept within narrow limits; it may become a real danger to liberty if too large a section of economic activity comes to be subject to the direct control of the state. But what is objectionable here is not state enterprise as such but state monopoly.

3. Furthermore, a free system does not exclude on principle all those general regulations of economic activity which can be laid down in the form of general rules specifying conditions which everybody who engages in a certain activity must satisfy. They include, in particular, all regulations governing the techniques of production. We are not concerned here with the question of whether such regulations will be wise, which they probably will be only in exceptional cases. They

will always limit the scope of experimentation and thereby obstruct what may be useful developments. They will normally raise the cost of production or, what amounts to the same thing, reduce over-all productivity. But if this effect on cost is fully taken into account and it is still thought worthwhile to incur the cost to achieve a given end, there is little more to be said about it. The economist will remain suspicious and hold that there is a strong presumption against such measures because their over-all cost is almost always underestimated and because one disadvantage in particular—namely, the prevention of new developments—can never be fully taken into account. But if, for instance, the production and sale of phosphorus matches is generally prohibited for reasons of health or permitted only if certain precautions are taken, or if night work is generally prohibited, the appropriateness of such measures must be judged by comparing the over-all costs with the gain; it cannot be conclusively determined by appeal to a general principle. This is true of most of the wide field of regulations known as "factory legislation."

It is often maintained today that these or similar tasks which are generally acknowledged to be proper functions of government could not be adequately performed if the administrative authorities were not given wide discretionary powers and all coercion were limited by the rule of law. There is little reason to fear this. If the law cannot always name the particular measures which the authorities may adopt in a particular situation, it can be so framed as to enable any impartial court to decide whether the measures adopted were necessary to achieve the general effect aimed at by the law. Though the variety of circumstances in which the authorities may have to act cannot be foreseen, the manner in which they will have to act, once a certain situation has arisen, can be made predictable to a high degree. The destroying of a farmer's cattle in order to stop the spreading of a contagious disease, the tearing-down of houses to prevent the spreading of a fire, the prohibition of an infected well, the requirement of protective measures in the transmission of high-tension electricity, and the enforcement of safety regulations in buildings undoubtedly demand that the authorities be given some discretion in applying general rules. But this need not be a discretion unlimited by general rules or of the kind which need to be exempt from judicial review.

We are so used to such measures being referred to as evidence of the necessity of conferring discretionary powers that it comes somewhat as a surprise that, as recently as thirty years ago, an eminent student of administrative law could still point out that "health and safety statutes are, generally speaking, by no means conspicuous for the use of discretionary power; on the contrary, in much of that legislation such powers are conspicuously absent.

. . . Thus British factory legislation has found it possible to rely practically altogether on general rules (though to a large extent framed by administrative regulation) . . . many building codes are framed with a minimum of administrative discretion, practically all regulations being limited to requirements capable of standardization. . . . In all these cases the consideration of flexibility yielded to the higher consideration of certainty of private right, without any apparent sacrifice of public interest."

In all such instances the decisions are derived from general rules and not from particular preferences which guide the government of the moment or from any opinion as to how particular people ought to be situated. The coercive powers of government still serve general and timeless purposes, not specific ends. It must not make any distinctions between different people. The discretion conferred on it is a limited discretion in that the agent is to apply the sense of a general rule. That this rule cannot be made completely unambiguous in its application is a consequence of human imperfection. The problem, nevertheless, is one of applying a rule, which is shown by the fact that an independent judge, who in no way represents the particular wishes or values of the government or of the majority of the moment, will be able to decide not only whether the authority had a right to act at all but also whether it was required by law to do exactly what it did.

The point at issue here has nothing to do with the question of whether the regulations justifying the actions of government are uniform for the whole country or whether they have been laid down by a democratically elected assembly. There is clearly need for some regulations to be passed by local ordinances, and many of them, such as building codes, will necessarily be only in form and never in substance the product of majority decisions. The important question again concerns not the origin but the limits of the powers conferred. Regulations drawn up by the administrative authority itself but duly published in advance and strictly adhered to will be more in conformity with the rule of law than will vague discretionary powers conferred on the administrative organs by legislative action.

Though there have always been pleas on the ground of administrative convenience that these strict limits should be relaxed, this is certainly not a necessary requirement for the achievement of the aims we have considered so far. It was only after the rule of law had been breached for other aims that its preservation no longer seemed to outweigh considerations of administrative efficiency.

4. We must now turn to the kinds of governmental measures which the rule of law excludes in principle because they cannot be achieved by merely enforcing general rules but, of necessity, involve arbitrary discrimination between persons. The most important among them are decisions as to who is to be allowed to provide different services or commodities, at what prices or in what quantities—in other words, measures designed to control the access to different trades and occupations, the terms of sale, and the amounts to be produced or sold.

So far as the entry into different occupations is concerned, our principle does not necessarily exclude the possible advisability in some instances of permitting it only to those who possess certain ascertainable qualifications. The restriction of coercion to the enforcement of general rules requires, however, that anyone possessing these qualifications have an enforcible claim to such permission and that the grant of the permission depend only on his satisfying the conditions laid down as a general rule and not on any particular circumstances (such as "local need") which would have to be determined by the discretion of the licensing authority. Even the need for such controls could probably be rendered unnecessary in most instances by merely preventing people from pretending to qualifications which they do not possess, that is, by applying the general rules preventing fraud and deception. For this purpose the protection of certain designations or titles expressing such qualifications might well be sufficient (it is by no means evident that even in the case of doctors this would not be preferable to the requirement of a license to practice). But it is probably undeniable that in some instances, such as where the sale of poisons or firearms is involved, it is both desirable and unobjectionable that only persons satisfying certain intellectual and moral qualities should be allowed to practice such trades. So long as everybody possessing the necessary qualifications has the right to practice the occupation in question and, if necessary, can have his claim examined and enforced by an independent court, the basic principle is satisfied.

There are several reasons why all direct control of prices by government is irreconcilable with a functioning free system, whether the government actually fixes prices or merely lays down rules by which the permissible prices are to be determined. In the first place it is impossible to fix prices according to long-term rules which will effectively guide production. Appropriate prices depend on circumstances which are constantly changing and must be continually adjusted to them. On the other hand, prices which are not fixed outright but determined by some rule (such as that they must be in a certain relation to cost) will not be the same for all sellers and, for this reason, will prevent the market from functioning. A still more important consideration is that, with prices different from those that would form on a free market, demand and supply will not be equal, and if the price control is to be effective, some method must be found for deciding who is to be allowed to buy or sell. This would necessarily be discretionary and must consist of *ad hoc* decisions that discriminate between persons on essentially arbitrary grounds. As experience has amply confirmed, price controls can be made effective only by quantitative controls, by decisions on the part of authority as to how much particular persons or firms are to be allowed to buy or sell. And the exercise of all controls of quantities must, of necessity, be discretionary, determined not by rule but by the judgment of authority concerning the relative importance of particular ends.

It is thus not because the economic interests with which such measures interfere are more important than others that price and quantity controls must be altogether excluded in a free system, but because this kind of control cannot be exercised according to rule but must in their very nature be discretionary and arbitrary. To grant such powers to authority means in effect to give it power arbitrarily to determine what is to be produced, by whom, and for whom.

5. Strictly speaking, then, there are two reasons why all controls of prices and quantities are incompatible with a free system: one is that all such controls must be arbitrary, and the other is that it is impossible to exercise them in such a manner as to allow the market to function adequately. A free system can adapt itself to almost any set of data, almost any general prohibition or regulation, so long as the adjusting mechanism itself is kept functioning. And it is mainly changes in prices that bring about the necessary adjustments. This means that, for it to function properly, it is not sufficient that the rules of law under which it operates be general rules, but their content must be such that the market will work tolerably well. The case for a free system is not that any system will work satisfactorily where coercion is confined by general

rules, but that under it such rules can be given a form that will enable it to work. If there is to be an efficient adjustment of the different activities in the market, certain minimum requirements must be met; the more important of these are, as we have seen, the prevention of violence and fraud, the protection of property and the enforcement of contracts, and the recognition of equal rights of all individuals to produce in whatever quantities and sell at whatever prices they choose. Even when these basic conditions have been satisfied, the efficiency of the system will still depend on the particular content of the rules. But if they are not satisfied, government will have to achieve by direct orders what individual decisions guided by price movements will.

The relation between the character of the legal order and the functioning of the market system has received comparatively little study, and most of the work in this field has been done by men who were critical of the competitive order rather than by its supporters. The latter have usually been content to state the minimal requirements for the functioning of the market which we have just mentioned. A general statement of these conditions, however, raises almost as many questions as the answers it provides. How well the market will function depends on the character of the particular rules. The decision to rely on voluntary contracts as the main instrument for organizing the relations between individuals does not determine what the specific content of the law of contract ought to be; and the recognition of the right of private property does not determine what exactly should be the content of this right in order that the market mechanism will work as effectively and beneficially as possible. Though the principle of private property raises comparatively few problems so far as movable things are concerned, it does raise exceedingly difficult ones where property in land is concerned. The effect which the use of any one piece of land often has on neighboring land clearly makes it undesirable to give the owner unlimited power to use or abuse his property as he likes.

But, while it is to be regretted that economists have on the whole contributed little to the solution of these problems, there are some good reasons for this. General speculation about the character of a social order cannot produce much more than equally general statements of the principles that the legal order must follow. The application in detail of these general principles must be left largely to experience and gradual evolution. It presupposes concern with concrete cases, which is more the province of the lawyer than of the economist. At any rate, it is probably because the task of gradually amending our legal system to make it more conducive to the smooth working of competition is such a slow process that it has had little appeal for those who seek an outlet for their creative imagination and are impatient to draw up blueprints for further development.

6. There is still another point we must consider a little more closely. Since the time of Herbert Spencer it has become customary to discuss many aspects of our problem under the heading of "freedom of contract." And for a period of time this point of view played an important role in American jurisdiction. There is indeed a sense in which freedom of contract is an important part of individual freedom. But the phrase also gives rise to misconceptions. In the first place, the question is not what contracts individuals will be allowed to make but rather what contracts the state will enforce. No modern state has tried to enforce all contracts, nor is it desirable that it should. Contracts for criminal or immoral purposes, gambling contracts, contracts in restraint of trade, contracts permanently binding the services of a person, or even some contracts for specific performances are not enforced.

Freedom of contract, like freedom in all other fields, really means that the permissibility of a particular act depends only on general rules and not on its specific approval by authority. It means that the validity and enforcibility of a contract must depend only on those general, equal, and known rules by which all other legal rights are determined, and not on the approval of its particular content by an agency of the government. This does not exclude the possibility of the law's recognizing only those contracts which satisfy certain general conditions or of the state's laying down rules for the interpretation of contracts which will supplement the explicitly agreed terms. The existence of such recognized standard forms of contract which, so long as no contrary terms are stipulated, will be presumed to be part of the agreement often greatly facilitates private dealings.

A much more difficult question is whether the law should ever provide for obligations arising out of a contract which may be contrary to the intentions of both parties, as, for example, in the case of liability for industrial accidents irrespective of negligence. But even this is probably more a question of expediency than of principle. The enforcibility of contracts is a tool which the law provides for us, and what consequences will follow upon concluding a contract is for the law to say. So long as these consequences can be predicted from a general rule and the individual is free to use the available types of contracts for his own purposes, the essential conditions of the rule of law are satisfied.

7. The range and variety of government action that is, at least in principle, reconcilable with a free system is thus considerable. The old formulae of laissez-faire or non-intervention do not provide us with an adequate criterion for distinguishing between what is and what is not admissible in a free system. There is ample scope for experimentation and improvement within that permanent legal framework which makes it possible for a free society to operate most efficiently. We can probably at no point be certain that we have already found the best arrangements or institutions that will make the market economy work as beneficially as it could. It is true that after the essential conditions of a free system have been established, all further institutional improvements are bound to be slow and gradual. But the continuous growth of wealth and technological knowledge which such a system makes possible will constantly suggest new ways in which government might render services to its citizens and bring such possibilities within the range of the practicable.

Why, then, has there been such persistent pressure to do away with those limitations upon government that were erected for the protection of individual liberty? And if there is so much scope for improvement within the rule of law, why have the reformers striven so constantly to weaken and undermine it? The answer is that during the last few generations certain new aims of policy have emerged which cannot be achieved within the limits of the rule of law. A government which cannot use coercion except in the enforcement of general rules has no power to achieve particular aims that require means other than those explicitly entrusted to its care and, in particular, cannot determine the material position of particular people or enforce distributive or "social" justice. In order to achieve such aims, it would have to pursue a policy which is best described—since the word "planning" is so ambiguous —by the French word *dirigisme*, that is, a policy which determines for what specific purposes particular means are to be used.

This, however, is precisely what a government bound by the rule of law cannot do. If the government is to determine how particular people ought to be situated, it must be in a position to determine also the direction of individual efforts. We need not repeat here the reasons why, if government treats different people equally, the results will be unequal, or why, if it allows people to make what use they like of the capacities and means at their disposal, the consequences for the individuals will be unpredictable. The restrictions which the rule of law imposes upon government thus preclude all those measures which would be necessary to insure that individuals will be rewarded according to another's conception of merit or desert rather than according to the value that their services have for their fellows—or, what amounts to the same thing, it precludes the pursuit of distributive, as opposed to commutative, justice. Distributive justice requires an allocation of all resources by a central authority; it requires that people be told what to do and what ends to serve. Where distributive justice is the goal, the decisions as to what the different individuals must be made to do cannot be derived from general rules but must be made in the light of the particular aims and knowledge of the planning authority. As we have seen before, when the opinion of the community decides what different people shall receive, the same authority must also decide what they shall do.

This conflict between the ideal of freedom and the desire to "correct" the distribution of incomes so as to make it more "just" is usually not clearly recognized. But those who pursue distributive justice will in practice find themselves obstructed at every move by the rule of law. They must, from the very nature of their aim, favor discriminatory and discretionary action. But, as they are usually not aware that their aim and the rule of law are in principle incompatible, they begin by circumventing or disregarding in individual cases a principle which they often would wish to see preserved in general. But the ultimate result of their efforts will necessarily be, not a modification of the existing order, but its complete abandonment and its replacement by an altogether different system—the command economy.

While it is certainly not true that such a centrally planned system would be more efficient that one based on a free market, it is true that only a centrally directed system could attempt to ensure that the different individuals would receive what someone thought they deserved on moral grounds. Within the limits set by the rule of law, a great deal can be done to make the market work more effectively and smoothly; but, within these limits, what people now regard as distributive justice can never be achieved. . . .

25. KEYNES
The End of Laissez-Faire

John Maynard Keynes (1883–1946) has been generally considered the most influential economist of the twentieth century. Keynes studied and later taught at Cambridge, where he was president of the Liberal Club. His concern with liberalism continued throughout his career but was especially close in the 1920's when he delivered the lecture "The End of Laissez-Faire."*

Keynes' major work in economics is *The General Theory of Employment, Interest and Money* (1936) which laid the foundation for selected governmental controls to achieve an optimal use of resources when the free market failed to do so. His influence, however, was not restricted to the impact of his works in economics. Keynes was a director of the Bank of England, an adviser to the British Treasury, and a major architect of the postwar international monetary structure.

I

The disposition towards public affairs, which we conveniently sum up as Individualism and *laissez-faire*, drew its sustenance from many different rivulets of thought and springs of feeling. For more than a hundred years our philosophers ruled us, because, by a miracle, they nearly all agreed, or seemed to agree, on this one thing. We do not dance even yet to a new tune. But a change is in the air. We hear but indistinctly what were once the clearest and most distinguishable voices which have ever instructed political mankind. The orchestra of diverse instruments, the chorus of articulate sound, is receding at last into the distance.

At the end of the seventeenth century the divine right of monarchs gave place to Natural Liberty and to the Compact, and the divine right of the Church to the principle of Toleration, and to the view that

* (London: Hogarth Press, 1926.) Used by permission.

a church is "a voluntary society of men," coming together, in a way which is "absolutely free and spontaneous."[1] Fifty years later the divine origin and absolute voice of duty gave place to the calculations of Utility. In the hands of Locke and Hume these doctrines founded Individualism. The Compact presumed rights in the individual; the new ethics, being no more than a scientific study of the consequences of rational self-love, placed the individual at the centre. "The sole trouble Virtue demands," said Hume, "is that of just Calculation, and a steady preference of the greater Happiness."[2] These ideas accorded with the practical notions of conservatives and of lawyers. They furnished a satisfactory intellectual foundation to the rights of property and to the liberty of the individual in possession to do what he liked with himself and with his own. This was one of the contributions of the eighteenth century to the air we still breathe.

The purpose of promoting the Individual was to depose the Monarch and the Church; the effect—through the new ethical significance attributed to Contract—was to buttress Property and Prescription. But it was not long before the claims of Society raised themselves anew against the individual. Paley and Bentham accepted utilitarian hedonism[3] from the hands of Hume and his predecessors, but enlarged it into social utility. Rousseau took the Social Contract from Locke and drew out of it the General Will. In each case the transition was made by virtue of the new emphasis laid on Equality. "Locke applies his Social Contract to modify the natural equality of mankind, so far as that phrase implies equality of property or even of privilege, in consideration of general security. In Rousseau's version equality is not only the starting-point but the goal."[4]

Paley and Bentham reached the same destination, but by different routes. Paley avoided an egoistic conclusion to his hedonism by a God from the machine. "Virtue," he says, "is the doing good to mankind, in obedience to the will of God, and for the sake of everlasting happiness"—in this way bringing back *I* and *others* to a parity.

[1] Locke, *A Letter Concerning Toleration*.

[2] *An Enquiry Concerning the Principles of Morals*, section lx.

[3] "I omit," says Archdeacon Paley, "much usual declamation upon the dignity and capacity of our nature, the superiority of the soul to the body, of the rational to the animal part of our constitution; upon the worthiness, refinement, and delicacy of some satisfactions, and the meanness, grossness, and sensuality of others: because I hold that pleasures differ in nothing but in continuance and intensity."—*Principles of Moral and Political Philosophy*, Bk. I, chap. 6.

[4] Leslie Stephen, *English Thought in Eighteenth Century*, ii, 192.

Bentham reached the same result by pure reason. There is no rational ground, he argued, for preferring the happiness of one individual, even oneself, to that of any other. Hence the greatest happiness of the greatest number is the sole rational object of conduct—taking Utility from Hume, but forgetting that sage man's cynical corollary: "'Tis not contrary to reason to prefer the destruction of the whole world to the scratching of my finger. 'Tis not contrary to reason for me to choose my total ruin to prevent the least uneasiness of an Indian, or person totally unknown to me. . . . Reason is and ought only to be the slave of the passions, and can never pretend to any other office than to serve and obey them."

Rousseau derived equality from the State of Nature, Paley from the Will of God, Bentham from a mathematical law of Indifference. Equality and altruism had thus entered political philosophy, and from Rousseau and Bentham in conjunction sprang both Democracy and Utilitarian Socialism.

This is the second current—sprung from long-dead controversies, and carried on its way by long-exploded sophistries—which still permeates our atmosphere of thought. But it did not drive out the former current. It mixed with it. The early nineteenth century performed the miraculous union. It harmonised the conservative individualism of Locke, Hume, Johnson, and Burke with the Socialism and democratic egalitarianism of Rousseau, Paley, Bentham, and Godwin.[1]

Nevertheless that age would have been hard put to it to achieve this harmony of opposites if it had not been for the *Economists*, who sprang into prominence just at the right moment. The idea of a divine harmony between private advantage and the public good is already apparent in Paley. But it was the Economists who gave the notion a good scientific basis. Suppose that by the working of natural laws individuals pursuing their own interests with enlightenment in conditions of freedom always tend to promote the general interests at the same time! Our philosophical difficulties are resolved—at least for the practical man, who can then concentrate his efforts on securing the necessary conditions of freedom. To the philosophical doctrine that Government has no right to interfere, and the divine miracle that it

[1] Godwin carried *laissez-faire* so far that he thought *all* government an evil, in which Bentham almost agreed with him. The doctrine of equality becomes with him one of extreme individualism, verging on anarchy. "The universal exercise of private judgment," he says, "is a doctrine so unspeakably beautiful that the true politician will certainly feel infinite reluctance in admitting the idea of interfering with it."—*Vide* Leslie Stephen, *op. cit.*, ii, 277.

has no need to interfere, there is added a scientific proof that its interference is inexpedient. This is the third current of thought, just dis-
coverable in Adam Smith, who was ready in the main to allow the
public good to rest on "the natural effort of every individual to better
his own condition," but not fully and self-consciously developed until
the nineteenth century begins. The principle of *laissez-faire* had arrived
to harmonise Individualism and Socialism, and to make at one Hume's
Egoism with the Greatest Good of the Greatest Number. The political
philosopher could retire in favour of the businessman—for the latter
could attain the philosopher's *summum bonum* by just pursuing his
own private profit.

Yet some other ingredients were needed to complete the pudding.
First the corruption and incompetence of eighteenth-century government, many legacies of which survived into the nineteenth. The Individualism of the political philosophers pointed to *laissez-faire*. The
divine or scientific harmony (as the case might be) between private
interest and public advantage pointed to *laissez-faire*. But above all,
the ineptitude of public administrators strongly prejudiced the practical
man in favour of *laissez-faire*—a sentiment which has by no means
disappeared. Almost everything which the State did in the eighteenth
century in excess of its minimum functions was, or seemed, injurious
or unsuccessful.

On the other hand, material progress between 1750 and 1850 came
from individual initiative, and owed almost nothing to the directive
influence of organised society as a whole. Thus practical experience
reinforced *a priori* reasonings. The philosophers and the economists
told us that for sundry deep reasons unfettered private enterprise
would promote the greatest good of the whole. What could suit the
businessman better? And could a practical observer, looking about
him, deny that the blessings of improvement which distinguished the
age he lived in were traceable to the activities of individuals "on the
make"? Thus the ground was fertile for a doctrine that, whether on
divine, natural, or scientific grounds, State Action should be narrowly
confined and economic life left, unregulated so far as may be, to the
skill and good sense of individual citizens actuated by the admirable
motive of trying to get on in the world.

By the time that the influence of Paley and his like was waning, the
innovations of Darwin were shaking the foundations of belief. Nothing
could seem more opposed than the old doctrine and the new—the
doctrine which looked on the world as the work of the divine Watch-

maker and the doctrine which seemed to draw all things out of Chance, Chaos, and Old Time. But at this one point the new ideas bolstered up the old. The Economists were teaching that wealth, commerce, and machinery were the children of free competition—that free competition built London. But the Darwinians could go one better than that— free competition had built Man. The human eye was no longer the demonstration of Design, miraculously contriving all things for the best; it was the supreme achievement of Chance, operating under conditions of free competition and *laissez-faire*. The principle of the Survival of the Fittest could be regarded as a vast generalisation of the Ricardian economics. Socialistic interferences became, in the light of this grander synthesis, not merely inexpedient, but impious, as calculated to retard the onward movement of the mighty process by which we ourselves had risen like Aphrodite out of the primeval slime of Ocean.

Therefore I trace the peculiar unity of the everyday political philosophy of the nineteenth century to the success with which it harmonised diversified and warring schools and united all good things to a single end. Hume and Paley, Burke and Rousseau, Godwin and Malthus, Cobbett and Huskisson, Bentham and Coleridge, Darwin and the Bishop of Oxford, were all, it was discovered, preaching practically the same thing—Individualism and *laissez-faire*. This was the Church of England and those her apostles, whilst the company of the economists were there to prove that the least deviation into impiety involved financial ruin.

These reasons and this atmosphere are the explanations, whether we know it or not—and most of us in these degenerate days are largely ignorant in the matter—why we feel such a strong bias in favour of *laissez-faire*, and why State action to regulate the value of money, or the course of investment, or the population, provoke such passionate suspicions in many upright breasts. We have not read these authors; we should consider their arguments preposterous if they were to fall into our hands. Nevertheless we should not, I fancy, think as we do, if Hobbes, Locke, Hume, Rousseau, Paley, Adam Smith, Bentham, and Miss Martineau had not thought and written as they did. A study of the history of opinion is a necessary preliminary to the emancipation of the mind. I do not know which makes a man more conservative— to know nothing but the present, or nothing but the past.

II

I have said that it was the economists who furnished the scientific pretext by which the practical man could solve the contradiction between egoism and socialism which emerged out of the philosophising of the eighteenth century and the decay of revealed religion. But having said this for shortness' sake, I hasten to qualify it. This is what the economists are *supposed* to have said. No such doctrine is really to be found in the writings of the greatest authorities. It is what the popularisers and the vulgarisers said. It is what the Utilitarians, who admitted Hume's egoism and Bentham's egalitarianism at the same time, were *driven* to believe in, if they were to effect a synthesis.[1] The language of the economists lent itself to the *laissez-faire* interpretation. But the popularity of the doctrine must be laid at the door of the political philosophers of the day, whom it happened to suit, rather than of the political economists.

The maxim *laissez-nous faire* is traditionally attributed to the merchant Legendre addressing Colbert sometime towards the end of the seventeenth century.[2] But there is no doubt that the first writer to use the phrase, and to use it in clear association with the doctrine, is the Marquis d'Argenson about 1751.[3] The Marquis was the first man to wax passionate on the economic advantages of Governments leaving trade alone. To govern better, he said, one must govern less.[4] The true cause of the decline of our manufactures, he declared, is the protection we have given to them.[5] "Laissez faire, telle devrait être la devise de toute puissance publique, depuis que le monde est civilisé." "Detestable principe que celui de ne vouloir notre grandeur que par l'abaissement de nos voisins! Il n'y a que la méchanceté et la malignité du

---

[1] One can sympathise with the view of Coleridge, as summarised by Leslie Stephen, that "the Utilitarians destroyed every element of cohesion, made Society a struggle of selfish interests, and struck at the very roots of all order, patriotism, poetry, and religion."

[2] "Que faut-il faire pour vous aider?" asked Colbert. "Nous laisser faire," answered Legendre.

[3] For the history of the phrase, *vide* Oncken, "Die Maxime Laissez-faire et laissez passer," from whom most of the following quotations are taken. The claims of the Marquis d'Argenson were overlooked until Oncken put them forward, partly because the relevant passages published during his lifetime were anonymous (*Journal Œconomique*, 1751), and partly because his works were not published in full (though probably passed privately from hand to hand during his lifetime) until 1858 (*Mémoires et Journal inédit du Marquis d'Argenson*).

[4] "Pour gouverner mieux, il faudrait gouverner moins."

[5] "On ne peut dire autant de nos fabriques: la vraie cause de leur declin, c'est la protection outrée qu'on leur accorde."

coeur de satisfaites dans ce principe, et l'intérêt y est opposé. Laissez faire, morbleu! Laissez faire!!"

Here we have the economic doctrine of *laissez-faire*, with its most fervent expression in Free Trade, fully clothed. The phrases and the idea must have passed current in Paris from that time on. But they were slow to establish themselves in Literature; and the tradition associating them with the Physiocrats, and particularly de Gournay and Quesnay, finds little support in the writings of this school, though they were, of course, proponents of the essential harmony of social and individual interests. The phrase *laissez-faire* is not be to found in the works of Adam Smith, of Ricardo, or of Malthus. Even the idea is not present in a dogmatic form in any of these authors. Adam Smith, of course, was a Free Trader and an opponent of many eighteenth-century restrictions on trade. But his attitude towards the Navigation Acts and the Usury laws shows that he was not dogmatic. Even his famous passage about "the invisible hand" reflects the philosophy which we associate with Paley rather than the economic dogma of *laissez-faire*. As Sidgwick and Cliff Leslie have pointed out, Adam Smith's advocacy of the "obvious and simple system of natural liberty" is derived from his theistic and optimistic view of the order of the world, as set forth in his *Theory of Moral Sentiments*, rather than from any proposition of Political Economy proper.[1] The phrase *laissez-faire* was, I think, first brought into popular usage in England by a well-known passage of Dr. Franklin's.[2] It is not indeed, until we come to the later works of Bentham—who was not an economist at all—that we discover the rule of *laissez-faire*, in the shape in which our grand-fathers knew it, adopted into the service of the Utilitarian philosophy. For example, in *A Manual of Political Economy*,[3] he writes: "The general rule is that nothing ought to be done or attempted by government; the motto or watchword of government, on these occasions, ought to be— *Be quiet.* . . . The request which agriculture, manufacturers, and commerce present to governments is as modest and reasonable as that which Diogenes made to Alexander: Stand out of my sunshine."

From this time on it was the political campaign for Free Trade, the influence of the so-called Manchester School and of the Benthamite Utilitarians, the utterances of secondary economic authorities, and

---

[1] Sidgwick, *Principles of Political Economy*, p. 20.

[2] Bentham uses the expression "*laissez-nous faire*," *Works*, p. 440.

[3] Written in 1793, a chapter published in the *Bibliothèque Britannique* in 1798, and the whole first printed in Bowring's edition of his *Works* (1843).

the educational stories of Miss Martineau and Mrs. Marcet, that fixed *laissez-faire* in the popular mind as the practical conclusion of orthodox Political Economy—with this great difference, that the Malthusian view of Population having been accepted in the meantime by this same school of thought, the optimistic *laissez-faire* of the last half of the eighteenth century gives place to the pessimistic *laissez-faire* of the first half of the nineteenth century.[1]

In Mrs. Marcet's *Conversations on Political Economy* (1817) Caroline stands out as long as she can in favour of controlling the expenditure of the rich. But by page 418 she has to admit defeat.

"*Caroline*.—The more I learn upon this subject, the more I feel convinced that the interests of nations, as well as those of individuals, so far from being opposed to each other, are in the most perfect unison.

"*Mrs. B*.—Liberal and enlarged views will always lead to similar conclusions, and teach us to cherish sentiments of universal benevolence towards each other; hence the superiority of science over mere practical knowledge."

By 1850 the *Easy Lessons for the Use of Young People*, by Archbishop Whately, which the Society for Promoting Christian Knowledge was distributing wholesale, do not admit even of those doubts which Mrs. B. allowed Caroline occasionally to entertain. "More harm than good is likely to be done," the little book concludes, "by almost any interference of Government with men's money transactions, whether letting and leasing, or buying and selling of any kind." *True* liberty is "that every man should be left free to dispose of his own property, his own time, and strength, and skill, in whatever way he himself may think fit, provided he does no wrong to his neighbours."

In short, the dogma had got hold of the educational machine; it had become a copybook maxim. The Political Philosophy, which the seventeenth and eighteenth centuries had forged in order to throw down Kings and Prelates, had been made milk for, babes, and had literally entered the nursery.

Finally, in the works of Bastiat we reach the most extravagant and rhapsodical expression of the Political Economist's religion. In his *Harmonies Economiques*, "I undertake," he says, "to demonstrate the Harmony of those laws of Providence which govern human society.

[1] *Cf.* Sidgwick (*op. cit.*, p. 22): "Even those economists, who adhered in the main to Adam Smith's limitations of the sphere of government, enforced these limitations sadly rather than triumphantly; not as admirers of the social order at present resulting from 'natural liberty,' but as convinced that it is at least preferable to any artificial order that government might be able to substitute for it."

What makes these laws harmonious and not discordant is, that all principles, all motives, all springs of action, all interests, co-operate towards a grand final result. . . . And that result is, the indefinite approximation of all classes towards a level, which is always rising; in other words, the *equalisation* of individuals in the general *amelioration*." And when, like other priests, he drafts his *Credo*, it runs as follows: "I believe that He who has arranged the material universe has not withheld His regard from the arrangements of the social world. I believe that He has combined and caused to move in harmony free agents as well as inert molecules. . . . I believe that the invincible social tendency is a constant approximation of men towards a common moral, intellectual, and physical level, with, at the same time, a progressive and indefinite elevation of that level. I believe that all that is necessary to the gradual and peaceful development of humanity is that its tendencies should not be disturbed, nor have the liberty of their movements destroyed."

From the time of John Stuart Mill, economists of authority have been in strong reaction against all such ideas. "Scarcely a single English economist of repute," as Professor Cannan has expressed it, "will join in a frontal attack upon Socialism in general," though, as he also adds, "nearly every economist, whether of repute or not, is always ready to pick holes in most socialistic proposals."[1] Economists no longer have any link with the theological or political philosophies out of which the dogma of Social Harmony was born, and their scientific analysis leads them to no such conclusions.

Cairnes, in the Introductory Lecture on "Political Economy and *Laissez-Faire*," which he delivered at University College, London, in 1870, was perhaps the first orthodox economist to deliver a frontal attack upon *laissez-faire* in general. "The maxim of *laissez-faire*," he declared, "has no scientific basis whatever, but is at best a mere handy rule of practice."[2] This, for fifty years past, has been the view of all

---

[1] *Theories of Production and Distribution*, p. 494.

[2] Cairnes well described the "prevailing notion" in the following passage from the same lecture: "The prevailing notion is that P.E. undertakes to show that wealth may be most rapidly accumulated and most fairly distributed; that is to say, that human well-being may be most effectually promoted, by the simple process of leaving people to themselves; leaving individuals, that is to say, to follow the promptings of self-interest, unrestrained either by the State or by public opinion, so long as they abstain from force and fraud. This is the doctrine commonly known as *laissez-faire;* and accordingly political economy is, I think, very generally regarded as a sort of scientific rendering of this maxim—a vindication of freedom of individual enterprise and of contract as the one and sufficient solution of all industrial problems."

leading economists. Some of the most important work of Alfred Marshall—to take one instance—was directed to the elucidation of the leading cases in which private interest and social interest are *not* harmonious. Nevertheless the guarded and undogmatic attitude of the best economists has not prevailed against the general opinion that an individualistic *laissez-faire* is both what they ought to teach and what in fact they do teach.

III

Economists, like other scientists, have chosen the hypothesis from which they set out, and which they offer to beginners, because it is the simplest, and not because it is the nearest to the facts. Partly for this reason, but partly, I admit, because they have been biassed by the traditions of the subject, they have begun by assuming a state of affairs where the ideal distribution of productive resources can be brought about through individuals acting independently by the method of trial and error in such a way that those individuals who move in the right direction will destroy by competition those who move in the wrong direction. This implies that there must be no mercy or protection for those who embark their capital or their labour in the wrong direction. It is a method of bringing the most successful profit-makers to the top by a ruthless struggle for survival, which selects the most efficient by the bankruptcy of the less efficient. It does not count the cost of the struggle, but looks only to the benefits of the final result which are assumed to be permanent. The object of life being to crop the leaves off the branches up to the greatest possible height, the likeliest way of achieving this end is to leave the giraffes with the longest necks to starve out those whose necks are shorter.

Corresponding to this method of attaining the ideal distribution of the instruments of production between different purposes, there is a similar assumption as to how to attain the ideal distribution of what is available for consumption. In the first place, each individual will discover what amongst the possible objects of consumption *he* wants most by the method of trial and error "at the margin," and in this way not only will each consumer come to distribute his consumption most advantageously, but each object of consumption will find its way into the mouth of the consumer whose relish for it is greatest compared with that of the others, because that consumer will outbid the rest.

Thus, if only we leave the giraffes to themselves, (1) the maximum quantity of leaves will be cropped because the giraffes with the longest necks will, by dint of starving out the others, get nearest to the trees; (2) each giraffe will make for the leaves which he finds most succulent amongst those in reach; and (3) the giraffes whose relish for a given leaf is greatest will crane most to reach it. In this way more and juicier leaves will be swallowed, and each individual leaf will reach the throat which thinks it deserves most effort.

This assumption, however, of conditions where unhindered natural selection leads to progress, is only one of the two provisional assumptions which, taken as literal truth, have become the twin buttresses of *laissez-faire*. The other one is the efficacy, and, indeed, the necessity, of the opportunity for unlimited private money-making as an *incentive* to maximum effort. Profit accrues, under *laissez-faire*, to the individual who, whether by skill or good fortune, is found with his productive resources in the right place at the right time. A system which allows the skilful or fortunate individual to reap the whole fruits of this conjuncture evidently offers an immense incentive to the practice of the art of being in the right place at the right time. Thus one of the most powerful of human motives, namely, the love of money, is harnessed to the task of distributing economic resources in the way best calculated to increase wealth.

The parallelism between economic *laissez-faire* and Darwinianism, already briefly noted, is now seen, as Herbert Spencer was foremost to recognise, to be very close indeed. Just as Darwin invoked sexual love, acting through sexual selection, as an adjutant to Natural Selection by competition, to direct evolution along lines which should be desirable as well as effective, so the individualist invokes the love of money, acting through the pursuit of profit, as an adjutant to Natural Selection, to bring about the production on the greatest possible scale of what is most strongly desired as measured by exchange value.

The beauty and the simplicity of such a theory are so great that it is easy to forget that it follows not from the actual facts, but from an incomplete hypothesis introduced for the sake of simplicity. Apart from other objections to be mentioned later, the conclusion that individuals acting independently for their own advantage will produce the greatest aggregate of wealth, depends on a variety of unreal assumptions to the effect that the processes of production and consumption are in no way organic, that there exists a sufficient foreknowledge of conditions and requirements, and that there are adequate opportunities of obtaining this foreknowledge. For economists generally reserve for a later stage of their argument the complications which arise—(1) when the efficient units of production are large relatively to the units of consumption, (2) when overhead costs or joint costs are present, (3) when internal economies tend to the aggregation of production, (4) when the time required for adjustments is long, (5) when ignorance prevails over knowledge, and (6) when monopolies and combinations interfere with equality in bargaining—they reserve, that is to say, for a later stage their analysis of the actual facts. Moreover, many of those who recognise that the simplified hypothesis does not accurately correspond to fact conclude nevertheless that it does represent what is "natural" and therefore ideal. They regard the simplified hypothesis as health, and the further complications as disease.

Yet, besides this question of fact, there are other considerations, familiar enough, which rightly bring into the calculation the cost and character of the competitive struggle itself, and the tendency for wealth to be distributed where it is not appreciated most. If we have the welfare of the giraffes at heart, we must not overlook the sufferings of the shorter necks who are starved out, or the sweet leaves which fall to the ground and are trampled underfoot in the struggle, or the over-feeding of the long-necked ones, or the evil look of anxiety or struggling greediness which overcasts the mild faces of the herd.

But the principles of *laissez-faire* have had other allies besides economic textbooks. It must be admitted that they have been confirmed in the minds of sound thinkers and the reasonable public by the poor quality of the opponent proposals—Protectionism on one hand, and Marxian Socialism on the other. Yet these doctrines are both characterised, not only or chiefly by their infringing the general presumption in favour of *laissez-faire*, but by mere logical fallacy. Both are examples of poor thinking, of inability to analyse a process and follow it out to its conclusion. The arguments against them, though reinforced by the principle of *laissez-faire*, do not strictly require it. Of the two, Protectionism is at least plausible, and the forces making for its popularity are nothing to wonder at. But Marxian Socialism must always remain a portent to the historians of Opinion—how a doctrine so illogical and so dull can have exercised so powerful and enduring an influence over the minds of men, and, through them, the events of history. At any rate, the obvious scientific deficiencies of these two schools greatly contributed to the prestige and authority of nineteenth-century *laissez-faire*.

Nor has the most notable divergence into centralised social action on a great scale—the conduct of the late war—encouraged reformers or dispelled old-fashioned prejudices. There is much to be said, it is true, on both sides. War experience in the organisation of socialised production has left some near observers optimistically anxious to repeat it in peace conditions. War socialism unquestionably achieved a production of wealth on a scale far greater than we ever knew in Peace, for though the goods and services delivered were destined for immediate and fruitless extinction, none the less they were wealth. Nevertheless the dissipation of effort was also prodigious, and the atmosphere of waste and not counting the cost was disgusting to any thrifty or provident spirit.

Finally, Individualism and *laissez-faire* could not, in spite of their deep roots in the political and moral philosophies of the late eighteenth and early nineteenth centuries, have secured their lasting hold over the conduct of public affairs, if it had not been for their conformity with the needs and wishes of the business world of the day. They gave full scope to our erstwhile heroes, the great businessmen. "At least one-half of the best ability in the Western world," Marshall used to say, "is engaged in business." A great part of "the higher imagination" of the age was thus employed. It was on the activities of these men that our hopes of Progress were centred. "Men of this class," Marshall wrote,[1] "live in constantly shifting visions, fashioned in their own brains, of various routes to their desired end; of the difficulties which Nature will oppose to them on each route, and of the contrivances by which they hope to get the better of her opposition. This imagination gains little credit with the people, because it is not allowed to run riot; its strength is disciplined by a stronger will; and its highest glory is to have attained great ends by means so simple that no one will know, and none but experts will even guess, how a dozen other expedients each suggesting as much brilliancy to the hasty observer, were set aside in favour of it. The imagination of such a man is employed, like that of the master chess-player, in forecasting the obstacles which may be opposed to the successful issue of his far-reaching projects, and constantly rejecting brilliant suggestions because he has pictured to himself the counter-strokes to them. His strong nervous force is at the opposite extreme of human nature from that nervous irresponsibility which conceives hasty Utopian schemes, and which is rather to be

[1] "The Social Possibilities of Economic Chivalry," *Economic Journal* (1907), xvii, p. 9.

compared to the bold facility of a weak player, who will speedily solve the most difficult chess problem by taking on himself to move the black men as well as the white."

This is a fine picture of the great Captain of Industry, the Master-Individualist, who serves us in serving himself, just as any other artist does. Yet this one, in his turn, is becoming a tarnished idol. We grow more doubtful whether it is he who will lead us into Paradise by the hand.

These many elements have contributed to the current intellectual bias, the mental make-up, the orthodoxy of the day. The compelling force of many of the original reasons has disappeared, but, as usual, the vitality of the conclusions outlasts them. To suggest social action for the public good to the City of London is like discussing the *Origin of Species* with a Bishop sixty years ago. The first reaction is not intellectual, but moral. An orthodoxy is in question, and the more persuasive the arguments the graver the offence. Nevertheless, venturing into the den of the lethargic monster, at any rate I have traced his claims and pedigree so as to show that he has ruled over us rather by hereditary right than by personal merit.

IV

Let us clear from the ground the metaphysical or general principles upon which, from time to time, *laissez-faire* has been founded. It is *not* true that individuals possess a prescriptive "natural liberty" in their economic activities. There is *no* "compact" conferring perpetual rights on those who Have or on those who Acquire. The world is *not* so governed from above that private and social interest always coincide. It is *not* so managed here below that in practice they coincide. It is *not* a correct deduction from the Principles of Economics that enlightened self-interest always operates in the public interest. Nor is it true that self-interest generally *is* enlightened; more often individuals acting separately to promote their own ends are too ignorant or too weak to attain even these. Experience does *not* show that individuals, when they make up a social unit, are always less clear-sighted than when they act separately.

We cannot therefore settle on abstract grounds, but must handle on its merits in detail what Burke termed "one of the finest problems in legislation, namely, to determine what the State ought to take upon itself to direct by the public wisdom, and what it ought to leave, with as little interference as possible, to individual exertion."[1] We have to discriminate between what Bentham, in his forgotten but useful nomenclature, used to term *Agenda* and *Non-Agenda*, and to do this without Bentham's prior presumption that interference is, at the same time, "generally needless" and "generally pernicious".[2] Perhaps the chief task of Economists at this hour is to distinguish afresh the *Agenda* of Government from the *Non-Agenda;* and the companion task of Politics is to devise forms of Government within a Democracy which shall be capable of accomplishing the *Agenda*. I will illustrate what I have in mind by two examples.

1. I believe that in many cases the ideal size for the unit of control and organisation lies somewhere between the individual and the modern State. I suggest, therefore, that progress lies in the growth and the recognition of semi-autonomous bodies within the State—bodies whose criterion of action within their own field is solely the public good as they understand it, and from whose deliberations motives of private advantage are excluded, though some place it may still be necessary to leave, until the ambit of men's altruism grows wider, to the separate advantage of particular groups, classes, or faculties—bodies which in the ordinary course of affairs are mainly autonomous within their prescribed limitations, but are subject in the last resort to the sovereignty of the democracy expressed through Parliament.

I propose a return, it may be said, towards medieval conceptions of separate autonomies. But, in England at any rate, corporations are a mode of government which has never ceased to be important and is sympathetic to our institutions. It is easy to give examples, from what already exists, of separate autonomies which have attained or are approaching the mode I designate—the Universities, the Bank of England, the Port of London Authority, even perhaps the Railway Companies. In Germany there are doubtless analogous instances.

But more interesting than these is the trend of Joint Stock Institutions, when they have reached a certain age and size, to approximate to the status of public corporations rather than that of individualistic private enterprise. One of the most interesting and unnoticed developments of recent decades has been the tendency of big enterprise to socialise itself. A point arrives in the growth of a big institution—particularly

---

[1] Quoted by M'Culloch in his *Principles of Political Economy.*
[2] Bentham's *Manual of Political Economy*, published posthumously, in Bowring's edition (1843).

a big railway or big public utility enterprise, but also a big bank or a big insurance company—at which the owners of the capital, *i.e.* the shareholders, are almost entirely dissociated from the management, with the result that the direct personal interest of the latter in the making of great profit becomes quite secondary. When this stage is reached, the general stability and reputation of the institution are more considered by the management than the maximum of profit for the shareholders. The shareholders must be satisfied by conventionally adequate dividends; but once this is secured, the direct interest of the management often consists in avoiding criticism from the public and from the customers of the concern. This is particularly the case if their great size or semi-monopolistic position renders them conspicuous in the public eye and vulnerable to public attack. The extreme instance, perhaps, of this tendency in the case of an institution, theoretically the unrestricted property of private persons, is the Bank of England. It is almost true to say that there is no class of persons in the Kingdom of whom the Governor of the Bank of England thinks less when he decides on his policy than of his shareholders. Their rights, in excess of their conventional dividend, have already sunk to the neighbourhood of zero. But the same thing is partly true of many other big institutions. They are, as time goes on, socialising themselves.

Not that this is unmixed gain. The same causes promote conservatism and a waning of enterprise. In fact, we already have in these cases many of the faults as well as the advantages of State Socialism. Nevertheless we see here, I think, a natural line of evolution. The battle of Socialism against unlimited private profit is being won in detail hour by hour. In these particular fields—it remains acute elsewhere—this is no longer the pressing problem. There is, for instance, no so-called important political question so really unimportant, so irrelevant to the re-organisation of the economic life of Great Britain, as the Nationalisation of the Railways.

It is true that many big undertakings, particularly Public Utility enterprises and other business requiring a large fixed capital, still need to be semi-socialised. But we must keep our minds flexible regarding the forms of this semi-socialism. We must take full advantage of the natural tendencies of the day, and we must probably prefer semi-autonomous corporations to organs of the Central Government for which Ministers of State are directly responsible.

I criticise doctrinaire State Socialism, not because it seeks to engage men's altruistic impulses in the service of Society, or because it departs from *laissez-faire*, or because it takes away from man's natural liberty to make a million, or because it has courage for bold experiments. All these things I applaud. I criticise it because it misses the significance of what is actually happening; because it is, in fact, little better than a dusty survival of a plan to meet the problems of fifty years ago, based on a misunderstanding of what someone said a hundred years ago. Nineteenth-century State Socialism sprang from Bentham, free competition, etc., and is in some respects a clearer, in some respects a more muddled version of just the same philosophy as underlies nineteenth-century individualism. Both equally laid all their stress on freedom, the one negatively to avoid limitations on existing freedom, the other positively to destroy natural or acquired monopolies. They are different reactions to the same intellectual atmosphere.

2. I come next to a criterion of *Agenda* which is particularly relevant to what it is urgent and desirable to do in the near future. We must aim at separating those services which are *technically social* from those which are *technically individual*. The most important *Agenda* of the State relate not to those activities which private individuals are already fulfilling, but to those functions which fall outside the sphere of the individual, to those decisions which are made by *no one* if the State does not make them. The important thing for Government is not to do things which individuals are doing already, and to do them a little better or a little worse; but to do those things which at present are not done at all.

It is not within the scope of my purpose on this occasion to develop practical policies. I limit myself, therefore, to naming some instances of what I mean from amongst those problems about which I happen to have thought most.

Many of the greatest economic evils of our time are the fruits of risk, uncertainty, and ignorance. It is because particular individuals, fortunate in situation or in abilities, are able to take advantage of uncertainty and ignorance, and also because for the same reason big business is often a lottery, that great inequalities of wealth come about; and these same factors are also the cause of the Unemployment of Labour, or the disappointment of reasonable business expectations, and of the impairment of efficiency and production. Yet the cure lies outside the operations of individuals; it may even be to the interest of individuals to aggravate the disease. I believe that the cure for these things is partly to be sought in the deliberate control of the currency and of credit by a central institution, and partly in the collection and dissemination on a great scale of data relating to the business situation, including the full publicity, by law if necessary, of all business facts which it is useful to know. These measures would involve Society in exercising directive intelligence through some appropriate organ of action over many of the inner intricacies of private business, yet it would leave private initiative and enterprise unhindered. Even if these measures prove insufficient, nevertheless they will furnish us with better knowledge than we have now for taking the next step.

My second example relates to Savings and Investment. I believe that some co-ordinated act of intelligent judgment is required as to the scale on which it is desirable that the community as a whole should save, the scale on which these savings should go abroad in the form of foreign investments, and whether the present organisation of the investment market distributes savings along the most nationally pro-ductive channels. I do not think that these matters should be left entirely to the chances of private judgment and private profits, as they are at present.

My third example concerns Population. The time has already come when each country needs a considered national policy about what size of Population, whether larger or smaller than at present or the same, is most expedient. And having settled this policy, we must take steps to carry it into operation. The time may arrive a little later when the community as a whole must pay attention to the innate quality as well as to the mere numbers of its future members.

V

These reflections have been directed towards possible improvements in the technique of modern Capitalism by the agency of collective action. There is nothing in them which is seriously incompatible with what seems to me to be the essential characteristic of Capitalism, namely the dependence upon an intense appeal to the money-making and money-loving instincts of individuals as the main motive force of the economic machine. Nor must I, so near to my end, stray towards other fields. Nevertheless I may do well to remind you, in conclusion, that the fiercest contests and the most deeply felt divisions of opinion are likely to be waged in the coming years not round technical questions, where the arguments on either side are mainly economic, but round those which, for want of better words, may be called psychological or, perhaps, moral.

In Europe, or at least in some parts of Europe—but not, I think, in the United States of America—there is a latent reaction, somewhat widespread, against basing Society to the extent that we do upon fostering, encouraging, and protecting the money-motives of individuals. A preference for arranging our affairs in such a way as to appeal to the money-motive as little as possible, rather than as much as possible, need not be entirely *a priori*, but may be based on the comparison of experiences. Different persons, according to their choice of profession, find the money-motive playing a large or a small part in their daily lives, and historians can tell us about other phases of social organisation in which this motive has played a much smaller part than it does now. Most religions and most philosophies deprecate, to say the least of it, a way of life mainly influenced by considerations of personal money profit. On the other hand, most men today reject ascetic notions and do not doubt the real advantages of wealth. Moreover, it seems obvious to them that one cannot do without the money-motive, and that, apart from certain admitted abuses, it does its job well. In the result the average man averts his attention from the problem, and has no clear idea what he really thinks and feels about the whole confounded matter.

Confusion of thought and feeling leads to confusion of speech. Many people, who are really objecting to Capitalism as a way of life, argue as though they were objecting to it on the ground of its inefficiency in attaining its own objects. Contrariwise, devotees of Capitalism are often unduly conservative, and reject reforms in its technique, which might really strengthen and preserve it, for fear that they may prove to be first steps away from Capitalism itself. Nevertheless a time may be coming when we shall get clearer than at present as to when we are talking about Capitalism as an efficient or inefficient technique, and when we are talking about it as desirable or objectionable in itself. For my part, I think that Capitalism, wisely managed, can probably be made more efficient for attaining economic ends than any alternative system yet in sight, but that in itself it is in many ways extremely objectionable. Our problem is to work out a social organisation which shall be as efficient as possible without offending our notions of a satisfactory way of life.

The next step forward must come, not from political agitation or premature experiments, but from thought. We need by an effort of the mind to elucidate our own feelings. At present our sympathy and our judgment are liable to be on different sides, which is a painful and paralysing state of mind. In the field of action reformers will not be successful until they can steadily pursue a clear and definite object with their intellects and their feelings in tune. There is no party in the world at present which appears to me to be pursuing right aims by right methods. Material Poverty provides the incentive to change precisely in situations where there is very little margin for experiments. Material Prosperity removes the incentive just when it might be safe to take a chance. Europe lacks the means, America the will, to make a move. We need a new set of convictions which spring naturally from a candid examination of our own inner feelings in relation to the outside facts.

IV

Nationalism, Revolution, and International Order

Although the prime focus of liberal theory has been directed to questions of domestic concern, liberal writers have generally been concerned with the implications of liberal theory for international order. The seven selections that follow provide only an introduction to the rich and complex liberal literature on war, colonialism, nationalism, revolutionary violence, and world order. In each case, the selection reflects the historical period in which it was written. Kant's "rationalistic" proposal for perpetual peace, for example, is rooted in the promise for international peace held out by the replacement of European dynastic regimes by "republican" governments. Adam Smith's calculation of the economic rationality of colonies is directed in part to British policy in the American War of Independence. The United Nations Declaration of Human Rights, phrased in the classic rhetoric of natural rights, is a product of the Second World War. It is a response to the demonstrated relationship between the domestic policies of totalitarian governments and their attacks on world peace.

What is striking about these documents is their continued relevance. Despite the enormous technological and international developments of the twentieth century and the great changes in the position of Western Europe in the world order, they retain their significance for contemporary problems.

Aleksandr Herzen was the first Russian exile to participate in revolutionary agitation from Western Europe against Russian authoritarianism. His exile began in 1847, a year before the nationalistic and democratic revolutions in Western Europe in 1848. Though analysis of socialism and communism were already on Herzen's agenda, these were not the movements of 1917; yet Herzen's stress on the priority of liberty of the individual within any program for social progress reads today like similar documents from contemporary newspapers. In his letters to the nineteenth-century anarchist Bakunin he assessed the price of revolution and of the ways in which means determine ends; his theses are continually being reformulated in contemporary writing.

Giuseppe Mazzini's rhetoric in his *Duties of Man* dates that work in the nineteenth-century heyday of romantic nationalism. Its central theme is the struggle for Italian unification, long since achieved. Yet the belief that individual expression can be manifest only through the growth of national self-consciousness and the program of revolutionary nationalism through organizational activism and guerilla warfare retains not only its operational significance but even its dynamism as a major secular religion of our century.

John Stuart Mill wrote the analyses of colonialism and internationalism presented here in the 1850's and 1860's. The relevance of his major themes—the dilemma of intervention in behalf of a small country's freedom in another country's sphere of influence; the conflict between international morality by reference to values of social welfare and by reference to strategic national interests; the responsibilities of a colonial power to the development of the colonial region consequent to its withdrawal of sovereignty—seems greater today than in his own times. Mill's detailed illustrations of 1859 which would presumably give to his topic a sense of the past, even on a perennial moral dilemma, actually heighten their immediacy since they related to Russian intervention in a Hungarian revolt for freedom and to foreign power control of the Suez Canal.

This contemporaneity of discussion of war and peace is in part the consequence of the failure of European liberalism to solve the problem of war and international order. Some of the problems may be insoluble and therefore will continually be transposed in new contexts, so that attention must then be focused not only on the problem but on the changing context.

The major feature of the transposition is the decline of a European role, and thereby of the role of European liberalism, in the fundamental issues of war and world peace. Another major feature, parallel with the decline of Europe is the emergence, to a marked degree because of the influence of liberal nationalism, of the Asian and African nations.

The attitudes and policies of liberalism were forged in a radically different context of nations and international order. The ideal values of liberalism in foreign affairs are well known. They include national self-determination, economic growth, minimization of suffering, widespread education, international unity. There is, however, no consensus today among European liberals on the type of foreign policy which would advance these values in the current arena of international politics.

26. KANT
Toward Perpetual Peace

It was a condition of the free exercise of reason, according to Kant, that society must allow full freedom of thought and that all states must admit of self-government. It was a corollary of the free experience of reason that wars among states would not be necessary. Although the idiom of Kant's argument, with its reference to the presupposition of human rationality and to the teleology of nature was characteristic of only one philosophical tendency within liberalism, the central conclusions of his analysis were widely shared by liberals from the eighteenth century to the present. Two of Kant's themes, the fundamental irrationality of war and the connection between liberal principles of self-government and international order, have been continually reformulated by liberals since Kant wrote *Toward Perpetual Peace* in 1795.

The selection is from the translation by W. Hastie.

FIRST SECTION

WHICH CONTAINS

THE PRELIMINARY ARTICLES OF AN ETERNAL
PEACE BETWEEN STATES

. . . "No State having an existence by itself—whether it be small or large—shall be acquirable by another State through inheritance, exchange, purchase or donation."

A State is not to be regarded as a property or patrimony like the soil on which it may be settled. It is a society of men, over which no one but itself has the right to rule or to dispone. Like the stem of a tree it has its own root, and to incorporate it as a graft in another State is to destroy its existence as a moral person; it is to reduce it to a thing, and thereby to contradict the idea of the original compact without which a right over a people is inconceivable. Everyone knows what danger the prejudice in favor of thus acquiring States has brought to Europe,—for in the other parts of the world it has never been known,—even down to our own times. It was considered that the States might marry one another; and hence, on the one hand, a new kind of industry in the effort to acquire predominance by family alliances, without any expenditure of power; and, on the other hand, to increase in this way by new possessions the extent of a country. Further, the lending of the troops of one State to another on pay to fight against an enemy not at war with their own State has arisen from the same erroneous view; for the subjects of the State are thus used and abused as things that may be managed at will.

"Standing armies shall be entirely abolished in the course of time."

For they threaten other States incessantly with war by their appearing to be always equipped to enter upon it. Standing armies excite the States to outrival each other in the number of their armed men, which has no limits. By the expense occasioned thereby, peace becomes in the long run even more oppressive than a short war; and standing armies are thus the cause of aggressive wars undertaken in order to get rid of this burden. Besides, it has to be considered that for men to be hired for pay to kill or to be killed appears to imply the using of them as mere machines and instruments in the hand of another, although it be the State; and that this cannot be well reconciled with the right of humanity in our own person. It is quite otherwise, however, as regards the voluntary exercise of the citizens in arms at certain appointed periods; for the object in view is thereby to protect themselves and their country from external attacks. The accumulation of treasure in a State would have the same sort of influence as regular troops, in so far as, being regarded by other States as a threat of war, it might compel them to anticipate such a war by an attack upon the State. For of the three powers known in the State as the power of the army, the power of external alliance and the power of money, the money power might well become the most reliable instrument of war, did not the difficulty of determining its real force stand in the way of its employment. . . .

"No State shall interfere by force with the constitution or government of another State."

For what could justify it in doing so? Perhaps the offense given by that State to the subjects of another State? Then the offending State should much rather serve as a warning by the example of the great evils which peoples have drawn upon themselves through their lawlessness. A bad example given by one free person to another is not an infringement of his right. But it is a different case where a State has become divided into two by internal disunion and when each of the parts represents itself as a separate State laying claim to the whole; for to furnish assistance to one of them under these circumstances might not be reckoned as the intervention of an external State with the constitution of another, as that other is then in a condition of anarchy. Yet so long as this internal dissension has not developed, such an intervention on the part of external powers would be a violation of the rights of an independent people that is only struggling with an external evil. It would, therefore, itself be a cause of offense, and would make the autonomy of all other States insecure.

"No State at war with another shall adopt such modes of hostility as would necessarily render mutual confidence impossible in a future peace; such as the employment of assassins or poisoners, the violation of a capitulation, the instigation of treason and such like."

These are dishonorable stratagems. For there must be some trust in the habit and disposition even of an enemy in war; otherwise no peace could be concluded, and the hostilities would pass into an internecine war of extermination. War, however, is only a melancholy necessity of asserting right by force—where, as in the state of nature, there is no common tribunal with the rightful power to adjudicate on causes of quarrel. In such circumstances neither of the two parties can be declared to be an unjust enemy as this presupposes a judicial sentence; but the issue of the conflict—as in the so-called "judgments of God"—has to decide on which side is the right. As between States, however, a punitive war, according to the principle of punishment, is inconceivable; because there is no relation of subordination between them, as between superior and inferior. Hence it follows that a war of extermination, in which the process of annihilation would strike at both parties, and likewise at all right at the same time, would reach perpetual peace only on the final Golgotha of the human race. Such a war, therefore, as well as the use of such means as might lead to it, must be absolutely unallowable. And that the means referred to inevitably lead to that result is apparent from the fact that when these hellish arts, which are debasing in themselves, are once brought into use they are not kept long within the limits of war. Such, for instance, is the employment of spies. In this case it is only the dishonesty of others that is employed, and, as such practices and habits cannnot be exterminated at once, they would be carried over into the state of peace, and thus its very purpose would be entirely frustrated. . .

SECOND SECTION

WHICH CONTAINS

THE DEFINITIVE ARTICLES OF AN ETERNAL PEACE BETWEEN STATES

A state of peace among men who live side by side with each other is not the natural state. The state of nature is rather a state of war; for although it may not always present the outbreak of hostilities, it is nevertheless continually threatened with them. The state of peace must, therefore, be established; for the mere cessation of hostilities furnishes no security against their recurrence, and where there is no guarantee of peace between neighbouring States—which can only be furnished under conditions that are regulated by law—the one may treat the other, when proclamation is made to that effect, as an enemy.

First Definitive Article in the Conditions of Eternal Peace

"The civil constitution in every State shall be republican."

A republican constitution is one that is founded, firstly, according to the principle of the liberty of the members of a society, as men; secondly, according to the principle of the dependence of all its members on a single common legislation, as subjects; and, thirdly, according to the law of the equality of its members as citizens. The republican constitution is thus the only one which arises out of the idea of the original compact upon which all the rightful legislation of a people is founded. As regards public law, the republican principles, therefore, lie originally and essentially at the basis of the civil constitution in all its forms; and the only question for us now is whether it is also the only constitution that can lead to a perpetual peace.

Now, in point of fact, the republican constitution, in addition to the purity of its origin as arising from the original source of the conception of right, includes also the prospect of realizing the desired object,—perpetual peace among the nations. And the reason of this may be stated as follows: According to the republican constitution, the consent of the citizens as members of the State is required to determine at any time the question whether there shall be war or not. Hence, nothing is more natural than that they should be very loath to enter upon so undesirable an undertaking; for in decreeing it they would necessarily be resolving to bring upon themselves all the horrors of war. And, in their case, this implies such consequences as these: to have to fight in their own persons; to supply the costs of the war out of their own property; to have sorrowfully to repair the devastation which it leaves behind; and, as a crowning evil, to have to take upon themselves at the end a burden of debt which will go on embittering peace itself and which it will be impossible ever to pay off on account of the constant threatening of further impending wars. On the other hand, in a constitution where the subject is not a voting member of the State and which is, therefore, not republican, the resolution to go to war is a matter of the smallest concern in the world. For, in this case, the ruler, who, as such, is not a mere citizen but the owner of the State, need not in the least suffer personally by war, nor has he to sacrifice his pleasures of the table or of the chase or his pleasant palaces, court festivals and such like. He can, therefore, resolve for war from insignificant reasons, as if it were but a hunting expedition; and, as regards its propriety, he may leave the justification of it without concern to the diplomatic body, who are always too ready to give their services for that purpose. . . .

Second Definitive Article in the Conditions of Eternal Peace

"The law of nations shall be founded on a federation of free States."

Peoples or nations regarded as States may be judged like individual men. Now men living in a state of nature independent of external laws, by their very contiguity to each other, give occasion to mutual injury or lesion. Every people, for the sake of its own security, thus may and ought to demand from any other that it shall enter along with it into a constitution, similar to the civil constitution, in which the right of each shall be secured. This would give rise to an international federation of the peoples. This, however, would not have to take the form of a State made up of these nations. For that would involve a contradiction, since every State, properly so called, contains the relation of a superior as the lawgiver to an inferior as the people subject to the laws. Moreover, many nations in one State would constitute only one nation, which is contradictory to the principle assumed, as we are here considering the right of nations in relation to each other, in so far as they constitute different States and are not to be fused into one.

The attachment of savages to the lawless liberty of rather being engaged to incessant conflict with each other than submitting to a legal constraint constituted by themselves is well known. Hence their preference of wild freedom to rational liberty is looked upon by us with profound contempt and characterized as barbarism, coarseness and a brutal degradation of humanity. Thus it might be thought that civilized nations, being each united into a State, would of necessity make all haste to advance as soon as possible out of any semblance to a condition that is so much condemned. Instead of this, however, we rather find that every State founds its majesty on not being subject to any external legal coercion; and the glory of its ruler or head is made to consist in the fact that, without his requiring to encounter any danger himself, many thousands stand ready to be sacrificed at his command for a cause which may be no concern of theirs. Thus the difference between the white savages of Europe and the red savages of America, consists mainly in this: that, while some tribes of the latter have been entirely eaten up by their enemies, the former know how to make a better use of the vanquished than to eat them, by rather adding them to the number of their subjects and thereby increasing the multitude of their instruments and means for still more extensive wars.

The depravity of human nature is exhibited without disguise in the unrestrained relations of the nations to each other, whereas in the legalized state of civil society it is greatly veiled under the constraint of government. In view of it, we may well wonder that the word 'law' has not yet been entirely banished from the policy of war as pedantic, and that no State has as yet ventured to declare itself publicly in favor of that doctrine. For Grotius, Puffendorf, Vattel and the others—miserable comforters all of them—are still always quoted cordially for the justification of an outbreak of war, although their philosophically or diplomatically composed codes have not, nor could have, the slightest legal force, since the States as such stand under no common legal constraint; and there is not an example of a State ever having been moved to desist from its purpose by arguments, although armed with testimonies of such important men. Yet the homage which every State thus renders—at least in words—to the conception of law still proves that there is to be found in man a higher and greater moral capacity, though it may slumber for a time; and it is evidently felt that this capacity will yet attain the mastery over the evil principle in him, the existence of which cannot be denied; and this gives a ground of hope to others. For the word 'law' would otherwise never enter into the vocabulary of States desirous to go to war with each other, unless it were merely to make a jest of it, in the manner of the Gallic prince who declared that "it is the prerogative of the strong to make the weak obey them."

The means by which States pursue their rights at present can never be by a form of process,—as if there were an external tribunal,—but can only be by war; but even the favorable issue of war in victory will not decide a matter of right. A treaty of peace may, indeed, put an end to a particular war, yet not to the general condition of war, in which a pretext can always be found for new hostilities. Nor can such a pretext under these circumstances be regarded as unjust; for in this state of society every nation is the judge of its own cause. At the same time, the position which, according to the law of nature, holds of men in a lawless condition, that "they ought to advance out of that condition," cannot according to the law of nations be directly applied to States; because as States they have already within themselves a legal constitution and have thus outgrown the coercive right of others to bring them under a wider legal constitution according to conceptions of law. And yet reason on the throne of the highest moral law-giving power absolutely condemns war as a mode of right, and, on the contrary, makes the state of peace an immediate duty. But the state of peace cannot be founded or secured without a compact of the nations with each other. Hence, there must be a compact of a special kind, which may be called a pacific federation, and which would be distinguished from a mere treaty or compact of peace in that the latter merely puts an end to one war whereas the former would seek to put an end to all wars forever. This federation will not aim at the acquisition of any of the political powers of a State, but merely at the preservation and guarantee for itself, and likewise for the other confederated States, of the liberty that is proper to a State; and this would not require these States to subject themselves for this purpose—as is the case with men in the state of nature—to public laws and to coercion under them. The practicability and objective realization of this idea of federalism, inasmuch as it has to spread itself over all States and thereby lead to perpetual peace, may be easily shown. For if happy circumstances bring it about that a powerful and enlightened people form themselves into a republic—which by its very nature must be disposed in favor of perpetual peace—this will furnish a center of federative union for other States to attach themselves to, and thus to secure the conditions of liberty among all States, according to the idea of the law of nations. And such a union would extend wider and wider, in the course of time, by the addition of further connections of this kind.

It is intelligible that a people should say: "There shall be no war among us: for we will form ourselves into a State and constitute of ourselves a supreme legislative, governing and judicial power which will peacefully settle our differences." But if this State says: "There shall be no war between me and other States, although I recognize no supreme legislative power which will secure me my right and whose right I will also secure,"—then there is no intelligible basis upon which any security for such rights could be founded unless it were a surrogate of the union embodied in civil society. And this can be nothing but a free federation of the states, which reason must necessarily connect with the idea of the law of nations if there is anything further to be thought in connection with it.

The notion of a right to go to war cannot be properly conceived as an element in the law of nations. For it would be equivalent to a right to determine what is just, not by universal external laws limiting the freedom of every individual alike but through one-sided maxims that operate by means of force. If such a right be conceivable at all it would amount, in fact, to this: that in the case of men who are so disposed it is quite right for them to destroy and devour each other, and thus to find perpetual peace only in the wide grave which is to cover all the abomination of the deeds of violence and their authors! For States viewed in relation to each other, there can be only one way, according to reason, of emerging from that lawless condition which contains nothing but occasions of war. Just as in the case of individual men, reason would drive them to give up their savage, lawless freedom to accommodate themselves to public coercive laws, and thus to form an ever-growing state of nations, such as would at last embrace all the nations of the earth. But as the nations, according to their ideas of international law, will not have such a positive rational system, and consequently reject in fact what is right in theory, it cannot be realized in this pure form. Hence, instead of the positive idea of a universal republic—if all is not to be lost—we shall have as result only the negative surrogate of a federation of the states averting war, subsisting in an external union and always extending itself over the world. And thus the current of those inclinations and passions of men which are antagonistic to right and productive of war may be checked, although there will still be a danger of their breaking out. . . .

Third Definitive Article in the Conditions of Eternal Peace

"The rights of men as citizens of the world in a cosmopolitical system shall be restricted to conditions of universal hospitality."

In this as in the previous articles, the question is not about a relation of philanthropy, but one of right. Hospitality here indicates the right of a stranger, in consequence of his arrival on the soil of another country, not to be treated by its citizens as an enemy. As a stranger he may be turned away, if this can be done without involving his death; but so long as he conducts himself peacefully in the place where he may happen to be, he is not to be dealt with in a hostile way. The stranger may not lay claim to be entertained by right as a guest,—for this would require a special friendly compact to make him for a certain time the member of a household; he may only claim a right of resort, or of visitation. All men are entitled to present themselves thus to society in virtue of their right to the common possession of the surface of the earth, to no part of which any one had originally more right than another; and upon which, from its being a globe, they cannot scatter themselves to infinite distances, but must at last bear to live side by side with each other. Uninhabitable portions of this surface are formed by seas and deserts; these present barriers to the fellowship of men in society; but they are of such a nature that the ship or the camel, "the ship of the desert," makes it possible for men to approach each other over these unappropriated regions, and thus to turn the right which the human species have in common to the surface of the earth into a means for social intercourse. The inhospitality, practiced for instance on the Barbary coasts, of plundering ships in the neighboring seas and making slaves of stranded mariners, or that of the sandy deserts, as practiced by Arab Beduins who regard their access to nomadic tribes as constituting a right to plunder them, is thus contrary to the law of nature. But this right of hospitality as vested in strangers arriving in another State does not extend further than the conditions of the possibility of entering into social intercourse with the inhabitants of the country. In this way distant continents may enter into peaceful relations with each other. These may at last become publicly regulated by law, and thus the human race may be always brought nearer to a cosmopolitical constitution.

If we compare the barbarian instances of inhospitality referred to with the inhuman behavior of the civilized, and especially the commercial, States of our continent, the injustice practiced by them even in their first contact with foreign lands and peoples fills us with horror, the mere visiting of such peoples being regarded by them as equivalent to a conquest. America, the Negro lands, the Spice Islands, the Cape of Good Hope, etc., on being discovered, were treated as countries that belonged to nobody; for the aboriginal inhabitants were reckoned as nothing. In the East Indies, under the pretext of intending merely to plant commercial settlements, the Europeans introduced foreign troops, and with them oppression of the natives, instigation of the different States to widespread wars, famine, sedition, perfidy and all the litany of evils that can oppress the human race.

China and Japan, having had experience of such guests, therefore, did wisely in limiting their intercourse. China permitted only access to her coasts but not entrance into the country. Japan restricted access to one European people, the Dutch, and even they were treated like prisoners by being excluded from social intercourse with the natives. The worst (or, regarded from the standpoint of a moral judge, the best) of all this is that no satisfaction is derived from this violence, as all these commercial societies are at present on the verge of ruin. The Sugar Islands—that seat of the cruelest and completest slavery—have yielded up no real profit, but have been only indirectly of account, and that in no praiseworthy relation. They have furnished only sailors for ships of war, and have thereby contributed to the carrying on of wars in Europe. And all this has been done by nations who make a great ado about their piety. . . .

But the social relations between the various peoples of the world, in narrower or wider circles, have now advanced everywhere so far that a violation of right in one place of the earth is felt all over it. Hence the idea of a cosmopolitical right of the whole human race is no fantastic or overstrained mode of representing right, but is a necessary completion of the unwritten code which carries national and international law to a consummation in the public law of mankind. Thus the whole system leads to the conclusion of a perpetual peace among the nations. And it is only under the conditions now laid down that men may flatter themselves with the belief that they are making a continual approach to its realization.

FIRST SUPPLEMENT

THE GUARANTY OF ETERNAL PEACE

The guaranty of eternal peace is furnished by no less a power than the great artist Nature herself. . . .

The problem of the institution of a State, however hard it may appear, would not be insoluble even for a race of devils, assuming only that they have intelligence, and it may be put as follows: "A multitude of rational beings all requiring laws in common for their own preservation, and yet of such a nature that each of them is inclined secretly to except himself from their sway, have to be put under order, and a constituion has to be established among them so that, although they may be antagonistic to one another in their private sentiments, they have yet to be so organized that, in their public relations, their conduct will have the same result as if they had no such bad sentiments."

Such a problem must be capable of solution. For it does not turn directly upon the moral improvement of men, but only upon the mechanism of nature; and the problem is to know how men can use the conditions of nature in order so to regulate the antagonism of the hostile sentiments at work among the people that the individuals composing it shall have to compel each other to submit to common compulsory laws, and that there shall thus be brought about a state of peace in which the laws will have full power. This process may be seen going on in the actually existing, although still very imperfectly organized, States. For in their external relations to one another they already approach what the idea of right prescribes, although the essential principle of morality is certainly not the cause of it; and indeed a good political constitution is not so much to be expected from that principle, but rather, conversely, the good moral culture of a people from such a constitution. Hence the mechanism of nature, as it works through selfish inclinations which are externally and naturally antagonistic in their operation to each other, may be used by reason as a means of making way for the realization of her own end by the application of a precept of right, and thereby of furthering and securing peace both internal and external, so far as it may lie within the power of the State to do so. It may then be said that nature irresistibly wills that right shall at last obtain the supremacy. . . .

The idea of international law presupposes the separation of several neighboring States that are independent of each other; and such a

condition of things is of itself already one of war, unless by their
federated union they can prevent the outbreak of hostilities. Such a
condition of things is, however, according to the idea of reason, better
than the fusion of all the States into a universal monarchy by one power
that has overgrown the rest and subjected them to its sway. This is so
because the laws always lose something of their definiteness as the
range of a government becomes enlarged; and soulless despotism, when
it has choked the seeds of good, at length lapses into anarchy. Nevertheless there is a desire on the part of every State, or of its sovereign, to
attain to a lasting condition of peace by subjecting the whole world,
were it possible, to its sway. But nature wills it otherwise. She employs
two means to prevent the peoples from intermingling, and to keep them
apart. These are the differences of their languages and of their religions,
which bring with them a certain tendency to mutual hatred and furnish
pretexts for war. However, as civilization increases, there is a gradual
approach of men to greater unanimity in principles and to a mutual
understanding of the conditions of peace even in view of these differences. This pacific spirit, unlike that despotism which revels upon the
grave of liberty, is developed and secured, not by the weakening of all
the separate powers of the States, but by an equilibrium which is
brought forth and guaranteed through their rivalry with each other.

Nature wisely separates the nations, which the will of each State,
even according to the principles of international law, would combine
into one by fraud or force. But, on the other hand, she again unites the
nations whom the idea of a universal cosmopolitan law would not have
secured from violence and war by regard to their mutual interests. This
is effected by the commercial spirit, which cannot exist along with war
and which sooner or later controls every people. Among all the means
of power subordinate to the regulation of the State, the power of money
is the most reliable; and thus the States find themselves driven to further
the noble interest of peace, although not directly from motives of
morality. Hence, wherever war threatens to break out in the world, the
States have an interest to avert it by mediations, just as if they stood
in a constant league with each other for this purpose. Thus, great
combinations with a view to war can but very rarely occur from the
very nature of things, and still more rarely can they succeed.

In this way nature guarantees the conditions of perpetual peace by
the mechanism involved in our human inclinations themselves; and
although this is not realized with a guarantee that is sufficient to enable
us to prophesy the future theoretically, yet the security involved is

sufficient for all practical relations. And thus it becomes a duty to labor for the realization of this purpose as not at all chimerical in itself.

27. SMITH
The Disutility of Colonialism

The general theory of *The Wealth of Nations*, as we have previously seen, supported the principle of free trade. Adam Smith developed the implications of his economic theory and of the principle of free trade for British colonial policy in the eighteenth century. Since the year of publication was 1776, it is not surprising that his most provocative illustration was that of the American colonies.

The selection is from Book IV, Chapter VII, of *The Wealth of Nations*, entitled "Colonies."

The common advantages which every empire derives from the provinces subject to its dominion consist, first, in the military force which they furnish for its defence; and, secondly, in the revenue which they furnish for the support of its civil government. The Roman colonies furnished occasionally both the one and the other. The Greek colonies, sometimes, furnished a military force, but seldom any revenue. They seldom acknowledged themselves subject to the dominion of the mother city. They were generally her allies in war, but very seldom her subjects in peace.

The European colonies of America have never yet furnished any military force for the defence of the mother country. Their military force has never yet been sufficient for their own defence; and in the different wars in which the mother countries have been engaged, the defence of their colonies has generally occasioned a very considerable distraction of the military force of those countries. In this respect, therefore, all the European colonies have, without exception, been a cause rather of weakness than of strength to their respective mother countries.

The colonies of Spain and Portugal only have contributed any revenue towards the defence of the mother country, or the support of her civil government. The taxes which have been levied upon those of other European nations, upon those of England in particular, have seldom been equal to the expense laid out upon them in time of peace, and never sufficient to defray that which they occasioned in time of war. Such colonies, therefore, have been a source of expense and not of revenue to their respective mother countries.

The advantages of such colonies to their respective mother countries consist altogether in those peculiar advantages which are supposed to result from provinces of so very peculiar a nature as the European colonies of America; and the exclusive trade, it is acknowledged, is the sole source of all those peculiar advantages. . . .

If the manufactures of Great Britain, however, have been advanced, as they certainly have, by the colony trade, it has not been by means of the monopoly of that trade but in spite of the monopoly. The effect of the monopoly has been, not to augment the quantity, but to alter the quality and shape of a part of the manufactures of Great Britain, and to accommodate to a market, from which the returns are slow and distant, what would otherwise have been accommodated to one from which the returns are frequent and near. Its effect has consequently been to turn a part of the capital of Great Britain from an employment in which it would have maintained a greater quantity of manufacturing industry to one in which it maintains a much smaller, and thereby to diminish, instead of increasing, the whole quantity of manufacturing industry maintained in Great Britain.

The monopoly of the colony trade, therefore, like all the other mean and malignant expedients of the mercantile system, depresses the industry of all other countries, but chiefly that of the colonies, without in the least increasing, but on the contrary diminishing that of the country in whose favour it is established.

The monopoly hinders the capital of that country, whatever may at any particular time be the extent of that capital, from maintaining so great a quantity of productive labour as it would otherwise maintain, and from affording so great a revenue to the industrious inhabitants as it would otherwise afford. But as capital can be increased only by savings from revenue, the monopoly, by hindering it from affording so great a revenue as it would otherwise afford, necessarily hinders it from increasing so fast as it would otherwise increase, and consequently from maintaining a still greater quantity of productive labour, and affording a still greater revenue to the industrious inhabitants of that country. One great original source of revenue, therefore, the wages of labour, the monopoly must necessarily have rendered at all times less abundant than it otherwise would have been.

By raising the rate of mercantile profit, the monopoly discourages the improvement of land. The profit of improvement depends upon the difference between what the land actually produces, and what, by the application of a certain capital, it can be made to produce. If this difference affords a greater profit than what can be drawn from an equal capital in any mercantile employment, the improvement of land will draw capital from all mercantile employments. If the profit is less, mercantile employments will draw capital from the improvement of land. Whatever, therefore, raises the rate of mercantile profit, either lessens the superiority or increases the inferiority of the profit of improvement; and in the one case hinders capital from going to improvement, and in the other draws capital from it. But by discouraging improvement, the monopoly necessarily retards the natural increase of another great original source of revenue, the rent of land. By raising the rate of profit, too, the monopoly necessarily keeps up the market rate of interest higher than it otherwise would be. But the price of land in proportion to the rent which it affords, the number of years purchase which is commonly paid for it, necessarily falls as the rate of interest rises, and rises as the rate of interest falls. The monopoly, therefore, hurts the interest of the landlord two different ways, by retarding the natural increase, first, of his rent, and secondly, of the price which he would get for his land in proportion to the rent which it affords.

The monopoly indeed raises the rate of mercantile profit and thereby augments somewhat the gain of our merchants. But as it obstructs the natural increase of capital, it tends rather to diminish than to increase the sum total of the revenue which the inhabitants of the country derive from the profits of stock; a small profit upon a great capital generally affording a greater revenue than a great profit upon a small one. The monopoly raises the rate of profit, but it hinders the sum of profit from rising so high as it otherwise would do.

All the original sources of revenue, the wages of labour, the rent of land, and the profits of stock, the monopoly renders much less abundant than they otherwise would be. To promote the little interest of one little order of men in one country, it hurts the interest of all other orders of men in that country, and of all men in all other countries. . . .

It is thus that the single advantage which the monopoly procures to a single order of men is in many different ways hurtful to the general interest of the country.

To found a great empire for the sole purpose of raising up a people of customers may at first sight appear a project fit only for a nation of shopkeepers. It is, however, a project altogether unfit for a nation of shopkeepers; but extremely fit for a nation whose government is influenced by shopkeepers. Such statesmen, and such statesmen only, are capable of fancying that they will find some advantage in employing the blood and treasure of their fellow-citizens to found and maintain such an empire. Say to a shopkeeper, Buy me a good estate, and I shall always buy my clothes at your shop, even though I should pay somewhat dearer than what I can have them for at other shops; and you will not find him very forward to embrace your proposal. But should any other person buy you such an estate, the shopkeeper would be much obliged to your benefactor if he would enjoin you to buy all your clothes at his shop. England purchased for some of her subjects, who found themselves uneasy at home, a great estate in a distant country. The price, indeed, was very small, and instead of thirty years' purchase, the ordinary price of land in the present times, it amounted to little more than the expense of the different equipments which made the first discovery, reconnoitred the coast, and took a fictitious possession of the country. The land was good and of great extent, and the cultivators having plenty of good ground to work upon, and being for some time at liberty to sell their produce where they pleased, became in the course of little more than thirty or forty years (between 1620 and 1660) so numerous and thriving a people that the shopkeepers and other traders of England wished to secure to themselves the monopoly of their custom. . . .

The maintenance of this monopoly has hitherto been the principal, or more properly perhaps the sole end and purpose of the dominion which Great Britain assumes over her colonies. In the exclusive trade, it is supposed, consists the great advantage of provinces, which have never yet afforded either revenue or military force for the support of the civil government, or the defence of the mother country. The monopoly is the principal badge of their dependency, and it is the sole fruit which has hitherto been gathered from that dependency. Whatever expense Great Britain has hitherto laid out in maintaining this dependency has really been laid out in order to support this monopoly. The expense of the ordinary peace establishment of the colonies amounted, before the commencement of the present disturbances, to the pay of twenty regiments of foot; to the expense of the artillery, stores, and extraordinary provisions with which it was necessary to supply them; and to the expense of a very considerable naval force which was constantly kept up, in order to guard, from the smuggling vessels of other nations, the immense coast of North America, and that of our West Indian islands. The whole expense of this peace establishment was a charge upon the revenue of Great Britain, and was, at the same time, the smallest part of what the dominion of the colonies has cost the mother country. If we would know the amount of the whole, we must add to the annual expense of this peace establishment the interest of the sums which, in consequence of her considering her colonies as provinces subject to her dominion, Great Britain has upon different occasions laid out upon their defence. We must add to it, in particular, the whole expense of the late war, and a great part of that of the war which preceded it. The late war was altogether a colony quarrel, and the whole expense of it, in whatever part of the world it may have been laid out, whether in Germany or the East Indies, ought justly to be stated to the account of the colonies. . . .

Under the present system of management, therefore, Great Britain derives nothing but loss from the dominion which she assumes over her colonies.

To propose that Great Britain should voluntarily give up all authority over her colonies, and leave them to elect their own magistrates, to enact their own laws, and to make peace and war as they might think proper, would be to propose such a measure as never was, and never will be adopted, by any nation in the world. No nation ever voluntarily gave up the dominion of any province, how troublesome soever it might be to govern it, and how small soever the revenue which it afforded might be in proportion to the expense which it occasioned. Such sacrifices, though they might frequently be agreeable to the interest, are always mortifying to the pride of every nation, and what is perhaps of still greater consequence, they are always contrary to the private interest of the governing part of it, who would thereby be deprived of the disposal of many places of trust and profit, of many opportunities of acquiring wealth and distinction, which the possession of the most turbulent, and, to the great body of the people, the most unprofitable province seldom fails to afford. The most visionary enthusiast would scarce be capable of proposing such a measure with any serious hopes at least of its ever being adopted. If it was adopted, however, Great Britain would not only be immediately freed from the whole annual expense of the peace establishment of the colonies, but might settle with them such a treaty of commerce as would effectually secure to her a free trade, more advantageous to the great body of the people, though less so to the merchants, than the monopoly which she at present enjoys. By thus parting good friends, the natural affection of the colonies to the mother country which, perhaps, our late dissensions have well nigh extinguished, would quickly revive. It might dispose them not only to respect, for whole centuries together, that treaty of commerce which they had concluded with us at parting, but to favour us in war as well as in trade, and, instead of turbulent and factious subjects, to become our most faithful, affectionate, and generous allies; and the same sort of parental affection on the one side, and filial respect on the other, might revive between Great Britain and her colonies, which used to subsist between those of ancient Greece and the mother city from which they descended. . . .

28.   J. S. MILL
Liberalism, Empire, and Intervention

It is one of the paradoxes of British liberalism that its anti-colonial stance was developed in many cases by utilitarians who were involved in colonial administration. John Stuart Mill in the concluding sections of *Considerations on Representative Government* asserted his belief in the long-term process of transforming colonies into independent nations. This work was published a few years after Mill's retirement in 1858 upon completion of thirty-five years of service in India House. The first selection is from Chapter XVIII of this work.

Mill published the second selection excerpted below, "A Few Words on Non-Intervention," in 1859. The point of departure of the article was the opposition of the British Foreign Secretary to the French construction of the Suez Canal, but Mill proceeded to discuss the general issues of expediency, morality, and intervention in foreign policy.

OF THE GOVERNMENT OF DEPENDENCIES
BY A FREE STATE

Free States, like all others, may possess dependencies, acquired either by conquest or by colonisation; and our own is the greatest instance of the kind in modern history. It is a most important question how such dependencies ought to be governed.

It is unnecessary to discuss the case of small posts, like Gibraltar, Aden, or Heligoland, which are held only as naval or military positions. The military or naval object is in this case paramount, and the inhabitants cannot, consistently with it, be admitted to the government of the place; though they ought to be allowed all liberties and privileges compatible with that restriction, including the free management of municipal affairs; and as a compensation for being locally sacrificed to the convenience of the governing State, should be admitted to equal rights with its native subjects in all other parts of the empire.

Outlying territories of some size and population, which are held as dependencies, that is, which are subject, more or less, to acts of sovereign power on the part of the paramount country, without being equally represented (if represented at all) in its legislature, may be divided into two classes. Some are composed of people of similar civilisation to the ruling country, capable of, and ripe for, representative government: such as the British possessions in America and Australia. Others, like India, are still at a great distance from that state.

In the case of dependencies of the former class, this country has at length realised, in rare completeness, the true principle of government. England has always felt under a certain degree of obligation to bestow on such of her outlying populations as were of her own blood and language, and on some who were not, representative institutions formed in imitation of her own: but until the present generation, she has been on the same bad level with other countries as to the amount of self-government which she allowed them to exercise through the representative institutions that she conceded to them. She claimed to be the supreme arbiter even of their purely internal concerns, according to her own, not their, ideas of how those concerns could be best regulated. This practice was a natural corollary from the vicious theory of colonial policy—once common to all Europe, and not yet completely relinquished by any other people—which regarded colonies as valuable by affording markets for our commodities, that could be kept entirely to ourselves: a privilege we valued so highly that we thought it worth purchasing by allowing to the colonies the same monopoly of our market for their own productions which we claimed for our commodities in theirs. This notable plan for enriching them and ourselves, by making each pay enormous sums to the other, dropping the greatest part by the way, has been for some time abandoned. But the bad habit of meddling in the internal government of the colonies did not at once terminate when we relinquished the idea of making any profit by it. We continued to torment them, not for any benefit to ourselves, but for that of a section or faction among the colonists: and this persistence in domineering cost us a Canadian rebellion before we had the happy thought of giving it up. England was like an ill-brought-up elder brother, who persists in tyrannising over the younger ones from mere habit, till one of them, by a spirited resistance, though with unequal strength, gives him notice to desist. . . .

It is now a fixed principle of the policy of Great Britain, professed in theory and faithfully adhered to in practice, that her colonies of European race, equally with the parent country, possess the fullest measure of internal self-government. They have been allowed to make their own free representative constitutions by altering in any manner they thought fit the already very popular constitutions which we had given them. Each is governed by its own legislature and executive, constituted on highly democratic principles. . . . Their union with Great Britain is the slightest kind of federal union; but not a strictly equal federation, the mother country retaining to itself the powers of a Federal Government, though reduced in practice to their very narrowest limits. This inequality is, of course, as far as it goes, a disadvantage ot the dependencies, which have no voice in foreign policy, but are bound by the decisions of the superior country. They are compelled to join England in war, without being in any way consulted previous to engaging in it.

Those (now happily not a few) who think that justice is as binding on communities as it is on individuals, and that men are not warranted in doing to other countries, for the supposed benefit of their own country, what they would not be justified in doing to other men for their own benefit—feel even this limited amount of constitutional subordination on the part of the colonies to be a violation of principle, and have often occupied themselves in looking out for means by which it may be avoided. . . .

Thus far of the dependencies whose population is in a sufficiently advanced state to be fitted for representative government. But there are others which have not attained that state, and which, if held at all, must be governed by the dominant country, or by persons delegated for that purpose by it. This mode of government is as legitimate as any other if it is the one which in the existing state of civilisation of the subject people most facilitates their transition to a higher stage of improvement. There are, as we have already seen, conditions of society in which a vigorous despotism is in itself the best mode of government for training the people in what is specifically wanting to render them capable of a higher civilisation. There are others, in which the mere fact of despotism has indeed no beneficial effect, the lessons which it teaches having already been only too completely learnt; but in which, there being no spring of spontaneous improvement in the people themselves, their almost only hope of making any steps in advance depends on the chances of a good despot. Under a native despotism, a good despot is a rare and transitory accident: but when the dominion they are under is that of a more civilised people, that people ought to be able to supply it constantly. The ruling country ought to be able to do for its subjects all that could be done by a succession of absolute monarchs, guaranteed by irresistible force against the precariousness of tenure attendant on barbarous despotisms, and qualified by their genius to anticipate all that experience has taught to the more advanced nation. Such is the ideal rule of a free people over a barbarous or semi-barbarous one. We need not expect to see that ideal realised; but unless some approach to it is, the rulers are guilty of a dereliction of the highest moral trust which can devolve upon a nation: and if they do not even aim at it, they are selfish usurpers, on a par in criminality with any of those whose ambition and rapacity have sported from age to age with the destiny of masses of mankind.

As it is already a common, and is rapidly tending to become the universal, condition of the more backward populations, to be either held in direct subjection by the more advanced, or to be under their complete political ascendancy; there are in this age of the world few more important problems than how to organise this rule, so as to make it a good instead of an evil to the subject people; providing them with the best attainable present government, and with the conditions most favourable to future permanent improvement. But the mode of fitting the government for this purpose is by no means so well understood as the conditions of good government in a people capable of governing themselves. We may even say that it is not understood at all. . . .

It is always under great difficulties, and very imperfectly, that a country can be governed by foreigners; even when there is no extreme disparity, in habits and ideas, between the rulers and the ruled. Foreigners do not feel with the people. They cannot judge, by the light in which a thing appears to their own minds, or the manner in which it affects their feelings, how it will affect the feelings or appear to the minds of the subject population. What a native of the country, of average practical ability, knows as it were by instinct, they have to learn slowly, and after all imperfectly, by study and experience. The laws, the customs, the social relations, for which they have to legislate, instead of being familiar to them from childhood, are all strange to them. For most of their detailed knowledge they must depend on the information of natives; and it is difficult for them to know whom to trust. They are feared, suspected, probably disliked by the population; seldom sought by them except for interested purposes; and they are prone to think that the servilely submissive are the trustworthy. Their danger is of despising the natives; that of the natives is of disbelieving that anything the strangers do can be intended for their good. These are but a part of the difficulties that any rulers have to struggle with who honestly attempt to govern well a country in which they are foreigners. . . .

NON-INTERVENTION

. . . It is the universal belief in France that English influence at Constantinople, strenuously exerted to defeat this project [the Suez Canal], is the real and only invincible obstacle to its being carried into effect. And unhappily the public declarations of our present Prime Minister not only bear out this persuasion, but warrant the assertion that we oppose the work because, in the opinion of our Government, it would be injurious to the interest of England. If such be the course we are pursuing, and such the motive of it, and if nations have duties, even negative ones, towards the weal of the human race, it is hard to say whether the folly or the immorality of our conduct is the most painfully conspicuous.

Here is a project, the practicability of which is indeed a matter in dispute, but of which no one has attempted to deny that, supposing it realized, it would give a facility to commerce, and consequently a stimulus to production, an encouragement to intercourse, and therefore to civilization, which would entitle it to a high rank among the great industrial improvements of modern times. The contriving of new means of abridging labour and economizing outlay in the operations of industry, is the object to which the larger half of all the inventive ingenuity of mankind is at present given up; and this scheme, if realized, will save, on one of the great highways of the world's traffic, the circumnavigation of a continent. An easy access of commerce is the main source of that material civilization, which, in the more backward regions of the earth is the necessary condition and indispensable machinery of the moral; and this scheme reduces practically by one half, the distance, commercially speaking, between the self-improving nations of the world and the most important and valuable of the unimproving. The Atlantic Telegraph is esteemed an enterprise of world-wide importance because it abridges the transit of mercantile intelligence merely. What the Suez Canal would shorten is the transport of the goods themselves, and this to such an extent as probably to augment it manifold.

Let us suppose, then—for in the present day the hypothesis is too un-English to be spoken of as anything more than a supposition—let us suppose that the English nation saw in this great benefit to the civilized and uncivilized world a danger or damage to some peculiar interest of England. Suppose, for example, that it feared, by shortening the road, to facilitate the access of foreign navies to its Oriental possessions. The supposition imputes no ordinary degree of cowardice and imbecility to the national mind; otherwise it could not but reflect that the same thing which would facilitate the arrival of an enemy, would facilitate also that of succour; that we have had French fleets in the Eastern seas before now, and have fought naval battles with them there, nearly a century ago; that if we ever became unable to defend India against them, we should assuredly have them there without the aid of any canal; and that our power of resisting an enemy does not depend upon putting a little more or less of obstacle in the way of his coming, but upon the amount of force which we are able to oppose to him when come. Let us assume, however, that the success of the project would do more harm to England in some separate capacity, than the good which, as the chief commercial nation, she would reap from the great increase of commercial intercourse. Let us grant this: and I now ask, what then? Is there any morality, Christian or secular, which bears out a nation in keeping all the rest of mankind out of some great advantage, because the consequences of their obtaining it may be to itself, in some imaginable contingency, a cause of inconvenience? Is a nation at liberty to adopt as a practical maxim, that what is good for the human race is bad for itself, and to withstand it accordingly? What is this but to declare that its interest and that of mankind are incompatible—that, thus far at least, it is the enemy of the human race? And what ground has it of complaint if, in return, the human race determine to be *its* enemies? So wicked a principle, avowed and acted on by a nation, would entitle the rest of the world to unite in a league against it, and never to make peace until they had, if not reduced it to insignificance, at least sufficiently broken its power to disable it from ever again placing its own self-interest before the general prosperity of mankind. . . .

There seems to be no little need that the whole doctrine of non-interference with foreign nations should be reconsidered, if it can be said to have as yet been considered as a really moral question at all. We have heard something lately about being willing to go to war for an idea. To go to war for an idea, if the war is aggressive, not defensive, is as criminal as to go to war for territory or revenue; for it is as little justifiable to force our ideas on other people, as to compel them to submit to our will in any other respect. But there assuredly are cases in which it is allowable to go to war, without having been ourselves attacked, or threatened with attack; and it is very important that nations should make up their minds in time, as to what these cases are. There are few questions which more require to be taken in hand by ethical and political philosophers, with a view to establish some rule or criterion whereby the justifiableness of intervening in the affairs of other countries, and (what is sometimes fully as questionable) the justifiableness of refraining from intervention, may be brought to a definite and rational test. Whoever attempts this, will be led to recognise more than one fundamental distinction, not yet by any means familiar to the public mind, and in general quite lost sight of by those who write in strains of indignant morality on the subject. There is a great difference (for example) between the case in which the nations concerned are of the same, or something like the same, degree of civilization, and that in which one of the parties to the situation is of a high, and the other of a very low, grade of social improvement. To suppose that the same international customs, and the same rules of international morality, can obtain between one civilized nation and another, and between civilized nations and barbarians, is a grave error, and one which no statesman can fall into, however it may be with those who, from a safe and unresponsible position, criticise statesmen. Among many reasons why the same rules cannot be applicable to situations so different, the two following are among the most important. In the first place, the rules of ordinary international morality imply reciprocity.

But barbarians will not reciprocate. They cannot be depended on for observing any rules. Their minds are not capable of so great an effort, nor their will sufficiently under the influence of distant motives. In the next place, nations which are still barbarous have not got beyond the period during which it is likely to be for their benefit that they should be conquered and held in subjection by foreigners. Independence and nationality, so essential to the due growth and developement of a people further advanced in improvement, are generally impediments to theirs. The sacred duties which civilized nations owe to the independence and nationality of each other, are not binding towards those to whom nationality and independence are either a certain evil, or at best a questionable good. The Romans were not the most clean-handed of conquerors, yet would it have been better for Gaul and Spain, Numidia and Dacia, never to have formed part of the Roman Empire? To characterize any conduct whatever towards a barbarous people as a violation of the law of nations, only shows that he who so speaks has never considered the subject. A violation of great principles of morality it may easily be; but barbarians have no rights as a *nation*, except a right to such treatment as may, at the earliest possible period, fit them for becoming one. The only moral laws for the relation between a civilized and a barbarous government, are the universal rules of morality between man and man. . . .

But among civilized peoples, members of an equal community of nations, like Christian Europe, the question assumes another aspect, and must be decided on totally different principles. It would be an affront to the reader to discuss the immorality of wars of conquest, or of conquest even as the consequence of lawful war; the annexation of any civilized people to the dominion of another, unless by their own spontaneous election. Up to this point, there is no difference of opinion among honest people; nor on the wickedness of commencing an aggressive war for any interest of our own, except when necessary to avert from ourselves an obviously impending wrong. The disputed question is that of interfering in the regulation of another country's internal concerns; the question whether a nation is justified in taking part, on either side, in the civil wars or party contests of another; and chiefly, whether it may justifiably aid the people of another country in struggling for liberty; or may impose on a country any particular government or institutions, either as being best for the country itself, or as necessary for the security of its neighbours.

Of these cases, that of a people in arms for liberty is the only one of any nicety, or which, theoretically at least, is likely to present conflicting moral considerations. The other cases which have been mentioned hardly admit of discussion. Assistance to the government of a country in keeping down the people, unhappily by far the most frequent case of foreign intervention, no one writing in a free country needs take the trouble of stigmatizing. A government which needs foreign support to enforce obedience from its own citizens, is one which ought not to exist; and the assistance given to it by foreigners is hardly ever anything but the sympathy of one despotism with another. A case requiring consideration is that of a protracted civil war, in which the contending parties are so equally balanced that there is no probability of a speedy issue; or if there is, the victorious side cannot hope to keep down the vanquished but by severities repugnant to humanity, and injurious to the permanent welfare of the country. In this exceptional case it seems now to be an admitted doctrine, that the neighbouring nations, or one powerful neighbour with the acquiescence of the rest, are warranted in demanding that the contest shall cease, and a reconciliation take place on equitable terms of compromise. Intervention of this description has been repeatedly practised during the present generation, with such general approval, that its legitimacy may be considered to have passed into a maxim of what is called international law. . . .

With respect to the question, whether one country is justified in help-ing the people of another in a struggle against their government for free institutions, the answer will be different, according as the yoke which the people are attempting to throw off is that of a purely native government, or of foreigners; considering as one of foreigners, every government which maintains itself by foreign support. When the con-test is only with native rulers, and with such native strength as those rulers can enlist in their defence, the answer I should give to the question of the legitimacy of intervention is, as a general rule, No. The reason is, that there can seldom be anything approaching to assurance that inter-vention, even if successful, would be for the good of the people them-selves. The only test possessing any real value, of a people's having become fit for popular institutions, is that they, or a sufficient portion of them to prevail in the contest, are willing to brave labour and danger for their liberation. I know all that may be said. I know it may be urged that the virtues of freemen cannot be learnt in the school of slavery, and that if a people are not fit for freedom, to have any chance of becoming so they must first be free. And this would be conclusive, if the intervention recommended would really give them freedom. But the evil is, that if they have not sufficient love of liberty to be able to wrest it from merely domestic oppressors, the liberty which is bestowed on them by other hands than their own, will have nothing real, nothing permanent. No people ever was and remained free, but because it was determined to be so; because neither its rulers nor any other party in the nation could compel it to be otherwise. If a people—especially one whose freedom has not yet become prescriptive—does not value it sufficiently to fight for it, and maintain it against any force which can be mustered *within* the country, even by those who have the command of the public revenue, it is only a question in how few years or months that people will be enslaved. Either the government which it has given to itself, or some military leader or knot of conspirators who contrive to subvert the government, will speedily put an end to all popular institutions: unless indeed it suits their convenience better to leave them standing, and be content with reducing them to mere forms; for, unless the spirit of liberty is strong in a people, those who have the executive in their hands easily work any institutions to the purposes of despotism. There is no sure guarantee against this deplorable issue, even in a country which has achieved its own freedom; as may be seen in the present day by striking examples both in the Old and New Worlds: but when freedom has been achieved *for* them, they have little prospect indeed of escaping this fate. When a people has had the misfortune to be ruled by a government under which the feelings and the virtues needful for maintaining freedom could not develop themselves, it is during an arduous struggle to become free by their own efforts that these feelings and virtues have the best chance of springing up. Men become attached to that which they have long fought for and made sacrifices for; they learned to appreciate that on which their thoughts have been much engaged; and a contest in which many have been called on to devote themselves for their country, is a school in which they learn to value their country's interest above their own.

It can seldom, therefore—I will not go so far as to say never—be either judicious or right, in a country which has a free government, to assist, otherwise than by the moral support of its opinion, the endeavours of another to extort the same blessing from its native rulers. We must except, of course, any case in which such assistance is a measure of legitimate self-defence. If (a contingency by no means unlikely to occur) this country, on account of its freedom, which is a standing reproach to despotism everywhere, and an encouragement to throw it off, should find itself menaced with attack by a coalition of Continental despots, it ought to consider the popular party in every nation of the Continent as its natural ally: the Liberals should be to it, what the Protestants of Europe were to the Government of Queen Elizabeth. So again, when a nation, in her own defence, has gone to war with a despot, and has had the rare good fortune not only to succeed in her resistance, but to hold the conditions of peace in her own hands, she is entitled to say that she will make no treaty, unless with some other ruler than the one whose existence as such may be a perpetual menace to her safety and freedom. These exceptions do but set in a clearer light the reasons of the rule; because they do not depend on any failure of those reasons, but on considerations paramount to them, and coming under a different principle.

But the case of a people struggling against a foreign yoke, or against a native tyranny upheld by foreign arms, illustrates the reasons for non-intervention in an opposite way; for in this case the reasons themselves do not exist. A people the most attached to freedom, the most capable of defending and of making a good use of free institutions, may be unable to contend successfully for them against the military strength of another nation much more powerful. To assist a people thus kept down, is not to disturb the balance of forces on which the permanent maintenance of freedom in a country depends, but to redress that balance when it is already unfairly and violently disturbed. The doctrine of non-intervention, to be a legitimate principle of morality, must be accepted by all governments. The despots must consent to be bound by it as well as the free States. Unless they do, the profession of it by free countries comes but to this miserable issue, that the wrong side may help the wrong, but the right must not help the right. Intervention to enforce non-intervention is always rightful, always moral, if not always prudent. Though it be a mistake to *give* freedom to a people who do not value the boon, it cannot but be right to insist that if they do value it, they shall not be hindered from the pursuit of it by foreign coercion. It might not have been right for England (even apart from the question of prudence) to have taken part with Hungary in its noble struggle against Austria; although the Austrian Government in Hungary was in some sense a foreign yoke. But when, the Hungarians having shown themselves likely to prevail in this struggle, the Russian despot interposed, and joining his force to that of Austria, delivered back the Hungarians, bound hand and foot, to their exasperated oppressors, it would have been an honourable and virtuous act on the part of England to have declared that this should not be, and that if Russia gave assistance to the wrong side, England would aid the right. It might not have been consistent with the regard which every nation is bound to pay to its own safety, for England to have taken up this position single-handed. But England and France together could have done it; and if they had, the Russian armed intervention would never have taken place, or would have been disastrous to Russia alone: while all that those Powers gained by not doing it, was that they had to fight Russia five years afterwards, under more difficult circumstances, and without Hungary for an ally. The first nation which, being powerful enough to make its voice effectual, has the spirit and courage to say that not a gun shall be fired in Europe by the soldiers of one Power against the revolted subjects of another, will be the idol of the friends of freedom throughout Europe. That declaration alone will ensure the almost immediate emancipation of every people which desires liberty sufficiently to be capable of maintaining it: and the nation which gives the word will soon find itself at the head of an alliance of free peoples, so strong as to defy the efforts of any number of confederated despots to bring it down. The prize is too glorious not to be snatched sooner or later by some free country; and the time may not be distant when England, if she does not take this heroic part because of its heroism, will be compelled to take it from consideration of her own safety.

29. MAZZINI

Revolutionary Nationalism

Giuseppe Mazzini (1805–72) was born in Genoa, where he first joined the movement for Italian unification. He was imprisoned there as a youth and in prison elaborated the plans for his own nationalist movement "Young Italy." By 1833 "Young Italy" was considered so dangerous that the Austrian government, ruling part of Italy, declared membership punishable by death.

Mazzini's military expeditions, aimed at organizing resistance and revolution for Italian national freedom, failed. He lived the life of a political exile and propagandist in Switzerland and England. The first four chapters of *Duties of Man* were written for an Italian journal which Mazzini published in England in 1844, and the concluding chapters appeared in 1858. It was written in the form of letters to the Italian workers.

The selection is from the "Introduction" and Chapter V of *Duties of Man* as translated by Ella Noyes in 1870.

TO THE ITALIAN WORKING CLASS

To you, sons and daughters of the people, I dedicate this little book, wherein I have pointed out the principles in the name and strength of which you may, if you so will, accomplish your mission in Italy; a mission of republican progress for all and of emancipation for yourselves. Let those who are specially favoured by circumstances or in understanding, and able to comprehend these principles more easily, explain and comment on them to the others, and may that spirit of love inspire them with which, as I wrote, I thought on your griefs and on your virgin aspirations towards the new life which—once the unjust inequality now stifling your faculties is overcome—you will kindle in the Italian country.

I loved you from my first years. The republican instincts of my mother taught me to seek out among my fellows the Man, not the merely rich and powerful individual; and the simple unconscious virtue of my father accustomed me to admire, rather than conceited and pretentious semi-knowledge, the silent and unnoticed virtue of self-sacrifice so often found in you. Later on I gathered from the history of our country that the true life of Italy is the life of the people, and that the slow work of the centuries has constantly tended, amid the shock of different races and the superficial transitory changes wrought by usurpations and conquests, to prepare the great democratic National Unity. . . .

Duties to Country

Your first Duties—first, at least, in importance—are, as I have told you, to Humanity. You are *men* before you are *citizens* or *fathers*. If you do not embrace the whole human family in your love, if you do not confess your faith in its unity—consequent on the unity of God—and in the brotherhood of the Peoples who are appointed to reduce that unity for fact—if wherever one of your fellowmen groans, wherever the dignity of human nature is violated by falsehood or tyranny, you are not prompt, being able, to succour that wretched one, or do not feel your-self called, being able, to fight for the purpose of relieving the deceived or oppressed—you disobey your law of life, or do not comprehend the religion which will bless the future.

But what can *each* of you, with his isolated powers, *do* for the moral improvement, for the progress of Humanity? . . . God gave you this means when he gave you a Country, when, like a wise overseer of labour, who distributes the different parts of the work according to the capacity of the workmen, he divided Humanity into distinct groups upon the face of our globe, and thus planted the seeds of nations. Bad governments have disfigured the design of God, which you may see clearly marked out, as far, at least, as regards Europe, by the courses of the great rivers, by the lines of the lofty mountains, and by other geographical conditions; they have disfigured it by conquest, by greed, by jealousy of the just sovereignty of others; disfigured it so much that today there is perhaps no nation except England and France whose confines correspond to this design. They did not, and they do not, recognise any country except their own families and dynasties, the egoism of caste. But the divine design will infallibly be fulfilled. Natural divisions, the innate spontaneous tendencies of the people will replace the arbitrary divisions sanctioned by bad governments. The map of Europe will be remade. The Countries of the People will rise, defined by the voice of the free, upon the ruins of the Countries of Kings and privileged castes. Between these Countries there will be harmony and brotherhood. And then the work of Humanity for the general ameliora-tion, for the discovery and application of the real law of life, carried on in association and distributed according to local capacities, will be accomplished by peaceful and progressive development; then each of you, strong in the affections and in the aid of many millions of men speaking the same language, endowed with the same tendencies, and educated by the same historic tradition, may hope by your personal effort to benefit the whole of Humanity.

To you, who have been born in Italy, God has allotted, as if favouring you specially, the best-defined country in Europe. In other lands, marked by more uncertain or more interrupted limits, questions may arise which the pacific vote of all will one day solve, but which have cost, and will yet perhaps cost, tears and blood; in yours, no. God has stretched round you sublime and indisputable boundaries; on one side the highest mountains of Europe, the Alps; on the other the sea, the immeasurable sea. Take a map of Europe and place one point of a pair of compasses in the north of Italy on Parma; point the other to the mouth of the Var, and describe a semicircle with it in the direction of the Alps; this point, which will fall, when the semicircle is completed, upon the mouth of the Isonzo, will have marked the frontier which God has given you. As far as this frontier your language is spoken and understood; beyond this you have no rights. Sicily, Sardinia, Corsica, and the smaller islands between them and the mainland of Italy belong undeniably to you. Brute force may for a little while contest these frontiers with you, but they have been recognised from of old by the tacit general consent of the peoples; and the day when, rising with one accord for the final trial, you plant your tricoloured flag upon that frontier, the whole of Europe will acclaim re-risen Italy, and receive her into the community of the nations. To this final trial all your efforts must be directed.

Without Country you have neither name, token, voice, nor rights, no admission as brothers into the fellowship of the Peoples. You are the bastards of Humanity. Soldiers without a banner, Israelites among the nations, you will find neither faith nor protection; none will be sureties for you. Do not beguile yourselves with the hope of emancipation from unjust social conditions if you do not first conquer a Country for yourselves; where there is no Country there is no common agreement to which you can appeal; the egoism of self-interest rules alone, and he who has the upper hand keeps it, since there is no common safeguard for the interests of all. Do not be led away by the idea of improving your material conditions without first solving the national question. You cannot do it. Your industrial associations and mutual help societies are useful as a means of educating and disciplining yourselves; as an economic fact they will remain barren until you have an Italy. The economic problem demands, first and foremost, an increase of capital and production; and while your Country is dismembered into separate fragments—while shut off by the barrier of customs and artificial difficulties of every sort, you have only restricted markets open to you—you cannot hope for this increase. Today—do not delude yourselves—you are not the working-class of Italy; you are only fractions of that class; powerless, unequal to the great task which you propose to yourselves. Your emancipation can have no practical beginning until a National Government, understanding the signs of the times, shall, seated in Rome, formulate a Declaration of Principles to be the guide for Italian progress, and shall insert into it these words, *Labour is sacred, and is the source of the wealth of Italy.*

Do not be led astray, then, by hopes of material progress which in your present conditions can only be illusions. Your Country alone, the vast and rich Italian Country, which stretches from the Alps to the farthest limit of Sicily, can fulfil these hopes. You cannot obtain your *rights* except by obeying the commands of *Duty*. Be worthy of them, and you will have them. O my Brothers! love your Country. Our Country is our home, the home which God has given us, placing therein a numerous family which we love and are loved by, and with which we have a more intimate and quicker communion of feeling and thought than with others; a family which by its concentration upon a given spot, and by the homogeneous nature of its elements, is destined for a special kind of activity. Our Country is our field of labour; the products of our activity must go forth from it for the benefit of the whole earth; but the instruments of labour which we can use best and most effectively exist in it, and we may not reject them without being unfaithful to God's purpose and diminishing our own strength. In labouring according to true principles for our Country we are labouring for Humanity; our Country is the fulcrum of the lever which we have to wield for the common good. If we give up this fulcrum we run the risk of becoming useless to our Country and to Humanity. Before *associating* ourselves with the Nations which compose Humanity we must exist as a Nation. There can be no association except among equals; and you have no recognised collective existence.

Humanity is a great army moving to the conquest of unknown lands, against powerful and wary enemies. The Peoples are the different corps and divisions of that army. Each has a post entrusted to it; each a special operation to perform; and the common victory depends on the exactness with which the different operations are carried out. Do not disturb the order of the battle. Do not abandon the banner which God has given you. Wherever you may be, into the midst of whatever people circumstances may have driven you, fight for the liberty of that people if the moment calls for it; but fight as Italians, so that the blood which you shed may win honour and love, not for you only, but for your Country. And may the constant thought of your soul be for Italy, may all the acts of your life be worthy of her, and may the standard beneath which you range yourselves to work for Humanity be Italy's. Do not say *I*; say *we*. Be every one of you an incarnation of your Country, and feel himself and make himself responsible for his fellow-countrymen; let each one of you learn to act in such a way that in him men shall respect and love his Country.

Your Country is one and indivisible. As the members of a family cannot rejoice at the common table if one of their number is far away, snatched from the affection of his brothers, so you should have no joy or repose as long as a portion of the territory upon which your language is spoken is separated from the Nation.

Your Country is the token of the mission which God has given you to fulfil in Humanity. The faculties, the strength of *all* its sons should be united for the accomplishment of this mission. A certain number of common duties and rights belong to every man who answers to the *Who are you?* of the other peoples, *I am an Italian*. Those duties and those rights cannot be represented except by one *single* authority resulting from your votes. A Country must have, then, a single government. The politicians who call themselves federalists, and who would make Italy into a brotherhood of different states, would dismember the Country, not understanding the idea of Unity. The States into which Italy is divided today are not the creation of our own people; they are the result of the ambitions and calculations of princes or of foreign conquerors, and serve no purpose but to flatter the vanity of local aristocracies for which a narrower sphere than a great Country is necessary. What you, the people, have created, beautified, and consecrated with your affections, with your joys, with your sorrows, and with your blood, is the City and the Commune, not the Province or the State. In the City, in the Commune, where your fathers sleep and where your children will live, where you exercise your faculties and your personal rights, you live out your lives as *individuals*. It is of your City that each of you can say what the Venetians say of theirs: *Venezia la xe nostra: l'avemo fatta nu*. [Venice is our own: we have made her.] In your City you have need of *liberty* as in your Country you have need of *association*. The Liberty of the Commune and the Unity of the Country—let that, then, be your faith. . . .

A Country is a fellowship of free and equal men bound together in a brotherly concord of labour towards a single end. You must make it and maintain it such. A Country is not an aggregation, it is an *association*. There is no true Country without a uniform right. There is no true Country where the uniformity of that right is violated by the existence of caste, privilege, and inequality—where the powers and faculties of a large number of individuals are suppressed or dormant—where there is no common principle accepted, recognised, and developed by all. In such a state of things there can be no Nation, no People, but only a multitude, a fortuitous agglomeration of men whom circumstances have brought together and different circumstances will separate. In the name of your love of your Country you must combat without truce the existence of every privilege, every inequality, upon the soil which has given you birth. One privilege only is lawful—the privilege of Genius when Genius reveals itself in brotherhood with Virtue; but it is a privilege conceded by God and not by men, and when you acknowledge it and follow its inspirations, you acknowledge it freely by the exercise of your own reason and your own choice. Whatever privilege claims your submission in virtue of force or heredity, or any right which is not a common right, is a usurpation and a tyranny, and you ought to combat it and annihilate it. Your Country should be your Temple. God at the summit, a People of equals at the base. Do not accept any other formula, any other moral law, if you do not want to dishonour your Country and yourselves. Let the secondary laws for the gradual regulation of your existence be the progressive application of this supreme law.

And in order that they should be so, it is necessary that *all* should contribute to the making of them. The laws made by one fraction of the citizens only can never by the nature of things and men do otherwise than reflect the thoughts and aspirations and desires of that fraction; they represent, not the whole country, but a third, a fourth part, a class, a zone of the country. The law must express the general aspiration, promote the good of all, respond to a beat of the nation's heart. The whole nation therefore should be, directly or indirectly, the legislator. By yielding this mission to a few men, you put the egoism of one class in the place of the Country, which is the union of *all* the classes.

A Country is not a mere territory; the particular territory is only its foundation. The Country is the idea which rises upon that foundation; it is the sentiment of love, the sense of fellowship which binds together all the sons of that territory. So long as a single one of your brothers is not represented by his own vote in the development of the national life—so long as a single one vegetates uneducated among the educated—so long as a single one able and willing to work languishes in poverty for want of work—you have not got a Country such as it ought to be, the Country of all and for all. *Votes, education, work* are the three main pillars of the nation; do not rest until your hands have solidly erected them.

And when they have been erected—when you have secured for every one of you food for both body and soul—when freely united, entwining your right hands like brothers round a beloved mother, you advance in beautiful and holy concord towards the development of your faculties and the fulfilment of the Italian mission—remember that that mission is the moral unity of Europe; remember the immense duties which it imposes upon you. Italy is the only land that has twice uttered the great word of unification to the disjoined nations. Twice Rome has been the metropolis, the temple, of the European world; the first time when our conquering eagles traversed the known world from end to end and prepared it for union by introducing civilised institutions; the second time when, after the Northern conquerors had themselves been subdued by the potency of Nature, of great memories and of religious inspiration, the genius of Italy incarnated itself in the Papacy and undertook the solemn mission—abandoned four centuries ago—of preaching the union of souls to the peoples of the Christian world. Today a third mission is dawning for our Italy; as much vaster than those of old as the Italian People, the free and united Country which you are going to found, will be greater and more powerful than Caesars or Popes. The presentiment of this mission agitates Europe and keeps the eye and the thought of the nations chained to Italy.

Your duties to your Country are proportioned to the loftiness of this mission. You have to keep it pure from egoism, uncontaminated by falsehood and by the arts of that political Jesuitism which they call diplomacy.

The government of the country will be based through your labours upon the worship of principles, not upon the idolatrous worship of interests and of opportunity. There are countries in Europe where Liberty is sacred within, but is systematically violated without; peoples who say, *Truth is one thing, utility another: theory is one thing, practice another*. Those countries will have inevitably to expiate their guilt in long isolation, oppression, and anarchy. But you know the mission of our Country, and will pursue another path. Through you Italy will have, with one only God in the heavens, one only truth, one only faith, one only rule of political life upon earth. Upon the edifice, sublimer than Capitol or Vatican, which the people of Italy will raise, you will plant the banner of Liberty and of Association, so that it shines in the sight of all the nations, nor will you lower it ever for terror of despots or lust for the gains of a day. You will have boldness as you have faith. You will speak out aloud to the world, and to those who call themselves the lords of the world, the thought which thrills in the heart of Italy. You will never deny the sister nations. The life of the Country shall grow through you in beauty and in strength, free from servile fears and the hesitations of doubt, keeping as its *foundation* the people, as its *rule* the consequences of its principles logically deduced and energetically applied, as its *strength* the strength of all, as its *outcome* the amelioration of all, as its *end* the fulfilment of the mission which God has given it. And because you will be ready to die for Humanity, the life of your Country will be immortal.

30. HERZEN
Revolution and Individual Freedom

Aleksandr Ivanovich Herzen (1812–70) was the first Russian exile in the West who propagandized for political and social revolution in Czarist Russia.

The first selection is the Introduction to Herzen's first work *From the Other Shore*,* a book of memoirs on the revolution of 1848 which Herzen had observed in Paris. It was published in 1849, just two years after Herzen's decision to become an expatriate.

The second selection,** written twenty years after the revolution, is the text of two letters by Herzen to the Russian anarchist and revolutionary Michael Bakunin.

FROM THE OTHER SHORE

PARIS

March 1st, 1849

Our parting will last for a long time yet—perhaps for ever. At the present moment I do not wish to return—whether it will be possible later I do not know. You have been waiting for me, you are still waiting, so I must give you an explanation. If there is anyone to whom I am obliged to account for my absence, for my actions, it is certainly you, my friends.

* A Meridian Book. (New York: George Braziller, Inc., 1956.) Used by permission.
** From "Letters to an Old Comrade," as published by the Soviet Academy of Sciences.

An unconquerable revulsion and a strong inner voice of prophecy do not permit me to cross the frontier of Russia, especially now, when autocracy, infuriated and frightened by everything that is happening in Europe, strangles with redoubled severity every intellectual movement, and brutally cuts off sixty million souls from the rest of mankind which is gaining its freedom, deflecting the last light which falls feebly on a few of them with its black iron hand caked with the blood of Poland. No, my friends, I cannot cross the border of this kingdom of darkness, lawlessness, silent death, mysterious disappearances, gagged and tortured prisoners. I shall wait until that time when the weary rulers weakened by vain efforts and by the resistance that they have provoked, recognize *something* worthy of respect in the Russian man.

Do not, I beg you, make a mistake: it is not happiness, not distraction, not rest, not even personal safety that I have found here; indeed, I do not know who could find in Europe today happiness or rest, rest in the midst of an earthquake, happiness in the midst of a desperate struggle.

You saw sadness expressed in every line of my letters; life here is very hard, venomous malignity mingles with love, bile with tears, feverish anxiety infects the whole organism, the time of former illusions and hopes has passed. I believe in nothing here, except in a handful of people, a few ideas, and the fact that one cannot arrest movement; I see the inevitable doom of old Europe and I feel no pity for anything that now exists, neither the peaks of its culture nor its institutions. . . . I love nothing in this world except that which it persecutes, I respect nothing except that which it kills—and I stay . . . stay to suffer doubly, to suffer my own personal anguish and that of this world; which will perish, perhaps, to the sound of thunder and destruction towards which it is racing at full steam. . . . Why then do I stay?

I stay because the struggle is *here*, because despite the blood and tears it is here that social problems are being decided, because it is here that suffering is painful, sharp, but *articulate*. The struggle is open, no one hides. Woe to the vanquished, but they are not vanquished without a struggle, nor deprived of speech before they can utter a word; the violence inflicted is great, but the protest is loud; the fighters often march to the galleys, chained hand and foot, but with heads uplifted, with free speech. Where the word has not perished, neither has the deed. For the sake of this open struggle, for this free speech, this right to be heard—I stay here; for its sake I give up everything; I give up you for it, a portion of my heritage and perhaps shall give my life in the ranks of an energetic minority of "the persecuted but undefeated."

For the sake of this freedom of speech, I have broken, or, better still, suppressed for a while my ties of blood with the people in whom I found so much response both to the bright and to the dark side of my soul, whose song and speech are my song and speech, and I stay among a people in whose life I am in deep sympathy only with the bitter tears of the proletariat and the desperate courage of its friends.

This decision has cost me dear . . . you know me . . . and you will believe me. I have stifled the inner pain; I have lived through the painful struggle and I have made my decision, not like an angry youth, but like a man who has thought over what he is doing . . . how much he has to lose . . . for months I have been calculating and pondering and vacillating, and have finally sacrificed everything to:

Human Dignity and Free Speech

The consequences are no affair of mine; they are not in my power, they are rather in the power of some arbitrary whim which has gone so far as to draw a capricious circle not only round our words but round our very steps. It was in my power not to obey—and I did not obey.

To obey against one's convictions when there is a possibility of not obeying—is immoral. Passive obedience becomes almost impossible. I have witnessed two upheavals, I have lived too long as a free man to allow myself to be chained again; I have lived through popular disturbances, I have become accustomed to free speech and I cannot accept serfdom again, not even for the sake of suffering with you. If it had been necessary to restrain oneself for the common cause, perhaps one might have found the strength to do so; but where at this moment is our common cause? At home you have no soil on which a free man can stand. How after this can you summon us? . . . If it were to battle—yes, then we would come: but to obscure martyrdom, to sterile silence, to obedience—no, under no circumstances. Demand anything of me, but do not demand duplicity, do not force me again to play at being a loyal subject; respect the free man in me.

The liberty of the individual is the greatest thing of all, it is *on this and on this alone* that the true will of the people can develop. Man must respect liberty in himself, and he must esteem it in himself no less than in his neighbour, than in the entire nation. If you are convinced of that, then you will agree that to remain here is my right, my duty; it is the only protest that an individual can make amongst us; he must offer up this sacrifice to his human dignity. If you call my withdrawal an escape and will forgive me only out of your love, this will mean that you yourselves are not wholly free.

I know all the answers that can be made from the point of view of romantic patriotism and formal civil responsibility, but I cannot allow these antiquated attitudes. I have outlived them, left them behind, and it is precisely against them that I am fighting. These *réchauffé* remnants of the Roman and Christian heritage are the greatest obstacles to the establishment of true ideas of freedom, ideas that are healthy, clear, mature. Fortunately, in Europe, custom and a long process of development partly counterbalance these absurd theories and absurd laws. The people who live here are living on a soil fertilized by two civilizations; the path traversed by their ancestors for the past two and a half thousand years was not in vain, many human virtues have developed independently of the external organization and the official order.

Even in the worst periods of European history, we encounter some respect for the individual, some recognition of independence, some rights conceded to talent and genius. Vile as were the German rulers of that time, Spinoza was not sentenced to transportation, Lessing was not flogged or conscripted. This respect not merely for material but also for moral force, this unquestioning recognition of the individual— is one of the great human principles in European life.

In Europe a man who lives abroad has never been considered a criminal, nor one who emigrates to America a traitor.

We have nothing similar. With us the individual has always been crushed, absorbed, he has never even tried to emerge. Free speech with us has always been considered insolence, independence, subversion; man was engulfed in the State, dissolved in the community. The revolution of Peter the Great replaced the obsolete squirearchy of Russia—with a European bureaucracy; everything that could be copied from the Swedish and German codes, everything that could be taken over from the free municipalities of Holland into our half-communal, half-absolutist country, was taken over; but the unwritten, the moral check on power, the instinctive recognition of the rights of man, of the rights of thought, of truth, could not be and were not imported.

With us slavery increased with education; the State grew and improved but the individual reaped nothing from it; on the contrary, the stronger the State, the weaker the individual. European forms of administration and justice, of military and civil organization, developed with us into a kind of monstrous and inescapable despotism.

Were it not that Russia was so vast, that the alien system of power was so chaotically established, so incompetently administered, one might have said without exaggeration that no human being with any sense of his own dignity could live in Russia.

Pampered authority, never meeting with any opposition, reached at times a degree of unbridled violence that has no equal in history. You can take its measure from the stories about that master of his trade, Tsar Paul. Take away the capricious, the fantastic element in Paul, and you will see that he is not original at all, that the principle that inspired him is not only the same as that of every tsar, but of every governor, every policeman, every landowner. The intoxication of arbitrary power has overcome every single one of the fourteen grades in the famous hierarchy. Every act of power, every relation of superior to inferior, reveals a brazen shamelessness, an arrogant display of moral indifference, the insulting conviction that the individual will endure anything: triple recruitment, the law about foreign passports, flogging in the Institute of Engineers. Just as Little Russia submitted to serfdom in the eighteenth century, so in the end the whole of Russia came to believe that men could be sold and re-sold and no one, not even those who were being sold, ever asked on what legal basis this was done. With us authority feels freer, more self-confident than in Turkey or Persia, nothing restrains it, no past of any kind; it has repudiated its own past and is not concerned with that of Europe. It has no respect for national principles, it knows no universal culture, and it fights against the present.

In the past the government at least felt shame before its neighbours, learnt from them. Now it feels called upon itself to act as an example to all oppressors: now it is itself the mentor.

We have seen, you and I, the most terrible development of imperial power. We grew up under the terror, under the black wings of the secret police, in its very claws; we were crippled by its merciless oppression; and just managed to survive. But is this enough? Is it not time to untie our hands and tongues for action, to set an example, is it not time to awaken the slumbering consciousness of the people? But can one do this if one speaks in whispers, in obscure hints, at a time when shouts and plain speech are barely heard? Brave, open acts are necessary. December 14th shook young Russia so strongly because it took place on St. Isaac's Square. Now not only a public square, but the printed word, the professorial chair—everything has become impossible in Russia. All that remains is individual work in retirement or individual protest from afar.

I remain here not only because I should find it abhorrent after crossing the frontier to wear handcuffs again, but because I want to work. To sit with hands folded is possible anywhere; here I have no other task but *ours*.

He who for more than twenty years has carried in his heart one single thought, who has suffered for it, and lived by it, and known many a prison and many a banishment, and owes it the best moments of his life, the brightest friendships, will not abandon it, will not subject it to the demands of expediency, to the geographical degree of latitude and longitude; quite the contrary: here I am more useful, here I am your uncensored voice, your free press, your chance representative.

All this seems new and strange only to us; actually there is nothing unusual about it. In every country, at the beginning of an upheaval, while thought is still feeble and material power unbridled, men of energy and devotion withdraw, their free speech rings out from the distance and this very *distance* gives their words strength and authority because behind their words lie deeds and sacrifices. The mightiness of their words grows with the distance, just as the force of attraction increases in a stone dropped from a high tower. Emigration is the first symptom of approaching upheaval.

Russians abroad have yet another task. It is really time to acquaint Europe with Russia. Europe does not know us, it knows our government, our facade—and nothing else. For this acquaintance circumstances are singularly favourable; haughty airs no longer suit Europe nor should she loftily wrap herself in the mantle of contemptuous ignorance. *Das vornehme Ignorieren* about Russia is out of date in Europe, now that she has experienced a bourgeois republic and the Cossacks from Algiers, now that from the Danube to the Atlantic she has been through a state of siege, now that the prisons and the galleys are full of men persecuted for their beliefs . . . let her learn to know better a people whose youthful force she has tried in battle, in battle from which it emerged victorious; let us tell her about this mighty and still unfathomed people which in its unobtrusive way has managed to create a state of sixty millions, which has grown in such a vigorous, marvellous fashion without losing the principle of community, and which was the first to maintain this principle through the initial upheavals of national development; about a people which has somehow miraculously contrived to preserve itself under the yoke of Mongol hordes and German bureaucrats, under the barrack-room discipline of the corporal's baton, and the degrading Tartar knout; which has retained the noble features, the lively mind and the generous sweep of a rich nature beneath the yoke of serfdom, and which, in answer to the Tsar's order to educate itself, replied a hundred years later with the prodigious phenomenon of Pushkin. Let the Europeans get to know their neighbour: they only fear him, but they should know what it is that they fear.

Until now we have been unpardonably modest and too conscious of our oppressive lack of rights, and have forgotten all that is good, full of hope and promise in our national life.... Will I succeed in achieving something? I do not know. I hope so.

And so farewell my friends for a long while. . . . Give me your hands, your support. For I need both. After that . . . who knows? What we have not seen of late! It may not be so *far away* as it may seem, that day when we shall all meet in Moscow as of old and shall fearlessly raise our glasses to the toast: "For Russia and sacred freedom."

My heart refuses to believe that that day will not come; it sinks at the thought of a parting for ever. Shall I really never see again those streets along which I used to walk so often, full of youthful dreams; those houses, so wrapped in memories; our Russian villages, our peasants, whom I used to think about with love in the very South of Italy? . . . It cannot be! . . . And yet, if it is—then I bequeath my toast to my children, and dying on alien soil, I shall preserve my faith in the future of the Russian people and bless it from the distant land of my voluntary exile.

TO AN OLD COMRADE

Letter One

> No matter how adequate the motives in themselves may be, they cannot produce the necessary effect without adequate means.
>
> *Jeremy Bentham*

One and the same question occupies our minds. As a matter of fact there is but one *serious question* on the historical agenda. All the others are either an expression of its growing force or of the maladies concomitant to its development, that is to say, growing pains by means of which the new and more perfect organism arises out of obsolete and narrow forms, adapting these to superior needs. For both of us the final

solution is the *same*. We by no means differ in principle or theory but
rather in method and practice, in the appraisal of forces, in the means
to be applied, in the time, and in our interpretation of the historical
material. The ordeals we have experienced since 1848 have affected both
of us but differently. You have not changed much, though sorely tried
by life. I got off with a few bruises. But you were far away while I was
right there. And if I have changed, remember that *everything has changed*.
The economic and social question is formulated today differently than
it was twenty years ago. It has outgrown its religious and ideal adoles-
cence as well as the age of clumsy attempts, and experimentation on a
small scale; the very period confined solely to complaint, protest,
criticism and accusations is drawing to a close. This is the important
sign of its maturity. We can see it in the process of growth; it has not
yet, however, reached it not only because of external obstacles or because of resistance but also because of internal reasons. The minority
marching in the vanguard has not arrived at manifest truths, at practical
means, at complete formulas of the future economic life. The majority
who suffered most endeavours through one group of its urban workers
to throw off this state but is restrained by the old, traditional outlook of
the other, more numerous group. Knowledge and understanding are not
to be acquired by any *coup d'état*, nor by a *coup de tête*. The sluggish-
ness, incoherence of the historical course of understanding exasperates
and depresses us; we find it intolerable and many of us, against our
better judgement, hurry ourselves and others. Is that good or bad?
That is the question.

Should we exert external pressure on the natural course of events in
order to hasten the internal process which is in evidence? Certainly a
midwife can hasten, lighten, eliminate the difficulties of travail, but only
within certain limits which are difficult to ascertain and dangerous to
exceed. This requires, over and above logical self-sacrifice, tact and
inspired improvisation. Moreover, not everywhere are the work or the
limits the same. Peter I and the Convention taught us to march in
seven-league boots, to pass directly from the first month of pregnancy
to the ninth and destroy, without discrimination, everything in our way.
Die zerstorende Lust ist eine schaffende Lust [The destructive desire is a
creative desire]—and forward we dashed in the steps of the unknown
god-destroyer, stumbling on broken treasures intermingled with all
kinds of rubbish and refuse.

. . . We have seen the frightful example of a bloody insurrection
which, at a moment of rage and despair, took to the barricades and only

then realized that it had no banner. The conservative world, rallied in one compact group, defeated it and the result was that regression which was to be expected. But what would have happened if the barricades had triumphed? Could those formidable combatants, at the age of twenty, have given voice to all that lay in their hearts? Their testament does not contain a single constructive, organic idea, and economic errors unlike the political ones which have an indirect effect, lead directly and deeply, to ruin, stagnation, and starvation.

Our days are precisely the days of thorough study which must precede the work of realization, just as the theory of steam preceded the introduction of railways. Previously, the force of courage, zeal, valour were applied to attain the end and it was a blind, haphazard attempt. We shall not act haphazardly.

It is plain to us that things cannot continue as they have been in the past, that the exclusive rule of capital and the absolute right of property has come to its end just as had the reign of feudalism and the aristocracy in its time. Just as the downfall of the medieval world began before 1789 with the realization of the unjust subjection of the middle estate, so today the economic revolution began with the realization of social injustice toward the workers. Just as the obduracy and degeneracy of the nobility contributed to its own downfall, so today the obstinacy and degeneracy of the bourgeoisie precipitates its end.

But the general terms in which the problem is formulated neither suggests the ways nor the means, nor even a favourable medium. They are not to be conquered by violence. Even if the whole bourgeois world were blown to bits, *some sort of bourgeois world* would arise after the smoke has dissipated and the ruins had been cleared away, though somewhat modified, because that world is *not yet dead* internally and *also because neither the world* that builds nor the new organization are yet so ready as to be able to perfect themselves as they come into being. Not a single pillar on which the modern system rests, and which must fall and be recreated, is affected enough or so shaky as to be torn up by force, to be debarred from life. Let every conscientious person ask himself if he is or is not ready. Is the new organization towards which we are moving as plain to him as the general ideals of collective property and solidarity and does he know the process (except for downright destruction) by means of which the old forms must be changed within it? Let him, if he is personally satisfied with himself, say whether that medium is ready which, due to its position, should be the first to act.

Knowledge cannot be gainsaid but it possesses no means of coercion.

Prejudices yield only to slow treatment; they have their phases and crises. Violence and terror are resorted to in order to disseminate religion and politics, to establish autocratic empires and indivisible republics. Violence permits one to destroy and clear the ground, but no more. By means of Peter the Great'ism the social revolution will not advance beyond the leveling of Gracchus Babeuf's hulks and of Cabet's system of communist corvée. The new forms must embrace everything and include all elements of modern activity and all human aspirations. Our world cannot be transformed either into a Sparta or into a Benedictine monastery. The future revolution should not strangle certain forces for the benefit of others but should be able to reconcile them all for the general benefit.

The economic revolution has an immense advantage over all religious and political revolutions in that its base is sound. Such should also be the paths it follows; and the manner of handling its problems. As it outgrows the state of vague suffering and discontent, it automatically plants its feet on *firm soil*. All other revolutions invariably found themselves with one foot resting on fantasies, mystic ideas, superstitions and unwarranted patriotic, juridical and other prejudices. Unlike these, economic questions are subject to mathematical laws.

Certainly, the law of mathematics contains, as a scientific law, its own proof and needs neither empirical justification nor a majority of votes. But in order to be *applied* the empiric aspect and all the external conditions of realization should come to the foregound. "No matter how adequate the motives in themselves may be, they cannot produce the necessary effect without adequate means." All this is so when human affairs are concerned but is disregarded by too impatient people in matters of such significance as social reconstruction. Any mechanic knows that his calculation, his formula will not enter the sphere of reality so long as the series of phenomena, handled by him, contain insubordinate elements, alien to it or else subject to other laws. These disturbing elements are, in the physical world, not generally complex and are easily introduced into the formula like the lines of the pendulum, the resistance of the medium in which it oscillates, etc. But this is not so simple in the domain of historical development. The processes of social growth, their digressions and deviations, their final results are so interwoven, are so deeply rooted in the popular consciousness, that they are by no means easy to approach and must be seriously considered. Treating them as a list of things to be rejected, proclaimed as an "order of the day of the social army," will yield nothing but confusion.

One cannot fight against false dogmas, against superstitions no matter how insane they are, simply by denying them no matter how much sense there is in this denial. To say "I do not believe" carries just as much weight and is, at bottom, just as ridiculous, as saying "I believe!" The old order of things is stronger than are the material forces that support it because it is *recognized*. This is seen most clearly where it possesses no punitive or coercive force, where it rests firmly on subjected conscience, on an uncultivated mind, on servile immaturity of new ideas, as in Switzerland and in England.

The popular consciousness, as it is, represents a natural product, crude and irresponsible, the result of diverse efforts, attempts, events, successes and failures, diverse instincts and conflicts; it should be accepted as a natural fact and combatted as we combat all that is unconscious by studying it, mastering it and adapting its means to our end.

On the whole, no one is to blame for the social absurdities of modern life and no one can be chastised with greater justification than the sea whipped by the Persian king, or the Veche Bell punished by Ivan the Terrible. To accuse, to punish, to deliver over to the executioner are all things beyond our comprehension. We should look at things more simply, physiologically and once and for all discard the criminal point of view which, unfortunately, continues to make itself felt and warps our understanding, introducing personal passions into the general cause and making us see the chance transposition of accidental happenings as a premeditated plot. Private ownership, the family, the church, the state were tremendous educational forms of human emancipation and development. We cast these off as the need for them disappeared.

To lay the blame for the past and the present on the last representatives of "the truth of other days" which became "the untruths of today," is no less an absurdity and injustice than the execution of French marquises simply because they were not Jacobins. It is even worse for we have not the same excuse the Jacobins had, a naive faith in the justice of their ideas, in their right. We change the fundamental principles of our views, condemning whole classes and, at the same time, rejecting the juridical responsibility of the individual. This is, in passing, so as not to return to it.

Former revolutions were made in the dusk; they lost their way, regressed, stumbled on and, because of their lack of inner clarity, exacted all manner of things, diverse beliefs and heroic deeds, a multitude of sublime virtues, patriotism, pietism. The social revolution requires nothing but *understanding and strength*, knowledge and means.

But understanding imposes a terrible obligation. It entails invariable compunctions, implacable reproaches of logic.

So long as the social idea was amorphous, its propagators who were themselves believers and fanatics, addressed themselves as much to the passions and the imagination as to the intelligence; they threatened the property owners with punishment and ruin, discredited and shamed them for their riches, exhorted them to a voluntary renunciation of their wealth by presenting pictures of frightful suffering. (A strange *captatio benevolentiae*—I grant you.) These are the means by which socialism was raised. We have to prove to property owners and capitalists not that property owning is sinful, immoral (a conception borrowed from a view quite alien to ours) but that the absurdity of its contradictions has reached the consciousness of the propertyless and it has thus become *impossible*. They should be shown that the struggle against the inevitable is a senseless waste of power and the more stubborn it is and the longer it lasts, the greater will be the losses and the destruction it will entail. The citadel of ownership and capital must be undermined by calculation, by double-entry book-keeping, by a clear balancing of assets and liabilities. The worst miser will not choose to drown with all his wealth if he can save part of it and himself by throwing the rest overboard. To achieve this it is essential that he see the danger *just as clearly* as he sees the *possibility of being rescued*.

The new order which will establish itself must be not only the avenging sword but also a protecting force. In dealing a blow to the old world, it not only must save all that is worth saving but leave intact that which does not interfere, which is different and ·original. Woe to that revolution, so poor in spirit and in artistic sense, which will reduce all the past and all that has been accumulated into a dull workshop in which all interest is concentrated on subsistence and subsistence alone. But this will not happen. Humanity has always shown, even in the very worst days, that its potentialities exceed its needs and that it possesses more power than it requires for the mere conquest of life. Development cannot suppress it. There are such treasures which people will not forego and which only despotic violence can wrest out of their hands and that only at times of passion and cataclysms. And who will say, without voicing a glaring injustice, that the past and the passing do not contain much that is beautiful and that they must sink together with the old ship?

Letter Four

Our iconoclasts do not stop short at the usual negation of the state and the destruction of the church. Their zeal makes them attack science as well. Here reason forsakes them completely.

The absurd statement made by Robespierre that atheism was aristocratic is supplemented by the one taxing science with being aristocratic.

No one asks how far such definitions fit or do not fit the subject at all. And, indeed, the entire dispute around "science for science's sake" and science as purely utilitarian is based on an extremely false approach to the question.

Applied science cannot exist without theoretical science.

Science is a force; it reveals relations between things, their laws and interaction, and it has no concern with the manner of its application. Science is not to blame if it is in the hands of the government and capital, as are the army, the court, and the executive organs. Mechanics offers the same service in the construction of railways as in the construction of cannons and *Zundnadelgewehre*.

The mind cannot be arrested at any one point and commanded to continue no further with its investigation until we have been liberated.

The mind cannot be prescribed only because the majority has no knowledge while the minority abuses its knowledge.

The savage clamour calling for the banning of books, the abandonment of science and the unleashing of the blind forces of destruction belong to the most unbridled and most baneful demagogy. It always provokes the worst passions, the *déchainement des mauvaises passions*. We make a joke of these fearful words without taking into the least consideration how greatly they injure the cause and those who hear them.

No, great revolutions are not made by unleashing evil passions. Christianity was preached by the apostles and their disciples who lived austere and pure lives, by ascetics and men who repressed all passions save one. Such were the Huguenots and the Reformers; such were the Jacobins of '93. Fighters for liberty, like the men in Cromwell's army, who took up arms for a cause, were always pure and therein lay their strength.

I do not believe that people who prefer destruction and brute force to evolution and to amicable agreements are really serious. Propaganda, unceasing, continual propaganda, is what people need regardless of whether they are workers, owners, farmers or bourgeois. We have a greater need for apostles than for vanguard officers, sappers of destruction. We need apostles who will preach not only to their own disciples but to their adversaries as well.

To preach to one's enemy is a great act of love. It is not the enemy's fault that he has found himself outside the modern flow of events, living on promissory notes, long overdue, on the morals of the past. I pity them as I would anybody suffering from a malady, as I would a cripple standing on the brink of a precipice and burdened down with wealth which will drag him down into the chasm. Their eyes should be opened rather than gouged out so that they can be saved if they wish to be saved.

The Greeks expressed themselves more explicitly than we: "The wise man has no need of a law; his mind is his law." Well, then, let us begin by "making" ourselves and others wise.

Nor do I pity people alone. I pity things as well, and *some things even more than some people.*

An outburst of unbridled savagery provoked by obstinacy will spare nothing; because of hardships which one might have personally undergone he will take revenge on the most impersonal chattels. Along with the capital amassed by the usurer will be wiped out that which has been transmitted from generation to generation and from nation to nation, a capital which bears the imprint of the personality and creativeness of different ages and which is itself an annal of human life and a crystallization of history. The unbridled forces of destruction will wipe out, along with the fences, those extreme mileposts of human power which mankind has attained in all directions since the dawn of civilization.

Christianity and Islamism have demolished enough of the antique world; the French Revolution has destroyed enough statues, pictures and monuments for us to be able to dispense with playing at iconoclasm.

How vividly I felt this as I stood dejectedly, almost shamefacedly, listening to some custodian's words: "All this was destroyed during the Revolution . . ." as he pointed to a bare wall, a broken statue, or a disinterred tomb.

31. GREEN

Right of the State over the Individual in War

Thomas Hill Green (1836–82) is one of a group of thinkers, which also includes L. T. Hobhouse, who sought to reconstruct liberal principles after their rejection of laissez-faire economies, utilitarianism, and John Stuart Mill's "atomic" individualism. In his *Lectures on the Principles of Political Obligation*, delivered in 1879-80 and published in 1882, Green developed a positive organic theory of the state under which a liberal could intervene in the life of the individual for reasons of public welfare. In the context of the growth of the powerful competing European nation-states of the late nineteenth century, however, Green argued against the right of the state over the individual in times of war. His characteristic liberal argument is that warfare by the state represents a regression to feudal or militaristic values. These have no place in the liberal states which can harmoniously form an international community. The selection is from the *Principles*.

169. It is nothing then in the necessary organisation of the state, but rather some defect of that organisation in relation to its proper function of maintaining and reconciling rights, of giving scope to capacities, that leads to a conflict of apparent interests between one state and another. The wrong, therefore, which results to human society from conflicts between states cannot be condoned on the ground that it is a necessary incident of the existence of states. The wrong cannot be held to be lost in a higher right, which attaches to the maintenance of the state as the institution through which alone the freedom of man is realised. It is not the state, as such, but this or that particular state, which by no means fulfils its purpose, and might perhaps be swept away and superseded by another with advantage to the ends for which the true state exists, that needs to defend its interests by action injurious to those outside it. Hence there is no ground for holding that a state is justified in doing

whatever its interests seem to require, irrespectively of effects on other men. If those effects are bad, as involving either a direct violation of personal rights or obstruction to the moral development of society anywhere in the world, then there is no ultimate justification for the political action that gives rise to them. The question can only be (as we have seen generally in regard to the wrong-doing of war), where in particular the blame lies. Whether there is any justification for a particular state, which in defence of its interests inflicts an injury on some portion of mankind; whether, e.g., the Germans are justified in holding Metz, on the supposition that their tenure of such a thoroughly French town necessarily thwarts in many ways the healthy activity of the inhabitants, or the English in carrying fire and sword into Afghanistan for the sake of acquiring a scientific frontier; this must depend (1) on the nature of the interests thus defended, (2) on the impossibility of otherwise defending them, (3) on the question how they came to be endangered. If they are interests of which the maintenance is essential to those ends as a means to which the state has its value, if the state which defends them has not itself been a joint-cause of their being endangered, and if they cannot be defended except at the cost of injury to some portion of mankind, then the state which defends them is clear of the guilt of that injury. But the guilt is removed from it only to be somewhere else, however wide its distribution may be. It may be doubted, however, whether the second question could ever be answered altogether in favour of a state which finds it necessary to protect its interests at the cost of inflicting an injury on mankind.

170. It will be said, perhaps, that these formal arguments in proof of the wrong-doing involved in war, and of the unjustifiability of the policy which nations constantly adopt in defence of their apparent interests, carry very little conviction; that a state is not an abstract complex of institutions for the maintenance of rights, but a nation, a people, possessing such institutions; that the nation has its passions which inevitably lead it to judge all questions of international right from its own point of view, and to consider its apparent national interests as justifying anything; that if it were otherwise, if the cosmopolitan point of view could be adopted by nations, patriotism would be at an end; that whether this be desirable or no, such an extinction of national passions is impossible; that while they continue, wars are as inevitable between nations as they would be between individuals, if individuals were living in what philosophers have imagined to be the state of nature, without recognition of a common superior; that nations

in short are in the position of men judging their own causes, which it is admitted that no one can do impartially; and that this state of things cannot be altered without the establishment of a common constraining power, which would mean the extinction of the life of independent states,—a result as undesirable as it is unattainable. Projects of perpetual peace, to be logical, must be projects of all-embracing empire.

171. There is some cogency in language of this kind. It is true that when we speak of a state as a living agency, we mean, not an institution or complex of institutions, but a nation organised in a certain way; and that members of the nation in their corporate or associated action are animated by certain passions, arising out of their association, which, though not egoistic relatively to the individual subjects of them (for they are motives to self-sacrifice), may, in their influence on the dealings of one nation with another, have an effect analogous to that which egoistic passions, properly so called, have upon the dealings of individuals with each other, On the other hand, it must be remembered that the national passions, which in any good sense is simply the public spirit of the good citizen, may take, and every day is taking, directions which lead to no collision between one nation and another; (or, to say the same thing negatively, that it is utterly false to speak as if the desire for one's own nation to show more military strength than others were the only or the right form of patriotism); and that though a nation, with national feeling of its own, must everywhere underlie a state, properly so called, yet still, just so far as the perfect organisation of rights within each nation, which entitles it to be called a state, is attained, the occasions of conflict between nations disappear; and again, that by the same process, just so far as it is satisfactorily carried out, an organ of expression and action is established for each nation in dealing with other nations, which is not really liable to be influenced by the same egoistic passions in dealing with the government of another nation as embroil individuals with each other. The love of mankind, no doubt, needs to be particularised in order to have any power over life and action. Just as there can be no true friendship except towards this or that individual, so there can be no true public spirit which is not localised in some way. The man whose desire to serve his kind is not centred primarily in some home, radiating from it to a commune, a municipality, and a nation, presumably has no effectual desire to serve his kind at all. But there is no reason why this localised or nationalised philanthropy should take the form of a jealousy of other nations or a desire to fight them, personally or by proxy. Those in whom it is

strongest are every day expressing it in good works which benefit their fellow-citizens without interfering with the men of other nations. Those who from time to time talk of the need of a great war to bring unselfish impulses into play, give us reason to suspect that they are too selfish themselves to recognise the unselfish activity that is going on all round them. Till all the methods have been exhausted by which nature can be brought into the service of man, till society is so organised that everyone's capacities have free scope for their development, there is no need to resort to war for a field in which patriotism may display itself.

172. In fact, just so far as states are thoroughly formed, the diversion of patriotism into the military channel tends to come to an end. It is a survival from a condition of things in which, as yet, the state, in the full sense, was not; in the sense, namely, that in each territory controlled by a single independent government, the rights of all persons, as founded on their capacities for contributing to a common good, are equally established by one system of law. If each separately governed territory were inhabited by a people so organised within itself, there would be nothing to lead to the association of the public spirit of the good citizen with military aggressiveness.... Patriotism, in that special military sense in which it is distinguished from public spirit, is not the temper of the citizen dealing with fellow-citizens, or with men who are themselves citizens of their several states, but that of the follower of the feudal chief, or of the member of a privileged class conscious of a power, resting ultimately on force, over an inferior population, or of a nation holding empire over other nations.

173. Standing armies, again, though existing on a larger scale now than ever before, are not products of the civilization of Europe, but of the predominance over that civilization of the old *dunasteiai* [the military-dynastic spirit]. The influences which have given rise to and keep up those armies essentially belong to a state of things in which mankind—even European mankind—is not yet thoroughly organized into political life. . . .

174. The more complete that organization becomes, the more the motives and occasions of international conflict tend to disappear, while the bonds of unity become stronger. The latter is the case, if for no other reason, yet for this; that the better organization of the state means freer scope to the individual (not necessarily to do as he likes, *e.g.* in the buying and selling of alcohol, but in such development of activity as is good on the whole). This again means free intercourse between members of one state and those of another, and in particular

more freedom of trade. All restrictions on freedom of wholesome trade are really based on special class-interests, and must disappear with the realization of that idea of individual right, founded on the capacity of every man for free contribution to social good, which is the true idea of the state. And as trade between members of different states becomes freer and more full, the sense of common interests between them, which war would infringe, becomes stronger. The bond of peace thus established is sometimes depreciated as a selfish one, but it need be no more selfish than that which keeps the peace between members of the same state, who have no acquaintance with each other. In one case as in the other it may be said that the individual tries to prevent a breach of the peace because he knows that he has more to gain than to lose by it. In the latter case, however, this account of the matter would be, to say the least, insufficient. The good citizen observes the law in letter and in spirit, not from any fear of consequences to himself if he did not, but from an idea of the mutual respect by men for each other's rights as that which should be an idea which has become habitual with him, and regulates his conduct without his asking any questions about it. There was a time, however, when this idea only thus acted spontaneously in regulating a man's action towards his family or immediate neighbours or friends. Considerations of interest were the medium through which a wider range of persons came to be brought within its range. And thus, although considerations of an identity of interests, arising out of trade, may be the occasion of men's recognising in men of other nations those rights which war violates, there is no reason why, upon that occasion and through the familiarity which trade brings about, an idea of justice, as a relation which should subsist between all mankind as well as between members of the same state, may not come to act on men's minds as independently of all calculation of their several interests as does the idea which regulates the conduct of the good citizen.

175. If the necessary or impelling power of the idea of what is due from members of different nations to each other is weak, it must be observed on the other hand that the individual members of a nation have no such apparent interest in their government's dealing unfairly with another nation as one individual may have in getting the advantage of another. Thus, so far as this idea comes to form part of the habit of men's minds, there ceases to be anything in the passions of the people which a government represents to stimulate the government to that unfairness in dealing with another government, to which an individual might be moved by self-seeking passions in dealing with another

individual, in the absence of an impartial authority having power over both. If at the same time the several governments are purely representative of the several peoples, as they should become with the due organization of the state, and thus have no dynastic interests of their own in embroiling one nation with another, there seems to be no reason why they should not arrive at a passionless impartiality in dealing with each other, which would be beyond the reach of the individual in defending his own cause against another. At any rate, if no government can ever get rid of some bias in its own favour, there remains the possibility of mediation in cases of dispute by disinterested governments. With the abatement of national jealousies and the removal of those deeply-seated causes of war which, as we have seen, are connected with the deficient organization of states, the dream of an international court with authority resting on the consent of independent states may come to be realised. Such a result may be very remote, but it is important to bear in mind that there is nothing in the intrinsic nature of a system of independent states incompatible with it, but that on the contrary every advance in the organisation of mankind into states in the sense explained is a step towards it.

32. UNITED NATIONS

Universal Declaration of Human Rights

The United Nations Declaration of Rights of Man was adopted by the General Assembly in Paris on December 10, 1948. No negative votes were cast although several nations abstained. The Declaration was proposed as a standard of achievement for all nations by the Third Committee of the General Assembly, the Committee that is concerned with social, cultural, and humanitarian problems. The draft proposal was first drawn up by the Human Rights Commission of the United Nations in 1946.

Both the form of the Declaration ascribing rights to all men and many of the substantive rights derive from the tradition of liberalism.

UNIVERSAL DECLARATION OF HUMAN RIGHTS

Preamble

Whereas recognition of the inherent dignity and of the equal and inalienable rights of all members of the human family is the foundation of freedom, justice and peace in the world,

Whereas disregard and contempt for human rights have resulted in barbarous acts which have outraged the conscience of mankind, and the advent of a world in which human beings shall enjoy freedom of speech and belief and freedom from fear and want has been proclaimed as the highest aspiration of the common people,

Whereas it is essential, if man is not to be compelled to have recourse, as a last resort, to rebellion against tyranny and oppression, that human rights should be protected by the rule of law,

Whereas it is essential to promote the development of friendly relations between nations,

Whereas the peoples of the United Nations have in the Charter reaffirmed their faith in fundamental human rights, in the dignity and worth of the human person and in the equal rights of men and women and have determined to promote social progress and better standards of life in larger freedom,

Whereas Member States have pledged themselves to achieve, in co-operation with the United Nations, the promotion of universal respect for and observance of human rights and fundamental freedoms,

Whereas a common understanding of these rights and freedoms is of the greatest importance for the full realisation of this pledge,

Now, Therefore,

THE GENERAL ASSEMBLY

proclaims

This Universal Declaration of Human Rights as a common standard of achievement for all peoples and all nations, to the end that every individual and every organ of society, keeping this Declaration constantly in mind, shall strive by teaching and education to promote respect for these rights and freedoms and by progressive measures, national and international, to secure their universal and effective recognition and observance, both among the peoples of Member States themselves and among the peoples of territories under their jurisdiction.

Article 1

All human beings are born free and equal in dignity and rights. They are endowed with reason and conscience and should act towards one another in a spirit of brotherhood.

Article 2

Everyone is entitled to all the rights and freedoms set forth in this Declaration, without distinction of any kind, such as race, colour, sex, language, religion, political or other opinion, national or social origin, property, birth or other status.

Furthermore, no distinction shall be made on the basis of the political, jurisdictional or international status of the country or territory to which a person belongs, whether it be independent, trust, non-self-governing or under any other limitation of sovereignty.

Article 3

Everyone has the right to life, liberty and security of person.

Article 4

No one shall be held in slavery or servitude; slavery and the slave trade shall be prohibited in all their forms.

Article 5

No one shall be subjected to torture or to cruel, inhuman or degrading treatment or punishment.

Article 6

Everyone has the right to recognition everywhere as a person before the law.

Article 7

All are equal before the law and are entitled without any discrimination to equal protection of the law. All are entitled to equal protection against any discrimination in violation of this Declaration and against any incitement to such discrimination.

Article 8

Everyone has the right to an effective remedy by the competent national tribunals for acts violating the fundamental rights granted him by the constitution or by law.

Article 9

No one shall be subjected to arbitrary arrest, detention or exile.

Article 10

Everyone is entitled in full equality to a fair and public hearing by an independent and impartial tribunal, in the determination of his rights and obligations and of any criminal charge against him.

Article 11

(1) Everyone charged with a penal offence has the right to be presumed innocent until proved guilty according to law in a public trial at which he has had all the guarantees necessary for his defence.

(2) No one shall be held guilty of any penal offence on account of any act or omission which did not constitute a penal offence, under national or international law, at the time when it was committed. Nor shall a heavier penalty be imposed than the one that was applicable at the time the penal offence was committed.

Article 12

No one shall be subjected to arbitrary interference with his privacy, family, home or correspondence, nor to attacks upon his honour and reputation. Everyone has the right to the protection of the law against such interference or attacks.

Article 13

(1) Everyone has the right to freedom of movement and residence within the borders of each state.

(2) Everyone has the right to leave any country, including his own, and to return to his country.

Article 14

(1) Everyone has the right to seek and to enjoy in other countries asylum from persecution.

(2) This right may not be invoked in the case of prosecutions genuinely arising from non-political crimes or from acts contrary to the purposes and principles of the United Nations.

Article 15

(1) Everyone has the right to a nationality.

(2) No one shall be arbitrarily deprived of his nationality nor denied the right to change his nationality.

Article 16

(1) Men and women of full age, without any limitation due to race, nationality or religion, have the right to marry and to found a family. They are entitled to equal rights as to marraige, during marriage and at its dissolution.

(2) Marriage shall be entered into only with the free and full consent of the intending spouses.

(3) The family is the natural and fundamental group unit of society and is entitled to protection by society and the State.

Article 17

(1) Everyone has the right to own property alone as well as in association with others.

(2) No one shall be arbitrarily deprived of his property.

Article 18

Everyone has the right to freedom of thought, conscience and religion; this right includes freedom to change his religion or belief, and freedom, either alone or in community with others and in public or private, to manifest his religion or belief in teaching, practice, worship and observance.

Article 19

Everyone has the right to freedom of opinion and expression; this right includes freedom to hold opinions without interference and to seek, receive and impart information and ideas through any media and regardless of frontiers.

Article 20

(1) Everyone has the right to freedom of peaceful assembly and association.

(2) No one may be compelled to belong to an association.

Article 21

(1) Everyone has the right to take part in the government of his country, directly or through freely chosen representatives.

(2) Everyone has the right of equal access to public service in his country.

(3) The will of the people shall be the basis of the authority of government; this will shall be expresssed in periodic and genuine elections which shall be by universal and equal suffrage and shall be held by secret vote or by equivalent free voting procedures.

Article 22

Everyone, as a member of society, has the right to social security and is entitled to realisation, through national effort and international co-operation and in accordance with the organization and resources of each State, of the economic, social and cultural rights indispensable for his dignity and the free development of his personality.

Article 23

(1) Everyone has the right to work, to free choice of employment, to just and favourable conditions of work and to protection against unemployment.

(2) Everyone, without any discrimination, has the right to equal pay for equal work.

(3) Everyone who works has the right to just and favourable remuneration ensuring for himself and his family an existence worthy of human dignity, and supplemented, if necessary, by other means of social protection.

(4) Everyone has the right to form and to join trade unions for the protection of his interests.

Article 24

Everyone has the right to rest and leisure, including reasonable limitation of working hours and periodic holidays with pay.

Article 25

(1) Everyone has the right to a standard of living adequate for the health and well-being of himself and of his family, including food, clothing, housing and medical care and necessary social services, and the right to security in the event of unemployment, sickness, disability, widowhood, old age or other lack of livelihood in circumstances beyond his control.

(2) Motherhood and childhood are entitled to special care and assistance. All children, whether born in or out of wedlock, shall enjoy the same social protection.

Article 26

(1) Everyone has the right to education. Education shall be free, at least in the elementary and fundamental stages. Elementary education shall be compulsory. Technical and professional education shall be made generally available and higher education shall be equally accessible to all on the basis of merit.

(2) Education shall be directed to the full development of the human personality and to the strengthening of respect for human rights and fundamental freedoms. It shall promote understanding, tolerance and friendship among all nations, racial or religious groups, and shall further the activities of the United Nations for the maintenance of peace.

(3) Parents have a prior right to choose the kind of education that shall be given to their children.

Article 27

(1) Everyone has the right freely to participate in the cultural life of the community, to enjoy the arts and to share in scientific advancement and its benefits.

(2) Everyone has the right to the protection of the moral and material interests resulting from any scientific, literary or artistic production of which he is the author.

Article 28

Everyone is entitled to a social and international order in which the rights and freedoms set forth in this Declaration can be fully realized.

Article 29

(1) Everyone has duties to the community in which alone the free and full development of his personality is possible.

(2) In the exercise of his rights and freedoms, everyone shall be subject only to such limitations as are determined by law solely for the purpose of securing due recognition and respect for the rights and freedoms of others and of meeting the just requirements of morality, public order and the general welfare in a democratic society.

(3) These rights and freedoms may in no case be exercised contrary to the purposes and principles of the United Nations.

Article 30

Nothing in this Declaration may be interpreted as implying for any State, group or person any right to engage in any activity or to perform any act aimed at the destruction of any of the rights and freedoms set forth herein.

Suggestions for Further Reading

The special virtue of an anthology is that it directs the interested reader to the works from which the selections are excerpted. The reader can find no better introduction to the study of liberal theory than further reading of the original sources of the theory. Most of the major primary sources have been presented or referred to in this work and I shall not repeat the references here.

The secondary literature is so large that criteria of selection are arbitrary. With emphasis on availability to the American student I suggest the following.

Among secondary works, Guido de Ruggiero's *History of European Liberalism* (Boston: Beacon Paperback, 1959) is an erudite, readable survey of liberalism in all European countries. It contains a very useful bibliography. John Plamenatz discusses the major theorists of liberalism in a direct and critical way in his two-volume history of political theory from Machiavelli to Marx, *Man and Society* (New York: McGraw-Hill, 1963). Recently Robert Cumming has offered a critical interpretation of the history of liberalism in *Human Nature and History* (Chicago: University of Chicago Press, 1969). From a different point of view, the British socialist Harold J. Laski provided a provocative Marxist analysis of the history of liberalism in *The Rise of European Liberalism* (London: George Allen & Unwin, 1936). One of the most stimulating analyses of the principles of liberalism is Isaiah Berlin's lecture "Two Concepts of Liberty" just republished in his *Four Essays on Liberty* (New York: Oxford University Press, 1969).

Customarily, studies of liberalism take as their theme particular national traditions. Frederico Frederici has provided a useful anthology of German Liberalism *Der Deutsche Liberalismus* (Zurich: Artemis, 1946) much of which is not yet available in English. The recent work of Bullock and Schock, *The Liberal Tradition* (Oxford: Clarendon Press, 1967), is very helpful in relating particular liberal theses to their historical context. John Plamenatz's anthology *Readings from Liberal Writers English and French* (New York: Barnes & Noble, 1965) presents some new materials of French liberalism. A very useful historical anthology of the democratic tradition in which the symbiosis between liberalism and democracy is documented is Charles M. Sherover's *The Development of the Democratic Idea: Readings from Pericles to the Present* (New York: Washington Square Press, 1968).

There have been innumerable major studies of particular national liberal traditions. Élie Halévy's work *The Growth of Philosophic Radicalism* (London: Faber & Faber, 1938) is a classic analysis of utilitarianism. A contrasting study of the same materials is John Plamenatz's *The English Utilitarians* (Oxford: Basil Blackwell, 1966).

Kingsley Martin's work *French Liberal Thought of the Eighteenth Century* (New York: Harper & Row, Torchbooks, 1963) retains its interest in showing the relationship of the French philosophers of the Enlightenment with modern liberalism. The particular theme of perfectibility in French thought is examined in a dramatic manner in Frank Manuel's *Prophets of Paris* (Cambridge, Mass.: Harvard University Press, 1962), and the most recent interpretation of the liberal heritage of the Enlightenment is in Peter Gay's *The Enlightenment: An Interpretation*, Vol. II, *The Science of Freedom* (New York: Alfred A. Knopf, 1969). J. Salwyn Schapiro has offered in *Liberalism and the Challenge of Fascism* (New York: McGraw-Hill, 1949) an historical analysis and spirited defense of liberalism with special emphasis on nineteenth-century French authors. A provocative interpretation of the tradition of Rousseau for democracy has been advanced by J. L. Talmon in his *Origins of Totalitarian Democracy* (New York: Praeger, 1960).

Recent scholarship provides new studies and analyses of the major figures of liberal tradition. Lewis Feuer, for example, in *Spinoza and the Rise of Liberalism* (Boston: Beacon, 1959) seeks to argue the significance of liberal political theory on Spinoza's thought and to reassess the impact of Spinoza's liberalism on the Continental tradition. Peter Laslett has edited the new manuscript of Locke's *Political Treatises* (New York: Cambridge University Press, 1960) to suggest a new interpretation of his significance for political theory. While the available literature of Russian liberalism is not too extensive, a new edition of Herzen's classic work *My Past and Thought* (New York: Alfred A. Knopf, 1968) has been prepared which casts fresh light on nineteenth century Russian liberal thought. I have found of special interest several essays in Simmon's *Continuity and Change in Russian Soviet Thought*

(Cambridge: Harvard University Press, 1955) especially M. Karpovich's "Two Types of Russian Liberalism" and I. Berlin's "Herzen and Bakunin on Individual Liberty."

The student may also trace some of the history of liberalism before the seventeenth century, the period which is our point of departure, in Henry Kamen's readable *The Rise of Toleration* (New York: McGraw-Hill, 1967), which contains significant documentation of the early sources of justification of resistance to tyranny and right of dissent. Kamen also provides a concise bibliography to the early literature of toleration. At the other extreme of our chronological limits, there have been several revaluations of liberal thought in the postwar period including Albert Camus' *The Rebel* (New York: Alfred A. Knopf, 1951), and Rolf Dahrendorf's *Society and Democracy in Germany* (Garden City, N.Y.: Doubleday, 1967).